Tested by Zion

The Bush Administration and the Israeli-Palestinian Conflict

This book tells the full inside story of the George W. Bush administration and the Israeli-Palestinian conflict. Written by a top National Security Council officer who worked at the White House with Bush, Dick Cheney, and Condoleezza Rice and attended dozens of meetings with figures like Ariel Sharon, Hosni Mubarak, the kings of Jordan and Saudi Arabia, and Palestinian leaders, it brings the reader inside the White House and the palaces of Middle Eastern officials. How did 9/11 change American policy toward Yasser Arafat and Sharon's tough efforts against the Second Intifada? What influence did the Saudis have on President Bush? Did the American approach change when Arafat died? How did Sharon decide to get out of Gaza, and why did the peace negotiations fail? In the first book by an administration official to focus on Bush and the Middle East, Elliott Abrams brings the story of Bush, the Israelis, and the Palestinians to life.

Elliott Abrams was educated at Harvard College, Harvard Law School, and the London School of Economics. After working on the staffs of the late Senators Henry M. Jackson and Daniel P. Moynihan, he served all eight years of the Reagan administration as an assistant secretary of state and received the Secretary's Distinguished Service Award from Secretary of State George P. Shultz. Abrams is former president of the Ethics and Public Policy Center in Washington, DC. He was a member and later chairman of the United States Commission on International Religious Freedom from 1999 to 2001, and he was reappointed to membership in 2012. He is currently a member of the U.S. Holocaust Memorial Council, which directs the activities of the U.S. Holocaust Memorial Museum. Abrams is the author or editor of six books. He served at the White House as a deputy assistant to the president and deputy national security advisor in the administration of President George W. Bush, where he supervised U.S. policy in the Middle East. Abrams is now a Senior Fellow for Middle Eastern studies at the Council on Foreign Relations and teaches about U.S. policy in the Middle East at Georgetown University's School of Foreign Service.

A Council on Foreign Relations Book

The Council on Foreign Relations (CFR) is an independent, nonpartisan membership organization, think tank, and publisher dedicated to being a resource for its members, government officials, business executives, journalists, educators and students, civic and religious leaders, and other interested citizens in order to help them better understand the world and the foreign policy choices facing the United States and other countries. Founded in 1921, CFR carries out its mission by maintaining a diverse membership, with special programs to promote interest and develop expertise in the next generation of foreign policy leaders; convening meetings at its headquarters in New York and in Washington, DC, and other cities where senior government officials, members of Congress, global leaders, and prominent thinkers come together with CFR members to discuss and debate major international issues; supporting a Studies Program that fosters independent research, enabling CFR scholars to produce articles, reports, and books and hold roundtables that analyze foreign policy issues and make concrete policy recommendations; publishing *Foreign Affairs*, the preeminent journal on international affairs and U.S. foreign policy; sponsoring Independent Task Forces that produce reports with both findings and policy prescriptions on the most important foreign policy topics; and providing up-to-date information and analysis about world events and American foreign policy on its website, www.cfr.org.

Tested by Zion

The Bush Administration and the Israeli-Palestinian Conflict

ELLIOTT ABRAMS

A Council on Foreign Relations Book

CAMBRIDGE
UNIVERSITY PRESS

CAMBRIDGE UNIVERSITY PRESS
Cambridge, New York, Melbourne, Madrid, Cape Town,
Singapore, São Paulo, Delhi, Mexico City

Cambridge University Press
32 Avenue of the Americas, New York, NY 10013-2473, USA

www.cambridge.org
Information on this title: www.cambridge.org/9781107696907

First published 2013

Printed in the United States of America

A catalog record for this publication is available from the British Library.

Library of Congress Cataloging in Publication data

Abrams, Elliott.
Tested by Zion : The Bush administration and the Israeli-Palestinian conflict / Elliott Abrams.
    p.   cm.
Includes bibliographical references and index.
ISBN 978-1-107-03119-7 (hardback) – ISBN 978-1-107-69690-7 (pbk.)
 1. United States – Foreign relations – Israel.   2. Israel – Foreign relations – United States.
3. United States – Foreign relations – 2001–2009.   4. Arab-Israeli conflict – 1993–   5. Al-Aqsa
Intifada, 2000–   6. Palestinian Arabs – Government policy – Israel.   I. Title.
E183.8.I7A26   2012
327.7305694–dc23   2012022617

ISBN 978-1-107-03119-7 Hardback
ISBN 978-1-107-69690-7 Paperback

"If liberty can blossom in the rocky soil of the West Bank and Gaza, it will inspire millions of men and women around the globe who are equally weary of poverty and oppression, equally entitled to the benefits of democratic government."

> George W. Bush, Speech in the Rose Garden, the White House, June 24, 2002

"Israel's population may be just over 7 million. But when you confront terror and evil, you are 307 million strong, because America stands with you."

> George W. Bush, Speech to the Knesset, Jerusalem, May 15, 2008

For Rachel, of course

Contents

Acknowledgments   *page* ix

    Introduction   1
1 Early Days   4
2 9/11 and the Search for a Policy   19
3 Roadmap to Disengagement   48
4 "New Realities on the Ground"   98
5 Arafat, Disengagement, Sharon   119
6 Olmert – Peace or War?   158
7 War in Lebanon – and Condi   179
8 From Mecca to Annapolis   212
9 The "Meeting" at Annapolis   244
10 Two Trips to Jerusalem   262
11 Final Days in Gaza and Turtle Bay   282
12 Lessons Learned   304
13 Conclusion   314

Index   321

Acknowledgments

Many people helped me bring this book to publication. I should start with President George W. Bush and Dr. Condoleezza Rice, who hired me in 2001 for the White House staff, and with Steve Hadley, the national security advisor in the president's second term. The many officials and former officials – mostly Americans, but also Israelis, Palestinians, and Jordanians – who agreed to be interviewed helped me immeasurably to reconstruct the relevant events of the Bush administration. Many of them are mentioned in the text, but doing my work in the White House also required the assistance of a number of people whose names do not appear here. These are the young officers, mostly from the State Department and CIA, who worked for me at the National Security Council (NSC) in the Bush years. Their dedication to advancing American interests in the Middle East and their ability to make their boss look good were enormous, as is my gratitude to them all.

Since leaving the government I have been a Senior Fellow for Middle Eastern Studies at the Council on Foreign Relations, probably the best place on the planet for writing a book. I thank CFR's president Richard N. Haass and its director of studies James M. Lindsay for their steadfast support and good advice during this entire project. While I was drafting the manuscript, reviewing written materials, and conducting interviews, Edward Stein was my research associate at CFR, and he deserves my thanks for his help and unfailing good cheer. Rachel Steyer, his successor, worked diligently on the final preparations of the manuscript. Rebecca Nagel of the Wylie Agency then took the manuscript and arranged for it to be published, and I greatly appreciate her unflagging support. Of course, none of this would be possible without the donors to my program – and especially without Roger Hertog, Paul Singer, James Tisch, Mortimer Zuckerman, and the Lynde and Harry Bradley Foundation – as well as those who support Middle East studies at CFR more broadly. Although I do not list all the donors here, I hope they all know how grateful I am for their generosity.

And as always, the person who gave me the best advice and most important support was my wife Rachel. No words can ever express my gratitude to her.

Introduction

For all its eight years, the administration of George W. Bush struggled to end violence between Israelis and Palestinians and lead them forward toward a peace agreement. The effort to help Israel end the intifada and then stop terrorism against Israeli citizens largely succeeded, and to this day the number of violent incidents remains low. Yet the effort to get a final status agreement that would bring a permanent peace failed, despite the immense amount of time and energy spent on it.

Many readers will wonder about or simply disagree with these statements, but the narrative that follows will, I hope, persuade some. The usual complaint about Bush policy – that the president and his staff paid little or no attention to the Middle East (or, in another version, paid no attention until the last years in office when it was simply too late to achieve much) – is nonsense, and this account will show, trip by trip and meeting by meeting, what we were up to and how much energy we devoted to this region.

At least it will show what happened from one vantage point. A memoir of years spent in the government is always the tale of what the author saw, and the full picture will be available only to historians, writing decades later when all the memoirs have been published, the memos declassified, and the emails opened to public review. As a deputy national security advisor and the NSC staff member at the White House who handled Israeli-Palestinian affairs day in and day out, my vantage point was pretty good. I do not doubt that I missed some events, but I doubt I missed much that was very consequential when it came to the Israelis and Palestinians. The account here is as complete as I can make it, thanks to dozens of former colleagues here and in the Middle East who helped me reconstruct events. Some of the telephone calls and meetings recounted here are painful to recollect even at the distance of 5 or 10 years; others are a source of lasting pride.

But this book is not a defense of all we did in those eight years. President Bush's key insights were keen and abandoned previous policy in critical ways. He believed that separation of Israelis and Palestinians into two states would benefit both – but only if the Palestinian state was peaceful and democratic. He therefore treated Yasser Arafat not as an honored guest at the White House but as a terrorist and failed leader who had to be removed from power. He believed that Israeli security was essential to any hope for peace in the region and strongly backed Israel's right to defend itself even when international criticism was deafening. He understood – and understood the need to say aloud – that in any peace agreement, Israel would keep the major settlement blocks and that Palestinian refugees would have to settle in Palestine rather than "return" to Israel.

Yet too often, diplomacy became the goal rather than the means, and building the institutions of a future democratic, peaceful, prosperous Palestine was subordinated to illusory efforts at the negotiating table. There was remarkable progress in the West Bank, where competent governance and decent security forces appeared for the first time and gave hope of what a Palestinian state might someday look like. Yet far more could have been accomplished had progress on the ground, in the actually existing Palestine between the Green Line and the Jordan River, been our central target. It seemed to me that too often we forgot that reality on the ground will shape an agreement, not vice versa.

In the Middle East and in Europe, the usual criticism of Bush's policy (after saying that we did nothing for eight years) was that we tilted to Israel. I am inclined to plead guilty, but it depends of course on what is meant by "tilt." President Bush was dedicated to helping the Palestinians escape the despotic, corrupt Arafat rule and create a fully democratic state that would be a model for the entire region. In his view, "supporters" of the Palestinians who were indifferent to the nature of the Palestinian state and focused only on its borders were doing the Palestinians no favors. He was well aware that, despite their endless speeches about Palestinian rights, most Arab leaders treated resident Palestinian populations badly and placed their own interests far above those of the "Palestine" they claimed to protect. Nor did he believe that staunch solidarity with Israel when its security was at risk meant he was favoring Israelis over the Palestinians. He knew that only a secure Israel would ever take the risk of withdrawing from the West Bank, so Israeli security was an essential step toward Palestinian self-government. He did not believe that endless pressure on Israel for concessions would yield as much as a partnership with its leaders, so he built one. He "tilted" to Israel but to the Palestinians as well, confident that he could do both and help both sides move toward peace and security in the process.

I believed in this policy – and fought for it even when at one moment of crisis or another the administration and its representatives seemed to me to sway from these principles. President Bush inherited a collapsed peace process and an Israeli-Palestinian conflict that during the intifada was killing hundreds on each side. He left behind a far deeper American relationship with Israel and the beginnings of state-building in Palestine. These pages follow the course of those events: how policy developed after 9/11, the struggle against Arafat, the partnership with Sharon, the Hamas electoral victory and takeover of Gaza, Israel's wars in Lebanon and Gaza, the reform of the Palestinian Authority, and the repeated but unsuccessful efforts to negotiate peace. In this book I also trace the struggles, sometimes emotional and tough, within the administration over Middle East policy.

Whenever I speak about my experiences in the White House and in Jerusalem and Ramallah, I am asked whether there is really any chance for peace. I often respond by telling this story. Visitors to Israel know that every Israeli now appears to have a Blackberry and an iPad, and hard data show there actually are more than one cell phone per person. But not long ago Israel had a telephone system that was best described as Balkan or Levantine. A central bureaucracy in the Ministry of Communications controlled everything and worked with all the inefficiency one would expect. The phones were clunky and black, lines were too few, repairs were always late, and getting a new line was a major challenge.

An American of my acquaintance made *aliyah* to Israel and set up there as a translator. When business became good enough he moved out of the place he had been sharing, rented an apartment, and went to the Ministry office to fill out the forms to get a phone. He lined up at the window and pushed his forms under the glass to the clerk, who briefly perused them and dropped them in a box. Before the clerk could say "Next," the American said, "Please wait. I'm new. I just made *aliyah*. I'm not sure I filled the forms out right, and I don't want to delay getting a phone because of some error I made. Please take another look." The clerk frowned, but did so and told him the forms were fine. "Great," said the American. "So when can I get a phone? I mean, I know you don't give appointments, but roughly when?" "I don't know," the clerk replied, "but roughly it should just be four months."

"Four months! Four months!" the American called out. "That's impossible. People have to call me to translate things. If they can't call, I'll starve. And my mother – my mother is sick. I call her every day and she has to be able to call me at any time. Four months! It's not possible. Isn't there any hope it can be less than four months?"

The clerk smiled through the glass and replied slowly, "Sure. Sure. Sure there's hope. There's no chance – but there's hope."

That seems to me the best summary today of the Middle East peace process: There is hope, but no chance. At least there is no chance for a magic formula conjured up in a diplomatic salon that will end decades of conflict. A peaceful, democratic Palestinian state will be built in the West Bank slowly, step by step, or it will not be built at all. How the Bush administration set about to help Israelis end the violence and help Palestinians build that state is the center of this story.

I

Early Days

No one suspected, on the day George W. Bush was inaugurated in 2001, that his presidency would become deeply entangled with events in the broader Middle East. He had no foreign policy expertise, and as a former governor of Texas his interests lay with domestic issues. "Compassionate conservatism" was a stronger message during his campaign than pledges to solve any international problem. Nearly eight years later, Bush explained to a gathering of American Jewish leaders at the White House that "[y]ou know I didn't campaign to be a foreign policy or a national security president. I didn't campaign to be a wartime president. I ran on a domestic agenda, but events happened."[1]

During the campaign Bush had said little about the Middle East, and his broad statements of support for Israel's security gave little insight into what he would actually do as president. Nor did he have the normal 10-week transition that might have provided time to focus on foreign policy matters: Because of contested ballots and "hanging chads" in Florida, the election results were not decided until the Supreme Court ruled on December 12, and a truncated transition process followed.

Yet on Inauguration Day itself, January 20, 2001, the Israeli-Palestinian crisis began to intrude on his presidency. Bill Clinton had ended his own years in office with a determined, sometimes desperate, effort to forge a peace treaty. He had devoted days and weeks of personal effort, meeting face to face with Israeli Prime Minister Ehud Barak and his team and with PLO leader Yasser Arafat and his. Although Clinton may have believed he was close to success several times, an agreement was impossible because of Arafat's unwillingness to sign any treaty. Clinton had invested in Arafat, and the investment went bust; as one of Clinton's top Middle East aides put it, "There is a common belief that 'we came close' to agreement at Camp David, but the truth is we were not close at all. After eight years, Clinton and our team surely should have known with whom we were dealing. Clinton had become dependent on the statesmanship of Yasser Arafat."[2] Clinton gives his own view of the Camp David negotiations in his memoir, *My Life*: "On the ninth day, I gave Arafat my best shot again. Again he said no.... I returned on the thirteenth day of discussions, and we worked all night again.... Again Arafat said no.... Right before I left office, Arafat, in one of our last conversations, thanked me for all my efforts and told me what a great man I was. 'Mr. Chairman,' I replied, 'I am not a great man. I am a failure, and you have made me one.'"³

In the Oval Office on January 20, Clinton used the brief and usually ceremonial meeting with his successor to vent his frustration. He told Bush and Vice President-elect Cheney that Arafat had torpedoed the peace process; Cheney often repeated later how bitter Clinton had been and how strongly he had warned the new team against trusting Arafat. As one of Cheney's top foreign policy assistants described it, "in the vice president's recounting, they couldn't get Clinton off the subject. I mean, it was the only thing Clinton wanted to talk about and it was, 'That son of a bitch Arafat,' you know, 'Don't, can't trust him,' 'I put too much weight on him,' 'Biggest mistake I made in my presidency,' was the way that they described it."⁴ The day before, on January 19, Clinton had called Colin Powell, the incoming secretary of state, to deliver the same message.

Stop the Intifada

The last gasp of the Clinton-era effort came in Israeli-Palestinian talks held January 21 to 27, 2001, in Taba, Egypt. Yet Clinton was no longer president; it seemed clear that Israel's impending elections would bring Ehud Barak's time in office to an end; and there was no reason to think Arafat would agree to conditions he had rejected just months before at Camp David.

In fact, "[w]hen the forty-second president departed the White House in January 2001 the Palestinian-Israeli peace process lay in smoking ruins."⁵ After the collapse of the Camp David talks in July, Arafat had turned back to terrorism: He had launched a new intifada that was bringing violence to Israeli cities and settlements. In 2010, one of the top leaders of Hamas admitted that "President Arafat instructed Hamas to carry out a number of military operations in the heart of the Jewish state after he felt that his negotiations with the Israeli government then had failed."⁶ The Israeli military's effort to stop the wave of terror was front-page news. With the negotiations over and violence flaring, what was the Bush policy to be, and who was to lead it?

Bush and his team had no appetite for a Clinton-style personal role for the new president: It had brought nothing but grief to Clinton, Clinton warned adamantly against trusting Arafat, and no one believed the collapsed talks could be revived. There was, moreover, a desire not to raise expectations unduly, another mistake the Bush team believed Clinton had committed. The intifada had grown bloodier in the months before the transition in Washington, and the team saw its task as reducing the level of violence. "When we took office, our goal was simply to calm the region," Condoleezza Rice writes in her memoir.⁷ The very first National Security Council Principals Committee meeting, or PC (where all NSC Principals – the secretaries of state and defense, CIA director,

national security advisor, chairman of the joint chiefs, and the vice president –
were present except the president; his presence would mean this was a formal
NSC meeting), covered the Middle East. Bruce Riedel, a career CIA official
who had been the NSC's senior director for the Middle East under Clinton
and continued in that role in 2001 under Bush, described the consensus at that
meeting:

> Now is not the time for peacemaking; now is the time for conflict management. See if we
> can dampen this down. And my understanding of my responsibility was that: conflict
> management. There was a great deal of interest in what happened at Camp David, what
> were the offers and what were the counteroffers, but mostly from a "let's understand the
> context of where we are" rather than "let's pick up the pieces and do this" viewpoint.
> That's the way I understood the administration in the beginning – conflict manage-
> ment.... The meeting was devoted to the question of Arab-Israeli, Israeli-Palestinian
> situation, what do we do about it, what's our posture going to be, and Powell dominated
> the meeting and he came out very sober: You know, we have a big difficult issue, we're
> not going to plunge into the negotiations process, chances of success there are very, very
> slim, we've already seen Taba was not going to produce a breakthrough, it was clear
> Barak was not going to survive as prime minister very long and that Sharon was going
> to come in. Our focus should be on trying to dampen down the fire and see if we can
> come up with a durable ceasefire and truce and then see, you know, what happens after
> that.[8]

Given the situation on the ground, no one in the new administration argued for
intense presidential involvement. The real issue was whether to try diplomacy
at all: Would there be anything resembling a "peace process," or was that
effort a waste of time? The director of policy planning at the State Department,
Richard Haass, later explained:

> I came to think two things: that the instinct of the administration was not to place what
> you might call a traditional emphasis on what we used to call the "peace process";
> but also analytically they had determined that there wasn't much for them to work
> with. They essentially didn't see a Palestinian partner. At most there was a very flawed
> Palestinian leadership. The administration was essentially prepared to let things drift
> until a better Palestinian leadership came along.[9]

Colin Powell opposed this drift and argued for *some* kind of diplomatic activity, no matter how slim the odds of success. After a trip to Mexico, Powell's
first overseas venture was to the Middle East, where he met with Israeli officials
as well as Yasser Arafat. In his view, he was engaging with all the parties, protecting the president, exploring what the new Israeli leadership thought, and
seeing what the collapse of the Camp David talks had meant to Arafat. As a
former State Department official who was close to him put it, Powell believed
that "you can't be the American government without a process or without
getting involved.... With no illusions about the personalities we were dealing
with, and no illusions that process can be more than process. But frankly,
that's very often what diplomacy is and what politics is all about: process,
and see if you can go somewhere with it. That was not the prevailing view

within the administration." Powell's disagreement with the consensus view at that PC meeting and his trip to the Middle East were the first inklings of a problem that would grow over time: the split between Powell's view of the region and his role in it, and the view of the White House. "State and the White House were not on the same page, and everyone in the region – and in Washington – knew it," Rice later wrote.[10] In Powell's vision, the administration had to be – or at least to appear – active, and that meant travel to the Middle East by the secretary of state. The earlier mentioned source close to Powell explained,

The new administration cannot come in and pretend there is no Middle East problem, which would've satisfied most of the president's other principal advisors. And so Powell did that and he asked George Mitchell to reengage. Remember Mitchell had started something for Clinton and then was wondering whether we wanted to continue. Powell called Mitchell in and said, "George, give me something to work with." And Mitchell came up with his sequential plan and so Powell tried to make something happen with that, a number of different ways.... Over the next several months we tried Mitchell, we tried Zinni [retired Marine general Anthony Zinni was also named a special envoy in 2001], and a couple of other attempts to see if we could not get something going. And we were not successful in getting something going, but we couldn't be accused of not being interested and not being engaged because Powell was, but he was the only one. The president had no theoretical or emotional engagement in this; nor did anybody else.[11]

Whatever Powell's vision of his activities, to many in the administration they seemed to be an unwanted continuation of the Clintonian approach: engaging with Arafat despite the terror he was fomenting, allowing him to pay no price for that terror, and supporting conventional plans (like Mitchell's) that were heavy on Israeli concessions but contained no vision of how to transform a disastrous situation on the ground.

Issued on April 30, 2001, the Mitchell Report (formally, *The Sharm el-Sheikh Fact-Finding Committee Report on the Middle East*) provided no answers. In their joint statement presenting the report, Mitchell and former Senator Warren Rudman stated, "First, end the violence.... The cycle of violent actions and violent reaction must be broken. We call upon the parties to implement an immediate and unconditional cessation of violence." Yet the report took a stance of total moral relativism between terrorists and those defending against them and was in that sense truly a product of pre-9/11 America. Moreover, it went on to equilibrate terrorism and Israeli settlements. The Mitchell-Rudman statement summarized that "[a]mong our recommendations are ... the PA should make clear through concrete action ... that terrorism is reprehensible and unacceptable.... The Government of Israel should freeze all settlement activity, including the 'natural growth' of existing settlements." On one side, murder; on the other, housing: To the Mitchell fact-finding committee, the moral responsibility was equally shared. Where the new administration could go with this report remained unclear.

"Every Arab in the World Wanted Bush to Win"

What did the Arabs and Israelis make of the new Bush administration? Arabs and Israelis shared the view – actually, for Israelis, the fear – that the new president would follow in his father's footsteps and would be far closer to Arab governments than to Israel. Clinton's last assistant secretary of state for the Near East, Edward S. Walker Jr., recalled that "every Arab in the world wanted Bush to win" in the 2000 election.[12] This included the Palestinians: As one member of the Palestinian negotiating team analyzed it, "there is a recurring pattern in Palestinian political thinking and behavior: tending to personalize the problem. So, the problem was Clinton and his special relations with Israel and the Jews, and now here comes Bush from a Texan oil background who has a special affinity with the Arabs. And so there was a sense of totally naïve elation."[13]

Powell's special efforts at outreach to Arab leaders may have reinforced this perception. Jordan's ambassador to the United States later described his first meeting with the new secretary of state this way:

At the start of the Bush administration we were actually hopeful that things will move on the Arab-Israeli conflict. And we were hopeful because the Bush administration signaled to us that it wanted to work with the region and not just, you know, with individual players. And I remember a meeting with Colin Powell a very few weeks after he started, when I was the ambassador. And our foreign minister . . . came early on to Washington to sort of gauge what the administration's views were. And we were received very warmly by Powell at the time. And so the impression then was that this would be a fresh start and that the administration would indeed give it more attention.[14]

This was, of course, not at all the view in the White House, where "more attention" was the last thing officials had in mind.

Bush himself was aware of Arab expectations. On May 31, 2001, he held a small dinner in the residential part of the White House for visiting Israeli President Moshe Katsav. At the dinner, Bush approached the head of a major American Jewish organization and told him, "The Saudis thought 'this Texas oil guy was going to go against Israel,' and I told them you have the wrong guy."

The Saudis and Arafat did think just that, as Bruce Riedel recalled:

Arafat had a different view which was that Bush II was going to be a replay of Bush I, and that he had gotten a good deal but he was going to get a *better* deal. And he looked at Powell, he looked at Bush, he assumed the father would have a role: "What's the hurry? Since Camp David they've been moving closer and closer. Now I'm [Arafat] going to get the best deal of them all." I also have a strong suspicion that the dean of the diplomatic corps in Washington, Prince Bandar, probably encouraged this belief: "I know the Bushies, I've been with them for a quarter-century, they'll want to do this even more than Clinton, don't be in any hurry." If so, [it was] a disastrous calculation by Arafat.[15]

It is even likely that this "disastrous calculation" about Bush's views played a role in the firing of the Saudi intelligence chief, Prince Turki, by the kingdom's de facto ruler Crown Prince Abdallah at the end of August 2001 (after twenty-five years in that position) and in the great tension that developed later in 2001 between the Saudi and American governments.

The initial Arab belief that Bush would be closer to their views than to those of the Israelis was shared in Jerusalem. There were few lines of communication to Israel, and there was no clear message coming from the new team in Washington. Shalom Tourgeman, then the deputy to Sharon's new diplomatic advisor Danny Ayalon, described the situation: "It was in the middle of the intifada; the Bush administration didn't know how to cope with it. They didn't prepare their policy yet. Most of the people were new on both sides. And there weren't any deep contacts yet with the administration. And we felt the perception that the administration is in a way continuing the previous administrations."[16] The quick Powell visit to see the newly elected Sharon and to meet with Yasser Arafat did nothing to dampen Israeli fears or Palestinian expectations about the Bush administration.

Yet if those who expected a "tilt" toward the Arab states were wrong about Bush, they were even more wrong about Cheney. The vice president had no strong ties to the Jewish community from his days as a Wyoming congressman, secretary of defense, or businessman in Dallas; in fact, his work in the private sector had substantially been in the Arab world. It was not surprising that Arab envoys should expect him to be a reliable ally, but Cheney turned out to be a staunch and reliable supporter of Israel's security during his eight years as vice president. In his memoir, he sums up his attitude, writing that he "did not believe, as many argued, that the Israeli-Palestinian conflict was the linchpin of every other American policy in the Middle East" and that it "would have been wrong to push the Israelis to make concessions to a Palestinian Authority (PA) controlled by Yasser Arafat."[17] Those views marked him as one of the most pro-Israel officials in the Bush administration.

"Sharon Was Very Concerned; He Was Very Worried"

Sharon was elected prime minister on February 6, 2001, formed a government in early March, and flew to Washington two weeks later. According to Tourgeman, Sharon was "very concerned; he was very worried about the Bush administration policy because in the perception in Israel, the Bush administration was the continuation of Bush the father, and this is after a very friendly administration of Clinton. I remember the preparation meetings to the visit where many experts told Sharon, 'Look, you are going now for four years of clashes with this administration.'"[18]

Sharon's March 20 visit was ill prepared by his new team and went poorly, as Tourgeman recalled:

We came to Washington, without real joint preparations, no real prior discussion on the agendas. The meeting and visit were not good also because everything was leaked to the press, including all the misunderstandings. These are the days of the intifada, many explosions in the streets of Israel, almost on a daily basis . . . and we fought terror without real understanding of the Americans at that period. The contacts were about how to prevent misunderstandings between us and the administration, and Sharon was concerned; he was concerned.[19]

Initially, Sharon did not seem to trust his own official team and used as his key contact with the U.S. government a personal friend, the Israeli-American businessman Arie Genger. Genger met with Powell and Rice repeatedly over the first 18 months Sharon and Bush were in office, until Sharon gained confidence in Danny Ayalon, whom he sent to Washington as his ambassador in 2002, and brought in Dov "Dubi" Weissglas as his chief of staff and chief "handler" of the U.S.-Israeli relationship.

But that came later. In late June 2001, Sharon returned to Washington to speak to the huge annual convention of AIPAC, the American Israel Public Affairs Committee, then and now the most significant pro-Israel lobbying organization. Once again the visit failed to establish a solid relationship between Sharon and Bush or between the two governments. In addition to Israeli suspicions about Powell, whom they saw as a representative of the classic State Department sympathy for Arab views, Sharon did not trust the new national security advisor, Condoleezza Rice. Sharon's military secretary, Gen. Moshe Kaplinsky, described Sharon's first impressions this way:

He was very concerned about the attitude of Condoleezza Rice. She was very, very tough with him at the first meetings. I believe that he didn't understand deeply the relations between Condoleezza and Bush. And one of the famous stories that I got was about the fact that in a pre-meeting – she met Sharon before he met the president – she asked him, "Let's see what we're going to talk about." And Sharon said, "I want to talk about releasing [convicted spy Jonathan] Pollard." And Condoleezza told him, "You're not going to raise this issue in the meeting." So he wasn't aware of their relations and he decided to raise it to President Bush. And Condoleezza shot him down immediately in the meeting, in the middle of the meeting. So he became aware after this meeting about the importance of coordinating with Condoleezza, but I believe for a long time he was suspicious about her attitude toward us. And he felt that between him and President Bush, he can manage it quite well. But he thought that Condoleezza is hurting the relations.[20]

At this meeting, the Israelis mistook Rice's assertion of control over their White House visit for an underlying hostility to Israel; later, they came to view Rice as an important counterbalance to Powell and the State Department.

It was after this visit that Rice decided to address the problem of communication with Israel herself rather than to leave it to the State Department diplomats. This was the first harbinger of her takeover of the Arab-Israel account, which started gradually in 2002 and was fully in place by 2003. Right after the Sharon visit, she initiated a channel to Danny Ayalon, which both allowed for candid conversations between these two top staff members and also permitted the quiet, confidential passing of messages between Sharon and Bush. This was the first direct channel between the Prime Minister's Office and the White House.

How was the relationship between Sharon and Bush faring? By the time Sharon's career was ended by a massive stroke in January 2006, a mythology had developed about his personal relations with President Bush. According to this storyline, which at times both sides favored, the two had formed a deep personal friendship when Bush, as governor of Texas, visited Israel in 1998. Sharon, then a government minister, had given Bush a helicopter tour of Israel, impressing him with the small size and great vulnerability of the country. Bush had emerged with a deeper understanding of Israel's security needs, as well as with an intimate friendship with Sharon.

The story is not false, but it is exaggerated. No great intimacy was achieved in the 1998 meeting; it lasted but a few hours, most of them spent in a helicopter where headphones made normal conversation impossible. However, Bush did come to understand Sharon's role in building the West Bank settlements, and that came to matter. Bush's chief speechwriter Michael Gerson explained:

The president would talk about the first time he met Ariel Sharon, and how they went on the helicopter tour. And he was very impressed by that trip. He recalls Sharon lining his finger up like this with one of the settlements, and saying, "I built that." He cites that as one of the reasons why, when Sharon was willing to give up settlements, that impressed him.... Sharon was so proud of his achievements but he saw the reality. I think that's one reason he kind of respected Sharon.[21]

Some moments in the early meetings in 2001, according to Danny Ayalon, suggest how each side made a real effort to bridge gaps and create a partnership. The Israeli team worked on ways for Sharon

to give a very vivid kind of impression for Bush so he could relate to terrorism. So, Sharon rehearsed it a couple of times before, and he said, "Mr. President, what would happen if you were governor of Texas and Texas would receive rockets coming out of Mexico? I'm sure, Mr. President, that in one hour there wouldn't be Mexico." And Bush said "Why an hour? Fifteen minutes!" So, this is when Sharon really began to like the guy.[22]

On the other side, Bush offered advice to Sharon:

Toward the end of the meeting, he took Sharon to the side and he told him, "I don't want you to have a problem with the Catholics; you don't want them to be on your back." What was the problem? A mosque that was being built in Nazareth. For political reasons some [Israeli] officials gave the Muslims the right to build the mosque just in front of the Church of the Annunciation. Big fiasco – it was crazy and we had to undo it, but nobody wanted to deal with it. And even when we took office, you know, it was a headache for us, but it wasn't something that took all our energies. Anyway, he took Sharon aside and he said, "Listen. There are 70 million Catholics here and there are a billion around the world. You don't want to make them an enemy." And he told Sharon about the story of this church. Sharon knew vaguely about it. Bush said, "You have to solve it." And Sharon said, "OK, Mr. President, we'll solve it." And then he came home, he formed a committee, and we made sure we fixed it.... [T]hese, I think, were the seeds for relations of trust and I would say almost affection later on.[23]

Such efforts show the desire for better communications and more trust, but achieving that was difficult – more for reasons of style than of substance. As Ayalon described it,

I think the – how should I say – the style, mental, age difference, whatever, was very obvious at that time. Although they had met before, during the campaign when Sharon took him on this famous helicopter ride, and they started this meeting by Sharon saying, "You know, I never thought next time I would meet you, you would be in the White House." And he [Bush] said, "I never thought you'd be the prime minister." It was a good rapport, but [it was] extinguished very quickly because Sharon was already hard of hearing, and I'm not sure he *really* was able to completely understand the Texan drawl of the President. . . . Phone calls between the two were very few and they weren't very good.[24]

Condi Rice's summary is the most apt: "You know how it was to talk to Sharon. I always said he's one of the few people I know who spoke English better than he understood it."[25] Sharon often spoke in formulas, using word patterns in English with which he was comfortable, to describe his positions on key questions. His hearing and his imperfect command of English meant that he missed some of the nuances; indeed, sometimes he missed the point of questions being put to him. His English was a barrier to effective communication, not a means to achieve it. Sometimes, he would realize that something important was escaping him and would turn to an aide and ask "Ma?" the Hebrew for "What?" Few aides would intervene and interrupt Sharon when he was conversing freely, but Dubi Weissglas often did, to be sure that Sharon understood fully what he was being asked. Weissglas, however, was not around for these early meetings in 2001, when relations between Sharon and the United States government were fragile and often difficult.

On March 26, 2001, shortly after Sharon's first visit, the Bush administration cast its first veto of a Middle East resolution in the United Nations Security Council. The resolution would have established an "observer force" to protect Palestinians from Israeli forces, and all the European nations in the Council abstained because of the resolution's imbalance: Palestinian terrorists were killing Israelis, but the UN was proposing to offer protection only to Palestinians and failing to condemn their terrorist actions. This U.S. veto must have reassured the Israelis, but other signals were mixed and confused both the Arabs and them. On April 30, the Mitchell Report was released and endorsed by the Bush administration; among other things, it called for a dead halt to Israeli construction activity in the settlements. CIA Director George Tenet continued the work he had begun in the Clinton days on security matters. It was clear that the Bush administration's main focus was security – lowering the level of violence and fostering some form of security cooperation between Israel and the PA – and that the new team believed no other forms of diplomatic progress were possible until the security situation improved. "Clinton inherited from Bush Sr. a young, promising peace process and bequeathed to Bush Jr. an Israeli-Palestinian war and a total collapse of the hopes that flourished in the

1990s," one of Israel's leading columnists wrote. "Under such circumstances, it is not surprising that the Republicans had no hopes, or illusions, that a comprehensive peace and an end to the conflict were just around the corner."[26] Still, it was not clear who was in charge of Bush policy or how the administration proposed to move forward. "Stop the violence" was hardly a Middle East policy.

And meanwhile the violence escalated: on June 1, a popular discotheque in Tel Aviv called the "Dolphinarium" was bombed, killing 21 and injuring 132 Israelis, most of them young people. Nine weeks later, on August 9, a bomb exploded in the Sbarro pizzeria at one of the busiest corners in Jerusalem, killing 15 Israelis and wounding 130. Yet these major attacks alone do not give an accurate sense of the terrorism Israelis faced during the intifada. The series of attacks in the single month of May 2001 give a better picture, and they occurred before the campaign of suicide bombings of buses in Israeli cities began to take a higher toll. There were attacks by terrorists on May 1, May 8, May 9 (two 14-year-old boys stoned to death), May 10, May 15, May 18 (bomb in a shopping mall killed 5, wounded more than 100), May 23, May 25 (65 wounded by a car bomb), May 27 (30 wounded by two car bombs), May 29, May 30 (8 wounded by a car bomb outside a school), and May 31.[27] And this does not count attacks prevented by successful police work.

The Bush administration was correct in concluding that ending this violence should be its main objective. No diplomatic progress would ever be possible while it continued. Stopping the terrorism was clearly the top priority for Ariel Sharon as well, but that did not mean he and the Americans saw eye to eye. Sharon doubted that the Americans truly understood the nature of this beast or shared his view that terrorism needed to be *fought* with the toughest military means available. The State Department's endless repetition of the old formula that the "cycle of violence must end" suggested to the Israelis that the administration was drawing no moral distinction between the terrorists and the Israeli police and soldiers trying to stop them.

On the Arab side, there were equally serious doubts as the new administration's early weeks turned into months and Israeli-Palestinian violence continued. The predicted "leaning" toward the Arab side was nowhere to be seen, and the Israel Defense Forces (IDF) efforts to crush the intifada meant that Palestinian blood was also flowing. There were fears that Israel would assassinate Yasser Arafat, and day after day IDF attacks flattened Palestinian official buildings and kept the PA leadership, including Arafat, under siege in their headquarters in the Muqata in Ramallah.

In late June, Sharon adopted a new line: There must be "seven days of quiet" before he would negotiate a ceasefire agreement with the Palestinians. If there were seven straight days in which the PA acted against terror and no acts of terror were committed, Israel would engage again, in accordance with the Tenet and Mitchell plans, in negotiations with the Palestinians and would undertake some unspecified confidence-building measures as well. Despite U.S. pressure, Sharon kept to this line until March 2002.

Letter from Riyadh

Enter the Saudis, who were viewed by other Arabs as having special influence
on and access (via their long-time ambassador in Washington, Prince Bandar)
to the White House. That perception proved correct, as Bruce Riedel explained:

In this saga, the party that is probably most important in affecting the president's mind
is the Saudis. As in any new administration, there is a rush to get your head of state
over here, to get a better reception than whomever he regards as his rival head of state.
The only player who categorically refused to come was [Crown Prince] Abdallah,[28] and
there was – I wouldn't say panic – but there was deep distress and we then resorted
to a series of attempts to see if we couldn't get him on board: a handwritten note
[to the Crown Prince from the president]....I thought it had a chance...it didn't
work; a phone call from Bush senior which was not my idea...did not work. It was
frankly pathetic listening to the father say, "He's my son, you can really trust him," and
the Crown Prince basically saying, "Nuh-uh...forget it." And he's basically saying,
"No, I'm not coming," because you're not doing enough on the Palestinians. Much
confusion: Is this really why? Is there something else? Have they taken affront over
something we've done? But the Saudis – the Crown Prince and then through surrogates
like Bandar and Prince Turki, who comes on a "private visit" – make very clear, "This
is the problem. We need to see some movement. Seeking a ceasefire is not enough. Give
us some vision of where you want to go." There's a lot of this "vision," references
to vision. "We don't want you to repeat the mistakes of the past, but we need to be
able to say that you know where you're going and that we're all going to the same
place."[29]

One may well question why so much attention was paid to Saudi views.
For one thing, the Saudi view was not idiosyncratic and did represent an
Arab consensus. The Jordanian, Egyptian, Saudi, and other ambassadors in
Washington remained in close touch with each other, and it was not wrong
to see the Saudi view as the broader Arab perspective. For another, the Saudis
spoke up, perhaps because unlike many of the other Arab regimes, they were
not recipients of U.S. foreign aid. They were not worried about offending
the administration or Congress and seeing the budget cut as a result. On the
contrary, the Saudis were a supplier of foreign aid to many Arab regimes,
which gave them considerable clout in Arab League circles. Finally, since the
Gulf War in 1991, U.S.-Saudi relations had remained close, and the kingdom
was the world's largest supplier of oil. On balance, then, it was not surprising
that a strong Saudi message was going to be heard carefully.

In the Arab view, the Bush administration was doing nothing in the Middle
East and certainly was not restraining Sharon's use of military force against
the Palestinians. On June 29, after a trip to Asia and the Middle East, Powell
met with Abdallah at the swanky George V Hotel in Paris. Riedel described the
event:

This meeting is very dramatic. They have turned one of the conference rooms of the
hotel into the equivalent of a Saudi Diwan [the ruler's executive council] with the chairs
all lined up, all around the room, nothing in the center. And at the beginning of the

meeting the Crown Prince hands Powell a stack of photographs which are pretty grisly, pretty grisly stuff. And he then goes on and says, "You have been a soldier, you are a diplomat now; how can you possibly tolerate such suffering? These are *your* weapons, and this is *your* ally, and they are doing... " He got pretty close to the edge of tears. I don't think this was for effect; I think he was really worked up. And Powell got pretty worked up too: "Hey, I didn't make this mess. You can't blame all of this on the United States of America and you certainly can't blame it all on me," at which point there was an "OK, let's not personalize this anymore" and step back a little bit.[30]

In the summer of 2001, the Saudis canceled a high-level defense meeting with little notice, telegraphing again that they would not let this issue drop. Prince Bandar was invited to the White House first for meetings with Condi Rice and then for a session with the president, and was asked in essence, "What gives? What do you want?" Bandar's reply was that the Crown Prince wanted some assurance that the president was involved with the Israeli-Palestinian issue and would pursue a peace agreement. The Saudis did not seek an immediate negotiation but rather a sense of shared objectives. "I would say that by August of 2001," Riedel recalled, "there is a sense of crisis in the U.S.-Saudi relationship and it revolves around the issue of doing something on the Palestinians."[31]

The Crown Prince then rocked the White House with a letter, held in absolute secrecy in that summer of 2001 and still secret today, that put U.S.-Saudi relations in the balance. Marwan Muasher, then the Jordanian ambassador to the United States, remembered it being described as a "very stern letter."[32] The letter's message, as recalled by the vice president's Middle East advisor, was "this is all intolerable, this violence, these massacres against the Palestinians, we can't sit by.... There already was a Saudi threat of some kind of fundamental reevaluation of the relationship unless America committed to doing something serious to stop the violence."[33]

The administration took the message seriously, given the context: Abdallah's refusal to schedule a visit, his emotional session with Powell, the firing of Turki as intelligence chief, the cancellation of a defense meeting, and the conversations with Bandar. Riedel and William J. Burns, previously Ambassador to Jordan and then coming on as the new assistant secretary of state for the Near East and Powell's top advisor for the region, developed the administration's response: The president would reply to the Crown Prince, endorsing establishment of a Palestinian state as an American policy goal.

In later years, this objective would come to seem a natural part of Bush's democracy initiatives in the region: He often cited the development of democratic states in Iraq, Lebanon, and Palestine as the key to creating a modern Middle East. Indeed, the development of a Palestinian state with new leaders – without Arafat – became a central part of his new approach: Statehood would be the Palestinians' reward for ridding themselves of a corrupt leadership, ending terrorism, and becoming capable of self-government. Yet that regional approach only developed later in 2002, and in the summer of 2001 the policy was simpler to describe: Responding to Saudi pressure, the United States would endorse Palestinian statehood.

A Palestinian State

This endorsement of Palestinian statehood was a new policy. The Camp David Accords signed during the Carter administration included no such reference. The Reagan administration had opposed statehood as "an outcome unacceptable to the United States" and favored a Palestinian association with Jordan.[34] President Reagan had, in his September 1, 1982, speech about the Middle East, made that plain: "Peace cannot be achieved by the formation of an independent Palestinian state. . . . So, the United States will not support the establishment of an independent Palestinian state in the West Bank and Gaza. . . . [I]t is the firm view of the United States that self-government by the Palestinians of the West Bank and Gaza in association with Jordan offers the best chance for a durable, just, and lasting peace."

The George H. W. Bush administration had pursued a policy of ambiguity on the issue of Palestinian statehood throughout the Madrid talks. Although the Clinton administration had embraced Palestinian statehood at the Camp David talks in 2000 and these talks often focused on what the new state's borders might be, the two-state solution never became the formal policy of the United States. Clinton's key negotiator on these issues, Dennis Ross, acknowledges in his memoir that President Bush's letter to Crown Prince Abdallah in the summer of 2001 "establish[ed] for the first time that the U.S. policy henceforth would be to support a two-state solution."[35]

It is not clear whether President Bush was told what a significant departure in U.S. policy this new position would be; according to some accounts, the president said several years later that he had not then known that no president had ever taken this line before. From later discussions, it seems more likely that the State Department played down the novelty in an effort to get the new approach approved – and the Saudis mollified. Riedel later argued that the two-state solution was obviously American policy under Clinton even if it was never formally stated and was not going to cause trouble with Sharon because he had also previously endorsed it – a claim that was inaccurate because Sharon's acceptance of Palestinian statehood came only in 2003. Even more striking is what the United States got, in concrete terms, in return for adopting this new policy: nothing. By describing support for Palestinian statehood as nothing new, those who pushed this new policy on the president were not only giving him an inaccurate picture of what American policy had been. They were also denying him the chance to demand concessions – from the Palestinians, the Saudis, or the Arab League – in exchange for adopting it. Yet because the Saudi letter and the Bush reply were held so closely, a full debate on these matters was never allowed. Most of the Cheney staff in particular were kept out of the loop, and they complained to Cheney that, even if the new policy was correct, to have adopted it in response to Saudi threats and to have demanded nothing for it beyond a withdrawal of those threats were policy mistakes. Even though Cheney and his top staffer, I. Lewis "Scooter" Libby, were in Wyoming on vacation during the key weeks, the vice president's office did inquire whether this endorsement of Palestinian statehood was not a significant policy change that could be sold to the Arabs for great value. No, came the response from Washington: It was nothing new.

A reply to Abdallah was drafted. Bandar was summoned back to the White House, as Riedel described:

It is now late August/early September. And the meeting takes place on the Truman Balcony. The waiter brought drinks out and everything, and I thought, "That's a little odd, but OK. This was a teetotalling country, Saudi Arabia, but OK." And Bandar read the letter and was quite a happy man, in fact immediately leading me to think, Did we put something in the letter that was too good? But I think that Bandar had read his boss and knew his boss was looking for something like this. This substantially changed the mood for the moment in the U.S.-Saudi relationship.[36]

How would the new policy of supporting Palestinian statehood be announced? The logical time and place were just weeks away: President Bush's forthcoming address to the United Nations General Assembly – always a dramatic moment for a new president. Drafts of that speech contained the key words, although discussion continued of whether the announcement might better be made separately in a speech devoted to the Middle East. The dramatic announcement of the new policy at the UN seemed on track as the final drafts were prepared early on September 11, for the president's talk scheduled on the morning of September 12. Then the first plane hit the World Trade Center.

Notes

1. Stephen J. Hadley, interview by the author, July 14, 2009, p. 6.
2. Martin Indyk, *Innocent Abroad: An Intimate Account of American Peace Diplomacy in the Middle East* (New York: Simon & Schuster, 2009), 337, 375.
3. Bill Clinton, *My Life* (New York: Vintage Books, 2004), 915, 925–26, 944.
4. Eric Edelman, interview by the author, July 17, 2009, p. 4.
5. Laura Zittrain Eisenberg and Neil Caplan, *Negotiating Arab-Israeli Peace: Patterns, Problems, Possibilities* (Bloomington: University of Indiana Press, 2010), 283.
6. Khaled Abu Toameh, "Arafat Ordered Hamas Attacks against Israel in 2000," *Jerusalem Post*, September 28, 2010, http://www.jpost.com/LandedPages/PrintArticle.aspx?id=189549.
7. Condoleezza Rice, *No Higher Honor* (New York: Crown Publishers, 2011), 54.
8. Bruce Riedel, interview by the author, January 13, 2010, pp. 2–3.
9. Richard Haass, interview by the author, October 7, 2009, p. 1.
10. Rice, *No Higher Honor*, 55.
11. Former State Department official, interview by the author, August 21, 2009 (name withheld by request), pp. 1–2.
12. Mark Matthews, *Lost Years: Bush, Sharon, and Failure in the Middle East* (New York: Nation Books, 2007), 73.
13. Ghaith al-Omari, interview by the author, February 4, 2010, p. 3.
14. Marwan Muasher, interview by the author, December 17, 2009, p. 1.

15. Riedel, interview, p. 2.

16. Shalom Tourgeman, interview by the author, June 25, 2009, p. 2.

17. Richard B. Cheney, *In My Time* (New York: Threshold Editions, 2011), 380.

18. Tourgeman, interview, p. 2.

19. Ibid., p. 3.

20. Moshe Kaplinsky, interview by the author, January 31, 2010, pp. 2–3.

21. Michael J. Gerson, interview by the author, July 16, 2009, p. 10.

22. Daniel Ayalon, interview by the author, October 21, 2009, p. 2.

23. Ibid., pp. 2–3.

24. Ibid., p. 2.

25. Condoleezza Rice, interview by the author, January 21, 2010, p. 6.

26. Aluf Benn, "Bush's Indelible Imprint," *Haaretz*, August 27, 2004.

27. "Chronology of Terrorist Attacks in Israel Part V: 2001," Wm. Robert Johnson, last modified April 5, 2003, http://www.johnstonsarchive.net/terrorism/terrisrael-5.html.

28. Due to the illness of King Fahd after a stroke in 1996, Abdallah had then run the kingdom as Crown Prince. On Fahd's death in August 2005, he became king.

29. Riedel, interview, p. 5.

30. Ibid., p. 7.

31. Ibid., p. 7.

32. Muasher, interview, p. 2.

33. John P. Hannah, interview by the author, July 14, 2009, p. 3.

34. George P. Shultz, *Turmoil and Triumph: My Years as Secretary of State* (New York: Charles Scribner's Sons, 1993), 48–49, 85.

35. Dennis Ross, *The Missing Peace* (New York: Farrar, Straus and Giroux, 2004), 688–89.

36. Riedel, interview, p. 8.

2

9/11 and the Search for a Policy

Within days of the 9/11 terror attack, the Bush administration began to regroup, but its focus was on Al Qaeda and the sanctuary the Taliban were providing it. As Bruce Riedel recalled,

It was, from the beginning of October until the middle of December, all Afghanistan. People now, as is usually the case, think this was easy and it unfolded like clockwork. This was all being made up on the spot. These were plays that were being called at the line of scrimmage, and it was a lot messier and a lot more confusing and didn't look like it was about to succeed until well into middle-late November. And that's what the president and vice president were focused on.[1]

Richard Haass, who had been in charge of the Middle East in George H. W. Bush's NSC eight years before, agreed that Israeli-Palestinian matters were peripheral at that moment: "After 9/11 what everyone focused on was counterterrorism, Afghanistan, homeland security; I was put in charge of Afghanistan, and there was no linkage to Israel and its neighbors. There was no way, no one, even the most fanatical peace processer, could claim that what motivated Osama bin Laden was his commitment to a Palestinian state. So it was all just pushed back."[2]

Yet some at the State Department did indeed make just that claim. There was much discussion of "why do they hate us so," and many of the proposed answers fit conveniently into boxes that had long filled the minds of "Arabists" in the department. Surely the Israeli-Palestinian conflict and America's "excessive" support for Israel were the explanation for Islamic terrorism, and surely a new "peace process" was the solution. Powell himself told the president that "we need a serious Arab-Israeli peace initiative" shortly after 9/11.[3] This came as no surprise, as Douglas Feith, then undersecretary of defense for policy, ruefully explained: "What does the State Department want to do? What it *always* wants to do. It wants a major Middle East initiative. This has been the case for decades, over and over again. When there was a Cold War, *that* was the reason to do it, and when the Cold War ended then *that* was the reason to do it. And before 9/11 *that* was the reason to do it and after 9/11 *that* was the reason to do it."[4]

The intellectual battle lines were becoming clear. If the problem was one of Islamic extremism, a "war of ideas" would be required, aimed at strengthening Islamic moderates in this battle within the Islamic world. We would need to focus on matters like Saudi financing of extremist groups, getting Islamic governments to silence mullahs who preached hatred and violence against America, and how new generations of young Muslims were being educated. Although this was an internal Islamic conflict and America as a majority Christian country had a limited role to play, the stakes were too high for us to sit by. The alternative view was that we were pursuing policies that made Muslims hate us, so we would need to review and perhaps change those policies. The problem was not Muslim extremism but Muslim anti-Americanism, and the antidote might be changes in American conduct, not least in America's "one-sided" support for Israel.

The consensus at State leaned to the latter view, fortified by a similar consensus in Europe – where support for Israeli security was lukewarm at best and protests against Sharon's actions to stop the intifada were widespread. Powell cited the European pressure for engagement in the "peace process" at a meeting with Bush held soon after 9/11, assuming this pressure would be a trump card. Here again, the split between Powell's and Bush's views and Powell's apparent inability or unwillingness to adjust even after 9/11 were evident, because Bush did not acquiesce: Instead, he replied, "You know, when I hear the Europeans talk about Israel, they just sound anti-Semitic."[5]

The War on Terror

As that reaction by the president suggests, 9/11 did not push President Bush and Vice President Cheney into a reexamination of U.S. support for Israel. Their attitude toward Israel's fight against terror did indeed change when America found itself in a similar struggle, but they became *more* supportive of Israel rather than more questioning of America's closeness to the Jewish State. Over time, for example, the White House abandoned the ritual intonation that "the cycle of violence must end" whenever Israeli actions against terror resulted in Palestinian casualties, and the White House then imposed the ban on State. In the Bush-Cheney view, we were not engaged in a futile "cycle of violence" but in a war imposed on us by enemies. Our actions in Afghanistan (and later Iraq) also brought civilian casualties; we and Israel were in the same boat, and it was a "war on terror," not a "cycle of violence." Similarly, criticism of Israeli assassinations of Palestinian terrorist leaders came easily at first, but once the United States began the hunt for Osama bin Laden and Mullah Omar, that criticism could not be justified. The White House abandoned it, substituting instead the formula, "Israel has a right to defend itself" – just as did the United States. In his memoir, President Bush sums it up: "I was appalled by the violence and loss of life on both sides. But I refused to accept the moral equivalence between Palestinian suicide attacks on innocent civilians and Israeli military actions intended to protect their people. My views came into sharper focus after 9/11. If the United States had the right to defend itself and prevent future attacks, other democracies had those rights, too."[6]

While the United States suffered only one terrorist attack in 2001, in Israel the intifada continued throughout that summer and fall. There were 12 attacks in July, 15 in August, and 11 more in September. On October 2, 2 were killed and 15 injured in a grenade and gun attack. For Ariel Sharon, the struggle against terrorism was the main task he faced, and any new policies being developed in Washington after 9/11 were as likely to be harmful as they were helpful. Although there was an evolution in Bush's thinking, Sharon could not yet see it. He knew that Arab states and America's European allies were pressing Bush to crack down on Israel and its efforts against the intifada, claiming that doing so was the key to fighting al Qaeda; he was aware of the calls for some new "peace process" as well. Gen. Kaplinsky explained that Sharon "felt that the American administration is going to sacrifice Israel in order to create a new coalition in the Gulf area. And he said, 'They're going to give the European countries what they want concerning Israel – put huge pressure on us.' And he understood that they want to achieve relations with the Saudi Arabia – better relations. Better relations with Egypt. And that's what led . . . to the 'Czechoslovakia' speech."[7] While his team fiercely debated what he might say, Sharon wrote out the words himself. On October 4, after a terrorist attack at a bus station, he voiced his intentions defiantly:

Today, Israel suffered another heinous Palestinian terrorist attack, which took a heavy toll – three dead and seven wounded. All efforts to reach a ceasefire have been torpedoed by the Palestinians. The fire did not cease, not even for one day. The Cabinet has therefore instructed our security forces to take all necessary measures to bring full security to the citizens of Israel. We can rely only on ourselves. We are currently in the midst of a complex and difficult diplomatic campaign. I call on the Western democracies, and primarily the leader of the Free World – the United States: Do not repeat the dreadful mistake of 1938, when enlightened European democracies decided to sacrifice Czechoslovakia for a 'convenient temporary solution.' Do not try to appease the Arabs at our expense – this is unacceptable to us. Israel will not be Czechoslovakia.[8]

The immediate American reaction was tough: The White House press secretary said, "The president believes that these remarks are unacceptable. Israel could have no better or stronger friend than the United States and no better friend than President Bush." In fact, Sharon's decision to refer to the Munich agreement with Hitler had been spurred not primarily by what was happening in Washington, but by a telephone call he had received from the German foreign minister, Joschka Fischer. Fischer reported on a conversation he had had with Syrian President Assad, who told him "he has always been against terror," and the call concluded with Fischer demanding of Sharon, "You have to make concessions to the Palestinians." A furious Sharon saw the pattern

emerging: Europeans and perhaps now Americans would believe the Arab propaganda, overlook the terror campaign against Israel, and demand that Israeli
concessions be the coin of appeasing the terrorists.[9]

Yet the final impact of the "unacceptable remarks" was positive because they
sparked more frequent contacts between U.S. and Israeli officials – between
Rice on the U.S. side, and Ayalon and Genger on the Israeli – to avoid
such public differences in the future and reach a better understanding of how
American policy was developing. Genger, as a private citizen, was especially
free to be undiplomatic: "Arie Genger, who was very close to the Prime Minister – because he came from the private sector and was not holding any official
position – he told Condi things that I think nobody else told her. He was very
straightforward, he told her exactly what he thinks, he could have told her
'you're making mistakes,' he shouted at her, and she shouted back."[10] This
became the key channel in U.S.-Israeli relations, not the established, official
communications via the State Department.

In Israel, terrorist attacks did not diminish. On October 17, a cabinet minister was assassinated by two shots to the head outside his room at the Jerusalem
Hyatt Hotel. On October 28, 4 were killed and 40 injured by a bomb at a
bus stop. On November 4, 2 more were killed and 45 injured in a shooting
attack on a bus in Jerusalem. When President Bush delivered his remarks to the
delayed opening session of United Nations General Assembly on November 10,
he spoke primarily of the war against terror. In passing, he addressed the situation in the Middle East, and although he did not speak directly to the terrorist attacks against Israel, his words did telegraph the policy that was to
come:

The American government also stands by its commitment to a just peace in the Middle
East. We are working toward the day when two states – Israel and Palestine – live
peacefully together within secure and recognized borders as called for by the Security
Council resolutions. We will do all in our power to bring both parties back into negotiations. But peace will only come when all have sworn off forever incitement, violence
and terror.[11]

Peace would not, in this understanding, come when new negotiations had been
concluded, and it was not the product primarily of diplomacy. Nor would it be
the product of additional Israeli concessions. Instead, peace would come only
when the Palestinians had abandoned terrorism. Yet the meaning of Bush's
words was far clearer in retrospect than it was at the time. The reaction to
his speech focused on the war on terror and America's campaign to topple
the Taliban, and the words about the Middle East – even the announcement
of support for a Palestinian state – were hardly noticed. To Colin Powell,
therefore, it was high time to explain more fully what American policy in the
region would be. A source close to Powell explained his view:

In the fall he felt under considerable pressure from his Arab friends and others and
people in the United States: "What is your policy?" And he felt a speech had to be
given. Somebody had to say what we were trying to do, where we were, what did we

think about Palestinians, what did we think about Israelis, what did we think about all of this. There had been not a single word that represented the administration's policy or point of view. So he arranged to give a speech . . . and everybody sort of went along.[12]

On November 19, Powell spoke at the University of Louisville in Kentucky, and the Middle East was his central topic. He made a clear and tough demand that Palestinian terror end:

The Palestinian leadership must make a 100 percent effort to end violence and to end terror. There must be real results, not just words and declarations. Terrorists must be stopped before they act. The Palestinian leadership must arrest, prosecute, and punish the perpetrators of terrorist acts. Whatever the sources of Palestinian frustration and anger under occupation, the *Intifada* is now mired in the quicksand of self-defeating violence and terror directed against Israel. And as President Bush has made clear, no national aspiration, no remembered wrong can ever justify the deliberate murder of the innocent. Terror and violence must stop and stop now.

Yet Powell also demanded that "[c]onsistent with the report of the committee headed by Senator George Mitchell, settlement activity must stop," used the terms "occupation" and "Israel's occupation of the West Bank and Gaza," and said flatly that "the occupation must end. And it can only end with negotiations." The security work of George Tenet and the recommendations of the Mitchell Report would be the basis for moving forward. The objective of U.S. policy was now clearly Palestinian statehood. Palestinian leaders "must make clear that their objective is a Palestinian state alongside Israel, not in place of Israel, and which takes full account of Israel's security needs," while Israel "must be willing to . . . accept a viable Palestinian State."

On the core issues, Powell was vague: Jerusalem was "a challenge"; for Palestinian refugees there must be "a just solution." Similarly vague was how to get to this new destination. Although Powell said that "the United States is ready to play an active leadership role," all he could offer was that "President Bush and I have asked Assistant Secretary of State for Near Eastern Affairs Bill Burns to return to the region later this week for consultations." To this he added, "Retired Marine Corps General Anthony Zinni has agreed to serve as a senior advisor to me, with the immediate mission of helping the parties achieve a durable cease-fire and to move along the lines of the Tenet security work plan and the Mitchell Committee Report." This was just more of the old medicine. Zinni was being sent to the region, where he would work with "senior-level committees" that Sharon and Arafat were forming. Although in this speech Powell was clearly reasserting his own bureaucratic ownership of the "peace process," how he intended to move forward remained unclear.

The speech did not evoke a strong reaction, and most responses were negative. Like Bush's mention of a Palestinian state in his UN address, the words Powell spoke were not viewed as earth-shaking. *Syria Times* said Powell "did not break much new ground"; the Jordanian government called the speech "serious" but added, "we are awaiting the practical procedural steps"[13]; a commentator in the Israeli paper *Maariv* claimed Powell "said nothing new or exciting" and that Powell's "vision" was "like reheated pasta."[14] The *Jerusalem Post* summarized that "Arabs and Europeans reacted coolly."[15] The coolness reflected a sense that the United States may have had an objective of Palestinian statehood, but it had no way forward to achieve it – for better or worse. These were just words, speeches, and "work plans," and there would be more visitors to the area: To Middle Easterners, it all sounded like more of the same.

Sharon reacted quietly because he had been told what was coming. As Shalom Tourgeman explained, after the 9/11 attacks, American attention was turned away from the Israeli-Palestinian conflict and then came back to it:

You were too busy with analyzing how it will be, and what are the implications of 9/11 on America. And Iraq – the focus was Iraq.... We entered a period where every week we had here a terror attack, and we had to deal with it. Then we started the thinking process of a Palestinian state, which was an idea that was agreed quietly with Sharon, but he wanted to see what are the reactions when you are spelling it out, and it was the first time that you mentioned it. The issue of a Palestinian state was first raised in the speech of Powell in Kentucky. And the administration called us before to prepare Sharon that this is something that Powell is going to do. And this was the first time and it was a big, big issue in Israel, that the Americans are supporting the establishment of a Palestinian state. He didn't get excited because he knew.[16]

Arafat's Ship Sinks Him

Nor could Sharon complain when visiting American officials, from Powell to Tenet and Zinni and Mitchell, met with Arafat because in his months as prime minister, he had been in frequent if indirect contact with Arafat. Shimon Peres, then Israel's foreign minister, had been sent to meet with the PLO leader, as had Sharon's older son Omri; Sharon and Arafat had even spoken on the telephone. But the terror did not stop. On November 27, 2 were killed and 50 injured in a shooting attack at a bus station. On November 29, a suicide bombing on a bus killed three and injured nine. On December 1, two suicide bombings at the largest pedestrian shopping street in Jerusalem, the Ben Yehuda mall, killed 11 and injured 180 people. The following day, 15 were killed and 40 injured by another suicide bombing in a bus, this time in Haifa. That was 26 dead in 24 hours. A week later on December 9, another bus bombing in Haifa injured 30 more Israelis. On December 12, 11 more people were killed and 30 injured in another bus bombing. The year was ending in a burst of Palestinian terrorist violence that Sharon could not seem to stop.

While the Israelis were maintaining contact with Arafat, they were also punishing him for these attacks: On December 4, for example, after the Ben Yehuda mall bombings, they had attacked his offices in both the West Bank and Gaza. They viewed him as a terrorist but were unable to break contact with him – in part because the United States and Europe seemed to view him as a statesman. In 1994, he had (with Shimon Peres and Yitzhak Rabin) received the Nobel Peace Prize for the Oslo Accords; during the Clinton years, he was invited to the White House a remarkable 13 times, more often than any other foreign leader. Israeli efforts to get the United States to see Arafat as a terrorist leader had failed before and, after 9/11, Arafat was eloquent in denying any connection to terror.

Yet on January 3, 2002, Israel seized a ship called the *Karine A*, and Arafat's world began to change. The freighter had been purchased in August 2001 by Adel Mughrabi, a Palestinian associated with Fatah and with Arafat, and had sailed to Sudan. There it picked up its regular cargo – and a new Palestinian crew. In November, in Yemen, some weapons were loaded on board. In December, it sailed near Iran, and a smaller vessel approached it and transferred 80 large wooden crates carrying 50 tons of Iranian arms for the PLO's use against Israel. Commanding the Iranian vessel ferrying the arms to the *Karine A* was Haji Bassem, the deputy of Hizballah's operations chief, the arch-terrorist Imad Mughniyah. Israeli naval commandos seized the ship in international waters in the Red Sea, on its way to the Suez Canal and thence to Gaza. In those crates on board, the Israelis found 345 Katyusha rockets, 735 hand grenades, 1,545 mortar shells, antitank missiles and mines, sniper rifles, Kalashnikov rifles, 700,000 rounds of small arms ammunition, and 2,000 kilograms of explosives. It was discovered that the chief procurement and finance officer of Arafat's Palestinian Authority, Fouad Shubaki, had handled payment for the weapons, inextricably tying Arafat to the episode.

The eventual result was a new American view of Arafat, who was now placed in the post-9/11 context: He was a terrorist, working with Iran and Hizballah, at the moment when America was in a global war against terror. After Israel's discovery of the ship's cargo, Sharon had summoned his aide Danny Ayalon and told him, "Call Rice." There were documents she needed to see, revealing who was behind the *Karine A*, who had paid for it, and what was on it. The intelligence attaché at the Israeli Embassy in Washington was Shlomo Mofaz, brother of IDF Chief of Staff Shaul Mofaz, and he brought the papers to the NSC offices personally. Steve Hadley, at the time deputy national security advisor to Rice, summed it up: "*Karine A* is a terribly important incident in our Middle East policy, because it confirms a view that the Israelis were pushing on us very hard, which was, 'You don't understand Arafat. Arafat is in fact a purveyor of terror.'"[17] General Zinni was in the Middle East that day and "actually watched news of the *Karine A*'s capture on television while Arafat was sitting beside him."[18] Arafat denied everything to Zinni's face. The whole affair had been fabricated to undermine Zinni's mission, Arafat said; he knew nothing about it. Initially, Zinni believed the denials, which made his anger at Arafat's lies even greater later on.

In retrospect, it is clear that the *Karine A* affair was a turning point in perceptions of Arafat, but the realization that he was permanently wedded to terror came slowly, at least for some: "One week after the seizure, Secretary of State Colin Powell could still be heard insisting that he had 'not seen any information that yet links [the *Karine A*] directly to Chairman Arafat.'"[19] In many ways, it is astonishing that as late as January 2002, the United States was dealing with Arafat as a possible peacemaker and desirable ruler of a new Palestinian state. After returning from Tunis as part of the Oslo Accords, Arafat had established a corrupt satrapy ruled by a web of "security forces" reporting only to him. He crushed the civil society that had come to life in the form of several hundred NGOs after 1967, when Israeli rule replaced that of Jordan.[20] Arafat led a one-man band, playing rivals and underlings off against each other and absolutely forbidding the establishment of political institutions that might have limited his personal power. There was no reason to believe that an independent state ruled by Arafat would be organized any differently. What is more, Arafat had been involved in terrorism for decades, from organizing the murder of the U.S. ambassador to Sudan in 1973 to leading the first intifada after 1987. Yet even after this latest episode, Arafat was viewed in some quarters as a man with whom business had to be done.

The State Department drafted a secret letter to Arafat, in essence telling him he needed to cut it out; henceforth, no more terrorism. Yet by focusing solely on the future, this draft would tacitly inform Arafat that he was to pay no penalty for the *Karine A*, a conclusion Arafat would reach instantaneously. Despite the war on terror, then, the draft of the letter would signal to him that he could engage in business as usual: terror, denials, more terror.

Rice kept the draft from the vice president's office, but a member of his staff overheard a reference to it and demanded to see the text. The result was a 45-minute confrontation between Rice and Powell on one side and the VP's chief of staff, Scooter Libby, on the other. Rice and Powell told Libby "we have a policy" and it includes dealing with Arafat; Libby's succinct reply was that the VP does not agree with the letter. Cheney took the issue to President Bush, and the letter was never sent.

So in the immediate aftermath of the *Karine A*, the administration neither reached out to Arafat nor did it publicly break with him. In a letter to Powell, Arafat denied any knowledge of or involvement in the arms shipment, a lie that again helped persuade Cheney and many others that Arafat was simply incorrigible. Bush states in his memoir that "Arafat had lied to me. I never trusted him again."[21] Yet at the State Department, there was equivocation: In the department's January 11 press briefing, its spokesman said Arafat must "provide himself a full explanation of what went on, and take action to ensure that it doesn't reoccur." There was a compelling case of PA involvement, so "Chairman Arafat has a responsibility as the leader of the Palestinian Authority to provide a full explanation, and a responsibility to take immediate action against those responsible."[22] It seemed that, for the State Department, Arafat could engage in such activity, lie about it, blame others, make believe he was punishing them, promise not to do it again, and all would be forgiven.

Yet for Sharon and for Bush, the Arafat who would – even after 9/11, even after the administration had endorsed Palestinian statehood, even while American envoys were visiting him regularly, even while Sharon sent secret emissaries to maintain contact – buy tens of millions of dollars worth of arms from Iran for use against Israel was a different figure after the *Karine A* incident. By late January, the president was blaming Arafat directly for promoting terror: "I am disappointed in Chairman Arafat. He must make a full effort to rout out terror... and ordering up weapons that were intercepted on a boat headed... for that part of the world is not part of fighting terror, that's enhancing terror."[23] Cheney added in a television interview days later that "[w]hat's most disturbing isn't just the shipment of arms, it's the fact that it came from Iran.... So what we have here is Yasser Arafat... doing business with Hizballah and Iran.... And it's difficult to take him seriously as an interlocutor in that peace process if he's going to conduct himself in that fashion."[24]

As shown by that CNN interview and his intervention to stop the Powell/Rice letter to Arafat, Cheney was concluding that Arafat was the problem, not part of the solution. To work with him was to turn a blind eye to Palestinian, Iranian, and Hizballah terror. Cheney's aide John Hannah explained that

Karine A is certainly critical in our universe because it does move the Vice President to finally say... you've got to get rid of Arafat, Arafat is a fundamental problem in terms of his support for violence, his role in terror, the kind of entity he's building in the West Bank.... *Karine A* I think really seals the deal for him that there is just no working with this guy; that he's incorrigible and cannot be redeemed and should not be redeemed – and in fact that he should be seen in the region as suffering a real price for promoting this kind of instability and violence, and being in bed with the Iranians and Mughniyah on *Karine A*. So I think the Vice President reaches a firm conclusion at that point.[25]

Cheney's intervention was a sign of another development that the *Karine A* affair had spurred: "Officials at the Pentagon and the White House... began wresting control of Israel policy from the State Department in mid-January."[26]

Terror and Candlelight

While officials in Washington mulled over Arafat's role and its implications for any future efforts at Middle East diplomacy, Palestinian terrorism escalated. On January 17, a shooting attack at a bar mitzvah reception killed 6 and injured 35. On January 22, a shooting attack at a Jerusalem bus stop on the busy Jaffa Road killed 2 and injured 40. On January 25, a suicide bombing injured 25 people near a café on a pedestrian mall in Tel Aviv. On January 27, a suicide bombing at almost the same spot as the January 22 attack killed one man and injured 150. In February, attacks came roughly every other day.

March was even worse, with almost daily attacks killing one or two Israelis. On March 2, 10 people were killed (including 6 children) and more than 50 injured when a suicide bomber detonated his explosives next to a group of women gathered around baby carriages outside a synagogue. Ten people, including seven soldiers, were killed in an attack at a roadblock on March 3. Fifteen people were injured by a suicide bombing on March 7.

The bloodshed was so great that Sharon lifted his year-old "seven days of quiet" demand, deciding on March 8 that negotiations with the Palestinians could recommence. He was responding to an American proposal that, in view of the extent of violence, the Tenet security plan should be implemented immediately. Yet on March 9, a bombing at the Café Moment in downtown Jerusalem, just blocks from the prime minister's residence, killed 11 and injured 54, while on the same day in Netanya, 2 were killed and 50 injured by two Palestinians using guns and grenades.

Sharon told IDF troops on March 10,

I have been demanding seven days of quiet as a precondition for entering into negotiations for a ceasefire. I know that I am now criticized for changing my mind. Due to the level of violence and the intensity of barbaric terrorist attacks inflicted on us – and the brave [counterterrorist] war being conducted by commanders and soldiers, there is no possibility at this stage of achieving a few days of quiet. I decided that since I had always attached great importance to the matter of achieving a ceasefire, I was also willing to change my position.

The policy shift by Sharon had no effect. A bus bombing in Jerusalem injured 25 people on March 17, and on March 20 an attack on a bus traveling from Jerusalem to Nazareth killed 7 and injured 30. On March 27, Palestinian terrorists exploded a bomb during a Passover seder at the Park Hotel in Netanya, killing 27 Israelis and injuring 140. Two were killed and more than 20 wounded by a bomb attack at a Jerusalem supermarket on March 29. On March 30, 1 was killed and 30 injured by a café bombing in downtown Tel Aviv. On the last day of the month, 14 people were killed and more than 40 injured by a suicide bomb in a Haifa restaurant.

In response, Sharon said the country "is at war" and Israel moved back into the West Bank in force – attacking terrorists and their workshops and PA buildings, declaring Ramallah a closed military zone, and surrounding Arafat in the Muqata – where electricity and water were cut off. IDF troops were but a few yards from Arafat's offices. All this activity turned out to be a public relations disaster because Arafat appeared on television throughout the world as the victim, not the terrorist. Lit by candlelight, he appealed for international pressure to stop Israel's attacks. The United States voted along with every other member of the Security Council (except Syria, which abstained) for a resolution calling for "immediate cessation of all acts of violence, including all acts of terror" and urging "the parties to halt the violence."[27] This was the kind of moral equivalence between terrorists and their Israeli victims that the United States would later come to reject. Yet in a news conference held the day after the UN vote, President Bush said, "I understand someone trying to defend themselves and to fight terror, but the recent [Israeli] actions aren't helpful."[28]

The Saudi Plan

In the midst of this paroxysm of violence in early 2002 came a peace proposal from an unlikely source: Crown Prince Abdallah of Saudi Arabia. Abdallah discussed his thoughts with Thomas Friedman of the *New York Times*, who wrote about them in a column on February 17. Abdallah's idea was "full withdrawal from all the occupied territories, in accord with U.N. resolutions, including in Jerusalem, for full normalization of relations." He told Friedman,

I have drafted a speech along those lines. My thinking was to deliver it before the Arab summit and try to mobilize the entire Arab world behind it. The speech is written, and it is in my desk.... I wanted to find a way to make clear to the Israeli people that the Arabs don't reject or despise them. But the Arab people do reject what their leadership is now doing to the Palestinians, which is inhumane and oppressive. And I thought of this as a possible signal to the Israeli people.

The Arab League summit on March 27 adopted a version of Abdallah's plan, which became "the Arab Plan." Ever since, Saudis and other Arabs have criticized both Israel and the United States for ignoring it and have argued that it would have provided a solution for the Israeli-Palestinian conflict – if only we had implemented it.

Having the Saudi head of government speak of normalization with Israel – under any circumstances whatsoever – was a significant step forward, but the Saudi claims that their ruler had provided a magic solution for the region were disingenuous. For one thing, this was no offer to negotiate with Israel: It was a "take it or leave it" statement. For another, its demand was clearly unacceptable: a complete return to the 1967 borders, which Israelis (and American officials) had long ago concluded were indefensible. Returning to the "1967 borders" also meant abandoning the Old City of Jerusalem, including the Western Wall of the ancient Temple, and every single settlement. The issue of Palestinian refugees, not mentioned by Abdallah, was added to the brew at the Arab summit in Beirut, making it even less potable for Israel: To accept millions of Palestinians into Israel would destroy the Jewish character of the society (which was presumably the goal of Syria and Sudan, who threw in this provision). Finally, although Abdallah had spoken only of Israeli-Palestinian peace, the "Arab Plan" adopted in Beirut required Israeli withdrawal not only from the Golan Heights but also from "the remaining occupied Lebanese territories in the south of Lebanon." This was a reference to the Sheba'a Farms area, which the United Nations itself had found to be Syrian, not Lebanese, territory, so adding a reference to it was yet another complication designed to be a killer amendment.

Then there was the issue of form. Given the American relationship with Israel, if Abdallah's proposal was meant to commence negotiations or a new peace effort, it is reasonable to think he might have given Washington a head's up or asked the administration to convey the proposal to the Israelis. He did not, laying out the plan in a column – not even a news story – in the *New York Times*. That was an odd way to put something on the table if he truly sought American backing.

Sharon's reaction, privately, was "[i]f it is a serious plan by the Saudis, let the Saudis talk to me about it." As Shalom Tourgeman put it, "What is the beginning of the Arab initiative? It is the Saudi plan that was launched. By

Tom Friedman writing about it, in the middle of a wave of terror. Now, how on the most critical and important issue to the future of our country, can one expect that we should rely on an editorial or an article written by a journalist from America? It wasn't serious."[29] Remembering the way Anwar Sadat's visit to Jerusalem had changed Israeli-Egyptian relations, perhaps a dramatic presentation of the plan in Jerusalem by a group of Arab leaders might have created a new dynamic. Yet no such visit came; instead, the original (and vague) terms suggested by Abdallah via Friedman were stiffened at the summit meeting on March 27 – and later that very same day came the "Park Hotel Massacre," the bloody and vicious bombing of a Passover seder in the coastal town of Netanya.

With Palestinian terrorism mounting and the list of victims growing, American diplomacy limped along almost aimlessly. Calls for Arafat to clamp down on the violence were endlessly repeated, as if it were not clear that he was in fact behind the violence. When Vice President Cheney visited several capitals in the Middle East in March, the schedule did not include a meeting with Arafat. Such a meeting had not been discussed in Washington. But once Air Force Two lifted off, Powell's man on the trip, Assistant Secretary Bill Burns, told Cheney he simply had to see the Palestinian leader – and facilitate his attendance at the Arab summit that was to be held March 27 in Beirut. As Eric Edelman, then Cheney's top foreign policy advisor, explained, "The idea was you'd get Sharon to agree that Arafat could go and come back, and then you'd get Arafat to agree that he would take some serious steps to deal with terror, and then the vice president would meet with him and he would go off to the Arab Summit." The VP's view was that most likely "Arafat wouldn't deliver, but there was a chance he might; but in the meantime you'd be able to tell Abdallah that we had done what we could for his peace plan."[30] Libby and Hannah on Cheney's staff argued against any meeting with Arafat: Especially after the *Karine A* incident, such a meeting meant business as usual with a terrorist and would undercut the entire war on terror.

The party reached a compromise: General Zinni was accompanying the VP in Israel, and if Arafat made certain firm antiterror commitments to Zinni, Cheney would see him later in the trip. As Cheney puts it in his memoir, "Would it be helpful, I asked, to set up a meeting with me as an inducement for Arafat's cooperation? Zinni said that it would, and so I offered to meet with Arafat provided he agreed to the conditions Zinni had set forth. Zinni was confident."[31]

Zinni believed that Arafat had already made these commitments orally, and he needed only to get the PLO chief to sign a piece of paper setting forth the agreed terms. Simple: Arafat signs and gets a visit from the VP in Ramallah. But when Zinni contacted him, Arafat would not sign. Zinni wanted more time. It was then agreed that if Arafat could be persuaded to sign, Cheney would see him at the very end of the trip, in Cairo. Still, and to Zinni's amazement, Arafat would not sign, so no meeting was held with the vice president. Shortly thereafter came the Park Hotel bombing of a Passover seder, and the Zinni mission was all but dead as well. In Zinni's words, "I knew immediately we had come to the end of the road."[32]

The Policy Mish-Mash

On March 29, Israel commenced what it called "Operation Defensive Shield," the largest military operation in the West Bank since the 1967 war. The goal: to stop terrorist attacks by hitting Palestinian targets, capturing terrorists, and making it nearly impossible for terrorists to plan and implement attacks. Arafat was put under siege at his headquarters in the Muqata in Ramallah. The IDF made incursions in all the major West Bank cities and into several refugee camps.

Immediately there were Palestinian claims of mass casualties, centering on the "Jenin Massacre" at the refugee camp there – where according to PLO officials, up to 500 people had been killed. It later emerged that, in fact, 52 Palestinians (mostly gunmen) and 23 IDF soldiers had died, but the Palestinian claims were picked up in the world media and by Arab governments. The latter began pressing Washington to stop the IDF and, according to Rice, "threatening all manner of retaliation if the Israelis didn't stop."[33] The Arab governments were also demanding that the United States protect Arafat, whom they believed (or in any event claimed) would be assassinated by the Israelis. President Bush did call Sharon to demand that the attacks on Arafat's Muqata stop and made the demand publicly as well. Ayalon recalled, "During *Defensive Shield* there were a few phone calls between Sharon and Bush that were not pleasant. When Bush said 'When I say now, I mean now,' it was after a phone call he made with Sharon. But Sharon didn't get the message and it wasn't a very good phone call."

Ayalon was referring to what were probably the roughest moments in U.S.-Israel relations in all eight Bush years; Rice called it "a deepening split with Israel."[34] On April 4, Bush said in a speech that "Israel is facing a terrible and serious challenge. For seven days, it has acted to root out terrorist nests. America recognizes Israel's right to defend itself from terror. Yet, to lay the foundations of future peace, I ask Israel to halt incursions into Palestinian-controlled areas and begin the withdrawal from those cities it has recently occupied.... Storms of violence cannot go on. Enough is enough." When Israel did not pull back, he repeated the message in tougher language on April 8: "I meant what I said to the Prime Minister of Israel. I expect there to be withdrawal without delay.... I repeat, I meant what I said about withdrawal without delay." Bush denounced terrorism with clarity and called on not only Palestinians but also the Arab states to act against it, but the confrontation with Sharon was clear. In Sharon's view, Israel and Israelis were under attack, and he would fight and win this war. For the Bush administration, concerned both about pressure from Arab allies and about picking up the pieces after the violence had diminished, an absolute demolition of the Palestinian political structure was unwise.

We were now seven months after 9/11, but in April 2002, U.S. policy in the Middle East remained a mish-mash, even though it had a new and concrete goal: Palestinian statehood. On March 12, the United States had supported a UN Security Council resolution (Resolution 1397) that for the first time explicitly called for two states, Israel and Palestine, living "side by side." Yet how that goal could be reached when the Palestinian leader was understood to be a terrorist himself was entirely unclear. Judging by the continuing trips to the region and the visits with Arafat, policy still seemed to revolve around re-creating conditions for a new peace negotiation between the PLO leader and the Israelis. On April 1, Rice called a small meeting to think through options. We have a policy that is "visibly different" from the past, she said; our goal is a Palestinian state, so a political solution exists in theory. Yet the creation of that state cannot appear to be the result of terror and violence, and it cannot be a terrorist state. She was grasping for a new approach.

In his April 4 remarks, the president announced that he was sending Secretary Powell on another visit to the region. This decision was less a reflection of policy than a substitute for one. At a meeting the following day to prepare for the trip, Rice warned Powell against falling back into the old "peace process" because the president was sympathetic with Israel's struggle against terrorism and nowhere called for new negotiations with Arafat. Yet it was clearer what Powell should *not* do than what he should: It seemed he was being sent only because the United States had to appear to be doing something to end the violence. As a biographer of Rice put it, "Bush had decided. . . . that there was little the United States could do to nudge the parties toward peace or even a suppression of hostilities. But he could also not be seen as indifferent to the downward spiral of events. By April 1, he concluded that he would have to send Powell to the Middle East. The Secretary of State did not want to go, and both he and the president knew that the trip would be futile."[35]

An official close to Powell described the event similarly:

In the spring of 2002 things turn rough because the Israelis move into the Muqata and they bottle up Arafat. He's [Powell's] getting tired of going over there knowing that he really has nothing in his caboose, nothing in his sheath. So he goes over there at the president's request. It's March and he doesn't want to go over there, but the president had suddenly realized he cannot ignore this stuff. The Israelis have cut off the power, they've cut off the water . . . the lights, everything, and Arafat's sitting in the dark with candles and AK-47s. And so we have a meeting in the Sit Room and the president says, "You know, I've got to do something and I think Colin has to go over and try to break this open." And we're walking out and the president says to Powell, "I really need you to do this. It's going to be hard, and I know that you're going to get beat up, but your credibility and your standing is such that you can afford to lose a little," which is right. And Powell replied, "I understand, Mr. President. That's the job."[36]

Powell began his Middle East visit on April 7, making several stops along the way in Europe and Morocco; at the stop in Madrid, he formed the "Quartet" (the United States, the European Union, Russia, and the UN Secretary General) that was to play a continuing role in Middle East negotiations. A State Department official explained,

He did create the Quartet. And the real reason for this is he wanted to show international backing for this trip he was taking. Secondly he was being driven nuts by every European foreign minister coming out with his own plan every day, especially Joschka Fischer. Every three days he had another German plan, or Igor Ivanov had a plan, and if he had a plan, Germany had to have a plan. And then the Brits were always saying, "We have to have a plan." But getting the EU as one entity relieved them of having to come up with plans all the time, so the Quartet served that purpose.[37]

Powell may have united the EU, but divisions in Washington were, in his view, not only clear but becoming nasty. A source very close to Powell described the scene from his perspective: "There was nobody behind him in the White House and as soon as the plane lifts off from Andrews Air Force Base, the NSC, the Vice President's Office, and everybody else in the White House was stabbing him in the back." Powell met Sharon on April 12 and was to see Arafat the following day. When another suicide bombing at a Jerusalem bus stop killed six, Powell did not cancel the meeting but merely postponed it by one day and met Arafat on April 14. A State Department official who traveled with Powell described how Powell spent his time in the region:

He went into the region, he went to the Muqata a couple of times, he spent a lot of time with Sharon. It was miserable because he knew that we're not going to have any breakthroughs here. We're able to break open Arafat and get him some running room from the Israelis; they kind of backed off. But he kept getting these rudder checks from Washington to make sure he didn't do anything. Just solve the problem, but don't do anything. You can talk about settlement freezes because that's our policy, but the president will not say anything along those lines. So he was in that terrible position where he was presenting what is official U.S. policy with the knowledge that the U.S. government would not support what he was saying was official U.S. policy, and they all knew it. And so after a while he got tired of it because he was being unfair to the process and he was being used by his own government. So he said to Arafat in their last meeting, "You've got to give me something. I can't keep coming back here. Nobody will see you in my government. I'm it. I am it." He saw Arafat twice in that three-day period. In the last meeting he said, "Goodbye if you don't give me something to work with other than your rhetoric ... you can't make statements that don't turn out to be true, you don't follow up on. If you don't give me something that I can take back and show real progress with, and not just another statement, then this is probably our last meeting." And Arafat said, "You're a general, I'm a general; I will obey." It was all crapola. Nothing really changed.

"He's Missed His Opportunities"

Arafat was playing the same games that had kept him at the top of Palestinian politics for decades and won him all those visits to the White House. But he had either not read or not taken seriously the rest of Bush's speech of April 4 dispatching Powell to the region to try and stop the violence. Rice, Rumsfeld, and others in the administration were beginning to focus on a new idea: that new Palestinian leadership was the key to moving forward.

In fact, Bush's speech had contained something that was new – a direct attack on Arafat. Finally, the frustrations that Bill Clinton had voiced in the Oval Office on January 20, 2001, were being expressed publicly and by the president himself:

> This can be a time for hope. But it calls for leadership, not for terror. Since September the 11th, I've delivered this message: everyone must choose; you're either with the civilized world, or you're with the terrorists. All in the Middle East also must choose and must move decisively in word and deed against terrorist acts.
>
> The Chairman of the Palestinian Authority has not consistently opposed or confronted terrorists. At Oslo and elsewhere, Chairman Arafat renounced terror as an instrument of his cause, and he agreed to control it. He's not done so.
>
> The situation in which he finds himself today is largely of his own making. He's missed his opportunities, and thereby betrayed the hopes of the people he's supposed to lead.
>
> I call on the Palestinian people, the Palestinian Authority and our friends in the Arab world to join us in delivering a clear message to terrorists: blowing yourself up does not help the Palestinian cause. To the contrary, suicide bombing missions could well blow up the best and only hope for a Palestinian state.
>
> No nation can pick and choose its terrorist friends. I call on the Palestinian Authority and all governments in the region to do everything in their power to stop terrorist activities, to disrupt terrorist financing, and to stop inciting violence by glorifying terror in state-owned media, or telling suicide bombers they are martyrs. They're not martyrs. They're murderers. And they undermine the cause of the Palestinian people.
>
> The Palestinian people deserve peace and an opportunity to better their lives. . . . They deserve a government that respects human rights and a government that focuses on their needs – education and health care – rather than feeding their resentments.[38]

The speech put Arafat and his leadership style – corruption, one-man rule, lack of any real political institutions, terrorism – front and center. Yet the debate over how much effort Bush should put into the Middle East continued inside the administration. Cheney and Powell faced off at a Principals Committee meeting on April 18, after Powell's return. Cheney was "kind of a hard realist oriented towards the security of Israel" and thought "the peace process was unlikely to have results."[39] When Cheney told Powell, "Don't get completely consumed with Arab-Israeli issues," Powell replied, "You're dreaming if you don't think the Arab-Israeli conflict is central to the region – central to whatever we want to do in Iraq. Don't underestimate the centrality of this crisis." The argument that "if you want to do anything in Iraq, you need an Israeli-Palestinian peace process" would be heard again and again. Rice told her colleagues it was time for a new look at all the "fundamental assumptions of ours that may no longer be right" given 9/11 and changes in the region.[40]

Powell agreed that it was time to rethink his approach: After his April trip, a close aide said, "He came back and that's when we decided we had to shut this off and that's when we started writing the June 24th speech. So we started working in that direction, because he wasn't about to go back over there just to be stiffed by both sides. He felt he was losing whatever he had left. The Quartet was around and we met from time to time, but it was nothing more than keeping a plate spinning; it wasn't progress."[41]

While at the White House on April 18, Powell reported to the Oval Office to tell Bush about his trip. After the briefing, Bush and Powell faced the press, and while cameras whirred, Bush took a notably pro-Israel stance. "Israel started withdrawing quickly after our call from smaller cities on the West Bank. History will show that they've responded," Bush said. "And as the prime minister said, he gave me a timetable and he's met the timetable." And Bush went further: "I do believe Ariel Sharon is a man of peace." This comment infuriated the Palestinian leadership, but they were not alone in reacting negatively: According to White House scuttlebutt, the president's father, George H. W. Bush, who seldom called him on policy matters, telephoned to complain vociferously about the president's choice of words. Nor was the former president alone: Rice "fully agreed at the time that the President had made a mistake" and "done long term damage to our relations in the Arab world," and Powell felt that even more strongly.[42] Yet Bush himself was not sorry: "The President's view – and it worked in some cases and didn't work in some cases – was very much, I'm going to show public faith in leaders so I can call them to account in private. He told me that after he said that about Sharon, he told him, 'You better live up to that. You know I'm going out on limb for you; you better live up to that.'"[43]

One week later came an intervention more consequential than that of George H. W. Bush: The Saudis became involved once again. Crown Prince Abdallah came to the president's ranch in Crawford, Texas, loaded for bear. President Bush's public remarks about the visit suggested a placid conversation: "One of the really positive things out of this meeting was the fact that the Crown Prince and I established a strong personal bond. . . . I made it clear to him that I expected Israel to withdraw, just like I've made it clear to Israel. And we expect them to be finished. He knows my position. He also knows that I will work for peace; I will bring parties along." Bush also noted that "Saudi Arabia made it clear that they will not use oil as a weapon," but he emphasized the personal side of the visit: "I had the honor of showing him my ranch. He's a man who's got a farm and he understands the land, and I really took great delight in being able to drive him around in a pickup truck and showing him the trees and my favorite spots. And we saw a wild turkey, which was good. But we had a very good discussion, and I'm honored he came to visit."

However, the visit had been anything but cordial: it was better described as a "spectacular showdown."[44] Abdallah bridled at the humiliation – for all Arabs, he said – of Israeli tanks surrounding an Arab leader in his capital and had demanded that Bush pick up the telephone and instruct Sharon to pull back his tanks and allow Arafat to move freely. He rejected Bush's explanation that this was impossible, that the United States did not have the ability to order the Israelis around this way; he was not mollified when Bush instructed Rice to call Sharon's chief of staff and discuss Arafat's situation and the president's desire to end the stand-off at the Muqata. The Crown Prince told Bush that the treatment of Arafat would affect U.S.-Saudi relations and made a direct threat: If nothing happened, he would publicly say that he had tried to do something to help the Palestinians, by going to Saudi Arabia's closest friend and ally, which is the United States, but the president of the United States was unable to help. As one member of the president's party recalled it,

He [Abdallah] was pretty strong in his views. He almost took it personally. He imagined any other Arab leader somehow surrounded and nobody is able to help; he just thought that this is totally unacceptable. I remember Abdallah was showing the president all kinds of pictures and images of Palestinian children affected by Israeli fire. And I remember the President also saying on the other side you also have very similar pictures and there are victims from every side; one side will not have a monopoly on pain and suffering.

Abdallah and his party began making preparations to leave, and the meeting would have ended with U.S.-Saudi relations in crisis; as the president later wrote, "America's pivotal relationship with Saudi Arabia was about to be seriously ruptured."[45] Bush called a break and said he would like to show Abdallah around the ranch. He drove the Crown Prince in his pickup truck, and after several minutes of driving toward one end of the ranch, a wild turkey crossed the path. As Bush tells the story,

We reached a remote part of the property. A lone hen turkey was standing in the road. I stopped the truck. The bird stayed put. "What is that?" the crown prince asked. I told him it was a turkey.... Suddenly I felt the crown prince's hand grab my arm. "My brother," he said, "it is a sign from Allah. This is a good omen." I've never fully understood the significance of the bird, but I felt the tension begin to melt.[46]

The mood changed instantly, the meeting resumed, and from that point on the relationship between the two men was cordial and indeed trusting. No doubt it helped that within days, on April 28, the Israeli cabinet did decide to move the tanks back and free Arafat; Abdallah presumably saw an American hand at work in that decision. Bush immediately issued a statement commending the Israelis and demanding that Arafat "now seize this opportunity to act decisively in word and in deed against terror directed at Israeli citizens."

Relations with both Sharon, momentarily rough after the president's "enough is enough" comments, and with Abdallah were on an even keel by the end of April, and the demands for Arafat to fight terror had been clear since the April 4 speech. But now what? How would the United States move forward? How would progress toward a Palestinian state be possible? When Ariel Sharon visited Washington on May 7, he said discussion of a Palestinian state was "premature" and instead focused on the need to stop terror, Israel's desire for peace, and "the need for reform in the Palestinian Authority." Bush recalled that "we had a good discussion about how to move forward" and reiterated his demands of Arafat: political reform, an end to terror, and unification of Palestinian security forces into one command structure (not the dozen or so separate fiefdoms Arafat had created). He also repeated his attack on the Palestinian leader: "I'll reiterate; I have been disappointed in Chairman Arafat. I think he's let the Palestinian people down. I think he's had an opportunity to lead to peace and he hasn't done so." No doubt intelligence and newspaper reports about Arafat's wealth – in 2003, *Forbes* estimated it as "at least $300 million"[47] and others suggested figures several times as high – also helped turn opinion against Arafat in Washington. But the lack of real progress in the region was dramatized when Sharon had to cut short his visit and rush home: A suicide bomber had detonated explosives in a Tel Aviv club, killing 15 Israelis and wounding more than 50.

Arafat was now making speeches about both political and security reform; he was not entirely deaf to the words coming from Washington. But despite the change in rhetoric, it was the old game: He was doing nothing to implement reforms – or to stop the terrorism. Three were killed and 50 injured at a market in Netanya on May 19. On May 22, 2 more were killed and 40 injured by a suicide bombing in Rishon Le Zion. On May 27, 2 were killed and 40 injured at an ice cream parlor in Petah Tikva, and 4 more Israelis were killed the following day in two more attacks. Finally, on June 5, 19 were killed and 74 wounded in a suicide bombing, in which a car laden with explosives drove into a bus at the Megiddo Junction in northern Israel.

For Sharon, that bombing was the last straw: Israeli troops attacked Arafat's compound and other West Bank locations again, this time eliciting a much quieter American reaction even when those troops entered and reoccupied the major towns. With terrorist attacks continuing almost daily, on June 15, Sharon announced a new plan: to build a fence 200 miles long separating Palestinians from Israelis and thereby thwarting suicide bombers.

Behind the scenes, Rice was thinking more about Palestinian reform. On May 21, she had met privately with a group of Catholic bishops, telling them the president had been clearer than anyone else about the need for a Palestinian state, but the issue was how to get there. Reform is the key, she said, because a corrupt terrorist state is impossible; we would not support it, and the Israelis would be right not to want to live next to such an entity. The occupation must end, but Palestinians needed a government that cares about their well-being. None of us, she told them, have addressed forthrightly the fact that the Palestinian leadership was failing its own people.

It is unlikely that the bishops understood what Rice was really telling them, which was that the administration was thinking through an entirely new approach: There would be an independent state of Palestine, but only if and when terrorism was abandoned and Arafat was gone. The key, then, was not diplomacy, not international conferences, nor was it Israeli concessions – it was Palestinian action.

Arafat was not immune from pressure, and on June 8 he appointed Salam Fayyad as finance minister. In the long run this would turn out to be an extremely significant move because Fayyad set about trying to clean up PA finances – the first time that had ever been undertaken. Serving in that post for three years, the U.S.-trained Ph.D. economist, a former International Monetary Fund official, became synonymous with honest and effective stewardship. Donors could, for the first time, begin to trace where their dollars went and could be sure they were not being stolen before reaching their intended aim. Fayyad computerized PA finances, gave financial reports, fought corruption – all previously unheard of. Naturally, he became a favorite of the United States and of the Europeans as well. But what Arafat would not do was give anyone similar influence over the security forces. Money was one thing, and he had plenty of that hidden away; guns were another. Though Arafat simultaneously named a new interior minister, Abdel Razak Yahya, Yahya resigned later in 2002 with the predictable complaint that Arafat had prevented him from undertaking any reforms or exercising control.

If there had been a glimmer of hope at the end of April that violence and terror would end, by June that hope was gone. With acts of terror almost daily and major Israeli action in the West Bank, could Bush continue to say and do nothing? The last time the president had dealt with the region, in April, the "action" he had taken was to announce he was sending Powell there again, but Powell's unsuccessful April trip took that option off the table. "The State Department again proposed a peace conference; the President again said no, not with Arafat," Rice recalled.[48] Cheney and Rumsfeld urged Bush to remain silent: He had given his views in the April speech and nothing would be gained by wading in again. From his own March trip to the region, Cheney had concluded that the Arab leaders were focused on the United States and Iraq, not the Israeli-Palestinian dispute. To Rumsfeld, the president was being set up for failure because the timing was poor: In June 2002, there was no chance for an Arab-Israeli peace. The risk was simply too high to attach the president's name to an initiative Rumsfeld viewed as a foolish push from the State Department.[49]

Those urging that the president speak again about the Middle East had a new argument: Iraq. However they phrased their argument, it amounted to a simple contention: If the United States was going to take action against Iraq, there had to be a credible "peace process" underway. "It was very much in the context of Iraq and Tony Blair's influence on the President," Mike Gerson recalled. "Because Blair from the very earliest in the preparations for Iraq was making the argument that kind of fulfilled the familiar foreign policy argument: at the same time we're doing this, we have to be doing the peace process, or you have all sorts of problems."[50] Doug Feith, Rumsfeld's undersecretary, thought the same: The June speech would be "what the President is going to do in answer to Colin Powell's saying you can't do Iraq unless you have a major Arab-Israeli position taken.... [Y]ou're viewed as being adrift, you're not engaged, Clinton was doing Camp David . . . and you're viewed as ignoring the Arab-Israeli conflict. . . . This was, as I understood it, the addressing of the Arab-Israeli conflict before the Iraq war."[51]

In his own memoir, Blair could not have been clearer that this was his view. To take action in Iraq, indeed to advance in the broader struggle against Islamic extremism, required an initiative on Israeli-Palestinian peace. He said this in his speech to the Labor Party conference shortly after 9/11 and repeats this theme in his memoirs:

[L]ike a broken record thereafter, I believed that resolution of the Palestinian issue was of essential strategic importance to resolving this wider struggle. It hadn't caused the extremism, but resolving it would enormously transform the battle lines in defeating it. . . . I made a major part of my pitch to George the issue of [the] Israeli-Palestinian peace process. To me this was the indispensable soft-power component to give equilibrium to the hard power that was necessary if Saddam were to be removed.[52]

According to Blair, this pitch worked; in April 2002 at Crawford, he received "George's commitment to me to re-engage with it."[53] Blair continued to make that pitch: in July, "I sent George another personal, private note . . . stressing again the Middle East peace process"[54]; in March 2003, "I stressed once again the seminal importance of the Middle East peace process."[55] Right up to the end of his tenure as prime minister and then afterward, as Quartet envoy, Blair peppered the president with advice about how to move things forward. Given his close relations with Bush, one must assume this pressure had some impact.

"Peace Requires a New and Different Palestinian Leadership"

The debate over whether to speak out at all in June 2002, and what to say, lasted weeks. Steve Hadley, then deputy national security advisor, described the process:

Very controversial – and the vice president and Rumsfeld . . . thought the speech should not be given. That was their position: There should be no speech. And the president said, "Well, let's work the process." And Mike Gerson and I had the responsibility to come up with a text that was true to the president's principles, advanced his policies, and as much as possible got everybody on board. We went over and over and over it, and I remember one session where we're actually in the Situation Room and the president is seated at the head table. We're all arrayed, I think it's the Principals, at least some Principals, and then Gerson and I at the other end of the table keeping book on the text – and we are going literally line-by-line through the speech telling the president what the disagreements are and getting some guidance from him as to how to resolve them. So, you know, we're *really* into the details of it and the president's into the details of it. But it's clear that while he wants to keep open the issue as to whether to give the speech, and he wants to try to bring his vice president and Secretary of Defense along, he wants to give the speech. And we go as far as we can to accommodate comments.[56]

The view from Powell's camp was similar, according to a top official at State:

The June speech was extremely controversial. It was drafted. Rumsfeld and Cheney were violently opposed to it – totally, to any speech. "You don't need too. You don't need to give a speech, Mr. President." And their basic objection to the speech is that if he was going to give a speech that laid out a position of the United States Government, he had to give something to the Palestinians. It can't just be "we fight terrorism along with our Israeli allies." He had to give the Palestinians some sense of evenhandedness and hope, and that was the sticking point. Cheney and Rumsfeld did not want to give them anything. Powell told him, you have to tell them what it is you believe in: a two-state solution, find a solution to Jerusalem, find a solution to the final borders, and the right of return – the three biggies – and you've got to put some timeline on it, and he did: "I want to see it in five years." But it was violently objected to by everybody. He gave it on a Monday. It was on Saturday afternoon when they were still debating whether he should give it, and Condi was getting hit from every side, and she called the Secretary [of State] at home. She said, "Well, what do you think?" She said, "I can't make this happen unless you are absolutely clear and forceful on the need for this." There were a lot of good reasons to do it and not to do it, so Powell read it again, added some more stuff in it for the Palestinians, and then called her back and said, "Tell the President I think he has to do this." We cannot just stand here staring at the sky. Powell felt he had to give a speech to show that he was interested in finding a two-state solution.[57]

Throughout, Bush was directly involved in drafting the text. As the chief speech-writer described, "This was not a Ronald Reagan policy process in which all the experts meet and then they write this speech and hash it out for six months to kind of figure out what to say. That was not the way it worked. The president participated in these meetings, came to very strong views, gave me direct direction, worked with me on the speech, and people made edits on the margins. We had a very White House-centric decision making process."[58] That was one way of putting it; Rice described it as "an interagency nightmare."[59] The speech went through 30 drafts and occasioned the unique phenomenon described by Hadley: an interagency meeting, chaired by the president himself, to debate the text of a speech. Doug Feith of the Defense Department attended the meeting and described it this way:

The president is being pushed on specifically the question of reviewing the final status issues. State, and I believe it was [Deputy Secretary Richard] Armitage – State was saying to the president that if you're going to give this speech, you've got to say something about boundaries, something about Jerusalem, something about refugees, something about water, the final status issues. The president said, "No. I don't want to do that." So Armitage came back again and argued that there's been all this diplomacy and you can't just leave it aside. People are going to be expecting you to address these final status issues. He was pushing the president to adopt diplomacy that the president was intent on repudiating. And the president got ticked, and he turned and he said, "I don't want to reinvent that diplomacy." He said, "I want to," I remember this *vividly*, he said, "I want to *change* the way people think about the Arab-Israeli conflict." He used the expression "change the way people think." This was not a case where the president was being told what to think by Condi or anybody else. The president came into this loaded for bear. The president did not like Arafat; I mean no-how. He really thought that Arafat was a crumb. The president also clearly believed that Israel and the United States were shoulder-to-shoulder in the same war.[60]

So did the vice president and the secretary of defense; as Bush later wrote, "Dick and Don were concerned that supporting a Palestinian state in the midst of an intifada would look like rewarding terrorism."[61] They did not favor giving any speech right then, but as the text emerged, they embraced it with enthusiasm while Powell thought it a great mistake. As draft followed draft, events in the region shaped the final outcome. On June 18, 19 people were killed and 74 injured, many of them young students, by the suicide bombing of a bus just outside Jerusalem. And the following day, 7 were killed and 50 injured in another suicide bombing, this time at a crowded bus stop in Jerusalem's French Hill neighborhood. Responsibility for the June 19 bombing was claimed by the "al-Aqsa Martyrs' Brigade," which was formally part of Arafat's Fatah movement. Days later, at a meeting in the final week before the speech, new intelligence was received showing that Arafat had authorized a $20,000 payment to the group – even as he was continuing to tell American officials he was opposed to terror and was stopping it. Yet even that evidence did not move everyone in the room: "Powell, actually, was pooh-poohing it all: 'Oh, you don't know, you can't believe this stuff, how do you know, you can't really lay it on his doorstep,' but finally the preponderance of evidence was just so heavy."[62]

Yet the proof that Arafat was still financing terror in June 2002 – 10 months after 9/11 and after the promises he had made to Bush, Powell, Zinni, and other American officials – did end the debate. To Bush, as Mike Gerson put it, the conclusion was inescapable: "Israel doesn't have a partner. None of the steps make much difference because there was no adequate partner on the Palestinian side. There was this, I think, a dawning recognition that Arafat was going to make this completely impossible. That it was literally *impossible* while he was there."[63] On Saturday afternoon, June 22, Bush himself added the sentence calling for Arafat's removal.

On Monday, June 24, Bush stood in the Rose Garden, flanked not only by Powell but also by Rice and Rumsfeld – a sign perhaps of the battles that lay behind the speech but also that the days of Powell's predominance in Middle East policy were numbered. The speech never mentioned Arafat by name, but the key passages were direct:

My vision is two states, living side by side, in peace and security. There is simply no way to achieve that peace until all parties fight terror.

Peace requires a new and different Palestinian leadership, so that a Palestinian state can be born.

I call on the Palestinian people to elect new leaders, leaders not compromised by terror.

I call upon them to build a practicing democracy based on tolerance and liberty. If the Palestinian people actively pursue these goals, America and the world will actively support their efforts.

If the Palestinian people meet these goals, they will be able to reach agreement with Israel and Egypt and Jordan on security and other arrangements for independence.

And when the Palestinian people have new leaders, new institutions and new security arrangements with their neighbors, the United States of America will support the creation of a Palestinian state, whose borders and certain aspects of its sovereignty will be provisional until resolved as part of a final settlement in the Middle East.

A Palestinian state will never be created by terror. It will be built through reform. And reform must be more than cosmetic change or a veiled attempt to preserve the status quo. True reform will require entirely new political and economic institutions based on democracy, market economics and action against terrorism.

Today the elected Palestinian legislature has no authority and power is concentrated in the hands of an unaccountable few.

Today, the Palestinian people lack effective courts of law and have no means to defend and vindicate their rights.

Today, Palestinian authorities are encouraging, not opposing terrorism.

This is unacceptable. And the United States will not support the establishment of a Palestinian state until its leaders engage in a sustained fight against the terrorists and dismantle their infrastructure.

This will require an externally supervised effort to rebuild and reform the Palestinian security services. The security system must have clear lines of authority and accountability and a unified chain of command.

America is pursuing this reform along with key regional states. The world is prepared to help, yet ultimately these steps toward statehood depend on the Palestinian people and their leaders. If they energetically take the path of reform, the rewards can come quickly.

If Palestinians embrace democracy, confront corruption and firmly reject terror, they can count on American support for the creation of a provisional state of Palestine.

With intensive effort by all of us, agreement could be reached within three years from now. And I and my country will actively lead toward that goal.[64]

In this speech, Bush was offering Palestinians both more and less. Previously, his support for Palestinian statehood had seemed more like a one-liner than a key policy objective, and here it was being given substance and a timetable, and turned into a direct pledge. But previously that support had seemed unqualified, and here the offer was being made conditional. Get rid of Arafat, abandon terror, start building a democracy, and then – but only then – the United States will support creation of a state – and even then, a state "whose borders and certain aspects of its sovereignty will be provisional" until there was a wider peace agreement in the region. Bush was describing a sequence: stop terrorism first, build decent Palestinian institutions, and then the United States would support a "provisional" state.

"The Arabists in the State Department were appalled" by Bush's remarks, Condi Rice reports in her memoir.[65] Within hours, a memo was circulating at the State Department's Near East Bureau suggesting that an immediate meeting with Arafat was needed to fix the damage done by the president's speech. Yet the president had done more than just broken with Arafat: He had also abandoned the approach to Arafat and to peacemaking that his own father, at the Madrid talks in 1991, and Bill Clinton at the Camp David negotiations, had embodied. Their goal had been to create a Palestinian state *without regard to what was within its borders.* That the state would be a dictatorship and a kleptocracy run by Yasser Arafat had been ignored; he was a "partner for peace" and his "flaws" or "idiosyncrasies" might be ignored as well. To Bush, this approach was immoral; it would replace Israeli occupation with another typical Arab tyranny. He wanted something better: As in Iraq and, later, Lebanon, he wanted a democratic, peaceful Palestine, and he wanted it not only because that would make Israel safer but also because Palestinians deserved it. The *nature* of the Palestinian state was now a greater priority than its territory.

Bush's thinking was now clear, and he recognized and described the moral realities on both sides. It was simply false that Israel was equally at fault for the violence and for the inability to achieve peace: Israel had sought a peace partner for years but instead had found in Arafat a terrorist. Israel had the right of any state to defend itself against such terror. For any progress toward peace, Arafat had to go – and Bush would clearly say so. But whatever the crimes of the Palestinian leadership, the Palestinian *people* also had moral claims – to an end to the occupation and the right to self-government. Bush would also say this clearly, in demanding Palestinian statehood as the objective.

Having delivered the speech and outlined an entirely new American approach, Bush jumped into Air Force One and left for the G-8 Summit in Canada. There he was viewed as the skunk at the picnic; as Hadley recalled, "He goes to the G-8 and he tells everybody, 'I'm not going to deal with Arafat anymore. He's a failed leader corrupted by terror.' And of course everybody is appalled."[66] Breaking with Arafat was considered outrageous and unthinkable. As the *Washington Post* reported, "Most of the leaders of the Group of Eight . . . issued statements distancing themselves from Bush's insistence that Yasser Arafat . . . be replaced before serious peace negotiations with Israel can begin." Even Bush's closest ally, Tony Blair, said, "It is for the Palestinians to elect their own leaders."[67] The BBC reported that "[t]he UK has refused to back US President George W. Bush's demand for the removal of Yasser Arafat as the price for a future Palestinian state. . . . Several UK newspapers say the issue could mark the first serious rift between the two leaders since September 11."[68]

Palestinian reactions were predictably sour, defending Arafat and their right to choose their own leaders and noting that Bush had not actually outlined any plan for moving forward. It did seem that peace negotiations were now indefinitely postponed, while the Palestinians addressed – or failed to address –

the political and security reforms Bush required of them. Conversely, the Israelis were delighted, and Sharon was amazed. Weissglas later explained, only partly in jest, that for Sharon, the world was divided into Jews and all the rest – and all the rest wanted to kill the Jews, some softly, some less softly. Sharon could hardly believe the change in the American attitude toward Israel and toward him personally. In 1991, when Sharon had visited the United States as minister of housing, not a single U.S. official would meet with him formally; he was not invited to one U.S. government office. Through the intervention of friends, HUD Secretary Jack Kemp finally agreed to see Sharon in the lobby of the hotel where he was staying. Now, he had visited the White House, he had been called "a man of peace" by the American president, and finally the United States was ending its romance with Arafat and adopting Sharon's own view of the PLO leader. When for the first time he heard an American president talk about the need to get rid of Arafat, Sharon could not believe his ears, Weissglas reminisced years later. The demand for an end to terrorism was the key: What Bush was doing, in Sharon's eyes, was to insist that the swamp of terrorism be drained before a political process could begin. Weissglas recalled that for the first time the principle was accepted that before we enter the negotiating room, the pistols have to be left outside.[69]

Various drafts of the speech had been shared with the Israelis, and the final draft was sent to them an hour before it was to be delivered. Even then Sharon was nervous, and told his staff, "Who guaranteed that they will stick to the script?" When Bush appeared on Israeli TV, he was impossible for Sharon to understand because of the clash of Bush's voice and the loud Hebrew voiceover. But immediately after Bush completed his remarks, one of Sharon's sharpest critics in the Israeli media, Karen Neubach, told viewers that Sharon had won a huge victory: Bush was practically repeating Sharon's campaign slogans. Then Sharon really believed what had happened. Weissglas recalled, "Immediately his expression changed into 'I told you so.' He became the proprietor of the project."[70] For Sharon, the only member of the Israeli delegation at Camp David who had refused to shake hands with Arafat, the American rejection of the PLO leader must have been a sweet moment.

And there was more in Israel's favor occurring during that last week of June. American demands that Israel leave the West Bank and Gaza were softened: Israel should leave "as conditions permitted" and security progress was achieved. Regarding Israel's attacks on Palestinian terrorists, there were no more cries about the "cycle of violence." The White House expressed regret about any innocent Palestinian casualties, but the bottom line was that "Israel has a right to defend itself."

Finally, a Policy

Now, finally, 17 months into his presidency and 9 months after 9/11, Bush had elaborated a Middle East policy. It had been obvious from January 20, 2001, that renewed negotiations were impossible: The Camp David and Taba talks had collapsed, and Arafat was leading a campaign of terrorism. The critical task was to reduce the level of violence. Clinton's experience – and, indeed, his advice – had taught Bush and his advisors that deep personal involvement in negotiations with Arafat would lead nowhere. So in the early months, Powell had made the usual statements and continued the usual approaches embodied by Tenet's security work, the Mitchell Report, and his own visits to the region. When the violence continued and the Saudis intervened, Bush had pledged to support Palestinian statehood and had said so publicly. But 9/11 and the advent of the war on terror had put both Palestinian terrorism and Israel's struggle against it into a new light, so Bush had had to figure out how he could square that circle. Doing so took the administration nine months, and now Bush believed he had it right. The real obstacles to peace negotiations and the building of a decent Palestinian state were the terrorism and corruption that were the trademarks of Arafat, who had to be sidelined. Once he was gone, in fact once the process of marginalizing him had begun, Palestinian reforms could take hold and diplomacy could play its traditional role. The road to a Middle East peace deal would be open and, in Palestine, an Arab democracy would arise, one that could be a model for the entire Arab world.

That was the theory. But in his speech, Bush had not explained how to move down that road. Would the United States sit back and wait until Palestinians moved against Arafat? Or would we take the lead in pressing for reforms in the Palestinian Authority, which actually governed the West Bank and Gaza, and in keeping up the pressure against Arafat? What role would other nations – the Arabs and the Europeans, above all – play in this drama? Bush believed he now had the right formula and in his speech had said, "I've asked Secretary Powell to work intensively with Middle Eastern and international leaders to realize the vision of a Palestinian state, focusing them on a comprehensive plan to support Palestinian reform and institution-building." Was this the beginning of something new for Powell or the return to more of the travel that had dispirited Powell and achieved so little in the winter and spring of 2002? Had Bush's speech been a prelude to "parking" the Palestinian issue until the administration had dealt with Iraq, or was it the beginning of a new period of intensive diplomacy?

Notes

1. Riedel interview, p. 11.
2. Haass, interview, p. 2.
3. Douglas J. Feith, interview by the author, July 30, 2009, p 2.
4. Ibid., pp. 4–5.
5. Ibid., p. 4.
6. George W. Bush, *Decision Points* (New York: Crown Publishers, 2010), 400.
7. Kaplinsky, interview, p. 2.
8. Ariel Sharon, "Statement by Israeli Prime Minister Ariel Sharon," Israeli Ministry of Foreign Affairs, October 4, 2001, http://www.mfa.gov.il/MFA/Government/

Speeches%20by%20Israeli%20leaders/2001/Statement%20by%20Israeli%20PM%20Ariel%20Sharon%20-%204-Oct-2001.

9. Shimon Schiffer and Nahum Barnea, "Sharon's Statement on Czechoslovakia: Background," *Yediot Ahronot*, October 7, 2001.

10. Tourgeman, June interview, p. 5.

11. Remarks to the United Nations General Assembly in New York City, 2 Pub. Papers 1375–1379 (November 10, 2001).

12. Former State Department official, interview by the author, August 21, 2009 (name withheld by request), p. 3.

13. Associated Press, "Syria, Jordan, Welcome Powell's Speech – with Qualifications," *Haaretz*, November 20, 2001, http://www.haaretz.com/news/syria-jordan-welcome-powell-s-speech-with-qualifications-1.75217.

14. "Israeli Press Finds Powell's 'Reheated Pasta' Speech Hard to Digest," *Al Bawaba News*, November 20, 2001, http://www.albawaba.com/news/israeli-press-finds-powells-%E2%80%98reheated-pasta%E2%80%99-speech-hard-digest.

15. Alistair Lyon, "Faint Praise for Powell Speech from Arabs and Europeans," *Jerusalem Post*, November 21, 2001, http://www.unitedjerusalem.org/index2.asp?id=66166&Date=11/20/2001.

16. Tourgeman, June interview, p. 8.

17. Hadley, interview, pp. 3–4.

18. Lawrence F. Kaplan, "Torpedo Boat," *The New Republic*, February 18, 2002.

19. Ibid.

20. See Elliott Abrams, "Israel and the 'Peace Process,'" in *Present Dangers: Crisis and Opportunity in American Foreign and Defense Policy*, ed. Robert Kagan and William Kristol (San Francisco: Encounter Books, 2000), 229–30.

21. Bush, *Decision Points*, 402.

22. Richard Boucher, "State Department Press Briefing," U.S. Department of State, January 11, 2002.

23. Exchange with Reporters in Portland, Maine, 1 Pub. Papers 115 (January 25, 2002).

24. Richard Cheney, interview by John King, *CNN*, January 28, 2002.

25. Hannah, interview, pp. 4–5.

26. Kaplan, "Torpedo Boat."

27. United Nations Security Council (SC) Resolution 1397, "The situation in the Middle East, including the Palestinian question," March 12, 2002, http://unispal.un.org/unispal.nsf/0/4721362DD7BA3DEA85256B7B00536C7F.

28. The President's News Conference, 38 Weekly Comp. Pres. Doc. 407–418 (March 13, 2002).

29. Shalom Tourgeman, interview by the author, October 26, 2009, p. 24.

30. Edelman, interview, p. 11.

31. Cheney, *In My Time*, 378.

32. Quoted in Elisabeth Bumiller, *Condoleezza Rice: An American Life* (New York: Random House, 2007), 176.

33. Rice, *No Higher Honor*, 138.

34. Ibid.

35. Ibid., 176–77.

36. Former State Department official, interview, August 21, 2009 (name withheld by request), p. 4.

37. Ibid., pp. 4–5.
38. Remarks on the Situation in the Middle East, 1Pub. Papers 546–548 (April 4, 2002).
39. Gerson, interview, p. 4.
40. Douglas J. Feith, interview by the author, August 19, 2009, p. 10.
41. Former State Department official, interview, August 21, 2009 (name withheld by request), p. 5.
42. Rice, *No Higher Honor*, 140.
43. Gerson, interview, p. 8.
44. Bumiller, *Condoleezza Rice*, 181.
45. Bush, *Decision Points*, 402.
46. Ibid., 403.
47. "Kings, Queens, & Despots," *Forbes*, February 24, 2003, http://www.forbes.com/2003/02/24/cz_royalslide_6.html.
48. Rice, *No Higher Honor*, 142.
49. Feith, July interview, p. 10.
50. Gerson, interview, p. 6.
51. Feith, July interview, p. 8.
52. Tony Blair, *A Journey: My Political Life* (New York: Vintage Books, 2010), 388–89.
53. Ibid., 401–2.
54. Ibid., 404.
55. Ibid., 443.
56. Hadley, interview, pp. 11–12.
57. Former State Department official, interview, August 21, 2009 (name withheld by request), pp. 5–6.
58. Gerson, interview, p. 6.
59. Rice, *No Higher Honor*, 143.
60. Feith, July interview, p. 13.
61. Bush, *Decision Points*, 404.
62. Edelman, interview, p. 16.
63. Gerson, interview, p. 5.
64. Remarks on the Middle East, 1 Pub. Papers 1059–1062 (June 24, 2002).
65. Rice, *No Higher Honor*, 145.
66. Hadley, interview, p. 5.
67. Karen de Young, *Washington Post*, July 26, 2002.
68. BBC News, "Blair and Bush 'Rift' over Arafat," *BBC News.com*, June 26, 2002, http://news.bbc.co.uk/2/hi/middle_east/2066560.stm.
69. Ari Shavit, "The Big Freeze," *Haaretz*, October 8, 2004, http://jewishpolitical chronicle.org/nov04/Big%20freeze.pdf.
70. Dov Weissglas, interview by the author, June 17, 2009, pp. 9–10.

3

Roadmap to Disengagement

The Bush speech was a clear statement of policy: When there was an end to terror and corruption, and the reform of Palestinian institutions was creating a democracy, the United States would lead the Palestinians to statehood. But how was all this to happen? How would the Palestinian reform, which required the marginalization of Arafat, be foisted on Arafat and his cronies in Fatah and the PLO? How would the reduction in terrorism, which Bush had made a prerequisite for progress, come to pass? And what roles would other states, Arab and European, play? For that matter, what role would the State Department play, after the arresting cameo on June 24 – not just Powell but also Rice and Rumsfeld appearing with the president as he spoke? The evolution of Bush's thinking had threatened not only Arafat and his coterie but also Powell and his, because Bush had rejected the traditional State Department approach. The "peace process," involving endless negotiating sessions with Arafat, had been declared bankrupt. Was it now to be U.S. policy to cheer for Palestinian reforms – or to impose them? The administration had no answers on June 24.

Yet one motivation for involvement in Israeli-Palestinian issues had been the coming confrontation with Iraq – by the time of the June speech, only nine months away. It was easy to argue, then, that silence and inactivity could not be the follow-on to the June speech, and it was not hard to persuade the president that some tactic or program was needed. For whatever other actors had in mind, the president was sincere: He believed he had found a formula, indeed the only workable formula, for achieving Middle East peace. If there were good ideas about how to make this experiment work, he was fully open to them. The potential vacuum was soon filled by several parties, beginning with Quartet activity at the United Nations, then involving more nations and international institutions like the World Bank, and finally coalescing around the production of a "Roadmap" toward Palestinian statehood.

On July 16, Powell convened a meeting of the Quartet he had formed in Madrid the previous winter. The meeting endorsed not only the approach Bush had taken in his speech but also his timeline: "Consistent with President Bush's

June 24 statement, the UN, EU and Russia express their strong support for the goal of achieving a final Israeli-Palestinian settlement which, with intensive effort on security and reform by all, could be reached within three years from now." That would mean a Palestinian state by mid-2005. The Quartet statement also spoke of a new Task Force on Reform that would work under its auspices and produce a "comprehensive action plan" for Palestinian reform.

For the State Department, such activities were a bureaucratic imperative. Seen from across the river at the Pentagon, the invention of the Roadmap had less to do with the Middle East than with Washington politics. As Douglas Feith described the initiative, "It got turned back to the State Department, and [Deputy Secretary of State] Armitage, with his colleagues, invented the Roadmap to retake the ground that he had lost in the June 24th speech. I remember having people at the State Department say to me, the purpose of the Roadmap is to win back in operation what was lost at the strategic level in the fight over the June 24th speech."[1] In the NSC, there was no doubt that "the Roadmap was the State Department's baby," as Rice's then-deputy Steve Hadley put it.[2] For Vice President Cheney's staff, the concern was not bureaucratic but programmatic: His foreign policy advisor Eric Edelman worried that "people who didn't like this – like the State Department – just wanted to walk away from that June 24th speech before the ink was even dry."[3]

The Roadmap to Peace

In fact, the State Department had not invented the Roadmap but had only seized on the idea after several other governments brought it forward. Oddly, the idea appears to have come first from Denmark, which was taking its six-month rotation as leader of the European Union during the second half of 2002. During that summer, Danish Foreign Minister Moeller visited the Middle East and presented to the Israelis a short draft, a three-chapter version of the Roadmap whose first chapter dealt with security.

The Jordanians were meanwhile pursuing the same path, working not with White House officials but only with the State Department, and urging that the steps leading to a two-state solution needed to be spelled out. Powell, their main interlocutor, was not encouraging in his discussion with Foreign Minister Muasher; perhaps his losing struggle over the content of the June 24 speech made him careful about predicting what he could push through the White House. "We're not there yet," he told the Jordanian. In July, the Saudi, Jordanian, and Egyptian foreign ministers were invited to meet with the Quartet in New York, at the United Nations, and the following day were asked to come to Washington to see President Bush in the Oval Office. In those meetings, the Jordanian minister again pressed for a Roadmap that outlined concrete steps, measures of performance, and timelines.

Ten days later, on August 1, King Abdullah of Jordan met with Bush. Preparing for the meeting, Muasher heard from Rice on July 31 precisely what he had been told by Powell: "This is a non-starter." The Palestinians needed to perform on security first "and then we will see." Muasher prepared the king for a tough meeting because the Americans were plainly rejecting the Roadmap concept. When King Abdullah presented the idea to Bush, the president replied as Rice had predicted: We are not ready for that yet; the Palestinians must work on security first. But this Roadmap is nothing new, the Jordanians argued; it is merely a way to translate your vision into steps. In a back and forth with Muasher, whom the king asked to explain what the Jordanians meant by a Roadmap, Bush began to come around. I don't think I have a problem with that, he finally said, and asked Muasher to work with Bill Burns on a proposal.

Both the Jordanians and the State Department leapt at the invitation and the drafting began. This was an unexpected gift for the State officials: In late June it had appeared that the traditional diplomatic approach was at an end, but only five weeks later the president was instructing them to reengage with their Arab and EU counterparts. In August and especially in September, when so many foreign ministries move to New York for the UN General Assembly, the preliminary Danish version was amended over and over again, and by the September 17 meeting of the Quartet, a near-final text was in hand. The White House had had little influence in these revisions; its supposed representative was a career CIA official detailed to the NSC and fully in sympathy with Burns and the Near East Bureau at State.

In mid-October, Sharon was to visit the White House again, and so it was time to reel in the Israelis. To that point the text had been developed entirely without their input, and indeed they did not even know of the American involvement in the Roadmap. At a preparatory meeting between American and Israeli officials shortly before the Bush-Sharon meeting in the Oval Office, Hadley handed over a few pages. Take a look at this, he told Weissglas and Tourgeman; it's something we've prepared. The pair had become Israel's two-man foreign ministry when it came to dealing with the United States, and between Weissglas's humor and panache and Tourgeman's brilliant mind and command of detail, they were perfectly balanced. A career diplomat who had served in London and Amman, Jordan, Tourgeman later succeeded Ayalon as diplomatic advisor and played a central role under Prime Minister Olmert as well.

The pair went back to Blair House, the presidential guest house across from the White House on Pennsylvania Avenue where Sharon was staying, made a few copies of what Hadley had handed them, and discussed the text with Danny Ayalon and others in the delegation. They told Sharon that the draft contained many problems for Israel. "It's a very bad document," Tourgeman told him. After reading the text and hearing all the comments, Sharon decided, "We are not going to respond to this document now. We will have to take it home, and we will examine it there. It is not something that should be part of the visit." When Hadley called to get the Israeli reaction, Weissglas replied, "Look, it's a six-page document. For you it's six pages. For us it's our life. It's our future. So we need to examine it, and cannot give you any response to it now."[4]

The sour Israeli reaction reflected, no doubt, their memory of the July Danish draft, which they had liked and had thought particularly strong in its handling of security issues. But it also reflected their anger at the way the text had been developed: without them. They were being presented by the United States with a fait accompli. They were asking themselves, "How is it that in our intimate dialogue with them they are presenting us with a document without even consulting us about it?"[5] Perhaps the answer lay in the choreography of the process: The idea had come from the EU and the Jordanians, and the president had then asked Burns to confer with Muasher, not with the Israelis. Still, as things had unfolded, the Israeli reaction was entirely predictable. It seemed that State was determined to develop a text without any Israeli input but with sufficient Arab and European support to make amendments impossible, and then to shove it down the Israelis' throats. These tactics worked, at least in that the final text was almost identical with the October draft. But they weakened Israel's desire to adhere to the Roadmap's conditions, which were always seen as imposed more than agreed to, and they certainly strengthened the Israeli view that Powell and Burns could not be trusted.

What did the Roadmap say? Its formal title – "A Performance-Based Roadmap to a Permanent Two-State Solution to the Israeli-Palestinian Conflict" – revealed immediately that, unlike the Arab Plan, it would address only Israeli-Palestinian and not Syrian or Lebanese issues (though these were given a nod at the end) and that it had a very clear objective: establishing a Palestinian state.

The document began by stating its ambitious goals:

The following is a performance-based and goal-driven Roadmap, with clear phases, timelines, target dates, and benchmarks aiming at progress through reciprocal steps by the two parties in the political, security, economic, humanitarian, and institution-building fields, under the auspices of the Quartet. The destination is a final and comprehensive settlement of the Israel-Palestinian conflict by 2005, as presented in President Bush's speech of 24 June.

There followed some language that was close to the Bush message of the June 24 speech, but also laid the foundation for endless debate in future years:

A two-state solution to the Israeli-Palestinian conflict will only be achieved through an end to violence and terrorism, when the Palestinian people have a leadership acting decisively against terror and willing and able to build a practicing democracy based on tolerance and liberty, and through Israel's readiness to do what is necessary for a democratic Palestinian state to be established, and a clear, unambiguous acceptance by both parties of the goal of a negotiated settlement as described below. The Quartet will assist and facilitate implementation of the plan, starting in Phase I, including direct discussions between the parties as required. The plan establishes a realistic timeline for implementation. However, as a performance-based plan, progress will require and depend upon the good faith efforts of the parties, and their compliance with each of the obligations outlined below. Should the parties perform their obligations rapidly, progress within and through the phases may come sooner than indicated in the plan. Non-compliance with obligations will impede progress. A settlement, negotiated between the parties, will result in the emergence of an independent, democratic, and viable Palestinian state living side by side in peace and security with Israel and its other neighbors.[6]

The Roadmap had three phases. In the first, all Palestinian violence and terrorism would end, the Palestinian political reform Bush had demanded would begin, there would be a new Palestinian constitution and free elections, Israel would withdraw from Palestinian cities in the West Bank, and Israel would freeze all settlement activity and remove settlement outposts erected after March 2001. The Quartet would monitor all these activities, which were supposed to be completed by June 2003 – an amazingly ambitious timetable.

The details of the text showed that the marginalization of Arafat was a goal in Phase I. On the security side, Palestinian security forces would be reorganized and removed from his control: "[A]ll Palestinian security organizations are consolidated into three services reporting to an empowered Interior Minister," not to Arafat. On the financial side, funds flowing to the Palestinian Authority would be sequestered and kept out of his hands. Politically, the Roadmap demanded "appointment of [an] interim prime minister or cabinet with empowered executive authority/decision-making body" and the "continued appointment of Palestinian ministers empowered to undertake fundamental reform" including "genuine separation of powers."

Phase II would come after Palestinian elections and would

end with possible creation of an independent Palestinian state with provisional borders in 2003.... Its primary goals are continued comprehensive security performance and effective security cooperation, continued normalization of Palestinian life and institution-building, further building on and sustaining of the goals outlined in Phase I, ratification of a democratic Palestinian constitution, formal establishment of office of prime minister, consolidation of political reform, and the creation of a Palestinian state with provisional borders.

The Roadmap noted the conditional nature of the timeline, however: "Progress into Phase II will be based upon the consensus judgment of the Quartet of whether conditions are appropriate to proceed, taking into account performance of both parties." Phase II also included a huge international conference designed to amass support for all these efforts, as well as the restoration of some Arab ties to Israel.

In Phase III, the Israeli-Palestinian conflict would end. A second international conference would be convened "leading to a final, permanent status resolution in 2005, including on borders, Jerusalem, refugees, settlements; and, to support progress toward a comprehensive Middle East settlement between Israel and Lebanon and Israel and Syria, to be achieved as soon as possible." The Arab states would then normalize relations with Israel, and decades of conflict in the Middle East would end.

Sharon and the Roadmap: "Security out of Thin Air"

The Roadmap would be cited thousands of times in later years, even after its timeline had long passed. What did it actually contribute? To Hadley,

The Roadmap was useful because it was concrete. It starts the notion that comes to fruition in Annapolis – that in order to have credible negotiations with Israelis and Palestinians, you need to have credible progress: Palestinians need to see their life getting better; Israelis need to see their lives getting more secure. That's a principle of the Roadmap. The second principle of the Roadmap, as interpreted by the Israelis, is that there will never be a state born of terror and if you don't have progress and cooperation on terror, you won't get the state. That also is an implicit principle of the Roadmap.[7]

No terror, visible progress for both sides: that was Hadley's view. But Sharon took a different view all along. In a later speech he described it this way:

The Roadmap is a clear and reasonable plan, and it is therefore possible and imperative to implement it. The concept behind this plan is that only security will lead to peace. And in that sequence. Without the achievement of full security – within the framework of which terror organizations will be dismantled – it will not be possible to achieve genuine peace, a peace for generations. This is the essence of the Roadmap. The opposite perception, according to which the very signing of a peace agreement will produce security out of thin air, has already been tried in the past and failed miserably. And such will be the fate of any other plan which promotes this concept. These plans deceive the public and create false hope. There will be no peace before the eradication of terror. The government under my leadership will not compromise on the realization of all phases of the Roadmap. It is incumbent upon the Palestinians to uproot the terrorist groups and to create a law-abiding society which fights against violence and incitement. Peace and terror cannot coexist. The world is currently united in its unequivocal demand from the Palestinians to act toward the cessation of terrorism and the implementation of reforms. Only a transformation of the Palestinian Authority into a different authority will enable progress in the political process. The Palestinians must fulfill their obligations. A full and complete implementation will – at the end of the process – lead to peace and tranquility.[8]

According to Sharon's interpretation of the Roadmap, the Israeli role largely disappears; the elimination of terror and indeed of Arafat by the Palestinians comes first and is a prerequisite for any Israel action. This Israeli view of the Roadmap was probably inevitable given the continuing terrorist attacks. During the summer of 2002, suicide bombings had recommenced: nine were killed on July 16 and three more on July 17. On July 31, a bombing at the Hebrew University cafeteria killed 7 and injured 85 students. On August 4, 9 were killed and 50 injured in a bus bombing in northern Israel, and on the same day 2 were killed and 16 wounded by a shooting attack at the Damascus Gate of the Old City of Jerusalem. There were smaller attacks (and other attacks failed or were halted by police) each week in August, and then another bus bombing, this time in the center of Tel Aviv, killed 6 and injured 70 on September 19. Israel responded throughout the summer and early fall with attacks on terrorists and on Arafat's infrastructure; the IDF surrounded the Muqata again on September 20 and destroyed more buildings there, withdrawing after 10 days. The next large terrorist attack came on October 21, when 14 were killed and 50 injured in yet another bus bombing. On November 15, 12 were killed and 15 injured in a shooting attack on Sabbath worshippers in Hebron. Six days later came another bus bombing in Jerusalem, this time killing 11 and wounding 50.

In the fall of 2002, as the Roadmap was drafted and its text put in final form and then leaked, Israel responded not with official comments but with a request for postponement. At the end of October, Sharon's coalition collapsed when the Labor Party withdrew – in a fight over the budget, not over the Roadmap or security issues. Sharon then argued that making the Roadmap an issue in the Israeli elections would kill it. It would become a political football, with politicians outbidding each other to denounce it and demanding that he and others do so. Without much contentious debate, the Bush administration and the Quartet agreed to postpone the release of the text. On November 5, Sharon announced that new elections would be held in January or early in February 2003. On November 14 the *New York Times* published a draft of the Roadmap (dated October 15), but the text remained "unofficial." The Roadmap was in suspension until Israel had a new government.

Sharon kept faith with President Bush: He did not criticize the Roadmap and indeed ended the year with a conditional endorsement of Bush's goal – establishment of a Palestinian state. In a speech on December 4 to the Herzliya Conference (an annual conference on security attended by many American and Israeli officials and former officials), Sharon described a very tough version of the Roadmap, based squarely on the June 24 speech, including its rejection of Arafat and demands for Palestinian reform. Sharon had hard words for Arafat, and for Israeli rivals of the left and right whom he accused of unrealistic assessments of where Israel's interests lay. But the bottom line was that a Palestinian state was acceptable – and this in a speech delivered during an election campaign.

First, here is what Sharon said about Arafat:

Twenty-seven months ago the Palestinian Authority commenced a campaign of terror against the State of Israel. This campaign of terror was not coincidental; it was meticulously planned and prepared by the Chairman of the Palestinian Authority.... The achievement of true coexistence must be carried out, first and foremost, by the replacement of the Palestinian leadership which has lied and disappointed, with different leadership which can – and more importantly – is willing to achieve real peace with the State of Israel. Unfortunately, there remain a few in Israel who believe that Arafat is still relevant. However, the U.S. Administration – with the world following in its footsteps – has already accepted our unequivocal position that no progress will be possible with Arafat as the Chairman of the Palestinian Authority. This man is not – and never will be – a partner to peace. He does not want peace.... The reconstruction of a Palestinian government should commence with governmental reforms which will ultimately lead to the establishment of a new, honest and peace-seeking administration, the removal of Arafat from his command of power and sources of financing, and from the decision-making process, and his relegation to a symbolic role.

Given this accusation that Arafat was behind the murders of so many Israelis, it is remarkable that Sharon was not calling for him to be sent into exile once again, much less for his incarceration. Instead, this was a "Hirohito strategy" – stay in place but with a symbolic role only, as power is given to others.

Then came Sharon's endorsement of the Bush vision for the Middle East and of Bush as well:

On June 24th this year, President Bush presented his plan for a true solution to our conflict with the Palestinians. The peace plan outlined in the President's speech is a reasonable, pragmatic and practicable one, which offers a real opportunity to achieve an agreement. We have accepted in principle the President's plan and the sequence presented therein.

Sharon then presented his understanding of the Roadmap, emphasizing Palestinian responsibilities:

The U.S. Administration has understood and agreed that the only way to achieve a true peace agreement with the Palestinians is progress in phases, with the first phase being a complete cessation of terror.... Only after a cessation of terror – and this is already agreed by most world leaders – will the commencement of peace negotiations between the parties be possible.... The American plan defines the parties' progress according to phases. The transition from one phase to the next will not be on the basis of a pre-determined timetable – which would have resulted in a build-up of heavy pressure on Israel towards the end of one phase and approaching the next phase. Rather, progress is determined on the basis of performance – only once a specific phase has been implemented, will progress into the next phase be possible. On the basis of lessons learned from past agreements, it is clear to all that Israel can no longer be expected to make political concessions until there is proven calm and Palestinian governmental reforms.... [T]he achievement of true and genuine coexistence must be a pre-condition to any discussion on political arrangements.[9]

Later the Israelis would rely heavily on the phrase "in the sequence of the Roadmap," insisting – even after Sharon was long gone from government – that the phrase be repeated by American officials. The sequence was first an end to terror, then Palestinian reform and the departure from power of Arafat, and only then the negotiations that would lead to Palestinian statehood. The Israelis said they would not talk and fight at the same time, and they relied on the Roadmap in refusing to do so.

In this December 2002 speech, Sharon specified that Arafat would no longer be the head of the Palestinian executive branch, and the security organizations ("the majority of which," Sharon noted, "are in fact involved in terror") would be dismantled and replaced with new organizations under an empowered minister of the interior, over whom Arafat would have no control. A new minister of finance would also be appointed, "taking the financial system out of Arafat's hands." A reformed judicial system would punish terrorists. After that, and only after that, should Palestinian elections take place:

The elections in the Palestinian Authority should be held only at the conclusion of the reform process and after proper governmental regulations have been internalized. The goal is that these will be true elections – free, liberated and democratic.

But Sharon made clear his decision to go forward:

The second phase of President Bush's sequence proposes the establishment of a Palestinian state.... As I have promised in the past, President Bush's sequence will be discussed and approved by the National Unity Government which I intend to establish after the elections.... I have said it before, and will say it again today: Israel is prepared to make painful concessions for a true peace.... These decisions are not easy for me, and I cannot deny that I have doubts, reservations and fears; however, I have come to the conclusion that in the present regional and international reality Israel must act with courage to accept the political plan which I described.

Arafat and the Roadmap: Elections Next Year?

On the Palestinian side, on July 12 Arafat had written to Powell to reiterate his commitment to reform. From an American perspective, these were just more Arafat lies, but Arafat was also responding to internal Palestinian pressures to reform. Powell met on August 8 with the PLO peace negotiator Saeb Erekat and other Palestinian leaders to discuss the reforms and elections that the Roadmap demanded. On September 11, Arafat's entire cabinet resigned; one effect of the Roadmap discussions had been to stir up Palestinian politics, and there was a showdown between Arafat and the Palestinian Legislative Council (PLC). The *Washington Post* called this incident "the stiffest internal challenge yet to his leadership. The Palestinian Legislative Council, which often has been at odds with Arafat, was only minutes away from a showdown vote against Arafat's cabinet."[10] A no-confidence vote in the PLC was imminent had Arafat not blinked because legislators were refusing to confirm a cabinet full of Arafat cronies renowned for corruption. Moreover, the demands President Bush was making for an end to Arafat's political monopoly and the establishment of a new and more democratic political system were reverberating: "[T]his week's upheaval shows that an increasing number of Palestinian politicians are demanding the creation of prime minister as an elected office," the *Christian Science Monitor* reported.[11] Terms like accountability and separation of powers were now being heard in Ramallah, for Bush had in fact judged the Palestinian political situation more accurately than his supposedly more sophisticated critics.

For Washington, these debates in Ramallah were all positive signs, revealing that there were Palestinians willing to stand up to Arafat and showing that U.S. accusations of his corruption and one-man rule were echoed by many who lived under his thumb – and wanted a government that was decent and democratic. When, after 1967, Palestinians found themselves living with Israeli democracy instead of Jordanian monarchical rule, they began to learn new habits. In fact, Palestinian civic life had taken off under the Israeli occupation, with a vast array of NGOs formed – in part to criticize the Israelis but also mirroring Israel's contentious civic culture. Arafat's return from exile in Tunis was the end of all that; he crushed civic life and built a satrapy for himself and his equally corrupt cronies.

This mini-rebellion in the summer of 2002 was a sign that Palestinians – at least, some Palestinians – might be tiring of Arafat and that efforts to marginalize him might have significant internal support. Arafat announced that there would be new elections – parliamentary and presidential – the following winter, on January 20. On October 29, the PLC voted for an interim cabinet that would serve until the forthcoming elections. Yet even at the time, this seemed more like a clever Arafat tactic than a real concession on his part: The Palestinian electoral register was way out of date, new election laws were needed, there was no independent electoral commission, and it was highly uncertain that elections could be held in January. Arafat had simply bought himself more time. Sure enough, on December 22, Arafat announced that the elections were to be postponed indefinitely.

The Importance of Iraq

These events transpired against the backdrop of ever clearer preparations for war in Iraq. The president sought both congressional authorization, which he obtained on October 10, and another UN Security Council resolution, adopted on November 8. Success in the November elections put the Senate back under Republican control, also strengthening Bush's hand. Iraq handed over a massive report on its alleged nuclear program in December, but the United States found that the report contained many errors and omissions and that Iraq was in "material breach" of its obligations under Security Council resolutions. The president's State of the Union speech on January 28, 2003, argued strongly that Iraq must and would be confronted: "If Saddam Hussein does not fully disarm for the safety of our people, and for the peace of the world, we will lead a coalition to disarm him."

As war came closer, Tony Blair pressed harder for more action on a Middle East "peace process." Blair later described his view in an interview:

Absolutely. Yes. I mean, I have always taken the view that although the Israel-Palestine issue is not the cause of the extremism, resolving it is a major part of helping with the broader strategy. And so particularly when we were going to have to do difficult things in Afghanistan, if we were going to have to do Iraq, our enemies would set this in the context of the West versus Islam; and the question is could we find a way of unifying the moderates in the cause of producing a different type of the Middle East. And to do that, I always thought Israel-Palestine was essential.[12]

It was evident by the end of 2002 that, barring a major concession by Saddam Hussein, we were headed for war in Iraq. So according to Blair's logic – and on this point he certainly had the full support of the State Department – progress in the Middle East was essential. For Powell, the mechanism for the "peace process" was clear; it would be achieved through the Roadmap and his diplomacy with the EU, Russians, and the UN Secretary General. At an NSC meeting on December 18, 2002, he called the Roadmap a "pretty good product" that reinforced the president's June 24 speech and the vision it presented. Yet Bush did not seem persuaded that the Roadmap would work and worried that the sequencing was off: He had argued for security first, and that insistence was being watered down. It undermines the message on terrorism, he said, if we all appear to be rushing forward regardless of terrorist attacks and the lack of security reform on the Palestinian side. And he noted that the PA was still run by Arafat alone and did not represent the Palestinian people. We need to make sure that the principles in the June 24 speech are reinforced and not undermined, Bush said. Bush's remarks were yet another sign that the president and his secretary of state were not on the same wavelength.

Two days later, Bush met with the Quartet at the White House. We need to move forward, he told them. Arafat was a failed leader and working with him would fail as it had in the past. The argument that "there is nobody else" was wrong; Palestinian democracy would produce new leaders. The others worried about Sharon, but Bush said he had spoken with Sharon and thought he would move forward – if the terrorism stopped, which was, again, why Bush had put security issues first. When Bush said he remained fully committed to establishing a Palestinian state, he was asked whether the 2005 timetable still stood. Not unless the terror stops, he answered. When Powell (interestingly, it was he and not the EU representatives or Kofi Annan who raised the issue) said the problem of Israeli settlement activity was sure to arise again soon, Bush shot him down and said that pushing the settlements issue at the wrong time would not yield anything. Anyway, Bush said, does anyone here believe that the terror would stop if Israeli settlement activity stopped? The key is to get a new Palestinian leadership that calls for peace and can deliver. Arafat is not that guy.

So, six months after the Bush speech of June 24, the year 2002 was ending with principles clearly stated and a strong desire for some forward movement – but little progress on the ground. The Roadmap text was finalized, though not yet published officially. The Quartet was in place and was now the main mechanism for coordinating the views of the Bush administration with those of the Europeans, the UN under Kofi Annan, and Russia. Yet Arafat remained in power and terrorist attacks continued, so the main demands of Bush's June 24 speech remained unmet. Perhaps the greatest progress had come on the Israeli side, where Prime Minister Sharon, the long-time leader of Israel's right wing and the head of Likud, its strongest right-wing party, had endorsed Bush's proposals. Like Bush, he had abandoned policies that flatly opposed Palestinian statehood and now accepted that goal – to be sure, under circumstances that would be difficult to reach. When the Israeli elections were over, the next task would be the one that had evaded the Americans and the Quartet: real Palestinian reform, of the sorts Bush had spoken about on June 24 and Sharon had demanded more belligerently on December 4.

The New NSC Staffer

I entered the scene in December 2002. I had been offered positions by both Powell and Rice in April 2001 and, having spent eight years at State in the Reagan administration, decided to take the White House job. The position was "Senior Director for Democracy, Human Rights, and International Organizations." In the NSC hierarchy, under Rice came her deputy Steve Hadley, and then the various senior directors (for geographical areas such as Africa, the Middle East, or Europe or for subject areas such as economics, counterterrorism, human rights, or intelligence). As the senior director for the small directorate known as "Democ," I handled the UN, foreign aid, and promotion of human rights and democracy.

In the Reagan State Department, I had been assistant secretary for human rights when George Shultz moved me to a regional slot – assistant secretary for inter-American affairs, in charge of Latin America. My history repeated itself at the NSC: In the fall of 2002, Rice moved me from a functional to a regional office, to be senior director for Near East and North African Affairs. Up to that point, the NSC staff members handling Israeli-Palestinian affairs had been from the CIA and had been Arabists, comfortable with the approach of State's Near East Bureau. By choosing me, Rice was choosing someone who had already revealed to her – with my private complaints to her in 2001 and 2002 about the way the NSC staff was handling Israel – my own views.

I was a Bush supporter, a Rice supporter, a "neocon," and a strong proponent of the closest possible relations between the United States and Israel. I worked far more closely with Vice President Cheney's staff than with the State Department. I had strong personal ties with most of the major American Jewish organizations. Although I had not written much about the Middle East, the book chapters and short pieces I had published made my position clear. So in selecting me in the fall of 2002 to be the "Middle East guy" at her NSC, Rice was staking out a position: closer to Cheney and Bush and farther from Powell and State. As the president's views and the lack of enthusiasm for them at State became clear, Rice was choosing a staff member who would be completely loyal to her and to the president and who would promote his views with enthusiasm.

To me it seemed clear that the path to peace was not through Israeli concessions and quickly assembled American peace plans. Ever since the smashing Israeli victory in the 1967 Six Day War, such approaches had been tried and had always failed. On the contrary, a strong Israel was in my view a valuable American ally and far more likely to reach peace agreements with its Arab neighbors. It was for that reason that I had, in 1972, taken time away from law school to work on Sen. Henry M. "Scoop" Jackson's initial presidential campaign and then had left law practice to come to Washington in the spring of 1975 to join his staff as he geared up for his 1976 presidential run. As his biographer wrote, "It was Jackson who introduced into the debate the idea that 'lasting peace in the Middle East lies in American support for a map of Israel with secure and recognized borders whose defense can be assured by the Israelis themselves.'"[13] Jackson led the fight for additional military aid to Israel and for the freedom of Soviet Jewry to emigrate there – the latter action earned him the scorn of Nixon and Kissinger but led the way to the emigration of a million Soviet Jews there and changed Israeli demography permanently. "Jackson saw Israel as a strategic bastion of the West," as I well knew; indeed, he was a far tougher defender of Israel than his colleagues Sens. Jacob Javits and Abraham Ribicoff, both Jews, and tougher than many leaders in the Jewish community.[14]

This was the perspective I brought to the NSC. Peace seemed possible to me if and only if the Arab states finally gave up the effort to destroy Israel – either to destroy it physically through war or to destroy its Jewish character through the return of millions of Palestinian refugees and their families. If and when the Arabs were willing to accept Israel as a Jewish state and a legitimate, permanent neighbor, I knew that Israelis would make great sacrifices for peace. I believed they would leave most of the West Bank and Gaza as soon as it was safe to do so because I knew few Israelis who believed it was possible or sensible to continue ruling millions of Palestinians forever. The effect of years of war and terror had been, I thought, to undermine permanently the old hopes for a "New Middle East" where Israelis and Palestinians would live together in peace; instead, I thought they would live apart in peace. Yet for the Arab governments and the Palestinian leadership to give up 50 years of delegitimizing, rejecting, attacking, and terrorizing Israel required the staunchest possible American backing for the Jewish state. With America now cast as the sole superpower, it was possible that the Arab leaders would finally reconcile themselves to peace with Israel and in turn that Israel could safely withdraw from much of the Palestinian territories. Yet it seemed clear to me that pressure on Israel was not the way to get there; pressure on the Arabs to stop supporting terrorism was the first step. Peace would come through security, not vice versa.

When Ariel Sharon defeated Ehud Barak in Israel's February 2001 elections, there was widespread chagrin in Washington, but I did not share it. At the time I had written that

Israel continues to face mortal peril, surrounded by enemies who wish its destruction. When Ehud Barak reached out for peace through concessions and compromises so great they threatened the nation's security, they were rejected out of hand by the Palestinian Authority. It has become clear to the great majority of Israelis that their Arab neighbors – today, as in 1948, 1967, and 1973, the years of Israel's major wars – continue to want not peace but victory, not compromise but surrender, not a Jewish State but another Arab state in Israel. So Israelis have chosen a leader who all along knew, and said, that the road to peace lies through strength instead of weakness, and firmness rather than unilateral concessions.[15]

It also seemed clear to me that the Palestinian side was not ready for state-hood, partly because of the crimes of Yasser Arafat. Arafat had created in Gaza and the West Bank a corrupt and violent satrapy that threatened Israel. There was no path to peace that led through a state he controlled and used as a terrorist base and fount of anti-Semitic propaganda. Palestinians needed to build the institutions of statehood, much as the Zionists had: school by school, courtroom by courtroom, policeman by policeman, road by road, and election by election. There were no shortcuts, and those who apologized for Palestinian terrorism and Arafat's tyranny did the Palestinian people no favors. This highly educated population was capable of self-rule, but a state needed to be built – not awarded to Arafat so that he would simply create yet another Arab tyranny.

So I was an enthusiastic supporter of the new Bush approach as expressed in the June 24 speech and of his desire to move the Israelis forward – not through the policy of pressure and antagonism that George H. W. Bush and Jim Baker had employed but through close cooperation and the building of confidence. I was wary about State's approach to the June 24 speech and expressed my concerns in a memo to Hadley soon after taking the Middle East portfolio. I worried that the Quartet and the Roadmap were not clear in requiring that Arafat be pushed aside and were thereby weakening the president's message. In fact, it seemed to me that every month Arafat stayed in power was a defeat for the president.

I was also an enthusiastic member of Condi's NSC staff, dazzled by her efficiency, lightning intelligence, and charm. Her way of treating everyone on the staff as intellectual equals while nevertheless asserting her own clear leadership brought out from all of us our best efforts – while maintaining the highest esprit de corps. We were all working 14 hours a day at least – I was up at 4:30 a.m. every morning and got to my desk at 6:00 a.m. – and this would have been intolerable had the mood at work been sour. Instead, it was wonderful because Condi knew how to motivate and care for a staff. She insisted that summer, for example, that every NSC staffer take two weeks' vacation, saying that given the pace at the White House, we and our families needed it. Two consecutive weeks with no excuses; email my secretary your vacation dates, she said, and you'll hear from me if you are not in compliance. Despite the immense pressures on her and the paperwork load, her desk was always clean, and she always had time to meet with her senior directors – and to make them feel she had nothing important going on but to listen to them and seek their advice.

"We Need to Get that Guy out of the Way"

Sharon predictably won his election on January 29, 2003, defeating a weak Labor Party candidate. Two days later the King of Bahrain visited the president, who made it clear to the king that his own views had not changed. We have an opportunity to move the peace process forward, Bush said, so the Palestinians will not have to depend on one man who is a failure. We need to get that guy out of the way so we can develop a state.

But the gears were grinding slowly. A month of negotiations lay before Sharon, as he tried to put together a new coalition. His Likud Party had won

38 seats in the Knesset, twice what Labor had won, but he needed 61 to govern. Not until February 24 was the bargaining concluded, and Sharon presented his new cabinet to the Knesset on the 27th – which included Benjamin Netanyahu as finance minister and Ehud Olmert as minister of trade and industry, with the added title of deputy prime minister. Meanwhile, he had sent his chief of staff, Weissglas, to Washington while the negotiations were underway, where Weissglas told Bush administration officials that the new coalition would be committed to the two-state solution. The problem on the Palestinian side, he told them, was Arafat, who was resisting the reforms called for in the Roadmap. Under immense European pressure, Arafat had finally agreed to allow the appointment of a prime minister. Now the jockeying was over who would fill the post, and the most likely candidate was Mahmoud Abbas, known as "Abu Mazen." Then would come the struggle over the powers of the post – which had none. Rice saw this as progress, step by step: Create the post and then get it some powers. We want to be able to move fast at the end of the Iraq war, she told the Israelis.

When Sharon and Bush spoke by telephone on February 26, Bush offered congratulations on the election victory and on forming a new coalition. Sharon was philosophical, saying, "I had 28 years in the military, and have now been in civilian life for 28 years. We've started talks with the Palestinians and we are moving forward toward peace." Bush continued his congratulatory approach to Sharon, telling him he was a great leader, a man of peace, in the hopes of pushing and pulling him forward. But Bush also repeated that new Palestinian interlocutors were needed: Arafat was just no good. When Rice met with EU ministers the following day, she pressed the Palestinian prime minister issue, calling on the Europeans to keep pushing for the post to be created and to be given serious powers.

For Bush, Palestinian reforms were fundamental matters. He believed Israelis would back a two-state solution if Arafat were gone and a decent Palestinian political structure was emerging. He believed Sharon would lead them in this direction but was not worried about what might happen if the old warrior changed his mind; Bush believed Israeli democracy would handle that shift, as he told Arab visitors who expressed grave doubts about Sharon: If he stands in the way of a decent peace settlement, he will be voted out; democracy was the answer. And democracy was the answer on the Palestinian side as well: If Arafat were gone, Bush could embrace the new Palestinian leadership that would emerge. On February 28 he told King Abdullah of Jordan that he was aching to open the door of the Oval Office to a new Palestinian political leader, but that could not happen until Arafat was gone.

To push harder for progress on that front, formal release of the Roadmap was delayed again. The idea had been to put it out right after the Israeli elections or at least after the formation of the new Israeli government, but now it became a tool to press for appointment of a Palestinian prime minister. The EU and United States agreed the release would be delayed until Arafat made good on his promise and a prime minister was in place. On March 10, the PLC approved Mahmoud Abbas for the post. President Bush called President Mubarak of Egypt, King Abdullah of Jordan, and Crown Prince Abdallah of Saudi Arabia on March 14 to tell them the Roadmap would finally come out when Abbas was formally appointed by Arafat, enlisting their help to make this happen. To several staff members gathered in the Oval Office for those calls, the president said he realized the Roadmap was just a tool. Peace depended on the willingness to make peace, which Arafat did not have, so we needed him out of the way. The reason I am so strongly for the Israelis, Bush said, is that they do want peace. So does Sharon, the president went on, but if I'm wrong about that, Israeli elections will take care of the problem. The task now is to push Arafat out of the way. Finally, on March 19, Arafat was forced to bow to pressure; he agreed to appoint Abbas as prime minister of the Palestinian Authority.

It was one day before the invasion of Iraq. A week earlier, Weissglas had visited Washington again, this time for sensitive discussions of the forthcoming war. He was told nothing about its timing; the subject was specifically how Israel would react if Saddam attacked Israel in response to the American assault. During the 1991 Gulf War, Saddam had shot SCUD missiles at Israel. What kind of Iraqi provocations would produce what kind of Israeli responses this time? Clearly, the United States wanted Israel to stay out of the conflict, but Bush also realized that significant Israeli casualties might make that impossible for Sharon. The meetings were conducted by Rice, not Powell or Rumsfeld or their staffs; the key relationships with Israel were now in the White House. And the tone of the meetings – quiet confidence, good humor, shared approaches – was increasingly the tone of the U.S.-Israel relationship at every level, including at the top.

On April 2, as the Iraq War continued, Bush met with Israel's new foreign minister, Silvan Shalom, who was never to be a powerful member of the government because Sharon kept control of foreign relations in the Prime Minister's Office. The conversation reflected Bush's focus on the prospects for progress if Arafat were truly starting to be pushed aside. No peace is possible with Arafat, Bush said, but Abu Mazen looks like progress; let's bet on him and help him. We want him to succeed. I need to talk to Sharon about him, the president said, and at some point I need to meet him. The foreign minister demurred: Abu Mazen has to act against terror, and we still do not know what authority he will have. Sure, Bush answered, but we have to help him; don't set conditions that almost guarantee his failure. You can make him succeed or destroy his chances.

"We've Broken the Middle East"

At this point, Bush was thinking through his options, not jumping forward: He was anxious to move, but understood that an embrace of Abbas could hurt the new prime minister, especially with the Iraq War raging. He would continually remind the Israelis that Abbas was their best hope for progress but realized that progress would only occur if Abbas asserted himself against Arafat.

My first meetings with the president in 2001 had shown, first of all, that he was completely in charge of his administration. Early on the press had offered the "Cheney as prime minister" line, suggesting that he was the power behind the throne. Yet it took me just a few minutes in the Oval Office in the summer of 2001, watching the president interrupt cabinet officers to pepper them with questions and tell them what he wanted, for me to see who was in charge. It was also obvious that the caricature of him as lacking in intelligence was itself a joke; like Condi and others he chose to surround himself with, he was razor sharp in seeing and evaluating both political and policy developments. I saw quickly, as well, that his view of international politics centered largely on leadership – his own and that of other heads of government, with whom he tried to build relationships that could later be used to American advantage. His tone was a patented combination of formality and informality: One could never appear in the Oval Office without a suit and tie out of respect for the office of president and the White House itself, but the banter was relaxed, the jokes frequent, the Texas references constant.

And the president was a constant: rarely moody, almost always fun to joke or chat with, always probing for more information and opinions, and amazingly well informed. To the formal briefings from CIA and others, he added his own network of contacts around the world, so that an update based on official reporting would often be met with a response based on a factoid he had picked up from some American businessman, author, or retired ambassador he knew. He read constantly, and several times I had the experience of reading some new history work (for example, on Air Force One in 2008 it was *Power, Faith, and Fantasy*, Michael Oren's history of the American role in the Middle East) only to have the president, walking by, tell me he had just finished it and wanted to know what I thought of it.

He was a constant in another way too: He spoke the same way to everyone who came through the Oval. I had a tendency to slow down and limit my vocabulary a bit when speaking with foreign officials to be sure they caught what I was saying. It was not condescension but an effort to communicate more effectively. In contrast, the president had one vocabulary, heavily salted with colloquialisms, and our interpreters were familiar with them and knew how to translate them. Foreign leaders who spoke some English, even good English, often wondered what was being said when the leader of the Free World asked if they were "ready to saddle up," or told them about someone who was "lying in the weeds," or commented that a certain other leader had "more hat than cattle." Their facial expressions of confusion were priceless, and if the president saw them he would laugh and translate his own remarks from Texan to English. If he did not see them, God only knows what these foreigners thought they were being asked or told.

Now the president wanted to be ready for action right after the conclusion of the Iraq War. Rice led planning meetings on April 9 and April 11. She was looking for something big when the war ended; we've broken the Middle East with this war, she would say, and now we need to show we know how to put it together again. The Israeli-Palestinian conflict is at the center of this effort, she said. She wanted a major push: Perhaps a big speech by the President? A regional economic initiative? A nonproliferation piece? Something bold – a significant democracy initiative, and of course something about terrorism. Perhaps, on the institutional side, a new organization modeled on the Organization for Security and Cooperation in Europe, which had both security and political dimensions. Rice was reaching for a positive and comprehensive agenda for the entire region after the Iraq War – encompassing human rights and democracy, fighting poverty, counterterrorism, security, and, of course, addressing the Israeli-Palestinian dispute. We need a bold agenda that displays American power as well as American values, she told the staff. It was Rice who formulated the idea of a grand meeting, one that would showcase both the new Palestinian leadership – because Arafat would not be invited – and Sharon's willingness to move on peace, and would be a demonstration of American leadership. She began a round of consultations with Arab leaders, by phone and in person, to see what the traffic would bear. Would the key leaders come to a meeting? Would they come if Sharon were there? And if Arafat were not? What would they say? What would Sharon and Abbas say? Rice and her staff spent scores of hours in April and May turning these ideas into a program for a summit meeting – or two summits, as it turned out. The timing was linked to the coming G-8 meeting in Evian, France, for that meant the president would be overseas in early June and already halfway to the Middle East.

But American power was proving more useful against Saddam than against Arafat. The post of prime minister had been created and Abbas had been selected, but Arafat was blocking his ability to choose a cabinet. If Abbas lacked all power, he could not be the interlocutor the president sought – for himself and for the Israelis. On April 14, Bush again called Mubarak and Crown Prince Abdallah, seeking their help to pressure Arafat to give in. As to sustained Palestinian action against terror – a Roadmap requirement and the key to progress – there was none. Arafat was fighting Abbas, not the suicide bombers. And he was far tougher and more resourceful than Abbas, his underling for decades. Arafat was battling over every inch of territory. Finally, the EU and Arab pressure again forced a concession; on April 29, Arafat swore in Abbas and his new cabinet. The PA had a prime minister. And according to plan, the text of the Roadmap was formally released on April 30.

"A Tiny Small Country"

Bush then sent Steve Hadley and me to Israel to see Sharon and confirm that he would move forward. Sharon would not be coming to the United States for a while, so it would be useful to sound him out. Hadley had a plan that reflected his own character and his insight into Sharon: Instead of the usual 45- to 60-minute meetings in his office, let's really listen to him. Let's go to his residence for some sessions that can last for hours and hours. Let him talk, let him explain himself. This is a man who has been a war hero and a pariah. This guy is one of the last of his generation of leaders. Let's hear him out, Hadley decided.

Hadley's plan worked; added to Bush's appreciation of Sharon, and Rice's and my own growing relationship with Weissglas, the sessions helped persuade Sharon that Bush and his people were different, that they really wanted to understand Israel and his view of its situation. Sharon liked being liked; under the gruff exterior was a man who cared what people thought, who could be wounded, who responded to respect and affection. Hadley gave Sharon a letter from Bush that thanked him for being willing to take risks for peace. After reading the letter, Sharon gave a long monologue that included stories of his parents and his own youth on an Israeli kibbutz and his views on Israel, its situation, and the demands being made of it.

I took risks personally, he said, but never took any risks with the security of the State of Israel. I appreciate Arab promises but will take seriously only tangible performance. For tangible performance I will take tangible steps. Israel is a tiny small country. From the Jordan River to Jerusalem is only 17.5 miles. Before 1967, the Knesset was in range of machine guns south of Jerusalem. From the Green Line to Tel Aviv is 11 miles. From the sea at Netanya to Tulkarm is 9 miles. Two-thirds of the Jewish population live in a narrow strip on the coastal plain. Between Haifa and Ashdod, which is 80 miles, are two-thirds of the Jewish population, our only international airport, and most of our infrastructure. The hills of Judea and Samaria overlook all of that area.

What does a settlement freeze "including natural growth" mean? Should we decree that settlers cannot have children? That pregnant women must have abortions? They live there, they serve in army elite units, they marry. Now what? They contribute to the society, and serve, and now tell them no more children – or move?

I am a Jew above all, he continued, and feel the responsibility to the future of the Jewish people on my shoulders. After what happened in the past, I will not let the future of the Jewish people depend on anyone, even our closest friends. Especially when you saw the crowds cheering Saddam, who killed even members of his own family and government. With the deepest friendship and appreciation, we do not choose to be the lamb, but not the lion either. I will not sacrifice the nation. I come from a farm family who settled here but I deal with these problems with a cold mind. I met with the Pope, Sharon concluded, who said this is Terra Sancta to all, but Terra Promisa for the Jews only.

The discussion of the route of the security fence Sharon was building was typical of these sessions. The United States had not been supportive of the move initially, but repeated suicide bombings had chipped away at American resistance – and over time the success of the barrier in stopping such attacks became an unanswerable argument. This day Sharon explained the proposed route at length and with maps. Having commanded troops in every part of

Israel, he knew the terrain almost by the square meter; he could explain why the route in one place or another could not be changed because "here there is a hill and you have to go around it; here there is a spring." Hadley told him of the widespread criticism that the fence and its route were an effort to create facts on the ground and prejudice final status negotiations. This is not a border, Sharon answered; it is just another means to control terror. You want us to withdraw from the West Bank towns; this allows us to do so without allowing more terror. And as to the critics who say this is just an Israeli land grab, Sharon replied that we don't want land; we want to protect people. Look, he said, you can't defend a nation based on what the *New York Times* will write.

A "Settlement Freeze"

By the end of this visit in early May, the American victory in Iraq was being celebrated; President Bush's "Mission Accomplished" landing on an aircraft carrier came on May 2. After the talks with Sharon, I thought I understood his intentions very well. Our discussion of settlements had revealed that he did not plan any new settlements, nor did he envision the physical expansion of the settlements that existed. There would be no need to include more land within settlement borders. Moreover, financial enticements to Israelis to move to the settlements were also on their way out, for budgetary reasons if for nothing else. We were stuck with the phrase "settlement freeze," which had appeared in the Mitchell Report in 2001 and in the Roadmap and been repeated endlessly by Powell and other State Department officials as well as by the president. After the conversations with Sharon, I told Rice and Hadley we could say we had an acceptable "settlement freeze" if Sharon did the following: announced a commitment to a viable Palestinian state, agreed that the security fence was for security only and was not meant to be a border, ended all subsidies to Israelis to move across the Green Line into settlements in the West Bank or Gaza, and said that said there would be no new settlements or taking of land for new settlements or physical expansion of existing ones, and that new construction in settlements would reflect only natural growth and be only in built-up areas. The last condition was simple: It did not prejudice Palestinians or block final status talks if Israelis built new houses or apartments *inside* existing settlements, using no additional land. Ma'ale Adumim had (at that time) perhaps 35,000 people, so adding another couple of thousand inside the settlement borders was not a major event. Building on new territory or at the edge of settlements, which would require security roads and perimeters to use additional land, was different – and to be avoided.

This was a formula that could work and represented a decent compromise between the United States and Israel without prejudicing Palestinian interests. Of course, the PA demanded an absolute halt to construction of any kind in the settlements and in Jerusalem, but no Israeli government would ever agree to that and the Palestinians knew it. The discussions we were holding with Israeli officials were moving toward a sensible compromise on the settlement issue.

Sharon's goals appeared to me to be to build the fence, stop the terrorism, and get to Phase II of the Roadmap. That would mean negotiations over the existence of a Palestinian state and of its provisional borders, and significant withdrawals in the West Bank and Gaza, but it would not mean dealing with all the most sensitive final status issues (including Jerusalem) or a full withdrawal to whatever the final borders would be. The borders of the Palestinian state would be provisional, but I thought Sharon envisioned this temporary situation as lasting for many years, perhaps decades – until the terrorist groups had truly been disbanded and a working Palestinian state structure was in place. Peace, quiet, and separation from the Palestinians were his goals, I thought, not a final status agreement. He seemed to me to be looking at the issues like an old general, not an ideologue; he wanted practical solutions and above all security.

On the Palestinian side, we still did not know whom we were dealing with – Arafat or Abbas. How successful the efforts to move power away from Arafat and his "security" gangs would be was still entirely uncertain. I did not think Abbas wanted a final status agreement any more than Sharon because then he would have to face extremely difficult compromises that he lacked the legitimacy to impose. Arafat, a charismatic leader with many means of persuasion at his disposal (including guns and cash), had backed away from such an agreement with Israel under Clinton. So perhaps the Palestinians too could find their way to an interim agreement that established a state with provisional borders and left the toughest issues for a later day. After all, that was the content of the Roadmap, to which all parties were now more or less pledged.

In fact, the Israelis had announced 14 objections to the Roadmap after its "official" publication. They insisted that it be clear Arafat was gone, not simply ruling from behind the scenes; they wanted clear action on terrorism, including arrests, arms seizures, and dismantling terrorist organizations; and they focused on an end to "incitement," which meant eliminating a broad category of Palestinian broadcasts, textbooks, and publications that demonized Israel and taught each new generation that war and "resistance" were the proper attitude, not peace and coexistence with the Jewish state. Most of all, they insisted on the sequencing: There must be full completion of one stage before the next is opened. All of their objections were based on reasonable points, but it was too late to reopen the text of the Roadmap in the spring of 2003. The Israelis (and Palestinians) had been promised all along that the Roadmap text they were seeing was a draft that was open to amendment, but the text as drafted in the early fall of 2002 was final. The Israelis had a right to feel misled; the best we could do in response was the statement I negotiated with Weissglas that promised all of Israel's objections would be "addressed fully and seriously." This left many Israelis, I was soon told, reaching for dictionaries;

why would we "address" their objections? Why did they need an address, and who would be mailing responses to whom?

Rice and the Red Sea Summits

By early May, Rice's plans for the post–Iraq War meeting had gelled. Right after the G-8 summit in France, Bush would continue on to Sharm el-Sheik, Egypt. There he would meet with key Arab leaders – Mubarak, Crown Prince Abdallah, King Abdullah of Jordan – and the new face in town: Prime Minister Abbas. The following day he would proceed to Aqaba, Jordan, where he would meet separately with King Abdullah, Sharon, and Abbas and then preside over a meeting with Sharon and Abbas together. It was critical that all of the parties say the right things about peace, so Rice engaged in a whirlwind of diplomacy. She browbeat the Saudi ambassador, Prince Bandar, into assuring that his head of government, the Crown Prince, would show up. She telephoned King Abdullah of Jordan on May 19 to get him to come to Sharm on June 3 and then hurry home to host his visitors the following day. She had the staff draft "parallel unilateral statements," statements that Abbas and Sharon would utter at Aqaba and that would reflect views compatible with the American approach. My computer contained dozens of drafts of these statements, and if the parties were amazed at the American chutzpah in proposing to put our words in their mouths, they did not say so. Perhaps it was Rice's warm but extremely firm approach; perhaps it was what appeared to be the smashing American victory in Iraq. But our parallel unilateral statements were never rejected; they were the basis for negotiations, word by word, line by line, because we wanted to be sure that Abbas made firm commitments against terror and Sharon equally firm ones about peace and Palestinian statehood. In these preparations, Rice entirely sidelined Colin Powell. As she notes in her memoir, "I took direct responsibility for overseeing U.S. efforts."[16] Powell attended the Sharm and Aqaba summits but was a marginal figure. The calls and the meetings, the cajoling and pressuring, and the planning of what the president would say, to whom, and when were all White House activities. At best, State was informed and asked to perform various helpful supportive roles. Increasingly, Rice rather than Powell was acting for the president and was in charge of Middle East policy. Assistant Secretary Bill Burns was involved in the practical arrangements for what were now being called the "Red Sea Summits," but neither he nor his boss was making policy; Burns was simply helping make sure the details were ironed out.

The president knew what he wanted: Terrorism must stop, which was not negotiable, and Abbas must say so in Aqaba. He could not stop 100% of the attacks, the president said, but the key is for Abu Mazen (the president never referred to him as Abbas) to show the world he is giving every ounce of effort to fighting terror. This was not an abstract argument: As we were planning for the Sharm and Aqaba meetings, Palestinian terror continued. On

May 18, 7 people were killed and 20 wounded in another suicide bombing
of a public bus, this time near French Hill in Jerusalem. The following day, a
suicide bomber attacked in a shopping mall in northern Israel, killing 3 and
injuring 70 more. These followed six smaller attacks in April and three earlier in May. Nor did Prime Minister Abbas believe he could stop them: When
Sharon (in a May 17 meeting between the two men) offered him a redeployment of IDF troops so that Palestinian forces could take greater responsibility
for security, he demurred. Instead, Abbas spoke of how weak his own position was; Sharon's notes of the meeting say, "They are not yet ready to take
responsibility."[17]

On May 20, the president called the newly installed Palestinian prime minister, noting that it was his first call to a Palestinian leader in two years. Bush
was warm and encouraging but clear about terror: Denounce terror and you
have a friend in me, he said. If you want peace we can work together, and this
is just the first of our calls and meetings. Bush told Abbas that Israel would
never compromise its security and he would never ask them to do so, but the
killers were the enemies of the Palestinians as well as Israelis. Abbas had the
right responses: He was committed to peace and against terrorism, and he
understood that without Israeli security there would be no peace. It was a good
start.

Bush also called Sharon that day. A planned Sharon visit to Washington
had been put off due to the terrorist attacks. Bush offered condolences for the
deaths and injuries and said he understood why Sharon was staying home. He
told Sharon he had spoken to Abu Mazen and thought the new prime minister
wanted to move forward to peace. The United States would never jeopardize
Israeli security, but we should help Abu Mazen; there is a chance for progress.
Not if the terror continues, Sharon replied, and Abu Mazen, whatever his
intentions, was doing nothing to stop it. Well, he just got there, Bush said; he
means well and we should help him succeed. Back and forth they went, Bush
noting the possibilities and the need to help Abu Mazen succeed, and each time
Sharon replying that he could not move during a wave of terror and while
Abu Mazen did nothing to end it. It was a conversation they would have over
and over during the next two years. Sharon said he would not compromise on
security; Bush agreed, but said we had a chance to marginalize Arafat now if
we could empower Abu Mazen. You can be a man of security *and* a man of
peace, he urged Sharon.

At its regular Sunday cabinet meeting on May 25, Israel's cabinet approved
the Roadmap – but not unanimously. The vote was 12 to 7, with 4 abstentions,
once again suggesting that Sharon's coalition was fractious indeed. A day later,
Sharon shocked allies and opponents alike by using the word "occupation" for
the first time to describe Israel's presence in the Palestinian Territories. Speaking
to a Likud audience in Haifa, he said Israel should seek a political arrangement
with the Palestinians and added, "The idea that it is possible to continue keeping
3.5 million Palestinians under occupation – yes, it is occupation, you might not
like the word, but what is happening is occupation – is bad for Israel and bad

for the Palestinians, and bad for the Israeli economy. Controlling 3.5 million Palestinians cannot go on forever."[18] Here was more evidence that Sharon was intent on a serious negotiation with Abbas and that he would say so at Aqaba.

As June began, Bush headed off in Air Force One for Evian, where the G-8 leaders pressed him for more action on the "peace process." He had a ready answer: The Red Sea Summits were the next step. They were Bush's first venture into Clinton-style diplomacy on this issue. The meeting in Sharm el-Sheik was an effort to showcase Arab support for the president's efforts, and it was noteworthy more because it happened than for anything said there. In fact, the meeting almost broke down before it began. The heads of state were to meet at a round table in the Movenpick resort, favored by President Mubarak for such sessions. They would discuss the issues privately before moving outside for the reading of a public statement by Mubarak, their host. When Mubarak, Bush, King Abdullah of Jordan, and Abbas (and the other invitee, King Hamad of Bahrain) arrived at the resort, they found that Crown Prince Abdallah of Saudi Arabia had not yet arrived. The minutes ticked by, but still no prince. More and more pressing inquiries were addressed to sweating Saudi diplomats, and finally the explanation was whispered: Abdallah had decided or been told that Sharon would be present – and the prince refused to meet with him.

Sharon was, of course, in Jerusalem, and after repeated efforts to reassure Abdallah of this fact, he finally appeared. But by then the discussion time had ended, and the press was gathered for the leaders' public appearance together. So after gathering at the roundtable, the leaders simply trooped outside onto the stage to listen together as Mubarak read the agreed statement. Viewers would have noticed that the audience and the press were absolutely wilting in the heat and sharp sunlight, while the leaders appeared – and remained – cool and fresh. This was not an optical illusion but a marvel of American technology. The stage on which the men stood was on the edge of the hill leading down to the sea; it was placed there because that location provided a gorgeous backdrop – Tiran Island and the Red Sea itself. But White House technicians had also brought air conditioning condensers down to the shore by boat and crane, and were piping cold air up the hill and under the stage. The audience saw nothing, but the icy air wafting up from the floor boards kept the leaders in a kind of cold bubble.

"The Goal Today Is to Strengthen Abbas"

From Sharm, the president made the short flight to Aqaba, which was to be a far more successful venture. There were three key events: the private meetings with Sharon and then with Abbas, and then public statements. Both men said what Bush wanted to hear. For the Palestinians, there had been debate over how to react to those American drafts of what Abbas should say. As an advisor to Abbas described it,

There were two schools of thought. One school of thought that said, "You know, this is unacceptable. Let's negotiate every word, every comma, every term." Another school of thought that said, "No. We're not going to turn this into one of these painful things – this is an opportunity to start building good rapport with the President. . . . [T]his is an opportunity to say, "Look, we're playing ball here." And the latter school of thought did prevail.[19]

Indeed it did. The Abbas speech did everything the White House wanted – in the key passages endorsing the two-state solution and new negotiations to reach it, renouncing terror and violence as a means of promoting Palestinian interests, and promising democratic reforms:

As we all realize, this is an important moment. A new opportunity for peace exists, an opportunity based upon President Bush's vision and the quartet's road map which we have accepted without any reservations. Our goal is two states, Israel and Palestine, living side by side in peace and security. The process is the one of direct negotiations to end the Israeli-Palestinian conflict and to resolve all the permanent status issues and end the occupation that began in 1967 under which Palestinians have suffered so much.

At the same time, we do not ignore the suffering of the Jews throughout history. It is time to bring all this suffering to an end.

Just as Israel must meet its responsibilities, we, the Palestinians, will fulfill our obligations for this endeavor to succeed.

We are ready to do our part. Let me be very clear: There will be no military solution for this conflict, so we repeat our renunciation and the renunciation of terrorism against the Israelis wherever they might be. Such methods are inconsistent with our religious and moral traditions and are a dangerous obstacle to the achievement of an independent sovereign state we seek. These methods also conflict with the kinds of state we wish to build based on human rights and the rule of law.

We will exert all of our efforts using all our resources to end the militarization of the intifada and we will succeed. The armed intifada must end, and we must use and resort to peaceful means in our quest to end the occupation and the suffering of Palestinians and Israelis. And to establish the Palestinian state, we emphasize our determination to implement our pledges which we have made for our people and the international community, and that is the rule of law, single political authority, weapons only in the hands of those who are in charge of upholding the law and order, and political diversity within the framework of democracy.

Our goal is clear and we will implement it firmly and without compromise: a complete end to violence and terrorism. And we will be full partners in the international war against terrorism.[20]

Sharon's speech also met the mark – in its key parts he clearly endorsed Palestinian statehood and the commencement of negotiations, and even mentioned the Roadmap:

As the Prime Minister of Israel, the land which is the cradle of the Jewish people, my paramount responsibility is the security of the people of Israel and of the State of Israel.

There can be no compromise with terror and Israel, together with all free nations, will continue fighting terrorism until its final defeat.

Ultimately, permanent security requires peace and permanent peace can only be obtained through security, and there is now hope of a new opportunity for peace between Israelis and Palestinians.

Israel, like others, has lent its strong support for President Bush's vision, expressed on June 24, 2002, of two states – Israel and a Palestinian state – living side by side in peace and security. The Government and people of Israel welcome the opportunity to renew direct negotiations according to the steps of the Roadmap as adopted by the Israeli government to achieve this vision.

It is in Israel's interest not to govern the Palestinians but for the Palestinians to govern themselves in their own state. A democratic Palestinian state fully at peace with Israel will promote the long-term security and well-being of Israel as a Jewish state.

There can be no peace, however, without the abandonment and elimination of terrorism, violence, and incitement. We will work alongside the Palestinians and other states to fight terrorism, violence and incitement of all kinds.

We can also reassure our Palestinian partners that we understand the importance of territorial contiguity in the West Bank, for a viable, Palestinian state. Israeli policy in the territories that are subject to direct negotiations with the Palestinians will reflect this fact.

We accept the principle that no unilateral actions by any party can prejudge the outcome of our negotiations.

In regard to the unauthorized outposts, I want to reiterate that Israel is a society governed by the rule of law. Thus, we will immediately begin to remove unauthorized outposts.

Israel seeks peace with all its Arab neighbors. Israel is prepared to negotiate in good faith wherever there are partners. As normal relations are established, I am confident that they will find in Israel a neighbor and a people committed to comprehensive peace and prosperity for all the peoples of the region.[21]

Before his private meetings with Abbas and Sharon, the president met briefly with King Abdullah, the host at Aqaba; in fact, all the meetings took place at his palace there. President Bush was impressed by Abbas's intentions but still worried about Arafat. If he reemerges, forget the peace process, he told Abdullah; the goal today is to strengthen Abbas, and in particular start getting him control over the security organizations. In this assessment Bush was absolutely correct because, as Sharon had repeatedly told him, there could be no "peace process" while suicide bombs were exploding weekly.

The president first met with Sharon before meeting with Abbas. Sharon was accompanied only by Dubi Weissglas. Dubi had been Sharon's lawyer for many years, since his libel lawsuit against *Time* magazine in 1983. He was a prosperous Tel Aviv lawyer who served Sharon now as his chief of staff inside the government and in effect as his foreign minister and chief interpreter – interpreter of the world to Sharon and of Sharon to the world. Dubi was famous in Israel, and soon enough to us as well, for his endless and often brilliant wisecracks and jokes, which he used to defuse any tense situation or to change the subject when he thought it useful to Israel that he do so. He was Sharon's best press agent and his key interface with the Bush administration. Perhaps most critically for us, Sharon trusted him and he truly spoke for the prime minister as no other Israeli official could. It was not surprising that for this key meeting with Bush, Sharon chose to come only with Dubi.

Bush began with flattery: I called you a man of peace, I meant it, and today you are proving me right. He then repeated his views of Arafat, knowing this too would reassure Sharon: I am never going to deal with him, he told the Israeli. He is no good; he has failed. And the president repeated his commitment to Israeli security, this time with a note of exasperation: Do not worry about that; in fact, if you are really worried about my commitment to Israel's security, which you keep mentioning over and over, take your plane and go home.

Sharon thanked Bush for calling him a man of peace and said that was his goal – but peace and security were inextricably linked. For real peace, peace that brought security, Sharon said he was ready to make "painful compromises." He had run on that platform and gotten a majority of the vote for it. He was ready for territorial concessions in the "cradle of the Bible." He then went back to security: The Palestinians must understand that if terror continues, they will not get anything. Bush did not argue but asked instead how the process could move forward; how can we make this work? Sharon, who had for so long resisted the Roadmap, now adopted its phases. If the terror ends in Phase I, we will move to an "interim" Palestinian state in Phase II and then can begin discussing the final phase. Sharon made it clear that he understood what Palestinian contiguity meant: the painful removal of settlements, which he always called "Israeli towns." But all this would have to come in stages: Israel would not negotiate peace first and then wait for terror to stop. Phase I came first, and only then Phase II. Sharon was adamantly opposed to making concessions first and then finding that Israel was still living under terror. I won't ask you to take risks with Israel's security, Bush told him again; you've mentioned this maybe 30 times so you must be nervous. Don't be.

There was also discussion of the settlements, worth noting in view of later denials (made by the Obama administration) that any real understanding had been reached. Weissglas said that as part of the U.S.-Israel understanding about a freeze, there would be no new building beyond the current construction line. Sharon added that there would also be no additional confiscation or expropriation of land. Rice asked about another part of the agreement, the end of subsidies; Weissglas replied that in the new Israeli budget, all subsidies to settlers would come to an end. This was no staff-level discussion but rather a meeting between Bush and Sharon, and both sides were fully cognizant of the agreement on settlements that had been reached.

The session ended with Sharon raising the so-called right of return. It had always been a central Palestinian demand – found in all their key documents – that all Palestinian refugees *and* their descendants, now numbering in the millions, had the right to "return" to Israel. Such a population movement would, of course, shift the ethnic/religious balance in Israel, whose population was then 20% Arab, and would mean the end of Israel as a Jewish State. It would finally defeat the partition declared by the United Nations in 1947 between a Jewish State and an Arab State and rejected since by every Arab nation.

Bush and Sharon had never discussed the issue before, but Sharon put it on the table before we adjourned. The official U.S. position had long been that there should be a "just settlement" of the refugee issue; we had no agreement with Israel that there would never be a right of return. The Bush reply must have surprised the Israelis: When Weissglas said the whole issue hit a raw nerve with the people of Israel, Bush's only comment was "No shit – here come three million people!" The Americans in the room could not have been surprised when later, in the spring of 2004, Bush made it official American policy that the refugee problem would be solved solely in a Palestinian state, and not by Palestinians "returning" to Israel.

In his meeting with Abbas, Bush first emphasized the need to stop terror. You've got to kick some terrorist ass, he told the mild-mannered prime minister, because it will be impossible to move forward if the terrorism continues. Abbas was accompanied by his security minister, Mohammed Dahlan, on whom Bush placed the burden for action: Tough things need to be done. Dahlan reminded Bush that the PLO had fought Hamas before, in 1996, and said it could do so again; the forces needed to be rebuilt, but this would not take long. (In this as in so many later promises, Dahlan proved to be what one very senior official called him that day – "just a bullshitter.") Abbas said the time for such a clash with the terrorists would come; it was inevitable. Bush spoke almost emotionally of his hopes for the Palestinians: A democratic Palestinian state would be a model for the entire Arab world, which had for so long mistreated the Palestinians. He promised to pressure Israel to move as well, though not by compromising its security, and told Abbas it was U.S. policy to make him and his new government steadily stronger.

In this meeting, the good and bad of Abbas came through clearly. He seemed to all of us, as we chatted later, a decent man who really did want to see the violence end. Nothing that Abbas said or did in the ensuing years ever led any of us to doubt that conclusion. He was always pleasant to work with, possessed a good sense of humor, and was fond of Americans. We had no evidence that he was personally corrupt, even if the rumors (and, later, information) about his sons were ultimately too strong to deny. But from the president on down, we doubted that day and ever after whether he could deliver on his pledges. He seemed better suited by nature to be a prime minister in some small and peaceful state in northern Europe than to lead the Palestinians. By 2002 and 2003, Palestinians were becoming tired of Arafat's corruption and his autocratic leadership style, but the political culture still placed a great premium on militancy. Those who had served time in Israeli prisons had a huge advantage over those who had not; those who had fired guns (or claimed to have done so or were urging others to do so) were elevated over those whose weapons were words. Could Abbas really wrest the mantle of leadership from Arafat and from gang leaders who urged confrontation with Israel? Could he persuade Palestinians to drop their weapons and make the compromises that peace would require, and then enforce any deal that was made? Those questions recurred throughout President Bush's efforts to move toward a peace agreement, and he himself repeatedly raised them, sometimes thinking aloud and sometimes directing them at visitors from the region.

In the trilateral meeting that day, he repeated the main points to Abbas and Sharon – the need to fight terror and the real chance to reach peace and Palestinian statehood. He told them he would send Ambassador John Wolf, a senior career diplomat, to live in Jerusalem and monitor progress, reporting to Powell and Rice. More remarkable were a few words whose import could not have escaped the other parties: "Condi will be my personal representative." Now the passing of the baton from Powell to Rice was not rumor: They had heard it from the president.

The Red Sea Summits had achieved all the White House wanted, symbolizing that the key Arab states, Sharon, and Abbas were on board for a new effort at peace. It had taken almost a year from the speech of June 24, 2002. Bush had judged correctly that no peace was possible with Arafat; in this he had applied the lessons taught by the Clinton administration, indeed by Clinton himself on January 20, 2001. Even while the global war on terror and the invasion of Iraq were said to monopolize his time, he had attended to the Israeli-Palestinian issue. Rejecting the old "peace process" of endless negotiations, he had developed an approach and he had moved it forward against the odds. Bush's refusal to deal with Arafat had been rejected by European and Arab leaders for months, as had his demands for Palestinian reform. But Palestinians were far more open to Bush's insistence on transparency and democracy, as political arguments among them had shown. And Israel's right wing leader had been reelected convincingly after endorsing Bush's approach – the two-state solution.

Now the key elements were clear: the marginalization of Arafat, new Palestinian leadership that would fight terror and undertake reforms, Israeli commitment to a viable Palestinian state, and new negotiations between the Israelis and Palestinians. At the end of the meetings on June 4, there was reason for cautious optimism. Unfortunately, it did not last the summer.

Arafat Strikes Back

On the Palestinian side, there was a serious backlash against what Abbas had pledged at Aqaba. Within two days of the Aqaba meetings, moderate Palestinians were privately warning us of trouble ahead. And, in the real world, the terrorists had a vote. On June 6, Hamas leaders ended talks they had been having with Abbas, claiming he had yielded too much in the summit meetings. Hamas leader Abdel Aziz Rantisi, in Gaza, slammed Abbas and said there would be no peace until Zionism was eradicated from Palestinian soil. On June 8, a terrorist attack killed four soldiers; four days later, Israel would attempt to assassinate Rantisi, who was held responsible for the attack, and in the process kill 2 civilians and wound perhaps 30 more. This elicited a sharp comment from President Bush: "I am troubled by the recent Israeli helicopter gunship attacks. I regret the loss of innocent life. I'm concerned that the attacks will make it more difficult for the Palestinian leadership to fight off terrorist attacks. I also don't believe the attacks help the Israeli security." On June 11, a suicide bomber blew up a Jerusalem bus, killing 16 and wounding more than 100 Israelis. Smaller lethal attacks continued almost every other day. For Sharon, each attack was new evidence that Abbas was simply incapable of action.

For the Bush administration, the immediate goal was to prevent terrorist acts and the Israeli responses to them from unraveling all that had been achieved at Sharm and Aqaba. The Israelis were asked to be careful and cautious in their own actions, avoiding civilian casualties; Abbas was pressed to get control of the security forces and use them to stop acts of terror. When Rice called Abbas, he made a proposal: Have the IDF pull back in Gaza and we will replace them with our own security forces. In Washington, we were skeptical they had the ability to do so, but it was worth trying. After all, Rice said to her team, Israel has tried to defeat Hamas alone and is failing, so why not try this new strategy?

While Israel's security-force presence in the West Bank was pervasive, in Gaza it was far less so: Israel conducted operations there but had no presence in Gaza's cities. On paper, the PA had 50,000 to 60,000 security men on the payroll and Hamas had 1,000. Dahlan told us that of the 50,000 to 60,000, perhaps 10,000 ever came to work. That bloated payroll was typical of Arafat's Palestine: He had used it to buy loyalty. Still, the ratio of PA to Fatah/PLO/PA forces was 10 to 1, so why not give Dahlan and his forces a chance? Israel did not want any form of truce with Hamas, which would be a form of recognition of the terrorist group. It wanted Abbas and Dahlan to act immediately, or the IDF would call up reserves and implement its own plans for a major incursion into Gaza. In a discussion with Weissglas, Genger, and Ayalon on June 16, Rice advised caution: It was not even two weeks since Aqaba, so give Abbas and his forces a chance. But Weissglas told her there were no "Abbas forces." All Palestinian meetings on security matters were still being held in Arafat's office, and it seemed he had *gained* strength since Aqaba. Still, at Rice's urgings, the Israelis agreed to wait and see what the PA forces could do in Gaza. Even a ceasefire between the PA and Hamas would be tolerable if it were part of a plan that would put the PA in charge. So the Israelis agreed to do less in Gaza and would be cautious in the West Bank as well, giving the PA some space. If it works, Rice said, we will build on it. The following day, John Wolf, now settled in Jerusalem, met with Dahlan to talk about Gaza. I have a plan and am ready to execute it, Dahlan told him, but Arafat is blocking everything, especially putting the security forces under Abbas's control.

As the terrorism continued, so did Israel's attacks on terrorist leaders. On June 21, Abdullah Qawasmeh, the man Israel thought to be behind the recent bus bombing, was killed in the West Bank; Powell denounced the killing the following day while visiting Jordan. But the forward momentum between Israel and the PA was sustained: Israel did agree on June 27 to pull its troops out of Gaza. On June 29, the PA announced a *hudna* or truce with the two largest terrorist groups: Hamas and Islamic Jihad said all attacks against Israelis would be suspended for three months.

At the end of June, Rice traveled to Israel and the West Bank to keep the momentum going. Rice began by disarming Sharon by taking a very hard line on security issues herself. We agree that a ceasefire alone is not enough; we agree that you cannot negotiate with terrorists. The president agrees that there can be no accommodation with terrorism. The Palestinians must go after and dismantle the terrorist organizations and unite their security forces under new leadership.

Her main message to Sharon was to give Abbas and the PA a chance, and his main response was to agree – but only within a narrow window. Sharon told her that Arafat was still in control of most of the security forces and was acting to undermine Abu Mazen. We understand that acting against terror takes time, he said – but not unlimited time. The PA must get started. The Israelis were trying a test: We had given Dahlan the names of 19 terrorists, and we will see what Dahlan does with them, said Sharon (who no doubt believed Dahlan would fail the test, as he did). It will be impossible to show restraint if terrorism continues.

Rice said no one was asking Israel to allow a ticking bomb to go off, but that was not the issue; the question was whether security could be made into a cooperative venture with the Palestinians. Give them some space; let's get them to act. Sharon agreed in principle, but said this test had never worked before: When before we gave them names of terrorists, they warned the people, who escaped and later went back to terror. Nevertheless, he agreed to try it. He added that it would be easier to undertake this experiment when the security fence was completed, construction of which had begun on June 16. Look, he told Rice, suicide bombers were not coming out of Gaza because the borders were closed, but in the past two years there had been scores of attacks from the West Bank.

At this point, Rice was still not persuaded about the value of the fence. We are very concerned about the fence, she said; the plans show it going farther and farther in the West Bank, cutting off Palestinian villages and lands. It would be a real problem and would not help security because it would undercut political progress. She urged Sharon to take another look at the route of the fence; it looks like it will be a huge political problem in the United States, and we cannot and will not remain silent if the fence cuts Palestinian lands and villages. Try to find solutions that are not so politically harmful. Take a really hard look. The fence will cause difficulty.

Sharon bristled at Rice's comments, reminding her that the president had asked in Aqaba if there was any possibility not to build the fence. I told him then that it is neither a political border nor even a security border. The only goal is to stop terror. It is very important for security. Near Jerusalem, I don't see any possibility not to build fences. We have to defend ourselves. Rice pushed back: You need to defend yourselves, but we are all going to try to deal with terrorism another way, to get the Palestinians to be active against terrorism. If the political situation is made more difficult by the route of the fence, we all lose. She proposed that John Wolf and Dubi Weissglas sit down and review the proposed route of the fence. I am ready to look again at the route of the fence, Sharon replied, but while it might cause some political problems, weigh this against funerals. We hope the United States will understand our problems and not pressure us not to defend ourselves.

The conversation began where it ended: Sharon would give the PA a little space to act against terrorism, but he did not believe they would do so. The discussion also showed that Rice and Sharon could argue forcefully – and respectfully. There were no bad feelings in this relationship. She showed a feeling of respect to Sharon, as Weissglas described it: maybe it was because of his age, because he really could have been her father or grandfather. And she was very sensitive to the way he approached her. Sometimes Sharon would call her on the phone and say, "Hey, how are you, Condi?" and sometimes it was "Dr. Rice;" if he was very upset, he would say "Madame Secretary." Weissglas remembered after one of those latter conversations, which ended with a very loud "Okay, thank you, Madame Secretary," she called him to say, "What have I done wrong now? Why I am downgraded back to Madame Secretary?"[22]

Abbas and Sharon Come to Washington

When Rice left Jerusalem, it seemed there was some momentum: On July 1, Sharon and Abbas met for the first time since Aqaba for a two-hour discussion, and the opening ceremony was broadcast live on Israeli and Palestinian TV. In both the West Bank and Gaza, Israeli troops were pulling back, allowing PA forces to take up positions and theoretically at least to stop terrorism. On July 2, the IDF pulled out of Bethlehem. The United States announced an additional $30 million in aid to the PA, targeted at work on the infrastructure in the West Bank and Gaza. But Sharon's sense of politics in the West Bank was correct: Arafat was not yielding to the pressure. On July 7, Abbas threatened for the first time to resign, in the face of orchestrated attacks from Arafat supporters criticizing his conduct at and since Aqaba. Abbas and Arafat kissed and made up a week later, and the resignation threat was withdrawn. Abbas then traveled to Washington for the first time as prime minister. It was now just six weeks since Sharm and Aqaba, but Bush wanted to keep things moving; that was why he had sent Rice to the region and why he was staying involved personally.

The symbolism of the trip was heavy: Arafat had visited the Clinton White House 13 times, but had never been invited to meet with Bush. (At the United Nations in 2002, Colin Powell had served as defensive tackle, literally pushing

Arafat back when he tried to get into a photo with Bush as the president moved down a General Assembly corridor.) Now a new Palestinian leader was standing in the Rose Garden and facing the world press alongside the U.S. president; in addition, Bush had given lunch to Abbas and his entire entourage, a clear sign of favor. In the meetings, Abbas told Bush he was meeting his Roadmap obligations but Israel was not. Although, of course, terrorist groups had not been dismantled in so short a time, the PA was regaining some control; people with masks and guns used to control the streets, but such people were no longer running around Palestinian cities. The problem was that Palestinians could not see any progress or reason for hope in Israel's actions. Israel was still building the fence, which Palestinians were already calling the "apartheid wall"; settlements were expanding; and Sharon was refusing to release any significant number of Palestinian prisoners out of the 7,000 Israel held. Bush responded with sympathy but also noted that, as concerned as he was about Roadmap implementation, he was equally concerned to see an end to violence and terrorism.

In the White House, we wanted to use this visit to give Abbas both pledges and symbols of U.S. support. In the Rose Garden remarks on July 25, the president said, "I'm honored to welcome Prime Minister Abbas to the White House. It is such an honor to have you here, sir. To break through old hatreds and barriers to peace, the Middle East needs leaders of vision and courage and a determination to serve the interest of their people. Mr. Abbas is the first Palestinian Prime Minister, and he is proving to be such a leader." Bush also announced that the United States would provide $20 million directly to the PA, a signal of trust in Abbas and his finance minister, Salam Fayyad, that the money would not be stolen or misused.

In his Rose Garden response to Bush, Abbas reiterated some of the themes of his Aqaba speech – "Reform and institution-building are an internal Palestinian priority. We do not merely seek a state, but we seek for a state that is built on the solid foundations of the modern constitution, democracy, transparency, the rule of law, and the market economy" – but also used the occasion to state the main Palestinian complaints against Israel:

We continue to negotiate with Israel on the implementation of its obligations. Some progress has been made, but movement needs to be made in terms of freeing prisoners, lifting the siege on President Arafat, Israeli withdrawal from Palestinian areas, and easing up freedom of movement to Palestinians.... Your vision, Mr. President... cannot be realized if Israel continues to grab Palestinian land. If the settlement activities in Palestinian land and construction of the so-called separation wall on confiscated Palestinian land continue, we might soon find ourselves at a situation where the foundation of peace, a free Palestine state, living side-by-side in peace and security in Israel is a factual impossibility. Nothing less than a full settlement freeze will do because nothing less than a full settlement freeze will work. For the sake of peace, and for the sake of future Palestinian and Israeli generations, all settlement activities must be stopped now, and the wall must come down.[23]

These were tough words that we thought would help Abbas at home. We did not understand clearly, however, how much Arafat would resent the very fact of Abbas's presence at the White House. Arafat had been undermining Abbas from the start, of course, and would have continued to do so under any circumstances, but in retrospect it seemed clear to me that Arafat's jealousy over the White House visit contributed to his desire to bring Abbas down – and soon.

Four days later, on July 29, the President hosted Sharon for their eighth meeting in Washington. We had met with Weissglas to set the stage, and he had argued that Abbas's descriptions of Israeli nonperformance were unfair. He minimized the impact of the security fence and said Sharon would tell Bush construction had to continue. Dubi also repeated the pledges about removing outposts and promised that all the understandings we had reached about limiting settlement construction would be kept.

On the White House lawn, Bush gave Sharon what he needed politically – tough language on terrorism and security:

America is firmly committed to the security of Israel as a Jewish state, and we are firmly committed to the safety of the Israeli people.... All parties agree that a fundamental obstacle to peace is terrorism, which can never be justified by any cause. Last month in Aqaba, Prime Minister Abbas committed to a complete end to violence and terrorism. The Palestinian Authority must undertake sustained, targeted and effective operations to confront those engaged in terror, and to dismantle terrorist capabilities and infrastructure.

He also added kind words for Sharon personally:

If we are ever to reach our common goal of two states living side-by-side in peace and security, leaders must assume responsibility. The Prime Minister is assuming responsibility.... I want to thank Ariel for all he's done to contribute to that friendship, for his leadership and his willing to make tough decisions in the cause of peace.

And there was credit and cajoling on what Sharon needed to do:

We have now a tremendous opportunity to add to Israeli security and safety, and add to the hopes of the average Palestinian citizen, by making tangible progress towards two states living side-by-side in peace.... I'm encouraged by the positive steps that Israel has taken since then to further the cause of peace, including prisoner releases. Prime Minister Sharon is now meeting regularly with Prime Minister Abbas, and that's positive. Israeli and Palestinian cabinet and security officials are meeting, as well. Israel has recently taken steps to make it easier for Palestinians to work in Israel, and to travel to their jobs and schools and families. And I thank the Prime Minister for these important actions. In our discussions, I encouraged the Prime Minister to take further steps to improve the daily conditions faced by Palestinians. Israelis and Palestinians deserve the same chance to live normal lives, free from fear, free from hatred and violence, and free from harassment. I also urged the Prime Minister to carefully consider all the consequences of Israel's actions as we move forward on the road to peace.

When his turn to speak came, Sharon congratulated Bush on Iraq and stressed their friendship:

Mr. President, it is a great privilege for me to be here at the White House for the eighth time. I am always pleased to visit, and feel that I am among friends, true friends of the state and the people of Israel. Mr. President, I congratulate you on the impressive victory in the Iraqi campaign and for removing Saddam Hussein from power, one of the most ruthless and tyrannical leaders in history. For 30 years, the free world has witnessed the recklessness and brutality of this dictator. Only you, Mr. President, have shown the courage, determination and leadership needed to spearhead the successful campaign to oust this ruthless, merciless despot, his dynasty an evil regime.

He then turned to his real talking points, about terror and the end of terror as a precondition for peace:

We are currently at an important juncture in our relations with our Palestinian neighbors. While relative quiet currently prevails in Israel, terror has not yet completely ceased. This relative calm was achieved, first and foremost, through the uncompromising activity of the Israeli security forces. . . . We are thankful for every hour of increased quiet and less terrorism, and for every drop of blood that is spared. At the same time, we are concerned that this welcome quiet will be shattered any minute as a result of the continued existence of terror organizations which the Palestinian Authority is doing nothing to eliminate or dismantle. Mr. President, I am confident that you, as the leader of the free world in this war against terror, will act to ensure that the Palestinians put a complete stop to the threat of Palestinian terrorism so that it will never rear its head again. I wish to move forward with a political process with our Palestinian neighbors. And the right way to do that is only after a complete cessation of terror, violence, and incitement, full dismantlement of terror organizations, and completion of the reform process in the Palestinian Authority.[24]

The two visits had, we thought, maintained the momentum established at the Red Sea Summits, and there was hope that slowly but surely progress would continue. We hoped the White House visit had helped build up Abbas and had perhaps persuaded Sharon to give the PA some more space. Sharon and Abbas planned to meet again soon and their teams would get together as well, and we were in the middle of a three-month stand-down by Hamas and Islamic Jihad that suggested there would be no acts of terror. Two weeks after returning to Israel, Sharon on August 15 announced that Israel would cede control of Jericho and Qalqilya, in the West Bank, to PA security forces. He also agreed to lift in part the siege of Arafat, who would be allowed to leave the Muqata for at least a brief visit outside. Further moves, the Israelis said, were contingent on no more terrorism. On August 12 there had been two suicide attacks, the first in more than a month, but "only" two Israelis had been killed and the Israeli government was not allowing these attacks to change its overall policy. In Washington, we planned out the fall with optimism: We would ask the Israelis to remove more checkpoints and roadblocks in the West Bank and to release more prisoners, assuming the truce held and there was no terrorism. We would see what the agreed "settlement freeze" looked like. We would push Abbas to continue financial and security reform. Assistant Secretary Burns would visit there in August, then Rice and later Deputy Secretary Armitage in September, followed by Powell after the UN General Assembly.

Abbas Resigns

Within weeks, however, Sharm and Aqaba would seem like mirages and the progress made in the two White House visits came to an end. A bloody suicide bombing on August 19, an attack on a crowded bus in Jerusalem, killed 23 people and injured more than 100. Sharon had repeatedly said he would not make gestures to the PA under fire and that everything depended on stopping terrorism. U.S. and Israeli views were congruent now: The PA must act. The reforms of the PA security forces that had been demanded month after month – taking control away from Arafat, consolidating the more than one dozen gangs into three professional forces – must be undertaken immediately. Once again, names of terrorists were passed to Dahlan so that the PA could act against them.

But Dahlan did nothing; he refused to take charge and made it clear that he would not act unless he had full political cover from Arafat. The PA forces sat on their hands. Behind the scenes, Abbas had a nasty meeting with Arafat, who refused to budge. The Egyptian intelligence chief Omar Soliman, a powerful force in Egypt and beyond in those days, called Arafat and told him it was time to agree that the security forces must be reorganized and consolidated; Arafat refused. Rice spoke with Weissglas, who said there was still time for the PA to act; at an Israeli cabinet session, the consensus had been that the process with the Palestinians was now over, but Sharon had pushed back. Now is the time for the PA to act, Dubi told Condi. We all agree on that, and so do all the newspapers, Rice said; it is time for the Palestinians to act. John Wolf, on the ground and visiting all the key players, told us Dahlan was sulking, his ego bruised by all the criticism – but he was doing nothing. Rice spoke with Omar Soliman directly and told him there was really nothing the United States could do if the PA was simply unable to move. But for Arafat, all these developments were wonderful: He was back at the center of attention. Arafat is in hog heaven, Wolf reported, playing the kind of political games he loves, having meetings all through the night at the Muqata. Nothing we are trying is working, Wolf told us. And except for the Soliman calls, the Arabs were AWOL. They were not supporting Abbas either publicly or privately, demanding action against terrorism, or trying to push Arafat aside. Calls from Powell and Rice to Arab leaders produced no responses.

After waiting 36 hours after the bus attack, Israel moved, assassinating a Hamas leader on August 21 and three days later conducting an air strike at a Hamas target in Gaza City. Abbas appeared impotent, a peripheral figure unable to command PA resources; he was not the "empowered prime minister" whose creation had been a key to the Roadmap and to peace. On September 6 he resigned, blaming both Arafat and Sharon for undermining him. Arafat declared a state of emergency and named another old crony, Ahmed Qurie (known as Abu Ala'a) to the post; he was installed formally on October 5. Ghaith al-Omari, an aide to Abbas, recalled the situation:

I think Arafat, from the day Abu Mazen was appointed, was working consistently and tirelessly in every way possible to undermine him.... Arafat was very politically intelligent in recognizing threats. And the moment Abu Mazen was appointed as prime minister, with even theoretical access to the security services, it was a threat to be eliminated. And you would notice that it was clear that Abu Mazen was imposed on him. So the minute that Abu Mazen was out, smartly Arafat did not abolish the position. He appointed Abu Ala'a with a clear understanding: "You're a prime minister that does nothing."[25]

The American consul general in Jerusalem, Jeffrey Feltman, was sent to see Abu Ala'a on September 8 to gauge his commitment to reform. I was concerned when I arrived and panicked when I left, Feltman reported back to Washington; there is a complete leadership vacuum. My own memos to Rice reflected this perspective: We were moving backward now, not forward, with the new Palestinian cabinet being more, not less, subservient to Arafat. In fact, there was no cabinet and in essence no PA during September and October; the new cabinet did not take office formally until it was approved by the PLC on November 12. As to security reform, there was to be a new National Security Council (NSC) in Ramallah, but any hope of real change was gone: Yasser Arafat was be the head, of course, of the Palestinian NSC. He was back in the saddle. Starting with Bush's speech of June 24, 2002, there had been a year and a half of politics, machinations, diplomacy, meetings, and pressure – all aimed at progress toward Israeli-Palestinian peace negotiations. The EU, the UN, the key Arab states had signed on; Ariel Sharon had brought along Israel's right to supporting establishment of a Palestinian state; Arafat had been forced to establish the post of prime minister and fill it with a decent candidate. But now in the fall of 2003, it was clear that there would be no such negotiations. Hamas and other terrorist groups were back at work, renouncing the truce they had undertaken in June. Mahmoud Abbas was gone, and the effort to sideline Arafat had failed.

"A Boom in Plans"

This situation was clear enough, but now what? Some Israelis and Palestinians acted outside their own governments to provide answers – "there is a boom in plans," Sharon described it – and of these the best known were the "People's Choice Plan" and the "Geneva Initiative." People's Choice (also known as "People's Voice") was an effort by Palestinian intellectual Sari Nusseibeh and by Ami Ayalon, a former commander of the Israeli Navy and later head of the Shin Bet, the internal security organization. It sought to get large numbers of Israelis and Palestinians to sign a petition committing to six principles for peace: the two-state solution; Jerusalem as an open city that would be the shared capital of both states; borders based on the 1967 lines with agreed one-to-one swaps; demilitarization of the Palestinian state; no "right of return" to Israel for Palestinian refugees, who would resettle only in the new Palestinian state; and an agreement that when all of these conditions are met, the conflict will be declared ended and all claims extinguished. Although drafted in the summer of 2002, People's Choice was not introduced at a press conference until June 25, 2003, and its authors hoped to affect politics on both sides by demonstrating vast public support. But over the following year and a half, People's Choice only signed up about 150,000 Israelis and 100,000 Palestinians, and by the end of 2007, its website went dark.

The Geneva Initiative got a great deal more publicity and became a center of attention and mobilization for the "peace camp" on Israel's left. Geneva included the following concepts: the two-state solution; one-to-one land swaps that would permit the major settlement blocks and the Jewish neighborhoods of East Jerusalem to be annexed by Israel but with the Old City open to all; a Multinational Force and International Verification Group to monitor and enforce its provisions; a solution to the refugee problem that included possible movement to Israel; and Palestine as a "non-militarized state." The full text and annexes took 500 pages and spelled out detailed plans on many issues, though not on security: The security annex was one tenth the length of the annex on the environment.

Included among its dozens of Israeli and Palestinian signers were prominent names: Yasser Abd Rabbo (a top PLO politician and advisor), Yossi Beilin (a former Knesset member and justice minister), David Kimche (a long-time Mossad official, now dead), Amnon Lipkin Shahak (a former IDF chief of staff), and Qaddurah Faris (a Fatah leader who had spent 14 years in Israeli prisons before being elected to the PLC). Teams of these and other signers toured the world, meeting with heads of government to promote their plan. In the United States, they went to the State Department for a session with Colin Powell on November 9. The Geneva Plan, which took more than two years to formulate, was finally presented to the public on December 1, 2003, at a ceremony attended by Jimmy Carter and blessed from a distance by UN Secretary General Kofi Annan.

The Geneva Initiative was a far better known effort than People's Choice, gathering support from the left in much of the world – and not surprisingly attracting criticism from the right in equal measure. Some of the criticism was detailed and programmatic: How many Palestinian refugees was Israel supposed to take, and why should it accept any blame for the refugee problem? What about dividing Jerusalem and removing Israeli sovereignty from the Old City? How could Israel trust the various international bodies and forces the Geneva Initiative would establish to treat it fairly, given the manifest biases at the UN and in much of Europe? Why would the settlement city of Ariel, with a population of 18,000, have to be abandoned?

The harsher criticism in Israel, however, was political: Who gave these private citizens the right to compromise Israeli positions? Sharon and his government saw all of this effort as pure subversion, waged by electoral losers unwilling to accept the rules of the democratic game and making common cause with the enemy. To the Israeli right, all the concessions to the Palestinians seemed rewards for terror. Moreover, entirely absent was any demand for Palestinian democracy; the state envisioned by Geneva would be run by Yasser Arafat, without the slightest need for reforms. In Washington, Powell greeted the plan in a letter to the organizers saying it was "important in helping to sustain an atmosphere of hope,"[26] but Bush was less enthusiastic, calling it "productive, so long as they adhere to the principles [to] fight off terror, that there must be security, and there must be the emergence of a Palestinian state that is democratic and free."[27] Arafat was still in his sights.

"A Forward Strategy of Freedom"

The Arafat "comeback" in the fall of 2003 came at precisely the moment when Bush was beginning to publicly promote his push for democratization in the Arab world. On November 6, 2003, Bush spoke at the National Endowment for Democracy, celebrating the 20th anniversary of the agency established by Ronald Reagan during the Cold War to fight for human rights and political freedom. Bush focused on the Middle East and lampooned generations of analysts who had said freedom was a Western conception that could not be exported beyond the Atlantic. He disagreed, saying, "It should be clear to all that Islam – the faith of one-fifth of humanity – is consistent with democratic rule. . . . More than half of all the Muslims in the world live in freedom under democratically constituted governments." He then turned to the real conditions in the Arab world, describing a "freedom deficit" with dictatorships that have left "a legacy of torture, oppression, misery, and ruin." This had to change: "The good and capable people of the Middle East all deserve responsible leadership. For too long, many people in that region have been victims and subjects – they deserve to be active citizens." He spoke about Iraq and Afghanistan but also addressed the Palestinian situation and then U.S. policy:

For the Palestinian people, the only path to independence and dignity and progress is the path of democracy. And the Palestinian leaders who block and undermine democratic reform, and feed hatred and encourage violence are not leaders at all. They're the main obstacles to peace, and to the success of the Palestinian people.

Sixty years of Western nations excusing and accommodating the lack of freedom in the Middle East did nothing to make us safe – because in the long run, stability cannot be purchased at the expense of liberty. As long as the Middle East remains a place where freedom does not flourish, it will remain a place of stagnation, resentment, and violence ready for export.

Therefore, the United States has adopted a new policy, a forward strategy of freedom in the Middle East. This strategy requires the same persistence and energy and idealism we have shown before. And it will yield the same results. As in Europe, as in Asia, as in every region of the world, the advance of freedom leads to peace.

The advance of freedom is the calling of our time; it is the calling of our country. From the Fourteen Points to the Four Freedoms, to the Speech at Westminster, America has put our power at the service of principle. We believe that liberty is the design of nature; we believe that liberty is the direction of history. We believe that human fulfillment and excellence come in the responsible exercise of liberty. And we believe that freedom – the freedom we prize – is not for us alone; it is the right and the capacity of all mankind.[28]

As these remarks show, Bush never bought into the idea – promoted by Tony Blair and virtually the entire State Department, including, in the second term, Secretary of State Rice – that progress toward democracy in the Middle East was closely related to solving the Israeli-Palestinian conflict. In his view, that was an excuse dictators used and behind which they hid.

These were powerful ideas, later to become the essence of Bush's Second Inaugural Address. Whatever critics and admirers made of them, it was clear to Bush that Arafat was part of the past, part of the group that had prevented progress in the Middle East. With words like these on the record, the notion of some compromise with the Palestinian leader was impossible. Arafat had to go – but he was not going, and the combined European and American efforts had not moved him aside.

"We Need Something to Break in the Region"

Inside the NSC, we tried to figure out where to go next. In November, the UN Security Council firmly endorsed the Roadmap in Resolution 1515, but this was a typical UN move: too little, too late. With Arafat immovable and Bush equally determined not to deal with him, a UN resolution was useless. The Roadmap was clearly stalled. Powell had met with the authors of the Geneva Initiative, although Rice had refused to do so, saying that stating what you think the outcome should look like doesn't actually get you any closer to that outcome. What are the steps to peace, she wondered. She spoke with Marwan Muasher, the Jordanian foreign minister, who agreed the central problem was that the Palestinians refused to empower a prime minister – and said there was no way to fix things until they did. This was Bush's view: After an Oval Office meeting, the president told the staff that he had spent some capital on backing Abu Mazen, but the minute that real progress had begun, he was booted out. We are in a waiting period for Palestinian leadership to stand up and say they are against terror. Bush said he fully believed the two-state solution was in Israel's interest, but he did not blame the Israelis for turning away from quick solutions that avoided the basic problems. I understand Sharon, he said; you have to sit in his chair and you would see his greatest responsibility is ensuring security.

Rice talked with Weissglas to see what the Israelis now thought. We need something to break in the region, she said; we need to shake up the dynamics.

What might it be? Is anything possible between Israel and Syria? Knowing that neither he nor Sharon would visit the United States soon, Weissglas suggested that Rice send me to see Sharon in Rome, where he would shortly be on a state visit, and we could talk it through. Rice readily agreed. Very few officials knew of the trip in either the Israeli or U.S. government – or the Italian government, for that matter. I made myself a hotel reservation on Expedia, landed on the morning of November 18, and went to my hotel for a rest and a shower. In the afternoon I walked over to Sharon's hotel, the Cavalieri Hilton, where one of his closest aides met me in the parking lot and escorted me through Italian and Israeli security up to Sharon's suite. The purpose of the trip was to discover Sharon's plans for dealing with Syria and with the Palestinians. He had made great progress, with full American support, in crushing the intifada. Now what?

As soon as Sharon appeared, he and I and Weissglas sat down in the dining room of Sharon's suite. I anticipated getting a terrific Italian meal, presumably catered for him by the best restaurant on the premises. Instead, a Sharon staffer brought us a platter covered by slabs of meat. Sharon immediately dug in, pulling over to his side of the table a large piece of pink meat and cutting a huge slice. It sure looked like ham to me, a food I did not eat and assumed Sharon could not, either. So I asked him, "What meat, exactly, is that?" As he brandished a large forkful, he replied "Elliott, sometimes it is better not to ask."

Sharon was, as usual, honest – and blunt. With Syria, there would be no negotiation, no matter what the Americans wanted. To start discussing the border with those murderers, he said, well, we did it before and it failed. We have to solve the Palestinian problem. We should not turn to another front and leave the Palestinian effort behind. A nation has only a certain ability to face problems. We should stick to the Palestinian issue; Israel cannot take another heavy burden on its shoulders. We cannot take it. It would be a major mistake. Don't drag Israel now into a new internal struggle. We don't trust the Palestinians and we are not sure something will happen. But we have to try and do that, he concluded.

I knew many of Israel's generals favored a negotiation with Syria, but they were not in charge. Sharon was, and the message I was to carry back to President Bush was clear: Starting a negotiation with Syria would shock Israel, and it has had enough shocks; it does not need another one right now.

Yet Sharon had a new view on the Palestinians and, for the first time, he unveiled his new approach. We might say that if it is quiet for a time we will dismantle some settlements in Gaza, Sharon told me. But this dismantlement would not be the product of a negotiation with the Palestinians, he made clear. I will take these new steps as unilateral steps, he said; I do not want to be in their hands, because they may not perform or there may be acts of terror.

Three months later, Sharon went public, suggesting he might order evacuation of some settlements in Gaza. His own Likud Party voted down the proposal in May 2004, the first step in a process that ultimately led Sharon to split Likud and create the new Kadima Party. But this conversation in Rome was the first inkling the U.S. government had of what later came to be called "disengagement." As Sharon reported to the Knesset later, in April 2004, "contacts between us and the U.S. Bush Administration on this issue . . . commenced during my visit to Rome, when I communicated to a White House representative my intention to initiate the Disengagement Plan."[29] We had once asked Weissglas, during a meeting in Rice's office, whether a withdrawal from Gaza was possible, and he had quickly said no. Clearly, Sharon had had a significant change of mind.

Sharon's military secretary, Gen. Moshe Kaplinsky, told me a story showing how far Sharon moved between 2002 and 2003:

In the mid-term of my tenure over there, I believe it was the beginning or so of 2002, he called me once and he said – he asked me, "You know, the status quo is very, very bad. The situation, when it's frozen, it's very, very bad. What do you think? How we can initiate some kind of process?" And I told him, "Can I be open with you?" "Sure you can. That's why I called you." And I told him, "Let's leave Netzarim." You know Netzarim was a very isolated settlement in the middle of the Gaza Strip; less than a hundred families, but a battalion of soldiers was on guard over there in order to secure this less-than-one-hundred families. "Let's remove Netzarim, let's leave Netzarim. By a small step, you can initiate a process where the entire world will support you and understand that you are serious." He almost threw me out of his office. He said, "What happened to you? What happened to you?"[30]

Sharon's disengagement policy answered the question the U.S. government and the Europeans were asking: After the resignation of Abbas – symbolic of the apparent collapse of all our plans for Palestinian reform, marginalizing Arafat, and then moving forward in accordance with the Roadmap – was there no way forward? Sharon and disengagement from Gaza are so familiar now that the depth of the change may be missed, but Arik Sharon was known as the father of the settlement movement. How had he moved so far?

Sharon's team later gave their own explanations for disengagement. The turning point, said Tourgeman, was the resignation of Abbas:

After the appointment of Abu Mazen, Sharon wanted to give it a real chance. That was the idea in Aqaba. Aqaba, for Sharon, was maybe the last time that he gave a chance to the Palestinians. We wanted to see if Abu Mazen can deliver as a prime minister, and we thought that it might work well. Arafat blocked him and blocked everything that he did also in regard to Israel. And then he resigned and in August Abu Ala'a became the prime minister. Abu Ala'a presented a different policy domestically and toward Israel. . . . Dubi and I went to meet with Abu Ala'a a few times when he was a prime minister, and we came to the conclusion that nothing will come out.

So we felt that we are going to a period where everything will be frozen. And, during Sukkot, it was the period of the Geneva Initiative. It was Sukkot [October 11 to 18, 2003]. In that period [the Europeans were] trying to create new initiatives – Geneva – which is going back to Clinton and final status issues, and there was the letter from the officers and pilots to the prime minister.[31] Dubi came to Sharon and told him, "Look, if you don't want any of those initiatives to take over, you should find another initiative." We had the Roadmap, we had our reservations to the Roadmap, we went through the elections in Israel, after the Roadmap was presented and the fact that Sharon went with the idea of a Palestinian state, we had Abu Mazen and the change of Palestinian leadership, we had discussions with him, very good discussions that might have been promising; Arafat blocked it. Abu Ala'a came as a prime minister and the channels to the Palestinians were blocked.

Now, the various initiatives and the fact that you cannot stand still, the Roadmap which is not being implemented, convinced the prime minister [Sharon] that we need to do something. The only thing that we should do is separation. And the only way to separate is to prepare a plan, and to decide we are separating from the Palestinians unilaterally, and doing it without them because we felt then that we don't have a partner when Abu Ala'a was prime minister. I'm not sure that this would have been the case if Abu Mazen would have continued.[32]

Weissglas, who was more intimate than Tourgeman with Sharon and his family, added that Sharon's sons were involved with disengagement from the beginning: "The first four people who spoke about disengagement were me, him, and his two children – his two sons." But for Weissglas as well, the departure of Abu Mazen as prime minister was the turning point.

In a later discussion, he reminded me of the timetable. At the end of August or early September, we had two suicide attacks in Jerusalem, he said, one after the other: 40 people killed in 2 weeks. Then Abu Mazen left, he quit, angrily accusing Arafat of preventing him any access to his security forces. Abu Ala'a took over and made it clear to us that he will not deal with security; control over security again was shifted to Arafat and everyone understood that nothing would come out, he said. Everything was deadlocked.

And then Condi said that she didn't know how or when or what, but something must be done to rock the boat – that is the term she used, Weissglas continued. So when I came back home from Washington, he said, I discussed it with Sharon for the first time. I said to him, Listen, this whole structure, the whole Roadmap – that he was so proud of, that he generally considered his most important political asset – was in jeopardy. Gaza cost us over 100 casualties that could not be explained, in the sense that he knew that in the long term we will not stay in Gaza. However the final status negotiations start or end, there will be no Israelis in Gaza. So, what are the casualties for? And as to the internal situation, public support and public opinion regarding the government, we were in the very worst shape we had ever been. He understood that if you want somehow to rock reality, Gaza is almost a natural address. You actually were the first U.S. official that he shared it with, Weissglas said to me. Before then it was discussed only in his kitchen. Then in December, Weissglas concluded, in the famous Herzliya speech, he made it public.[33]

The basic idea behind disengagement was to make a virtue out of the sad fact that there was, in Israeli eyes, no negotiating partner so long as Arafat led the Palestinians. That had been clear since Camp David and it precluded any negotiated settlement. This gave the Israelis an opportunity to attempt to shape their future unilaterally, which had other advantages: While negotiations with the Palestinians could always be (and often were) blown up by terrorist acts, unilateral Israeli action need not be. Continuing with unilateral actions, such as disengagement from Gaza, could be explained as something undertaken for Israeli interests that the government of Israel would therefore not permit Hamas to stop or slow.

Eival Giladi, an IDF general who then directed the IDF Strategic Planning Division, worked hard to develop alternatives to the apparently frozen Roadmap. Unless Israel acted, the situation would remain "a low level of terror," he later explained, and this could not be the best Israel could achieve and offer its people. It was clear to him that a final status agreement was not then possible. He and his staff did a good deal of the analysis and planning that surrounded disengagement. As he recalled,

I came to Sharon, I said, "OK, we understand that we cannot achieve final status agreement. But are we in the best possible point? OK, we move to something which is not perfect, but it's much better; politically, security, economically. You know, instead of complaining all the time there is no partner," which is true, I truly believe that we have no partner, "why don't we take advantage of the fact that there is no partner and shape the future unilaterally." You can do whatever you want if you're strong. But if you do something which is right, which is morally right, legally right, the Israeli public accepts it and the international community accepts it, it will work. And I thought instead of negotiating with them, let's think ourselves. What would we like to achieve had we had a partner to discuss with? And if this is what we think is right and balanced and fair and honest, let's do it unilaterally. And at some point the other side will mature the leadership that we can negotiate with; then we'll finalize it.

At the very initial stage I'm not talking about the West Bank; I'm talking about pulling out of Gaza and I suggest one settlement in the West Bank to send a signal. I was trying to find the right balance because I understood Sharon that he didn't want to move to a final status agreement.[34]

Giladi's explanation clarifies several points about the disengagement policy. The timing of the initiative certainly reflected the resignation of Abbas as PA prime minister and the reassertion of control by Arafat. This is what made Rice as well as the Israelis believe that the Roadmap was blocked; there could no longer be progress toward final-status negotiations. And the timing reflected as well Sharon's desire to head off other plans being developed to fill the now-empty space. But for the Israelis, disengagement from Gaza was more than an effort to fill the vacuum; it was also part of a new attitude toward the Palestinians on the part of Sharon and the Israeli right. As Giladi put it, "For me the disengagement is the first step in a much larger concept. How would we like to see the region? What is Israel at the end of the day?"[35] The intifada and the collapse of what had been decent, even intimate, relations with the Palestinians had caused a sea change in Israeli attitudes. The visions of peace and integration that Shimon Peres and much of the Israeli left had entertained – the "new Middle East" of Peres's speeches – were dying fast, killed off by the terrorism. The security fence that prevented terror also prevented economic and social integration; no longer did hundreds of thousands of Palestinians cross the Green Line each day to work in Israel. And separation was motivated by more than security. Even if there were perfect peace, did Israel want to advance toward integration into the Arab world? Did it not prefer that Palestinians shop in Amman, rather than Tel Aviv? My own view was that Israelis had decided that the Arab hostility was so fierce that a Palestinian state was desirable for Israel because separation from the Palestinians was desirable; the security barrier was the temporary physical manifestation of what would eventually be a deeper and more permanent division.

Demography must have played a role in Sharon's decision: With the Palestinian population growing fast in the West Bank and even faster in Gaza, it was not sensible to think of uniting those territories permanently with Israel – not if one wanted to maintain Israel as a democracy and as a Jewish State. The Muslim population west of the Jordan River would sooner or later be nearly as large as or larger than the Jewish population, which suggested separation – moving settlers out of Gaza, building the separation fence, and moving West Bank settlers back into the major settlement blocks that would someday be annexed by Israel. To this demographic argument could be added a military one. Sharon, the 75-year-old general who had fought all over Israel's terrain, knew that holding the small Gaza settlements was a thankless, endless strain on the IDF, as was holding small settlements spread out all over the West Bank. His strategic goals had long included holding the hills – for example, those overlooking Israel's only international airport – as well as the Jordan Valley but did not include taxing the IDF to protect every small settlement and outpost placed in the middle of Judea and Samaria, far from Israel's cities and amidst the towns and villages of millions of Palestinians. Sharon the general was looking for defensible borders.

He was also looking for defensible policies. Dubi Weissglas defended the disengagement policy, then under wide attack on the Israeli right, in a lengthy interview in *Haaretz* in October 2004:

When Arafat undermined Abu Mazen at the end of the summer of 2003, we reached the sad conclusion that there is no one to talk to, no one to negotiate with. Hence the disengagement plan. Because in the fall of 2003 we understood that everything is stuck. And even though according to the Americans' reading of the situation, the blame fell on the Palestinians and not on us, Arik grasped that this state of affairs would not last. That they wouldn't leave us alone, wouldn't get off our case. Time was not on our side.

The concern was the fact that President Bush's formula was stuck and this would lead to its ruin. That the international community would say: You wanted the president's formula and you got it; you wanted to try Abu Mazen and you tried. It didn't work. And when a formula doesn't work in reality, you don't change reality, you change the formula. Therefore, Arik's realistic viewpoint said that it was possible that the principle that was our historic policy achievement would be annulled – the principle that eradication of terrorism precedes a political process. And with the annulment of that principle, Israel would find itself negotiating with terrorism. And because once such negotiations start it's very difficult to stop them, the result would be a Palestinian state with terrorism.

[Disengagement] places the Palestinians under tremendous pressure. It forces them into a corner that they hate to be in. It thrusts them into a situation in which they have to prove their seriousness. There are no more excuses. There are no more Israeli soldiers spoiling their day. And for the first time they have a slice of land with total continuity on which they can race from one end to the other.... And the whole world is watching them – them, not us. The whole world is asking what they intend to do with this slice of land.[36]

This was the view in Sharon's camp, but to many Israelis, Sharon's new plan seemed like a betrayal of everything he had stood for and they still believed in: the right of Israelis to live wherever they pleased in the West Bank and Gaza and the strategic necessity of placing settlements everywhere. Palestinian reactions were equally unhappy: Sharon was acting unilaterally, and there were fears that he would follow up the departure from Gaza by annexing parts of the West Bank. Arafat's reaction was said to be "Seventeen trailers? What, so they can replace them with another one hundred and seventy?" As another high Fatah official put it, "Sharon's plan is dangerous ... He is trying to sidestep ... the Roadmap.... He is sending the message that the Palestinians are a people who do not deserve a state. These steps would abort the chances of creating a Palestinian state in the West Bank and the Gaza Strip."[37]

In fact, Sharon's disengagement plans remained incomplete. Removing settlers and settlements did not necessarily mean removing the IDF and its bases. Patrolling the thin "Philadelphi Strip" that separated Gaza from Egypt would allow Israel to block illegal movement of people and arms, but leaving Gaza while keeping that thin road would be a significant military challenge. On one side was Egypt, which Israeli troops could not enter; on the other was not a barren area easy to patrol but rather jumbles of houses where thousands of Gazans lived. Those who favored total removal of the IDF – all bases and personnel – argued that Israel could achieve anything it wanted there militarily by air strikes and by lighting, in-and-out ground attacks. After all, Gaza was not the West Bank, where the IDF presence had been constant and ubiquitous, even in the cities; Israeli troops were not present in Gaza's cities. Moreover, maintaining an IDF presence would undermine the achievement of "getting out of Gaza." On the West Bank, whether Sharon would remove any settlements was also uncertain, as was the route of the fence: There were many disputes over its twists and turns around Palestinian villages and towns and Israeli settlements.

"The 'Disengagement Plan' Will Include a Change in the Deployment of Settlements"

The goal agreed in the Roadmap, Palestinian statehood, remained the same, though the path would now change: Israel would withdraw from Gaza and perhaps a few token locations in the West Bank. In his initial public remarks about disengagement, at the Herzliya Conference on December 18, Sharon spoke carefully:

We wish to speedily advance implementation of the Roadmap towards quiet and a genuine peace. We hope that the Palestinian Authority will carry out its part. However, if in a few months the Palestinians still continue to disregard their part in implementing the Roadmap – then Israel will initiate the unilateral security step of disengagement from the Palestinians.

We are interested in conducting direct negotiations, but do not intend to hold Israeli society hostage in the hands of the Palestinians. I have already said – we will not wait for them indefinitely.

The "Disengagement Plan" will include the redeployment of IDF forces along new security lines and a change in the deployment of settlements, which will reduce as much as possible the number of Israelis located in the heart of the Palestinian population. We will draw provisional security lines and the IDF will be deployed along them. Security will be provided by IDF deployment, the security fence and other physical obstacles. The "Disengagement Plan" will reduce friction between us and the Palestinians.

This reduction of friction will require the extremely difficult step of changing the deployment of some of the settlements. I would like to repeat what I have said in the past: In the framework of a future agreement, Israel will not remain in all the places where it is today. The relocation of settlements will be made, first and foremost, in order to draw the most efficient security line possible, thereby creating this disengagement between Israel and the Palestinians. This security line will not constitute the permanent border of the State of Israel, however; as long as implementation of the Roadmap is not resumed, the IDF will be deployed along that line. Settlements which will be relocated are those which will not be included in the territory of the State of Israel in the framework of any possible future permanent agreement. At the same time, in the framework of the "Disengagement Plan," Israel will strengthen its control over those same areas in the Land of Israel which will constitute an inseparable part of the State of Israel in any future agreement. I know you would like to hear names, but we should leave something for later.[38]

In what he said and what he did not say, Sharon was in fact hinting at a great deal that became clear to Israelis only later. For one thing, he did not speak of "Gaza disengagement," and the principles he outlined applied to the West Bank settlements as well as the few in Gaza. But Sharon was not committing to disengagement at all; instead, he was "threatening" to take that route if there were no change on the Palestinian side. He declared his commitment to the Roadmap and to direct negotiations, but then said he would move unilaterally if the Palestinians, in his words, continued to disregard their obligations. With domestic politics in mind, he presented disengagement to the Israeli audience as a way of fighting terror and as an act of defiance. But he was saying something that had to be music to the ears of American and European statesmen: He was prepared to remove settlements.

Sharon also added one line about the settlement agreement he had reached with the United States, simply spelling out its terms: "Israel will meet all its obligations with regard to construction in the settlements. There will be no construction beyond the existing construction line, no expropriation of land for construction, no special economic incentives and no construction of new settlements."

As 2003 ended, Ariel Sharon was the center of action. This had certainly not been predictable when he became prime minister in 2001 during the intifada, nor even after 9/11; it seemed then that he would fight terror and repeat over and over that Israel needed security. He seemed to be immovable and ideologically motivated, a view his closest advisors always thought to be a misreading of the pragmatic leader they saw. They were right: Sharon had watched carefully as Bush's thinking evolved after the terrorist attacks on the United States and had understood that Bush's changed view of Arafat created a new situation. He had not fought the United States when we formally endorsed Palestinian statehood but had rolled with that punch. His own thinking evolved toward separation from the Palestinians, and he came to agree that once Arafat was out of power, progress toward Palestinian statehood was desirable. In 2003 he won reelection in January, soon after came to Washington in February to cement relations with Bush, accepted the Roadmap in May, and then appeared at Aqaba in June to deliver the words Bush wanted to hear. He met with Abbas in July and appeared ready to give American- and Quartet-backed negotiations a chance, but meanwhile began building the security barrier to prevent the plague of suicide bombings. When Arafat's tenacious grip on power proved unbreakable and the Americans were stumped, Sharon moved: He would act unilaterally to break the deadlock, prevent the adoption of other plans that involved too many concessions or abandoned the struggle against Arafat, and begin to move Israel in the direction he wanted. Indeed, Sharon was abandoning the idea of a "Greater Israel," an Israel of which many on its right wing had long dreamed. The idea of disengagement fit perfectly with the security fence itself because roughly 90% of the West Bank was beyond that fence. Sharon was tacitly acknowledging that while he intended the major settlement blocks to become part of Israel, those beyond the fence were expendable; he was dividing settlers between the vast majority who would be rescued by his plans and the small minority, perhaps 15%, who would be abandoned politically and forced to move back westward.

And Sharon was guaranteeing continued, strong American support for Israel and for himself. He had not used the Palestinians' troubles and Bush's clear demands that Arafat be sidelined to abandon the two-state solution. In Herzliya, he stated flatly that direct negotiations were the preferred route, and nothing he was doing – not the fence and not disengagement – contradicted or undermined the Roadmap. He was in a sense being faithful to his promises to Bush and at the same time rescuing the Americans from a predicament we could not solve. Nothing could move while Arafat remained in charge, we had said, but there he still was. We were stuck. At Herzliya, Sharon showed us a way forward.

Notes

1. Feith, July interview, p. 16.
2. Hadley, interview, p. 10.
3. Edelman, interview, p. 14.
4. Tourgeman, June interview, p. 9.
5. Tourgeman, October interview, p. 11.
6. BBC News, "A Performance-Based Roadmap to a Permanent Two-State Solution to the Israeli-Palestinian Conflict," *BBC News*, April 30, 2003, http://news.bbc.co .uk/2/hi/2989783.stm.
7. Hadley, interview, p. 15.
8. Ariel Sharon, "Address by Prime Minister Ariel Sharon at the Fourth Herzliya Conference," press release, Israel Ministry of Foreign Affairs, December 18, 2003, http://www.mfa.gov.il/MFA/Government/Speeches+by+Israeli+leaders/ 2003/Address+by+PM+Ariel+Sharon+at+the+Fourth+Herzliya.htm.
9. Ariel Sharon, "Speech by Prime Minister Ariel Sharon at the Herzliya Conference," Israeli Ministry of Foreign Affairs, December 4, 2002, http://www.mfa.gov.il/MFA/ Government/Speeches+by+Israeli+leaders/2002/Speech+by+PM+Sharon+at+the+ Herzliya+Conference+-+4.htm.
10. Molly Moore, "Cabinet Resigns as Legislators Challenge Arafat; Some Palestinians Welcome Move as Start of Reform," *Washington Post*, September 12, 2002.
11. Ilene R. Prusher, "Arafat's Critics Rise from among Ranks of Former Friends," *Christian Science Monitor*, September 13, 2002.
12. Tony Blair, interview by the author, October 21, 2009, p. 1.
13. Robert G. Kaufman, *Henry M. Jackson, A Life in Politics* (Seattle: University of Washington Press, 2000), 263.
14. Ibid., 264, 268.
15. Elliott Abrams, "Why Sharon?" *Beliefnet*, February 2001, http://www.beliefnet .com/Faiths/2001/02/Why-Sharon.aspx?p=1.
16. Rice, *No Higher Honor*, 219.
17. Gilad Sharon, *Sharon: The Life of a Leader* (New York: Harper Collins, 2011), 561.
18. Conal Urquhart, "Sharon's Stance Puzzling to Peers," *Newsday*, May 28, 2003.
19. Al-Omari, interview, p. 11.
20. Mamoud Abbas, "Aqaba Summit Speech," June 4, 2003, transcript, 15:30 PM, Beit al Bahar, Aqaba, Jordan, http://georgewbush-whitehouse.archives.gov/news/ releases/2003/06/20030604-1.html.
21. Ariel Sharon, "Statement by Prime Minister Ariel Sharon after the Aqaba Summit meeting," Israeli Ministry of Foreign Affairs, June 4, 2003, http://www.mfa.gov.il/ MFA/MFAArchive/2000_2009/2003/6/Statement%20by%20PM%20Ariel%20 Sharon%20after%20the%20Aqaba%20Summi.
22. Weissglas, interview, p. 16.
23. The President's News Conference with Prime Minister Mahmoud Abbas "Abu Mazen" of the Palestinian Authority, 2 Pub. Papers 930–935 (July 25, 2003).
24. The President's News Conference with Prime Minister Ariel Sharon of Israel, 2 Pub. Papers 946–950 (July 29, 2003).

25. Al-Omari, interview, p. 9.
26. Aluf Benn, "Powell Lends Support to Geneva Accord," *Haaretz*, November 9, 2003.
27. Nathan Guttman, "Bush: Geneva is 'Productive,'" *Haaretz*, December 5, 2003.
28. Remarks on the 20th Anniversary of the National Endowment for Democracy, 2 Pub. Papers 1468–1474 (November 6, 2003).
29. Ariel Sharon, "Speech by Prime Minister Sharon to the Knesset on his Visit to the United States and the Disengagement Plan," *Jewish Virtual Library*, April 22, 2004, http://www.jewishvirtuallibrary.org/jsource/Peace/sharonknesset.html.
30. Kaplinsky, interview, p. 9.
31. In September 2003, 27 Israeli Air Force pilots wrote an open letter to the prime minister protesting strikes in Gaza that caused civilian casualties during targeted killings. In December 2003, 27 commandos from the highly elite unit "Sayeret Matkal" wrote an open letter to the prime minister decrying the "occupation of the territories" due to the "deprivation of basic human rights" it caused and saying they would refuse to serve there.
32. Tourgeman, June interview, pp. 14–15.
33. Weissglas, interview, pp. 2–4.
34. Eival Giladi, interview by the author, December 3, 2009, pp. 11, 5.
35. Giladi, interview, p. 7.
36. Ari Shavit, "The Big Freeze," *Haaretz*, October 8, 2004, http://jewishpoliti calchronicle.org/nov04/Big%20freeze.pdf.
37. Hatem Abdel Qader, "Israeli-Palestinian Conflict," ProCon.org, last modified May 18, 2008, http://israelipalestinian.procon.org/view.answers.php?questionID= 000557.
38. Ariel Sharon, "Address by Prime Minister Ariel Sharon at the Fourth Herzliya Conference," Israeli Ministry of Foreign Affairs, December 18, 2003, http://www.mfa.gov.il/MFA/Government/Speeches+by+Israeli+leaders/2003 /Address+by+PM+Ariel+Sharon+at+the+Fourth+Herzliya.htm.

4

"New Realities on the Ground"

If Ariel Sharon had been vague in his Herzliya speech of December 2003, he did not wait long to spell out his intentions to Israelis and to the world. On February 2, 2004, he told an interviewer from the Israeli newspaper *Haaretz* that he would remove all 17 settlements and every Israeli (there were roughly 7,500) from Gaza. "It is my intention to carry out an evacuation – sorry, a relocation – of settlements that cause us problems and of places that we will not hold onto anyway in a final settlement, like the Gaza settlements," Sharon said, though he gave no timetable. "I am working on the assumption that in the future there will be no Jews in Gaza."[1]

Sharon met with Likud members of the Knesset in the days after his *Haaretz* interview, and reactions from many on Israel's right were loud: Sharon was abandoning a lifetime of commitment to settlements, was betraying his party, and was rewarding terror. A few weeks before the interview, on January 12, 2004, the Settlers' Council had organized an anti-disengagement mass rally in Tel Aviv that attracted 120,000 people. In the days and weeks after the interview, Gaza settlers picketed at Sharon's ranch in the Negev, angrily denouncing him. A council of rabbis declared a day of fasting to "annul the evil decree." The National Religious Party said it would pull out of the government coalition if he moved forward, though Sharon's majority of 73 in the 120-seat Knesset gave him a cushion against such threats from outside Likud; his real problem would prove to be the party itself, where opposition was quickly building: "The turmoil in the Likud turned into an uprising,"[2] according to a biography of Sharon. A criticism repeated often by the Israeli media was that Sharon was trying to distract the public's attention from a serious police investigation of the funding of his most recent campaign. There had already been one indictment, and it was unclear whether the scandal would touch Sharon himself.[3] One Knesset member from the National Union Party, himself a settler, told reporters that "the prime minister's sole motivation now is the police investigations. The progress of the investigation will determine the extent of uprooting" of settlers and settlements in Gaza; "the more investigations, the more evacuations."[4]

Sharon himself was sympathetic to the settlers. He told *Haaretz* that "there are people who are third generation there. The first thing is to ask their agreement, to reach an agreement with the residents." In later conversations, I found that his determination to carry out his plan and defeat his political enemies never translated into resentment of the settlers themselves. His mistake was that he never told them clearly what he told me and other American officials: that he viewed the settlers as people sent by the State of Israel and motivated by the best Zionist principles – they were people to be appreciated and thanked, and to be persuaded that just as they had made sacrifices to build their settlements, so now the state required further sacrifices of them. Instead, what the government of Israel conveyed was annoyance at the settlers' resistance and a sense that they were fanatics who had to be pushed out of the way. This made Sharon's political battle even harder than it needed to be.

State Is Cold; the White House Is Warm

The initial American reaction to the plan had been cold. The State Department at first refused comment and then reiterated over and over that it wanted progress on the Roadmap – period. "To get progress, we need to see the parties carry out their obligations of the roadmap," the State Department spokesman said on February 3; "we're not looking for any steps by the parties to prejudge final status issues.... [T]here are certainly unilateral actions that we would be opposed to that do attempt to prejudge final status issues." The following day the spokesman said, "We're looking for action on settlements that moves us in the direction of the President's vision" and "the kind of negotiated settlement that the parties have committed to." Unilateral steps were not welcome: "[R]emoving settlements...can help us move down the road towards the vision, but it can't be seen in isolation...from other steps on settlements and other steps...that both parties need to take to achieve a negotiated solution." The tune did not change immediately: On February 13, State was still saying that the Gaza disengagement "needs to be placed in the context of reaching a negotiated solution.... [Y]ou can't really resolve the fundamental issue without a negotiation." Four days later, the spokesman said discussions with Israel were aimed at "how to get going on the Roadmap."

This was nonsense. There was no negotiation, and there was not going to be one with Yasser Arafat, who had frozen the Roadmap by pushing out Abbas and stopping reforms. Journalists who spoke with NSC officials had a better insight than those who simply listened to official State Department pronouncements. By the end of February, the *Washington Post* was reporting that the Bush administration would "embrace Israel's proposal" as a "fresh approach...an acknowledgment that productive talks between Israel and Palestinian leaders are not possible at this moment and that unilateral steps proposed by Prime Minister Ariel Sharon...could provide an interim step that presents the best hope of progress toward ultimate success."[5] The story noted that Sharon appeared willing to consider adjustments in the fence route and the delay or abandonment of some sections of the security fence as well.

Although the entire Gaza plan had been Sharon's alone, the White House did in fact come to view it as a very positive move: It was shaking things up in the way Rice had hoped. However, we were reluctant to offer military advice, with some of us backing complete removal of the IDF from Gaza and others in favor of partial withdrawal. Yet our hopes were clear enough: We told Sharon and his team that we advised a clean break, a complete departure, from Gaza, if that were militarily possible. And we had strong advice on another point: Do something in the West Bank as well. Getting out of Gaza did not necessarily imply that progress in the West Bank was possible; some Palestinians thought it implied the opposite. Sharon had been suggestively vague at Herzliya, but if he then did nothing in the West Bank, conclusions would be drawn: that Israel would keep every square inch, every settlement was permanent, and no negotiated peace was possible. So we urged that something be done, indeed as much as he could do politically, to counter those claims. As Sharon's son later described our efforts, "[W]hat had become clear from those talks was that if the Disengagement Plan did not include any parts of Judea and Samaria, the Americans would not offer any type of reward for the initiative, nor would it receive their backing."[6] Sharon set teams to work on both issues: the withdrawal of the IDF from Gaza and particularly the Philadelphi Strip, and the West Bank issue. We also told Sharon to take another look at the fence route, so that it encircled as few Palestinians as possible and kept as few as possible from roads and lands they needed to reach. Finally, we urged the Israelis to work with the Palestinians to the extent possible on the Gaza pullout, for obvious pragmatic reasons as well as equally obvious political ones.

Sallai Meridor, Israel's ambassador to the United States from 2006 to 2009, years later gave a thoughtful comment on Bush's possible calculations about disengagement:

I've tried to think about Bush. He's inheriting broken negotiations, terrible terror; he has to make a judgment on how he is dealing the matter. He is struggling whether he should continue with Arafat, should decide that Arafat is a terrorist and just ignore him, to what extent he feels he wants to support Israel in its efforts to put an end to terror. September 11 is in the background, America's engagement in Afghanistan and Iraq is dealing with the same issues. . . . He makes a decision, from 2002 onward – that on the one hand he is accepting the endgame, at the same time he is loyal to his principles that you fight terror and you fight terror and you fight terror, and you cannot build a state with no democracy or it's not worth supporting and it cannot go along with terror. So – for me – he's doing two things: on the one hand, he is articulating the notion of two states and [at] the same time, it cannot be phony, it cannot be corrupt, it cannot be based on terror so there is a Roadmap to get there. Then there is terror and Israel is fighting terror and you have to support Israel in its fight against terror. And you have Arafat there and there is nobody to talk to. Then you have Sharon with the idea of disengagement. And he [Bush] has to make a call whether to support it or not, and he made a call to support it because there is no alternative with Arafat and because this is something which may change the equation in some ways.[7]

I agreed. As I saw it, Arafat had crushed the hopes of 2002 and 2003; obviously, there would be no significant reform while he was in charge – and we had failed to push him aside. After the Abbas visit to the White House, Arafat had gotten rid of Abbas. There would be no negotiations between Israel and Arafat, nor did we seek any. Progress on the Roadmap was impossible because it was evident that Arafat would not fight terror; he was a master terrorist, and at least since the *Karine A* incident, it had been clear to us that he viewed terror as he viewed speeches or monetary payments: just one tool in his kit. Indeed, the terrorism, by groups related to Arafat and by other Palestinian terrorist organizations, had continued in the fall of 2003 and into 2004. In addition to smaller attacks every week, larger and even more deadly acts occurred. On October 4, 2003, 21 Israelis were killed when a beachfront restaurant was blown up in Haifa. The totals were 30 dead in October, 5 in November, and 6 in December; on Christmas Day, a suicide bombing at a bus stop east of Tel Aviv killed 4 and injured 15. And then it started again: There were attacks on January 13 and 14, 2004, and on January 29, 11 Israelis were killed and more than 50 injured in the suicide bombing of a bus in Jerusalem by the Al Aqsa Martyrs Brigades, a part of Yasser Arafat's Fatah party.

"It Looks Like a Kind of Civil War Here"

So Sharon's new initiative was the only game in town. The president sent Steve Hadley and me off to see Sharon on February 18 and 19 to assess exactly what he had in mind. During our preliminary talks, Weissglas explained that Sharon's intentions for Gaza were clear: The plan was to get out totally. As for the West Bank, that was under discussion: Sharon's long-term goal was to remove the minimum number of settlements while allowing the Palestinians maximum contiguity, and he would move the IDF westward toward the fence. How and when this could be achieved was not certain, but it was, of course, reassuring to us that Sharon was thinking so seriously about the West Bank. But Weissglas also recounted Sharon's political problems: For example, on February 2, he had won a no-confidence vote in the Knesset by the slim margin of 41 to 40. Sharon's own foreign minister, Silvan Shalom, vocally opposed withdrawing from Gaza.

We then met with Sharon, who had a message for the president. Sharon explained that he felt negotiations were impossible now: Abu Ala'a did not control the Palestinian security forces, Arafat did, which meant there would be no Palestinian actions against terrorism. That situation is what led to this new plan, he said. The steps he planned were very complicated internally, he told us: At Aqaba and elsewhere, he had talked of painful compromises in exchange for peace, but this would be disengagement without peace. Menachem Begin had pulled out of Sinai to secure peace with Egypt, but this would be the first time a prime minister dared to withdraw without a peace agreement. It looks like a kind of civil war here, he said of Israeli politics. It doesn't stop me, but it's very complicated. Sharon commented that he had been defending Jews all his life, but now the security services had to surround him to protect him from Jews.

The real problem is in Likud, he went on. He was not so worried about small parties leaving the coalition, so long as Likud was steady – but would it be, if other right-wing parties left? Those are my problems, he said. It's very complicated and difficult, and there's only one way I'll be able to carry out the withdrawal – if Israel gets political backing. I've got to persuade people here, he continued, that though we are giving up land, we are getting support, political support. You want me to make some moves in the West Bank? That depends on U.S. support, so that I can show we are getting something for disengagement. We're not getting peace, after all. I am not doing this for you or for the Palestinians, but for Israel, and I would not have entered this minefield unless I were fully decided to do it. Sharon repeated this thought two or three times: I decided to do it, and I will. But, he concluded, how far I can go depends on you. That was the message we were to take back to the president, plus a request to visit Washington soon.

We did take the message back, and discussions continued in both Jerusalem and Washington. The concept Hadley and I developed was "more for more," which simply meant that the more Sharon could do, the more President Bush could offer support. Weissglas, of course, saw it the other way: The more public support from Bush, the more Sharon could do. We very clearly wanted Sharon to make a clean break with Gaza and to include the West Bank in his withdrawal plans; he very clearly sought some American help to get there. We knew that Sharon's NSC had drawn up a variety of plans, including withdrawal from zero West Bank settlements, one or two, three or four, or more and larger ones. Our assessment of the political situation was that he was not bluffing: Resistance to his proposals on the Israeli right, and especially within Likud, appeared to be growing.

Meanwhile, the terror continued, which weakened his hand further: Opponents said Israel should never withdraw under fire and that by disengaging, Sharon was giving in to terror. On March 14, a double-suicide bombing killed 10 and wounded 16 more in an attack on the port of Ashdod; Hamas and Fatah claimed "credit" for the bombing.

On March 22, Israel retaliated by assassinating the Hamas leader Sheikh Yassin, one of the organization's founders. Rice viewed this as a great error; Yassin was 67 and confined to a wheelchair by paralysis. Kofi Annan and Tony Blair, among many others, publicly condemned the killing. The official U.S. position was that we were "deeply troubled," but at the United Nations, the United States vetoed a resolution condemning Israel on the grounds that the text did not also condemn Hamas terrorism. Rice and Weissglas had an angry shouting match over the assassination of Yassin, which she told him was a terrible mistake; her criticism outraged the Israelis. But Sharon and his team also noticed the different tone Bush himself took: "There needs to be a focused, concerted effort by all parties to fight terror. Any country has a right to defend itself from terror. Israel has the right to defend herself from terror. And as she does so, I hope she keeps consequences in mind as to how to make sure we stay on the path to peace."[8] This was perhaps the first time the Sharon team noted a gap between the president and Rice on such issues.

"Sharon Needs Something from Us"

The continuing terrorism, and the Israeli responses to it, did not deter the Sharon and Bush teams from continuing negotiations on the goal we shared: giving Sharon the political support he needed to pull off the disengagement and to include withdrawal from some part of the West Bank in it. A Likud referendum on disengagement was scheduled for May 2, and we knew we needed to act before then. On March 31, Hadley and I headed back to Jerusalem, with Assistant Secretary Bill Burns, this time to negotiate the text of what became known as the April 14 letter. In hour after hour of meetings with Weissglas and Tourgeman, the draft began to take shape. At a meeting with Abu Ala'a, Hadley was frank about the failure to advance reform and reduce Arafat's powers: You've missed an opportunity, he said, and the president is disappointed. At meetings with the Jordanians and Egyptians on this trip, Hadley explained, in general terms, what was coming: some words from President Bush that would assist Sharon in winning his internal battles and proceeding with disengagement. We asked Egyptian officials what would happen in Gaza after the Israelis left, and they told us not to worry: However strong Hamas might be there, Egypt would never allow Hamas to take over Gaza. If need be, Egypt had police and armed forces that could be used – and would be. That was a last resort, to be sure, something to be avoided, but Egypt's national interests and its security were at stake, so they would act if they had to. Egypt's powerful intelligence chief, Omar Soliman, pounded on the table as he assured Hadley and me of Egypt's control of Gaza. (Events in 2007, when Hamas took over Gaza while Egypt did nothing, proved how far off the mark these comments were.)

When we met with Sharon, he pleaded again for U.S. help and support. There was a nasty and energetic campaign against him and his plans. If what the president says isn't clear, he told us, I won't be able to win the battle in Likud. And that would be the end of disengagement, he added; if he could not pull it off, no one could. The left can't act, and the right won't act, he said. That would be the end of his own political career, but never mind that; it would mean no progress for years. And he reminded us that while his plan was unilateral, it did not foreclose future options: If at some point Arafat was pushed aside and a new Palestinian leadership was acting against terror and ready to negotiate, nothing he had done under his disengagement plan would make it harder to move forward.

That was increasingly the White House view. The president wanted to help Sharon achieve disengagement. The opposition Sharon was facing only deepened his desire to help because Bush was always impressed above all by courageous political leaders – Sharon, Blair, John Howard in Australia, Koizumi in Japan – people who did not get themselves elected only to then spend their time worrying mostly about reelection. He was willing, indeed eager, to assist Sharon in meeting the challenges and getting disengagement done. After all, not only was it the only game in town in 2004 but we felt it was also a strong basis for the future. If Sharon would pull entirely out of Gaza and do something as well in the West Bank, he was laying the foundation – as Weissglas and others told us, and as many on the Israeli right feared – for further moves in the West Bank.

If in subsequent years Sharon withdrew to the security fence line, removing settlements beyond it, he and Bush would leave office with the Israeli-Palestinian situation transformed. There had been no such move since 1967; although Israel had removed settlements in Sinai under Begin, no such withdrawal had ever been made with respect to the Palestinians. If such a withdrawal was made, Bush could look ahead to a second term where, even if Arafat remained in power, there would be substantial change on the ground, an achievement that had eluded Clinton and every other predecessor who had tried to push for an Israeli-Palestinian agreement. Sharon's unilateralism could be the path toward peace, and as Sharon had accurately told Hadley and me, it did not in any way preclude a return to the Roadmap, to direct negotiations, should a new Palestinian leadership arise that fought terror. By the time we left Jerusalem, Sharon had agreed to move on the West Bank: Four very small settlements in the north, in Samaria, would go. A visit to Washington for Sharon was arranged for mid-April.

The calendar already showed a mid-April visit to the ranch in Crawford by President Mubarak, but that was no problem: Bush would receive Mubarak, then return to the White House to see Sharon a day or two later. This proved to be a mistake with a lasting impact because Mubarak stayed in the United States for several days after his Crawford visit and felt upstaged and embarrassed by the Sharon visit and then the announcement of the April 14 letter. But the conversations at the ranch went well enough, and U.S. officials explained to Mubarak about the forthcoming Sharon visit and the release of the letter. Mubarak's position was that any withdrawal would be welcome but should be the product of negotiations. In response, Powell told him there would be no negotiations; once Arafat had pushed Abu Mazen out, there was no responsible Palestinian partner left with whom to negotiate. We all learned a lesson from what Clinton went through, Bush added. We were dead in the water, said Rice. Now, this is the first withdrawal since 1967 except for Sinai, and it is a sea change, and we all have to keep our eyes on the big picture and recognize what is happening. This is a precedent for future withdrawals. They then explained to Mubarak that in a letter to Sharon, to be announced when he visited the White

House, there would be strong language about Palestinian refugees: They would be expected to settle in the Palestinian state, not "return" to Israel. Mubarak said an issue like that should be left to negotiations, but Bush pushed back: We are now in favor of creating a Palestinian state, we changed the policy, and we have to say why. Why create a Palestinian state? This is the answer – it is a place for the refugees to go. Sharon needs something from us, and he'll get a statement. Later, Mubarak would complain that he had not been told what was coming, but that was false. He had to claim ignorance, we at the NSC thought, to escape any accusation that he had been fully informed but indifferent or insufficiently influential to stop Bush.

By the time Sharon arrived, the text of the April 14 letter was nearly complete, as was the letter we demanded of Sharon. When they met, Bush did not negotiate details with Sharon; he was more interested in learning how Sharon the political leader had come to the decision to disengage. He still believed the Roadmap was the way to go in the long term, Sharon replied, but in the previous year he had seen a stalemate and a vacuum develop. There was no one with whom to negotiate. It was dangerous, so he decided to try something new: I'm an old soldier, I tried the Roadmap, it didn't move, so I decided on a detour. As he had said in Aqaba, Israel should not be ruling millions of Palestinians. Disengagement is the beginning of a process, not the end of the Roadmap, he said; we can always go back to the Roadmap later. The Arabs are saying that we will start in Gaza and end in Gaza, but that's not my intention, Sharon told Bush. Once the Palestinians start fighting terror, and Arafat is gone, we can continue with the Roadmap. (Bush then reminded Sharon of his repeated insistence to the Israelis that they absolutely not assassinate Arafat, whatever the provocation. In Bush's view, such a move would only inflame Arab opinion and lead to demonstrations and rioting across the Arab world, some of which would be aimed at imagined American complicity in the killing.) I am insisting that disengagement isn't part of the Roadmap, Sharon continued, because I don't want anyone to say we've abandoned the Roadmap now. You haven't abandoned it and this may be the way to jump-start it, Bush replied; this is real leadership.

The president was aware, as were we all, of the accusations that Sharon was playing this "peace card" to escape police investigations at home. We were also aware of another cynical interpretation of his actions: that he had no intention to move forward in Gaza and was simply buying time. We did not buy these theories; we thought Sharon would move in Gaza and that only Sharon could do so. We also thought that the speeches at the UN and elsewhere about moving forward now on the Roadmap and starting negotiations were foolish. If there was cynicism, it was from those who preferred to repeat old formulas rather than face the reality that they had failed.

The April 14 letter had elicited much nervousness on the international scene, not least in Jordan and in Britain. What exactly would Bush say? How far would he go, and would American allies be able to follow him there? And would

Sharon say what we needed? There were many drafts, as words, phrases, and paragraphs came in and out and shifted position; my own notes, stored in the Bush Library, show the hourly changes.

"The State of Israel Intends to Relocate Military Installations and All Israeli Villages and Towns in the Gaza Strip, as Well as Other Military Installations and a Small Number of Villages in Samaria"

Sharon's letter to Bush recommitted himself and Israel to the June 24, 2002, vision of a two-state solution and to the Roadmap. In fact, Sharon hugged the Roadmap tight, emphasizing its "correct sequence" and calling it "the sole means to make genuine progress." He repeated this sentiment several times:

We are committed to this formula as the only avenue through which an agreement can be reached. We believe that this formula is the only viable one. . . . Progress toward this goal must be anchored exclusively in the roadmap and we will oppose any other plan. . . . This initiative, which we are not undertaking under the roadmap, represents an independent Israeli plan, yet is not inconsistent with the roadmap. . . . The execution of the Disengagement Plan holds the prospect of stimulating positive changes within the Palestinian Authority that might create the necessary conditions for the resumption of direct negotiations.

Sharon unsurprisingly reiterated the need to end terror and jumped on the bandwagon for Palestinian reform: "As you have stated, a Palestinian state will never be created by terror, and Palestinians must engage in a sustained fight against the terrorists and dismantle their infrastructure. Moreover, there must be serious efforts to institute true reform and real democracy and liberty, including new leaders not compromised by terror."

Sharon explained that given the current impasse, "I have decided to initiate a process of gradual disengagement," which he described in terms meant to reassure Israelis (but that would equally offend European and Palestinian audiences):

The Disengagement Plan is designed to improve security for Israel and stabilize our political and economic situation. It will enable us to deploy our forces more effectively until such time that conditions in the Palestinian Authority allow for the full implementation of the Roadmap to resume. . . . The Disengagement Plan will create a new and better reality for the State of Israel, enhance its security and economy, and strengthen the fortitude of its people.

Then came the "meat" of the plan: "The State of Israel intends to relocate military installations and all Israeli villages and towns in the Gaza Strip, as well as other military installations and a small number of villages in Samaria." Thus, Sharon was announcing that the West Bank would be included but was not giving a final decision on pulling the IDF out of the Philadelphi road area on the border with Egypt: Note that he said "military installations," not "all" military installations.

On the security barrier, at our request Sharon, repeated that "[t]he fence is a security rather than political barrier, temporary rather than permanent, and therefore will not prejudice any final status issues including final borders." And at our request he also added, "The route of the fence, as approved by our Government's decisions, will take into account, consistent with security needs, its impact on Palestinians not engaged in terrorist activities." On settlements and outposts, he acknowledged "the responsibilities facing the State of Israel. These include limitations on the growth of settlements [and] removal of unauthorized outposts." The limitations on settlement growth were those negotiated by us with Weissglas, but of course Sharon's phrasing – limitations on settlement growth, not an end to it – suggested that a complete freeze "including natural growth" was not in the cards. (On removing the outposts, Sharon never fulfilled his pledge, which he acknowledged and for which he apologized face to face with the president a year later.)

So we had gotten what we needed from Sharon: a complete pullout from Gaza (and later, perhaps unwisely, he included the Philadelphi road border with Egypt); withdrawal from four very small settlements in the West Bank, proving this was not "Gaza only"; and a recommitment to the Roadmap and to direct negotiations for Palestinian statehood. Then in return he got what he needed from Bush.

"In Light of New Realities on the Ground, Including Already Existing Major Israeli Populations Centers, It Is Unrealistic to Expect that the Outcome of Final Status Negotiations Will Be a Full and Complete Return to the Armistice Lines of 1949"

The April 14 letter was, along with Bush's speech to the Knesset in 2008, a high point in his relationship with Israel and support for its security and its future. It addressed, most significantly, the refugee and border issues. Bush began by restating his commitment to the two-state solution as presented in his speech of June 24, 2002, and to the Roadmap. He then welcomed Sharon's disengagement plan, noting that it included the West Bank as well as Gaza. Bush then continued, "The United States appreciates the risks such an undertaking represents. I therefore want to reassure you on several points." This was, then, the reward and the incentive for Sharon.

First, Bush "reassured" Sharon that the Roadmap, including its sequence of fighting terrorism first before negotiating over final status issues, would remain U.S. policy: "[T]he United States remains committed to my vision and to its implementation as described in the roadmap. The United States will do its utmost to prevent any attempt by anyone to impose any other plan." Bush then reiterated that the Palestinians must, under the Roadmap, undertake "comprehensive and fundamental political reform that includes a strong parliamentary democracy and an empowered prime minister" and must fight terror. They "must undertake an immediate cessation of armed activity and all acts of violence against Israelis anywhere, and . . . must act decisively against terror, including sustained, targeted, and effective operations to stop terrorism and dismantle terrorist capabilities and infrastructure."

Second, Bush restated a firm pledge to support Israel's security: "The United States reiterates its steadfast commitment to Israel's security, including secure, defensible borders, and to preserve and strengthen Israel's capability to deter and defend itself, by itself, against any threat or possible combination of threats." There were two key phrases in this one sentence. "Defensible borders" was a familiar code phrase for suggesting that a return to the "1967 borders" – which were in reality simply the armistice lines that existed when fighting stopped in 1949 – was not likely. "Defend itself, by itself" suggested both the continuation of American military aid and agreement with the Israeli doctrine that its defense should not depend on international forces or UN troops.

Third, Bush restated, as he had been saying almost since 9/11, that "Israel will retain its right to defend itself against terrorism, including to take actions against terrorist organizations." He then added that Israel's coming withdrawals in Gaza and the West Bank would not change "existing arrangements regarding control of airspace, territorial waters, and land passages of the West Bank and Gaza" – meaning Israel would retain control of them.

Fourth, Bush turned to the refugee issue. Because the United States "is strongly committed to Israel's security and well-being as a Jewish state," he explained, "[i]t seems clear that an agreed, just, fair and realistic framework for a solution to the Palestinian refugee issue as part of any final status agreement will need to be found through the establishment of a Palestinian state, and the settling of Palestinian refugees there, rather than in Israel." Here, an American president was, for the first time, stating clearly that the "right of return" was dead. Moreover, Bush explained why: because the United States saw Israel as Israel saw itself, as a Jewish State, and we understood that the "return" of millions of Palestinian "refugees" would destroy the state's Jewish character. Bush did not exactly use normative language – he did not say that a solution for the refugee problem "must" be found in the Palestinian state – but he came so close that the meaning was the same. The neutral phrase "it seems clear" was in fact far from neutral; it meant that any fair-minded observer, any reasonable person, would have to agree.

Fifth, Bush addressed the settlement and border issues. Borders would emerge from negotiations between the parties as part of a final peace settlement. But he had this caveat:

In light of new realities on the ground, including already existing major Israeli population centers, it is unrealistic to expect that the outcome of final status negotiations will be a full and complete return to the armistice lines of 1949, and all previous efforts to negotiate a two-state solution have reached the same conclusion. It is realistic to expect that any final status agreement will only be achieved on the basis of mutually agreed changes that reflect these realities.

This was another bombshell. Bush was accepting and saying that there would be no return to the 1949 lines *because* Israel would keep some of the settlements. This was widely acknowledged and had been on the table at Camp David, but in this letter, Bush was setting it forth publicly: Israel would keep the major settlement blocks. Moreover, his use of the term "armistice lines of 1949" rather than "1967 borders" was another statement that the sacrosanct 1967 lines were not sacrosanct at all – and would go. There were qualifications: This was not normative language at all, and Bush was "merely" predictive, stating what was realistic and what was unrealistic. Moreover, he repeated that final borders could only emerge from negotiations, not be imposed by Israel. But the headline was clear: There would be no return to 1967 and Israel could keep the major settlement blocks.

Bush then reiterated the commonly expressed position about the fence: "[t]he barrier being erected by Israel should be a security rather than political barrier, should be temporary rather than permanent, and therefore not prejudice any final status issues including final borders, and its route should take into account, consistent with security needs, its impact on Palestinians not engaged in terrorist activities." The Palestinian state, he said, must be "viable, contiguous, sovereign, and independent, so that the Palestinian people can build their own future." He pledged U.S. help to build that state and its institutions.

He concluded by describing disengagement as "a bold and historic initiative" and called it "a courageous decision which I support. As a close friend and ally, the United States intends to work closely with you to help make it a success." Later, the Senate and House would add their own support by lopsided margins: The votes were 95 to 3 in the Senate on June 23, and 407 to 9 in the House of Representatives on June 24.

A beaming Sharon saw the April 14 letter as a great victory for his disengagement strategy. Weissglas told us that all senior ministers (including the Likud ministers) were now on board; if Bush was for it, they would go along. The Israeli press, however, adopted a mixed view: Some said he had come to Washington and now returned home in triumph because the president had said "no" to the right of return and "yes" to keeping the major blocks. Others in the press were less overwhelmed and focused on the language: Bush had not said "no right of return" and "no 1967 borders"; he had said "it seems clear" and "it is unrealistic." Were these formulations strong enough? Would they bind future presidents? Doubts on the Israeli right ran along the same lines. Weissglas had once lectured us on the language he called "Likudish." It was a difficult tongue, he had told us as we drafted the April 14 letter, not sensitive to subtlety, demanding absolute clarity and direct language. Perhaps the careful wording of the letter would not be enough to satisfy those who spoke "Likudish."

"As Far as I'm Concerned, Sharon and Bush Can Decide to Cancel Ramadan"

Not surprisingly, Arab reactions were sour. President Bush "is the first president who has legitimized the settlements in the Palestinian territories," Prime

Minister Qurie (Abu Ala'a) said. "We as Palestinians reject that, we cannot accept that."⁹ "As far as I'm concerned, Sharon and Bush can decide to cancel Ramadan," the Muslim holy month, said Saeb Erekat, a Palestinian negotiator then and now. "But that doesn't mean that Muslims will not fast."¹⁰ The head of the Arab League called the Bush letter "negative and very regrettable." From all over the Arab world came similar, and often much nastier, comments.

There were similarly negative comments from Europe. President Chirac of France called the disengagement plan an "unfortunate and dangerous precedent," and EU spokespeople stressed that matters between Israel and the Palestinians could be settled only in direct negotiations, not by Israel and the United States in speeches in Washington. Only Tony Blair, who as always had a better understanding of what President Bush was seeking, gave real support when he visited the White House on April 17. "If there is disengagement by Israel from the Gaza and from parts of the West Bank," Blair said in a White House press conference alongside Bush, "that gives us the opportunity to help the Palestinian Authority with the economic, the political and the security measures they take and they need to take in order to get to the point where the concept of a viable Palestinian state becomes a real possibility."¹¹

A small crisis in relations with Jordan ensued as well because King Abdullah was visiting California when the letter was released. In preparations for that release, the American team had visited Jordan; here is how Foreign Minister Muasher later described it:

You came to Jordan . . . March 30, 2004. And you talked to us about the assurances you wanted to give to Sharon, which scared the hell out of us, because to us it changed a longstanding US position on the outcome of a settlement. So, we wrote a letter to President Bush on April 8 in which we made the Jordanian position clear that we do not accept this – that any changes to the border must be minor and reciprocal, etcetera. . . . The King was going to come to the United States. He was already on the west coast, California.¹²

With the April 14 letter to Sharon already delivered, the Jordanians suggested that the president now write a letter to the king, in essence undoing what he had done on April 14. Then the king would come to the White House to receive it, replicating the drama with Sharon. A letter was drafted, and a version of it appears in Muasher's 2008 memoir, *The Arab Center*.

I worked hard on the language, attempting to give them whatever we could without watering down what the President had just said: an impossible task, in the end. But we were saved: the Jordanians pushed too hard and quickly ran into a stubborn Rice. She saw the advantages of giving the Arabs something, and doing so through the moderate Jordanian king, but she saw with equal clarity that the President would look weak and foolish if he appeared in any way to undermine his own statements just days later. The Jordanians made the tactical error of threatening that the king would cancel his visit to Washington if they did not get the language they demanded. This got Rice's back up immediately, for she would not permit the President to be cornered this way. So the editing of the letter stopped, and the visit was delayed; Abdullah came a month later, in May, when tempers had cooled.

President Mubarak's temper did not cool so quickly. He had remained in the United States after his Crawford visit, and believed that the White House ceremony with Sharon and the promulgation of the April 14 letter while he was still in the United States was an embarrassment and an insult. One result was that he declined the President's invitation for the G-8 Summit meeting then just around the corner in June at Sea Island, Georgia, where the Middle East had been selected as the main topic. Given the emphasis on reform and democracy at Sea Island, Mubarak must later have regarded this as a wise decision.

Lest anyone believe the Middle East had changed overnight, on April 17, the Israelis assassinated Abdel-Aziz Rantisi, who had replaced Sheik Yassin as leader of Hamas. In Israel, Sharon spoke to the Knesset on April 22, explaining and defending the disengagement plan in its entirety. Israel would withdraw from Gaza and four small settlements in the northern West Bank, relocating "communities in areas which will clearly not be under Israeli control in any future permanent status arrangement." He also mentioned the security fence and a new security line where the IDF would deploy, and he argued that "the U.S. President has expressed his sweeping support of the plan." For the Palestinians, he said, "[t]he rules of the game have changed. If they do not uphold their commitments, Israel will continue to act alone." He told the Knesset he had considered a national referendum on disengagement but had opted for a Likud vote, which reflected the party's "genuine internal conflict."

On May 2, in an especially ugly terrorist incident, a pregnant Israeli woman and her four daughters were shot to death at close range near their home in a settlement in Gaza. Later that day, despite Bush's endorsement of the disengagement plan, Sharon lost the Likud Party vote on it. Perhaps the savage terrorist attack that day had affected the result: 193,000 Likud members voted 60/40 against the plan. They did not believe it would improve Israel's security. They did not see their vote as a repudiation of Sharon, nor of Bush, but they simply did not want to get out of Gaza in return for nothing from the Palestinians. The April 14 letter had not solved Sharon's Likud problem.

King Abdullah of Jordan did come to visit on May 4, restoring both the U.S.-Jordanian relationship and his personal relationship with the president to their normal warmth. The president was not, however, backing away from what he had said. In fact, he told the king ruefully, the international reaction was mostly the product of his own and Sharon's low popularity. This is a real opportunity, he said to the king, and people are losing sight of it; under any other circumstances, everyone would have said "hallelujah" at Israel's decision to get out of Gaza.

Two weeks later, Rice and her team met with the Palestinian prime minister Ahmed Qurie, known as Abu Ala'a, in Berlin. Qurie told her there were serious reforms under way, of which a key part was elections. The PA would ask the Quartet, he said, to choose the right timing for both presidential and PLC balloting. Rice was not buying. She sternly told Qurie that there was a chance for a breakthrough but not if all the PA did was hold meetings. Instead, it had to act on security matters. As we had been saying for months and months, it was time to unify the security forces into just three groups and put them under the prime minister – in other words, take them away from Arafat. With Israeli withdrawal from Gaza coming, the effectiveness of the Palestinian security forces was critical. How do we achieve that?

In the Berlin meeting with Rice and her team, Qurie's answer to that question was, in effect, we don't. We can only unify the security forces under the prime minister after the Israeli withdrawal. Nothing can be done to change Arafat's role; he is the symbol of our independence movement. Right now he is under siege by the Israelis, so why should he cooperate anyway? Our political system is a strange one, and it cannot achieve what you want. Rice then returned to security issues: Could the PA handle Hamas and the other groups? The PA would absorb them, Qurie said, not confront them. Rice told him there would be no international force in Gaza, so the PA needed to face its responsibilities and show that terrorism would not be tolerated. We are not proposing a civil war, but you have to show that the armed struggle is over. Qurie replied by moving away from the topic of security again: What we need now, he said, are final status negotiations. This idea of building political institutions is fine, but it is not central. Our real business is preparing for final status talks; building institutions follows later.

To say that Rice and Qurie were talking past each other is a gross understatement; there was little common ground in that meeting. In essence, Qurie was saying, "Give us a state and then we'll see about reform" – the approach that had marked the Clinton administration. Those days were long gone in Washington, but apparently he had not noticed.

Rice rejected his approach and told him, Abu Ala'a, look around you. We're in *Berlin. Berlin!* You are telling me nothing can be accomplished until you negotiate final borders and have a state. Germany had no final borders until 1990 – but it built a prosperous democratic state. Rice suggested that final status talks were not in the cards right now, and anyway, talks had gone on forever and not produced anything. The disengagement plan could give the PA land to govern. If it reformed its institutions and governed that territory well, it would not be a great leap from there to final status. So she urged him to get started – prepare to govern Gaza and govern it well.

The session ended with no meeting of the minds – except on one aspect: elections. Everyone in the Palestinian party demanded full American support for elections, to rejuvenate the leadership and show that the Palestinians were ready for self-government. Rice responded with complete agreement and pledged U.S. support.

In June, shortly before the Sea Island summit, the Israeli cabinet approved (14 to 7) a version of the disengagement plan, but Sharon had been forced to compromise. There would have to be a separate vote on the dismantling of each settlement, meaning Sharon's political struggle would go on and on for months more. Worse yet for Sharon, two National Religious Party cabinet members resigned their posts as soon as the cabinet approved disengagement; later, the entire party left Sharon's government, meaning he now had a minority coalition in the 120-member Knesset. For us in Washington, this turn of events had one reassuring side: Sharon really had needed the April 14 letter. His arguments about the necessity for strong American backing were not ploys designed merely to improve his political situation. We were working together to achieve the disengagement and move toward the vision the president had sketched out in June 2002.

Sea Island

President Bush hosted the G-8 summit from June 8 to 10 at Sea Island, Georgia, using the meeting to promote a new "Partnership for Progress and a Common Future with the Region of the Broader Middle East and North Africa." The official Chair's Summary of the meetings began, "We met at Sea Island for our annual Summit to advance freedom by strengthening international cooperation to make the world both safer and better." The entire effort was part of Bush's larger approach to the Broader Middle East and North Africa region, called BMENA for short, which as we defined it included every country from Morocco to Afghanistan. (Initially, we had called it the "Greater Middle East" until German foreign minister Joschka Fischer pleaded that in German, the term smacked of Nazi-era locutions.) The Sea Island declarations reflected Bush's promotion of democracy and institutional reform, which he had outlined in his National Endowment for Democracy speech in November 2003. The president was also proposing establishing a U.S.-Middle East Free Trade Area by 2013. In addition, the G-8 backed a Democracy Assistance Dialogue bringing together governments and NGOs and a Forum for the Future in which "G-8 and regional Foreign, Economic, and other Ministers" would meet annually "in an ongoing discussion on reform, with business and civil society leaders participating in parallel dialogues."

An odd mix of regional leaders attended the summit – from Afghanistan, Algeria, Bahrain, Iraq, Jordan, Turkey, Yemen – and the degree of enthusiasm from governments in the region and in Europe for the Sea Island declarations was equally mixed. The most common criticism was that nothing could be achieved in the Middle East unless and until the Israeli-Palestinian conflict was resolved. Zbigniew Brzezinski's reaction was typical of the criticism we had been getting all year: "Democracy right now is a slogan. Probably worse than that, it is a deceptive device to justify postponement in the peace process."[13] Critics also argued that this democracy initiative would end up like the Roadmap and the June 24, 2002, speech: It would fail because the Bush administration would not give it the attention and energy it needed. Needless to say, we in the White House saw such criticisms as reflecting hostility based partly on opposition to the war in Iraq and partly on a startling misreading of the Middle East situation. There had been no lack of attention and energy in the White House, but they were met by a successful effort by Arafat to block any of the reforms that were essential for progress. The Israelis were not going to negotiate a peace agreement with Arafat, and we were not going to ask them to do so. Critics who ignored what Clinton had gone through, and then the *Karine A* incident and all the other proofs of Arafat's continuing support for terrorism, were not serious; they were substituting slogans for realistic efforts to move toward peace and Palestinian statehood. And like Brzezinski, they were, for the most part, totally uninterested in bringing about democracy in the Arab world.

Yet Bush's insistence after 9/11 on reform and on freedom – stated in speeches such as his address to the National Endowment for Democracy the previous June (2003) and after the launching and funding of the Middle East Partnership Initiative (MEPI) in 2002 – was eliciting reactions from NGOs and civic leaders gathered in various places in the region and outside. Both the "Sana'a Declaration" made at Sana'a, Yemen, in January 2004 and the "Alexandria Statement" in Alexandria, Egypt, in March demanded democracy, human rights, and free elections. The 2002 *Arab Human Development Report*, published by the UN Development Program in 2003 and written by teams of Arab intellectuals, had begun to challenge what it called a "freedom deficit" in the region:

There is a substantial lag between Arab countries and other regions in terms of participatory governance. The wave of democracy that transformed governance in most of Latin America and East Asia in the 1980s and Eastern Europe and much of Central Asia in the late 1980s and early 1990s has barely reached the Arab States. This freedom deficit undermines human development and is one of the most painful manifestations of lagging political development.[14]

So the declarations coming from Sea Island were not lone voices in the wilderness, even if many Arab rulers were not keen on hearing them. For Bush, the G-8 summit provided an occasion to advance his own view that reform in the region was essential; he would make this the theme of his Second Inaugural Address six months later. Ritual bows were made in the Sea Island documents to the traditional view that the Israeli-Palestinian conflict was central: The Chair's Summary stated, "Our support for reform in the region will go hand in hand with our support for a just, comprehensive, and lasting settlement to the Arab-Israeli conflict." But the G-8 welcomed "the prospect of Israeli withdrawal from all Gaza settlements and from parts of the West Bank, following the Israeli Cabinet decision to endorse Prime Minister Sharon's initiative." A statement on disengagement noted that the "G8 looks forward to the implementation of this decision in 2005."

Summer of Politics

Both Sharon and Qurie were struggling with internal politics that summer of 2004. On July 12, Sharon asked the leader of the Labor Party, Shimon Peres, to join a coalition that would have a majority in the Knesset needed to go forward with disengagement. That day, Hadley and I were back in the region to meet with Sharon and Qurie. The latter told us what he had told Rice in Berlin: The Palestinian people want elections, and he was for them. He figured that the majority of the population was moderate and would vote for moderate candidates. Elections should be held, he thought, in January or February 2005. He expressed no worry about Hamas as a political rival; Fatah could beat them. Nor was he worried about an armed struggle between the PA and Hamas: Dahlan was preparing for one, and if it came, he would win. The Israelis came to the same conclusion: If there ever were a confrontation, defeat was possible, but the PA should win. In our meeting with Sharon, he explained his political problems. He was now presiding over a minority government, and he lacked a majority in his own party, Likud, either for disengagement or to bring Labor into the government. He urged us to be patient and assured us he was not deterred. That the political situation was very confused was an advantage, he said; it gave him more room to maneuver.

Shortly after our return home, on July 17, Qurie offered Arafat his resignation, a result of many of the same frustrations that Abbas had experienced. Arafat was refusing to cede any real power to the office of prime minister. Ten days later, on July 27, he withdrew the resignation when Arafat agreed that the prime minister would have some control of the security forces. It is unlikely that anyone in the PA, in the Government of Israel, or in Washington actually believed this would happen. For us at the White House, the same pattern appeared month after month: A beleaguered, dogged, determined Sharon plowed forward against tough opposition, while on the Palestinian side, Arafat blocked anything resembling progress and reform. There was danger of a stalemate on the Israeli side, but Sharon was beating those who tried to stop progress. On the Palestinian side, the stalemate was real. Qurie was in essence doing nothing, perhaps correctly gauging his strength against Arafat. But this meant that the disengagement might not have the impact we sought. Rice told a visitor that she had thought Gaza disengagement itself would shake up things well enough, be enough of a shock to the system; now that seemed dubious. I returned to the region in early August on a working vacation, and Palestinian officials told me we could not rely on Egypt to "pull our chestnuts out of the fire" in Gaza if things went wrong there. The Egyptians are pulling back, they explained. They are backing away because of controversy about the disengagement plan – criticism by Palestinians and opposition within Egypt. Gaza seems to them chaotic and they will not take it on, whatever they told you Americans. And they want to see who wins your November elections, anyway.

On August 18, we had further proof of the challenge Sharon faced: Likud, which voted in May against the disengagement plan in a party referendum, now voted against Sharon's intent to form a coalition with the Labor Party. Sharon needed Labor votes to get a majority in the Knesset for his plan, and that was exactly what Likud politicians wanted to keep from him. At the end of August, I urged Rice in a memo to spell out our agreement with Sharon on settlements. It seemed to me this would help Sharon make his case for disengagement, which was in part that Israel was giving up peripheral settlements in order to keep the main blocks. We had agreed that Israel could build in settlements as long as there were neither new settlements nor expansion of settlement land areas. (Once again, it is worth noting that the fact that we had an agreement was clear to all.) Sharon recorded one victory in mid-September: On September 14, the Knesset approved the Gaza compensation bill, giving funds to settlers so they could relocate. And Sharon kept his steamroller moving: Six weeks later, on October 26, the Knesset gave preliminary approval (voting 67 to 45) to the entire disengagement plan. Every vote was a compromise and a battle, but somehow Sharon was finding the votes to keep moving forward.

Sharon's battle for votes was conducted against a background of continuing violence. On August 31, two suicide bombers, acting within minutes of each other, attacked buses in Beersheba, killing 16 people and wounding about 100. Hamas claimed responsibility. There were smaller attacks on September 8, 14, 22, 23, 24, and 30. As October began, Sharon ordered what became a 17-day offensive into Gaza, both in response to these attacks and to stop the rockets that were being fired into Israeli settlements. For Sharon, it was critical to prove that he would not be withdrawing from Gaza under fire – so he was determined that the firing would stop.

But a more significant development occurred at the end of October: On the 29th, Yasser Arafat was flown to Paris for medical treatment. Rumors were swirling as to what ailed him – cancer, AIDS, blood poisoning – and whether he would recover. Our role had been to assure that Israel would let him travel abroad for medical treatment, but the Israelis were too smart to get in the way of that. We had all been watching his health fade, but just how badly off he was remained a secret. Many sources of information were clearly biased and unreliable.

The New White House

On November 2, President Bush was reelected by a wide margin. I had given no thought to what I would do if he lost and had no thoughts whatsoever of leaving if he won. Now the only question was whether to stay at the NSC or go with Condi Rice to State – as several friends and colleagues from the NSC were doing. I discussed the matter with Hadley, who was quickly (as expected) named her successor, and with Rice. We discussed jobs at State seriously, but Hadley persuaded me to stay at the White House with two powerful arguments. First, the president preferred that I stay; it was not helpful if the whole NSC decamped with Condi.

Second, Hadley argued that Middle East policy is always, in every administration, ultimately made at the White House. I should stay close to the president, he said; that is where the policy comes from. If I wanted to have influence on policy making, I was already in the right place. Finally, he offered a sweetener: a promotion, from senior director for the Near East and North Africa, to deputy national security advisor. I would oversee both the Democracy, Human

Rights, and International Organizations directorate I had initially headed, as well as the Near East directorate, and be given a new title, which I needed to invent, that stressed the president's democracy initiatives. My wife and I tried out a dozen variations and settled on deputy national security advisor for global democracy strategy, which was both too long and too ambiguous. In the end, it did not matter: In diplomatic shorthand, I was the White House Middle East guy. Whether Hadley had been right that Middle East policy was always made in the White House was another matter, as time would teach me, because Rice was not Powell. As one biographer of Rice later wrote, "when Rice became secretary of state, the Israeli portfolio followed her back to Foggy Bottom."[15] Her relationship with the president was uniquely close and her influence uniquely powerful. Moreover, she was not opposed at the NSC by a power-hungry rival; in Hadley she had a former deputy who understood that she was and would remain the president's top foreign policy advisor. Even in discussions in November and December, as Condi prepared for her confirmation hearings, it was plain that the Middle East "peace process" would be a focus for her.

But in November 2004 there were not yet significant policy differences inside the Bush administration: We all favored the course the president had been taking since his June 2002 speech. As my own key NSC colleague on Israeli-Palestinian matters at that time, Rob Danin, and I put it in a memo to Condi on November 8, it was clear that any final status negotiations in the near future would fail. Instead, this was a ground game: Step by step, new Palestinian leadership must emerge, and it must take power over the security forces. With Arafat in charge, this would be a long and trying process, but there were no quick fixes.

Notes

1. "Sharon Promises to Remove Jewish Settlements from Gaza," *CBCNews*, February 4, 2004, http://www.cbc.ca/world/story/2004/02/02/sharon_settlements040202.html#ixzzowIXXqkxo.
2. Nir Hefetz and Gadi Bloom, *Ariel Sharon: A Life* (New York: Random House, 2006), 445.
3. In the end, one contributor and Sharon's older son Omri were convicted and Omri was jailed. Sharon himself was never convicted of any wrongdoing.
4. Joel Greenberg, "Sharon Calls for Shutting Outposts; Plan of Evacuation Ordered for Gaza," *Chicago Tribune*, February 3, 2004.
5. Glenn Kessler, "U.S. Views Gaza Proposal as Possible Interim Step; Israel's Plan to Vacate Gaza Settlements Could Prod Talks," *Washington Post*, February 26, 2004.
6. Sharon, *Sharon*, 583.
7. Sallai Meridor, interview by the author, October 20, 2009, p. 5.
8. Remarks Following a Cabinet Meeting and Exchange with Reporters, 13 Weekly Comp. Pres. Doc. 40 (March 23, 2004).
9. Greg Myre, "The Mideast Turmoil: Reaction; Palestinians and Other Arabs Assail Bush for Stand on Israel," *New York Times*, April 14, 2004.

10. James Bennet, "The Mideast Turmoil: News Analysis; Sharon Coup: U.S. Go-Ahead," *New York Times*, April 15, 2004.
11. Richard W. Stevenson, "Blair Visits White House, Says Commitment in Iraq Steadfast," *New York Times*, April 17, 2004.
12. Muasher, interview, p. 12.
13. Glenn Kessler and Robin Wright, "Arabs and Europeans Question 'Greater Middle East Plan," *Washington Post*, February 22, 2004.
14. United Nations Development Program, "Arab Human Development Report," July 2, 2002, http://www.arab-hdr.org/publications/other/ahdr/ahdr2002e.pdf.
15. Glenn Kessler, *The Confidante: Condoleezza Rice and the Creation of the Bush Legacy* (New York: St. Martin's Press, 2007), 27.

5

Arafat, Disengagement, Sharon

Our expectations changed on November 11, when Yasser Arafat died in a military hospital in Paris. He was buried in Ramallah after a chaotic funeral, and Mahmoud Abbas was quickly chosen to head the PLO. In accordance with the PA's "Basic Law," elections were to be held within 60 days for a new president of the Palestinian Authority. If an internal battle had been expected among Palestinians, it did not materialize; it was made clear very soon that Abbas would also be the candidate for president of the PA, replacing Arafat there as well.

Bush's immediate public reaction, one we thought through carefully, was not to shed crocodile tears for Arafat but to look forward. Blair was back at the White House on November 12, the first visit of a foreign leader since the president's reelection, and Bush used their scheduled press appearance to emphasize the positive. "I think it is fair to say that I believe we've got a great chance to establish a Palestinian state," the president said. "And I intend to use the next four years to spend the capital of the United States on such a state. . . . We seek a democratic, independent and viable state for the Palestinian people. . . . We are committed to the security of Israel as a Jewish state. . . . I look forward to working with the Palestinian leadership that is committed to fighting terror and committed to the cause of democratic reform."[1] Arafat had been the barrier to real reform, we thought, and his removal from the scene now opened the path forward. No longer would he be there to block the creation of more unified and professional security forces, to steal or divert aid funds (and a global search for the funds would soon be underway), or to prevent democratic institutions from developing. In December, Steve Hadley and I once again visited Jerusalem and found that Sharon shared this view. He told us he would see Abbas right after the Palestinian elections and that he was optimistic: With Arafat gone, he would have someone with whom to talk.

Why did the Palestinians decide to hold an election? The Basic Law was, after all, not the U.S. Constitution, and it was ignored whenever that was convenient. An advisor to Abbas explained that it was not obvious that there *had* to be an election:

I believed that Abu Mazen could have governed easily without an election. It was a time of political instability and you could have easily packaged an unelected president – especially if it's the PLO chairman and all of that kind of thing. Abu Mazen insisted on it; he knew very well that he needed that election.... He needed it for legitimacy purposes. He needed it in the long term. His position will be more assailable without an election. It will empower him and he was going to win anyway.[2]

Given the later complaints about the PLC election in 2006, it is worth recalling that, all along, Palestinian leaders like Qurie and Abbas had favored elections; they had even insisted on them as a means of legitimating their leadership. With Arafat – the charismatic, recognized leader – now gone, they concluded that elections were critical.

We had been working closely with Abbas for two years, and he still struck us all as a nice man; the question was whether he would provide the leadership needed to combat Palestinian terrorist groups and Islamist extremists. Reasonably pious and apparently moderate in his religious and political views, Abbas was not a hero. Arafat had not shown any courage on the one occasion when it mattered most – at Camp David; he had refused to accept compromises with the Israelis that he knew would bring vicious criticism from Hamas and others. Would Abbas do any better? Would he actually sign a final status agreement that, even in versions viewed as favorable to the Palestinian cause (such as the Geneva Initiative), required giving up the "right of return," dividing Jerusalem, and accepting that many Israeli settlements would stay forever? These were questions for later because no such talks were then before us. But these were the questions we asked ourselves repeatedly during Bush's second term, as we met dozens of times with Abbas.

Disengagement Marches On

What is striking in retrospect is that we never considered deviating from the path we were then on: backing Sharon's disengagement plan. Literally no one at the White House suggested that we take a different path. Nor was it raised, it seems, in Jerusalem. As recounted by Eival Giladi, "We announced the disengagement before Arafat passed away and we don't even reconsider should we do it, should we do it as planned, should we do it in the same time frame. We move on."[3] That may now appear strange: After all, disengagement had been the product of Arafat's obduracy. Progress toward realizing the June 24 vision and movement on the Roadmap had been made impossible by Arafat's refusal to reform. Abbas himself had resigned in protest when Arafat made it clear that the prime minister's post was, to him, a source of danger that would never be allowed any power. Sharon had decided to move unilaterally only after it was clear that negotiations – which he had begun by meeting with Abbas in the summer of 2002 – were dead. So, why not now go back to June

24 and the Roadmap? Why not leap directly to final status negotiations with Abbas?

There were several reasons not to do so. Abbas was newly on top and had spent his life playing second (sometimes third or fourth) fiddle to Arafat. How likely was it that he would wish to jump instantly into final status talks? He certainly never proposed it to us; no PA official suggested that it was time to stop disengagement and go immediately to final status negotiations. We noted that Abbas had been chosen as leader of the PLO immediately and as the candidate for the PA presidency but had not managed to seize the reins at Fatah: there, Farouk Qaddoumi became and remained chairman. Qaddoumi was an unreconstructed hardliner, promoting the armed struggle and waging an endless campaign against Abbas, and Abbas's inability to do much about this rival suggested the limitations on his own power. Moreover, there was now momentum behind the disengagement plan: Sharon was winning, battle by battle, vote by vote. To abandon that plan seemed like folly: Instead of achieving, in 2005, the removal of Israeli settlements in Gaza and of the IDF there, and having territory the PA could then govern by itself, we would probably have nothing but endless and likely unsuccessful negotiations. So it seemed better to everyone to continue on the path toward disengagement. Sallai Meridor recalled Sharon's struggles to implement disengagement and the impact of Arafat's death:

In the middle Arafat dies. Sharon doesn't decide, maybe was not even asked to consider to stop from moving onward on the decision that was taken based on the existence of Arafat and no other alternative. And because he's already on the way and the concern is he will never be able to get there if any side wind now is interfering with his movement. So regardless, notwithstanding the fact that Arafat is not – the reason to go this way does not exist anymore, everybody supports the movement.[4]

The Palestinians after Arafat: Sympathy and Cash

So no one viewed Arafat's death as a reason to abandon disengagement. But in fact the death of Arafat was a huge event for President Bush and the way in which he, and Washington more generally, perceived the Palestinian leadership. Arafat was a man on the wrong side of the war on terror, an enemy of democracy and good governance and therefore of the president's repeated calls for reform in the Arab world and for the advance of democracy, and a famously corrupt leader who had stolen hundreds of millions of dollars of aid donations. With his death, perceptions of the Palestinians were transformed. As the president had said to Abbas and Qurie in the summer of 2002, they could become a model for the Arab world of good government and progress. He would soon place them with the Iraqis and Afghans – who had elected Karzai as president on October 9, 2004 – as tomorrow's democracies. (And soon, Lebanon would be added; after the murder of Rafik Hariri in February 2005, free elections were held for the first time in 30 years without the presence of Syrian troops.) It is not so much that the Palestinians were now seen solely through rose-colored glasses, as that their failings were transformed into additional reasons to help them. At worst they were sad sacks, unable to perform efficiently; there were few Fayyads. But this shortcoming only suggested that we should give them more help, more financing, and more encouragement. Now, it seemed, they were on our side too, working for a moderate, democratic state that would take its place in the Middle East we hoped would emerge. When they failed, we reacted with regret, not with anger; they were not betraying the cause but merely exposing their own sad weaknesses – the results less of moral failings than of the local pathologies President Bush had discussed in his NED speech and elsewhere. They had suffered from decades under Arafat, seen more as his victims than as his colleagues and abettors. They had been the victims as well, in this view, of Western prejudices that assumed Arabs were uninterested in or incapable of democratic governance. Now all this would change.

Perversely, the "balance of sympathy" that had tilted toward Israel while Arafat ruled was further tilted toward the Palestinians by the great reduction in terrorist attacks. The vicious bus bombings and other suicide attacks had elicited sympathy everywhere for Israel and for the steps it took to defend itself. Even those who criticized specific Israeli responses admitted that any government would act to save its citizens from such relentless assaults. But after Arafat's passing (and presumably not coincidentally) and given Sharon's great success in crushing the intifada, the toll was far lower. From 220 deaths at the hands of terrorists in 2002, Israel experienced a 90% drop by 2005: In that year, 22 citizens were killed by terror, and the number dropped again to 15 in 2006.[5] The sympathy Israelis had won as victims of violence dissipated.

On January 9, 2005, Abbas was elected president of the PA, running as the Fatah candidate, with 62% of the vote. It was on the surface a good election: There was free campaigning and other candidates criticized Abbas. It seemed that the ballots were counted accurately. Turnout was also about 62%, lower than some had predicted, but Hamas and many Palestinians living in East Jerusalem had boycotted the election. We did not think so at the time, but it is fair to wonder whether the inability to gather that other 40% of the vote so soon after Arafat's death suggested more profound weaknesses in Fatah, which later became obvious. In Washington and in the EU, we also played down the departure of the head of the independent Central Election Commission, who along with several dozen members of his staff resigned in protest right after the election. Fatah had illegally pressured the Commission to extend voting by two hours and allow some unregistered voters to cast ballots, both efforts designed to achieve a larger turnout and a greater victory margin for Abbas.

In his State of the Union speech on February 2, 2005, the president empha-sized the centrality of democracy in U.S. foreign policy – and displayed the new attitude toward the Palestinians:

We've declared our own intention: America will stand with the allies of freedom to support democratic movements in the Middle East and beyond, with the ultimate goal of ending tyranny in our world. . . . And because democracies respect their own people and their neighbors, the advance of freedom will lead to peace. That advance has great momentum in our time, shown by women voting in Afghanistan, and Palestinians choosing a new direction, and the people of Ukraine asserting their democratic rights and electing a president. We are witnessing landmark events in the history of liberty. And in the coming years, we will add to that story.

The beginnings of reform and democracy in the Palestinian territories are now showing the power of freedom to break old patterns of violence and failure. Tomorrow morning, Secretary of State Rice departs on a trip that will take her to Israel and the West Bank for meetings with Prime Minister Sharon and President Abbas. She will discuss with them how we and our friends can help the Palestinian people end terror and build the institutions of a peaceful, independent, democratic state. To promote this democracy, I will ask Congress for $350 million to support Palestinian political, economic and security reforms.[6]

So Arafat's death had led to a request that, in addition to the $150 million in funds we had been giving to help Palestinians – through agencies of the United Nations, for example – Congress grant $200 million more in a supplemental appropriation. These were big numbers, but the president had large ambitions. Combine Sharon's tenacity and his disengagement plan with new Palestinian leadership, and real progress seemed possible. Despite a significant terrorist attack in Gaza on January 13 and a threat by Sharon not to meet with the new Palestinian leadership until it acted against terrorist groups, in fact Sharon and Abbas did meet on February 8 – at Sharm el Sheik, in a session jointly hosted by King Abdullah of Jordan and President Mubarak. It was the first such Israeli-Palestinian "summit" in years. Abbas and Sharon declared an end to violence (though obviously Abbas did not control the Palestinian terrorist groups) and looked forward to future negotiations under the Roadmap. Egypt and Jordan immediately announced they would send their ambassadors back to Israel, after a four-year absence. The mood in the region was upbeat. The United States invited both Abbas and Sharon to visit Washington. Perhaps disengagement would indeed shock the system, as we had always hoped, and provide real momentum to keep it going: disengagement, good PA governance of Gaza as a model for a future Palestinian state, and a return to negotiations. Things were again looking up.

We believed progress was now possible. Condi Rice had visited London in late January, for the first time as secretary of state, and had told the British that the follow-on to the Gaza withdrawal should be final status talks. She was committed; we'll go all out, she said. Both the Gaza withdrawal (in the summer) and the Palestinian parliamentary elections (July 15) were scheduled. In another trip, Rice met with Sharon on February 6, and he repeated that he thought there might be a real opportunity now, with Arafat gone. He complained about Israeli politics, telling her again that the left cannot get anything done and the right is against getting anything done – but he would persevere. His political troubles had been striking: He had lost two no-confidence votes in November, and in the fall of 2004, 10 cabinet ministers had either resigned or been fired.[7] Sharon complained as well that Abbas and his security forces were still doing nothing against terrorism. Rice told him we had decided to find a U.S. general to serve as security coordinator, with the task of pushing the Palestinians into greater action and greater reform. The next day she met with the new Palestinian leadership, or perhaps the more apt description is the "newly promoted" leadership – for there were no new faces. This was the Arafat crew without Arafat. Only in Fayyad did we see a real commitment to change.

I continued to accompany Rice on all her trips to the region, now as the "White House guy" on a State Department plane rather than as her subordinate. After that trip, I reported to Hadley, now the national security advisor. There was optimism in the region, I wrote, but there is also a dilemma. Israel complains that Abbas is not confronting Hamas and is pressing him to do more. His slow and nonconfrontational approach produces quiet, about which the Israelis then complain, but which helps Sharon in his own internal political battle. Confronting Hamas would produce more violence, which neither Abbas nor Sharon want right now.

On February 11, the president met the army officer who had been selected as security coordinator, Gen. William E. "Kip" Ward – a U.S. Army three-star general with experience mostly in Europe. In the end, Ward would serve only until December 2005 and then go on to become deputy commander of the U.S. European Command, but his work established this new and significant position. The president wanted to see him and let him know what his commander in chief thought of the situation in the Middle East before he headed there. The president harkened back to Aqaba and said Abu Mazen – he still called Abbas by his "nom de guerre" despite his elevation to president of the PA – had not acted after all the fine words he said at that summit. He could not be blamed for that because Arafat had prevented it, but the president noted that Abu Mazen had never told him to anticipate zero progress. Maybe the election changed things and he would act now. Sharon, he told Ward, was a tank driver and a gruff old general but wanted peace. The thing is, he has no confidence in the Palestinian leadership now, and he is waiting to take the measure of Abu Mazen. So am I, Bush said, and he asked Ward to give us his thoughts after a few months in the field. You tell me: Who does the PA see as the enemy? Who are its forces fighting? Before we get to a settlement, we need to see Palestinian security forces taking on Palestinian terrorists. Bush viewed Abbas as well meaning but had little confidence in his ability to force change and lead to statehood. Was he tough enough? Would he be the father of a Palestinian state? Bush's doubts had appeared early and were never satisfied. He was hopeful but never convinced.

On February 14, a massive terrorist bomb blew up the motorcade of Rafik Hariri, the former prime minister and still the most important man in Lebanon. This murder would lead to huge demonstrations on March 14 in favor of Lebanese self-rule, and the popular and international revulsion against Hariri's killing soon forced an end to 30 years of Syrian occupation of Lebanon. Free elections were then held in May. In Washington, we were enthusiastic backers of these developments, increasing aid to Lebanon and becoming champions of its new government after elections later that spring and summer.

On February 16, the Knesset passed a compensation law, and on February 20, the Israeli cabinet again approved the withdrawal from Gaza, voting 17 to 5. (Natan Sharansky, unwilling to support the forced evacuation of Jews from their homes in Gaza, resigned at this point.) If opponents were using salami tactics, trying by one vote after another to defeat Sharon, he was still winning these votes. But around the corner was an event, the London Conference on March 1, that was giving Sharon fits. Tony Blair organized this conference ostensibly to help move the PA forward toward reform and statehood. As I saw it, the conference would be marginally helpful to the Palestinians, at least in keeping up a sense of momentum, but was mostly helpful to Blair. He was under attack in the United Kingdom for being too close to Bush and too close to Israel and for backing Sharon's disengagement plan. This conference would showcase his pro-Palestinian side, and the Israelis, by agreement, would not even be present: It was all about the PA, not about Israeli-Palestinian relations. That focus is what annoyed Sharon and his crew. To them, Abbas was so far doing nothing and risking nothing, while Sharon was risking his party and his political career – and Europe was applauding Abbas. So was the United States because Rice would be present at the conference. And in his first trip to Europe since beginning his second term, Bush had spoken in Brussels on February 21 about the London Conference:

Next month in London, Prime Minister Blair will host a conference to help the Palestinian people build the democratic institutions of their state. President Abbas has the opportunity to put forward a strategy of reform which can and will gain support from the international community, including financial support. I hope he will seize the moment. I've asked Secretary Rice to attend the conference and to convey America's strong support for the Palestinian people as they build a democratic state.

For the first time since before the June 24 speech two and a half years earlier, the Israelis were in a sour mood about something we were doing. They noted carefully that Bush had spoken in Brussels the day after the Israeli cabinet had approved disengagement but had remained silent about that vote. Where were the thanks and the encouragement for them, they asked.

Still, things were moving. The PA took control of Jericho on March 16 and of Tulkarm on March 21, in accordance with an Israel-PA agreement giving it control of five West Bank towns. Of greater importance was an agreement between Fatah and Hamas, announced in Cairo. Hamas agreed to a truce – a suspension of attacks on Israel – and to participation in the forthcoming parliamentary elections in July, after boycotting elections for 10 years. A mixed electoral system was to be implemented, with half of the seats chosen by districts and half from national lists of candidates. To a degree we did not appreciate at that moment, Abbas was deciding that he wanted Hamas in, not out; that whatever his rhetoric in private with us about confronting Hamas, about having to take them on in the end, he was avoiding any such action as well as the Roadmap requirement to "dismantle terrorist organizations."

Who Runs Palestine, and the Blue Curtain

The announcement about the Palestinian elections spurred no real debate at that point in Washington, although there were voices – to become louder later – challenging the right of Hamas to participate. Ken Wollack, head of the National Democratic Institute (NDI) for International Affairs, the Democratic Party's democracy-promotion arm, shook his head and warned us. NDI had many programs in the Palestinian Territories, as in countries throughout the world, aimed at helping build modern democratic political parties. This would be a terrible precedent, he argued, with ramifications far beyond Palestine; people must be forced to give up their guns before they can compete in elections, not be permitted to shoot their way to political power. But the argument was theoretical at that point; it did not much engage the attention of the administration's top ranks at the time. And there were counterarguments, pragmatic if not theoretical ones. Fatah expected to win, and its victory would have the same impact as Abbas's own victory in the presidential election: As that success had legitimized his personal leadership, so would the electoral victory over Hamas legitimize Fatah's own continuing leadership after Arafat's death. To exclude Hamas, we heard over and over again from Palestinians, would mean that the election not only would not serve to legitimize the new Palestinian leadership but would also actually serve to *de*-legitimize it. Without Hamas, the election would be like those in Syria or Egypt or elsewhere in the Arab world, in which "republics" functioned without permitting opposition parties to challenge the rulers. Such an election would prove that all the fine words about democracy were phony.

I returned yet again to the region, this time with the new assistant secretary of state for the Near East, David Welch, who had just ended his tour as ambassador to Egypt; Bill Burns was off to Moscow to serve in his new position as ambassador there. David and I heard the same Israeli complaints that Abbas was not acting against terrorist groups, and now we heard – for the first time – Israeli officials complain that Hamas should not be permitted to field candidates in the July elections. Tzipi Livni, already a minister in Sharon's cabinet, was adamant then and later: How could a terrorist group be allowed to keep all its arms and affirm its commitment to the armed struggle and still be permitted to run candidates? In earlier meetings in Washington, she had told us that "she had looked at the constitutions of dozens of countries and had studied the transition to power in Northern Ireland, Afghanistan, and other hot spots. Armed militias were always required to give up their arms before they could participate in the political process."[8] Moreover, the Oslo Interim Agreement, Weissglas said when we sat with him, prohibited the involvement of groups like Hamas: "The nomination of any candidates, parties or coalitions will be refused, and such nomination or registration once made will be canceled, if such candidates, parties or coalitions: (1) commit or advocate racism; or (2) pursue the implementation of their aims by unlawful or non-democratic means."⁹ Everyone knew this meant Hamas, the Israelis told us. Yet Weissglas told us that the Palestinian elections might be postponed anyway. He was more concerned about the forthcoming Sharon visit to Crawford. Look, he said, for leaving Gaza and those little settlements in the West Bank, we get zero from the Palestinians. The only compensation is from you, from the president, in those words he spoke on April 14 last year. Those words are our only tool to beat the opposition, he said. So any deviation from them in Crawford will be caught by the Israeli press and used against Sharon by his opponents. There must, there must, be a faithful repetition of the exact words of the April letter. I promised to relay this concern to Hadley and could already see the frowns of the speechwriters as we told them to lay off the word-smithing and just repeat the old language again.

When we met with the Palestinians, their real concern was the elections, then only four months away: There was a division in the leadership over whether they were ready for them. Abbas and Qurie said they wanted to go forward and could be ready and that Fatah could win. Dahlan disagreed, arguing that the timing is bad and they should be postponed. Welch wondered about holding elections just one month before the Israeli pullout from Gaza, with its likely *sturm und drang*. Would postponement be better? Privately, other Palestinians told us that Fatah was divided and unprepared and that postponement was essential to enable them to get their act together. My post-trip memo to Hadley said things were not as good as they looked on the surface. Abbas was certainly not confronting terrorism; there was zero preparation for the withdrawal of the Israelis from Gaza; and there was no reform in the Fatah party whatsoever, in preparation for the elections.

In fact, there was never much in the way of reform in Fatah – not then, not at any point during Bush's time in office, and not later. At one level this was understandable: When had a ruling party in any Arab country democratized itself and allowed opponents to mount a real challenge? In Tunisia, Egypt, Algeria, and Syria, ruling parties ruled and fixed elections. The party was run by the president and was an arm of the government, not a democratic party as that was understood in the West, competing for power against others and alternating in power with them. The Palestinians had leapt ahead with their January 2005 presidential election, which by regional standards had been remarkably fair, and Abbas had only won 62% of the vote. But that was easy compared to parliamentary elections, which required selection of candidates and mobilization of support for them all across Gaza and the West Bank. Selection of candidates meant rejection of others and here, Fatah was hopeless; seniority, corruption, and connections won out, as they always had, and there was little understanding of what democratic, competitive politics meant.

That year we sent an experienced political hand from the administration to help out with the elections, and he came back shaking his head at the impossibility of the task. He felt they barely understood what he was talking about. He did achieve one victory: In the hall where press conferences were held, the backdrop to the podiums was a dirty white wall with a giant photo of Arafat. Not the image they wanted to project, he suggested, so he persuaded them to move the Arafat photo higher up – out of camera range when the lens was focused on a speaker – and to put in a richly colored blue curtain behind the speakers. Year after year I would return to Ramallah and sit in that hall listening to Abbas and Rice and others address the press and think ruefully that all we had achieved by way of "Fatah reform" was that blue curtain.

Years later, I asked Jake Walles, who had been our consul general in Jerusalem throughout the Bush second term, why Fatah reform had been so difficult. "You know," he answered, "there was a lot of resistance within Fatah to any reform." He continued,

Clearly the old guard didn't want to give up; that was one factor.... And Abu Mazen, I think, his heart was with the young guard and the "reformers" but he also wasn't prepared to have a knock down/drag out with the old guard who were part of his generation; they shared experiences and things like that. It wasn't his personality to do it. I'm not sure he had the power to do it – just to come in and say, "That's it. You guys are done." So that's one factor.

Second, I don't think we as outsiders ever really were in a position to do much within Fatah. I remember this very early from my time as Consul General, beginning of the second term of the Bush administration – we were trying through NDI in particular. There were programs, but I never felt the programs were very effective. Part of it was because NDI's approach was fairly technical: organizing seminars on how you market ideas, and a big project in computerizing the Fatah rolls, which [is] a mechanical thing. It doesn't change the culture of the organization.... I don't think we ever really were in a position where we could, in a practical way, affect very much of what was going on.[10]

At that time, we did not contemplate a more radical approach: turning against Fatah. Why, one might ask, was it good policy to "save Fatah?" The president himself had doubts that Abbas was a strong enough leader to take the Palestinians to the promised land of statehood. The rest of Fatah was worse: It remained the party Arafat had built. It was already becoming clear to us that the kind of modern, reformist leadership we wanted was not to be found within that party, and at least in theory we could have turned to other figures a generation younger than the Abus who had been Arafat's cronies – Fayyad, who was effective as finance minister, and Mustafa Barghouti, who had gotten 20% of the vote running against Abbas for president, are two examples – and supported an effort to create a new party. But that was easier said than done, considering personal rivalries and the lack of resources (while we gave aid to the PA, we gave none to Fatah as a party and to its campaign coffers, nor could we have given any to competing parties). The struggle for power seemed to be between Fatah, now led by "moderates" like Abbas, and Hamas plus the other terrorist and Islamist organizations. What is more, despite the very high literacy rate among Palestinians, their political culture glorified violence.

A new generation of technocrats was unlikely to compete successfully against men who had spent years in Israeli jails for their actions in the "resistance." It was an irony that always made me smile ruefully that the older generation (of both professionals and of Fatah leaders) spoke English well, while that younger generation of Fatah fighters often spoke excellent Hebrew, learned during years in Israeli jails. Moreover, the younger generation of competent technocrats and professionals was far better represented among PA leaders than in the Fatah party ranks.

This situation left us in 2005, and leaves the United States still, confronting the bizarre division of power and responsibility among the Palestinians. Negotiations with Israel are conducted by the PLO, which Israel and the United States recognized after the Madrid Conference in 1991 as the party with whom Israel would negotiate peace – and which had been designated in 1974 by the Arab League as the "sole legitimate representative of the Palestinian people." The West Bank (and, until the Hamas coup in 2007, Gaza) is governed by the Palestinian Authority, formed under the Oslo Accords in 1994. The Fatah Party was formed, by Arafat among others, in 1954 and by the late 1960s was the most powerful faction in the PLO. Arafat headed all three – PA, PLO, and Fatah – but after his death, the differences among the three organizations became consequential. The United States was giving aid to the PA but none to Fatah as a party. Israel was negotiating with the PLO, not with Fatah or the PA. While under Fayyad, first as finance minister and later as prime minister, PA official structures were beginning real reforms, Fatah remained a 1950s Arab political movement struggling in the face of competitive elections. We often wondered why Fatah did not capitalize on Fayyad's successes and claim them as its own – good government, less corruption, economic progress: Was this not the best platform? Yet that was a very Western viewpoint, we soon saw, for the Fatah pols hated Fayyad; he stood for everything they viewed as a threat, not least this business about fighting corruption. And what did good government mean, except that they and their relatives and their cronies could no longer get well-paid government jobs in the PA ranks?

We understood all of this better as the months and years went by, but in the spring of 2005, just months after Arafat's death and Abbas's election, we did not understand it. We were able to work with the PA, and over time its finances, its ministries, and even its security forces showed real change, but Fatah was immune to U.S. efforts. We did not then foresee what that resistance to change would mean when parliamentary elections were finally held.

Sharon in Crawford: "Sometimes God Helps"

In April, Ariel Sharon visited the president's ranch. The ranch was not so easy to get to if you were not president of the United States, and especially if you set out from Israel. Sharon's plane had had to stop for refueling, and it then landed in Waco on April 10, where Hadley, Rice, and I joined Sharon for dinner to prepare for the next day's meeting with the president. Sharon had had a rotten flight and had a bad cold. He should probably have gone right to bed; after all, he was 77 years old. He was irritable, he felt we did not appreciate the depth of the divisions inside Likud over disengagement, and some comments by Rice about settlement expansion set him off. Usually very gracious and even courtly with Rice, this time he literally pounded the flimsy hotel dining table as he lectured her:

People in Israel don't understand, for example, why we can't build in Gush Etzion, an old community where everyone was killed in the 1948 War.[11] NEVER will this area be handed to the Palestinians. NEVER. I am not going to negotiate this area. As to negotiations under the roadmap: something must come before. Israel will never agree to withdraw pursued by terrorists. Economic and social and humanitarian steps for the Palestinians should be taken, but they want negotiations under the roadmap. I am not going to do it. We are not in the roadmap, but the pre-roadmap. The roadmap will not start as long as there is terror. I am not going to withdraw pursued by terror. The basic problem is that the Arabs have not recognized the basic right of the Jewish people to a homeland. The peace agreement with Egypt is with the leaders, not the people; many organized groups boycott us. Jordan, we are under boycott there too. How do we solve this? Only by education. But what they are teaching children about us? For real peace, you need education. Their maps still show no Israel. But on the major blocs, the Palestinians will NEVER be able to come there – NEVER; they already destroyed it one time, and murdered hundreds.

Once Sharon had gotten all this off his chest and gotten a night's sleep, the meeting with the president the next day went smoothly. Bush, forewarned, began by congratulating Sharon for the political courage and leadership he was showing. He acknowledged that since Aqaba he had not seen the commitment and leadership he expected from Abbas, but told Sharon we must all help him: If he fails we all fail, and if he succeeds we all do. Sharon answered that he remained committed to peace, and then to retirement back at his farm. He noted that since the two men had met a year before, Bush had been reelected and Arafat had died. Recalling how many times he had told Sharon not to harm Arafat, Bush thanked him for not being the reason why he's gone. Sharon quickly replied, "Sometimes God helps!" And he spoke with hope. Bush had eliminated Saddam Hussein and changed Iraq. Lebanon was changing. People were starting to speak about democracy. I am optimistic, said Sharon. Turning to disengagement, he reiterated his commitment to see it through and detailed the many complications – political and practical – of moving thousands of people out of their homes.

Conversations with the President were never stilted and formalistic, even with leaders who tried to stick to a script. So Bush reacted to Sharon's comments by asking the question he had posed back in April at the White House: How did Sharon come to his decision to leave Gaza? I support it, the president said; it's a good decision, but what was the logic behind it?

We had no negotiating partner in Arafat, Sharon replied, but it was dangerous not to try to move forward, and I saw that Gaza disengagement could pave the way to the Roadmap. Some people advised me to "destroy the PA." Some said "do nothing." Some said, "You have a solid majority, wait until after new elections." I didn't want to wait, and I didn't want other people, even you with all the problems you have, to press me. It was better to take steps ourselves; it was not right to sit and do nothing. I rose through the ranks from private in the IDF, and saw my best friends killed in wars; I fought in all our wars, was badly injured twice, and saw the horrors of war. The only condition for peace is quiet. I am ready for painful compromises but not without security. I greatly appreciate that you always understood that there can be no compromises with terror. Maybe my generation, that saw the great victories and defeats, could take these responsibilities on our shoulders. And I had no partner when Arafat was alive, but I saw we had to make an effort, unilaterally, to relocate – maybe to help move forward.

If this was just a line it was a good one, but the president did not think it was just a line and I fully agreed with him. When he had so controversially said Sharon is a man of peace, he had been right; he had seen through to the Sharon that lay under the years of abuse and vilification as some kind of warmonger. He had seen the Sharon whom Hadley and I had seen when we sat with him for hours in his living room in Jerusalem: one of the last leaders from the founding generation, who had spent his life at war and wanted peace. And he believed that his generation, and he personally, had a responsibility to try to get peace.

Sharon and the president talked about Gaza for some time. Bush clearly saw Gaza as a start, a precedent for disengagement in the West Bank and further moves toward a peace settlement. But he told Sharon he saw the other side of that coin too. If this experiment failed, if the Palestinians could not rule Gaza, Sharon would have proved to the world that moving forward in the West Bank was not possible. And it would have proved that to us as well: The United States was not interested in moving toward any final status agreement if there is no progress in Gaza, Bush told Sharon. Later, in 2007 and 2008, that position would change: Despite disaster in Gaza, a complete PA failure, and a Hamas takeover, the Bush administration did indeed push hard for final status talks. But by then Sharon was gone from power and could not have recalled the comment made in April 2005 at the ranch.

After the visit to Crawford, Sharon came to Washington, where he told Vice President Cheney that the Palestinian elections were on his mind. He was strongly opposed to allowing Hamas (and others, like Palestinian Islamic Jihad [PIJ]) to participate. If they win something, how can we then go forward?, he asked. He suggested postponing the PLC elections because they could very well weaken Abbas and "already he is not Samson." Fatah is not yet strong enough to take on Hamas in elections, Weissglas added.

On April 19, Welch and I returned to Jerusalem and Ramallah, and Abbas told us he had made no final decision about the elections. One issue was the date; another, arising again, was whether to have people run in constituencies, as in the United States, or to have a national poll and proportional representation of the winning percentages. Perhaps he would go for a mix of the two, he said. As to Gaza, we asked how coordination between Israel and the PA was going; the Israeli withdrawal was only four months away. There was not much coordination, we were told, but things were quiet. That's because we're not attacking Hamas, the Palestinians explained, and Hamas too wants the quiet; if we listened to the Israelis and their demand for "action against terror," that would be the end of the quiet.

Pep Talks

When I saw Sharon on April 20 in his office in Jerusalem, he was in an unhappy mood, in part because of American statements criticizing new construction in settlements. Whenever there was an announcement of new construction from Jerusalem, it was followed by one in Washington, repeating that the Roadmap required a freeze on construction and that new construction was not helpful, not constructive, troubling (a favorite State Department term), or words to that effect. For Sharon, the problem was that he had described the Bush letter of April 14, 2004, as giving Israel the major settlement blocks. That was the compensation, the only compensation, for wrenching nearly eight thousand Israelis from their homes in Gaza and moving out of the four settlements in the West Bank. So how was it that the Americans – in Washington and in Israel, where he especially disliked U.S. Ambassador Daniel Kurtzer, and (rightly) saw him as a political enemy – were criticizing every time a wheelbarrow moved in one of the major blocks that Israel would clearly keep?

You are causing me more and more problems daily, Sharon told me, and if elections were held now, I would lose. I ask that you not make daily announcements. Do you understand the situation here? Now only 50% believe what the president said about the major blocks. If this criticism continues, I won't be able to do Gaza disengagement. I want you to understand: If there were elections now, primaries in Likud, I would lose. Maybe the U.S. criticism is said to please the Arabs but it endangers Gaza disengagement. Leave me alone for several months now. I understand your position; do you understand mine? Leave it quietly now. I am on the edge of my ability to implement. If there is a vote of no confidence I have to have an election, and I am not going to win. Let me finish this burden. If I don't do it, it will not be implemented. Sharon spoke in exasperation, not anger, and he viewed me as an ally against enemies he and the president shared. My trip report to Hadley said Sharon was beleaguered and wondered if we understood how close to failing he was.

President Abbas came to visit Washington the following month, on May 26, and the schedule of these visits is a reminder of President Bush's continuing involvement and interest. That this was not the only issue on his plate would be a laughable understatement even considering only Iraq and Afghanistan, but it was never off his plate. Sharon and Abbas visited repeatedly, as did other Arab, Muslim, and European leaders with all of whom he discussed Israeli-Palestinian affairs at length. On top of that were frequent telephone calls to leaders like President Mubarak, the kings of Jordan and Saudi Arabia, and European heads of government. I was in the Oval Office for very many of those calls to the

Europeans – to Merkel and Blair and even Putin – even though my portfolio was the "Near East and North Africa," because so often the Middle East was on the agenda. It is fair to say that hardly a day went by when Israeli and Palestinian issues were not discussed with the president.

During the Abbas visit, the president announced that we would give $50 million in cash to the PA. This was a remarkable gesture of faith in the new, post-Arafat PA leadership because we had never given the PA budgetary support but had only given aid indirectly, through the United Nations or other groups. In theory, these funds were being given now to help them prepare for the Gaza disengagement and their coming complete control over Gaza. I had had a personal role in making this support possible. House Majority Leader Tom DeLay had strong doubts about handing this cash over, and I was sent up to see and reassure him, and it worked: If I trusted that Fayyad would be sure the money was not stolen or misspent, he would go along. (It turned out that hardly any of the money was spent at all. In 2006, when events led us to demand that any unspent portions be returned, we got back more than three-quarters of the money.)

In addition to cash, the president gave Abbas some public support, reacting to Palestinian complaints that the April 14, 2004, letter to Sharon had seemed to go too far. "Changes to the 1949 armistice lines must be mutually agreed to," he said, and a two-state solution meant "contiguity of the West Bank" for a "state of scattered territories will not work."[12]

During their private meetings, the president gave Abbas what can only be described as a pep talk. I'll help all I can, he said, but you have to make the hard choices. I can't make them for you. I'll do what I can but the tough decisions are yours. You can do all of this, I believe this will work, but you've got to do the hard things. Gaza was the test case: Get it right and you'll persuade the whole world, and I'll persuade the Israelis, that you can build a peaceful democracy in Palestine. Bush also made it clear that he admired Sharon, who was driving forward against all odds and at the cost of his own party's support.

The president also told Abbas that Secretary Rice was totally committed to achieving Palestinian statehood. In fact, he said, when I asked her to be secretary of state, she told me she would only do it if I would stay focused on this issue. That was the only time I ever heard the president confirm a rumor that floated constantly at State and NSC: that Rice had put this marker down when she agreed to stay on another four years and move to the State Department. In her memoir, Condi confirms this: When the president offered her the State Department job, the only substantive policy issue she raised was the Middle East. She told the president that "we need to get an agreement and establish a Palestinian state."[13] Events certainly did not contradict this commitment: In fact, as the years of the second term went by, much to my chagrin, Hadley's Fall 2004 claim that the White House is always in charge of Middle East policy seemed increasingly disputable.

But in the spring and summer of 2005, there were two issues to watch and on those, the entire Bush team saw eye to eye: getting Gaza disengagement done and moving to Palestinian elections. On the latter, Abbas on June 18 announced a postponement. We were not shocked by the decision, given previous discussions, nor were we alarmed by the delay. One could make a good argument that holding them in the middle of disengagement was foolish and that a delay of a few months was sensible; one could also argue that the departure of the Israelis would help Fatah, which would claim credit – and anyway would be ruling Gaza. Perhaps this all would give Fatah leaders greater confidence that they would win the elections.

The Greenhouse Effect

Meanwhile, the date of disengagement came closer. Actual Israeli-Palestinian cooperation was very limited but not nonexistent. There was much discussion of practical issues: Would the settlement housing be destroyed or left standing? If destroyed, would the Israelis remove the rubble? What about the synagogues that would be left behind? What would become of any light industrial buildings or greenhouses? The story of the greenhouses would later come to characterize, for many Israelis and Americans, the tragic situation in Gaza. The approximately 1,000 acres of crops and greenhouses were worked on by 3,600 people, the vast majority of them Palestinians, and they earned tens of millions of dollars. The PA had decided the settlement housing should be destroyed because it could not think of any fair and politically acceptable way to allocate these homes should they be left intact. But it was not sensible to destroy the greenhouses because they provided employment and income and should be a building block of Gaza's future agro-industry. The settlers demanded compensation; why should they simply walk away from what they had built and have people they viewed as terrorists take it over, they asked. They preferred to destroy it all, unless compensation was paid. But the PA leaders told us they could not pay; it was politically impossible to "reward" the settlers this way.

Into this void stepped James D. Wolfensohn, who had left the presidency of the World Bank at the end of March and become the Quartet's Special Envoy for Gaza Disengagement. Wolfensohn raised the $14 million that was needed, contributing a half-million dollars himself and raising much of the rest from American Jews. The theory of his Quartet appointment was that Wolfensohn knew about development and could help the Palestinians turn Gaza into a productive economy, but his record at the World Bank gave few hints of this. A well-financed public relations effort had had a great deal to do with Wolfensohn's reputation; what solid advice he could offer, when not accompanied by scores of flacks and real economists, was unclear. What was clear from the outset was that he viewed this minor role, helping Gaza disengagement, as beneath him; it was simply a means of continuing his hobnobbing with world leaders despite having left the World Bank job. Wolfensohn had asked for far more: "The terms of reference originally proposed would have given Wolfensohn a writ, essentially covering the entire peace process, much wider than the narrower one that emerged," wrote Alvaro de Soto, the UN's under secretary general handling the Middle East peace process. Nevertheless, his appointment meant that when the Quartet Principals – Rice, Kofi Annan, EU leaders, and Russian foreign minister Lavrov – met, Wolfensohn had a reason to join them; he had a reason to be chatting on the phone with Putin or Blair or coming to see George Bush. Wolfensohn envisioned that, after the minor matter of Gaza was successfully behind him, he would be the leader of efforts at a peace deal; as de Soto put it, "Wolfensohn did little to hide his aspiration to broaden his mandate," and it seemed to me he could see his Nobel Peace Prize glimmering in the distance.[14] I had been in Washington for 30 years and had never met anyone with a larger ego.

Rice returned to the region yet again in June and met with the same Sharon I had left in April: beleaguered. The Palestinian elections were postponed, but no decision had been made on excluding Hamas, he said; they should not be allowed to field candidates. The PA leaders are doing nothing against terror. Fatah's decline is continuing. Would Gaza disengagement go smoothly? Sharon was assembling a huge force of Israeli police and IDF troops to make sure it did, and to handle possible resistance – including possible violent resistance – by settlers and their supporters and to react if there were acts of terrorism. I will not run away under fire, he told us; the terrorists could still force us to abort all the plans. Gen. Amos Gilad, chief of planning for the IDF, told us that "we live on luck."

Rice's message to Abbas in our subsequent meeting with him was firm: Get ready to take action. Deploy forces in Gaza right after disengagement, in serious numbers. Take control. Abbas's reply was typical: We understand fully what we are up against, but now is not the time to act. The IDF should not make things worse; we all have to wait.

There were more and more accusations in Israel, in June and July, that Sharon was holding the IDF back from acting against terrorists because he did not want to upset his disengagement plans. Condi asked me to call Abbas, which I did on July 17, to repeat what she had told him in June; I got the same answer she had. But in the course of July, we began to see some real confrontations between PA forces and Hamas, which gave hope to us and the Israelis that something better was around the corner. Perhaps when the Israelis were out of the way, the PA would assert itself in Gaza, as Dahlan had long been promising.

Rice traveled to the Mideast again in July. The greenhouse deal was being worked out, though endless complications forced it to be recast every week. The greater worry was what we heard from Dahlan this time. All of a sudden he told us he had only 2,000 men in Gaza, or at least only 2,000 reliable ones. Don't be misled by the impression we have created that the PA is strong: Hamas and Palestinian Islamic Jihad and the gangs are stronger. This was not what we had been hearing from him and his colleagues for the previous months, and we wondered if finally he was telling the truth or merely understating his situation in an effort to gild the coming victory as a greater triumph. Again during this trip, there were lengthy discussions of the role of Hamas in elections and also a return to discussion of the Philadelphi Strip. Israel had never announced its final decision: stay or leave? Weissglas told us privately that Sharon wanted to get out, to leave Gaza fully, and was weighing the pros and cons of leaving the Philadelphi Strip.

When we met with Sharon, he told us he would go through with disengagement, even under fire. He would fire back, harshly, with artillery, but the withdrawal would happen. And he had made a decision about Philadelphi: He would leave. But, he added, Gaza would not be the first step but the last one we can take, if the PA did not then act in Gaza against Hamas and the others and reform what he called the "security/terror organizations" of the PA itself. As to Hamas's participation in the elections, he was adamant. I reject it totally, he said; we are totally against it. Why? Once they participate in elections, they won't be regarded as a terrorist organization any more. An armed terrorist group can't be part of a democratic system, he warned Rice. I've lost my majority, Sharon concluded, and am just maneuvering now. I am walking on eggshells, he told Rice with a smile, and I am too heavy to do that.

The following day we went down to his farm in the northern Negev – close enough to Gaza to be hit occasionally by rockets – for a late breakfast. By Israeli standards, this was a large farm, roughly 1,000 acres; by Texas standards, Bush's 1,500-acre Crawford ranch was minuscule. Sharon gave Rice a tour of the citrus and vegetable fields and showed her the flocks of sheep, and then we sat down. Sharon sat silently for a while, as he often did, eating huge amounts of food while he listened to the conversation. Several of the Israelis were criticizing the Palestinians and their leaders harshly: their actions, their political culture, their history. Eventually, Sharon jumped in and said, I am going to defend the Palestinians. After a moment of shocked silence at that development, Weissglas, who joked with Sharon as no one else could, looked across to Rice and said, "I hear the footsteps of the Messiah." Sharon continued, saying that I have known the Palestinians my whole life. I was raised with them here. Of all the Arabs, the Palestinians are the most talented, and they have the best sense of humor. But, he said, there are two problems: their desire to murder and their taste for Jewish blood, and their treacherous ingratitude. This comment again was met with dead silence for a moment, until Weissglas drily noted, "And remember, that is the defense." It was an extraordinary moment because we had been discussing practical details of the Gaza withdrawal and PA takeover for most of the meal. We had been arguing about what exactly the PA security forces were doing, and not doing, and how to force them and/or help them to do more. But here was a remarkable glimpse of the layers underneath, at what Sharon really thought he was dealing with. He wanted peace, he was taking enormous political risks for peace, but it was clear as I thought about the remark over and over that to him the best that could be hoped for was an armed peace. Whatever dreams others may have had about a new Middle East, Sharon saw his work as defending Jews from people who would murder them, as they had been murdered throughout history. Now Jews had a state and they could and would defend themselves, and he would create new lines and new separations that would, he hoped, make that perpetual task far easier.

Would the PA be able to rule Gaza; did they have the forces? Dahlan and others now claimed they would soon have 5,000 men there and were busily organizing them. General Ward scoffed at this claim, as did the Israelis. But on August 7, a week before disengagement was scheduled to commence, the final Israeli cabinet approval was secured. From the beginning of 2004, Sharon had faced test after test in his cabinet and the Knesset and had plowed forward; this was the last vote. The repeated voting had been designed partly to allow opponents of disengagement to remain in the cabinet while telling supporters they would resign in the end. That is what happened: the finance minister, Benjamin Netanyahu, resigned in protest. It was widely thought that Netanyahu would soon challenge Sharon for the leadership of Likud, where it was clear that despite Sharon's personal popularity, a majority opposed his Gaza plan.

"I Need Support and Understanding"

I was back in Israel, alone this time, in August, and saw Weissglas and Sharon. Dubi repeated previous Sharon themes: Look at what Sharon has gone through, and look at the credit he is getting: nothing. He told Israelis that the compensation for getting out was the April 14 letter, and its statements about Israel keeping the major settlement blocks. Yet every time someone moves a bulldozer, Ambassador Kurtzer condemns it. Tell him to stop, to keep quiet, or Sharon is finished. When I saw Sharon alone on August 11 a few days before the withdrawal, he looked tired and pale. That was the first time I had ever been struck by his physical condition; he looked crummy, I thought. Weissglas ushered me into the prime minister's office – small and plain in comparison to the Oval Office or the digs at the Elysée in Paris or Number 10 Downing Street in London. Sharon sat behind his desk, a wall of books in Hebrew and English behind him, facing his guests. On the wall on his right were just two photos: one of David Ben-Gurion and one of Yitzhak Rabin.

The political situation is very complicated, he said, and his main problem was that it appeared Israel was getting nothing for leaving Gaza and that therefore he had lied. He had said Israel could keep the major blocks, but every time a shovel was lifted in them, the United States attacked it. He delivered the following soliloquy:

I have lost my majority in the polls for withdrawing from Gaza, and there are calls for early primaries in Likud. I am behind in all the polls 10–15% and it's hard to bridge so large a gap. I'm in a real minority in the Likud Central Committee. You in the US have tended to understate the political problems I am facing. You relied on me to solve them, but you have not fully understood the challenge. I could succeed in withdrawing from Gaza and still lose my post as prime minister. If that happens, starting on the roadmap, the second phase, is gone.

How am I going to overcome all this? I need support and understanding. I reached an agreement with President Bush, the April 14th letter, but now people are saying there are no commitments at all in that letter and that I was lying about the major blocs. People don't believe something changed, because all settlements are treated the same. I have serious problems now. I could lose it. That would be the end of plans. What I need urgently is to make the distinction between the major blocs and the rest. Elliott, I tell you as a friend: if I can't speak about some construction in the major blocs I don't think I'll be in power in three months. This is used against me daily. I must have this distinction. It's urgent. Because I don't have anything to show that this was done.

It is not sensible to use the construction zones rule for a remote little settlement, and the major blocs. I am not speaking about major construction, but small scale – but zero cannot be the Israeli government's position. That means that the Bush letter means no construction, and no future. The current rules are impossible politically. The understandings with the US, the letter, have led to a worse situation not better. President Bush is a politician. I need his immediate support. What is said is that consideration for withdrawing from Gaza does not exist. That's a strong complaint. Bibi says it – that we did Gaza for nothing, that Sharon has not got the major blocs. The Likud primary is mid-November. The Central Committee will meet in mid-September unless I can avoid it. I need support before the primary. I don't plan any major construction; I agree to limits. The problem is credibility. That's how I won in the past, and that's what's attacked here. The agreements with the US will have undermined us because there is no ideological compensation perceived.

These remarks and many others like them contradict those who said, in later years, that there was never any settlement agreement between Israel and the United States. Sharon perceived himself to be under constraints. In fact, the great expansion of Israeli settlements came under Labor governments, not under Sharon. Whether Sharon needed exactly the relief he asked for here – the ability to build anywhere in the major blocks, even outside the existing construction zones – is a different matter. No doubt it would have made life easier for him, but the Israelis never demonstrated to us that there was inadequate space in and near already built-up areas to accommodate housing demand in the major blocks. It seemed to me that we could help him by simply not taking an antagonistic position, by not looking for fights over construction in the major blocks. On this I agreed with Sharon and with his criticism of our ambassador, Dan Kurtzer, who was clearly in the Labor Party camp and seemed to go out of his way to make trouble for Sharon.

And Sharon seemed to me correct: There was an anomaly in the U.S. position. We had said that Israel would, realistically, be keeping the major blocks. But we were treating construction in the major blocks we all knew Israel would keep exactly as we treated construction in small settlements beyond the security fence that would become part of the eventual Palestine. The explanation for the anomaly was simple enough: First, there were no agreed borders, so it was not agreed which blocks exactly were "the major blocks Israel would keep." Second, even if there were agreed-on borders, Israel would win the unlimited right to build only when a final agreement with the Palestinians was signed; it was one of the rewards for reaching a final status agreement.

Weissglas proposed a different deal. Our agreement on settlements allowed Israel to build within the construction line in every existing settlement. What if Sharon said he would impose a freeze on all construction in settlements beyond the fence line, in return for the ability to build without these limitations in the major blocks? This would help Sharon politically, he said, by strengthening his argument that he had really won something in return for getting out of Gaza; this was the ideological compensation of which Sharon often spoke. Like the inclusion of four small West Bank settlements in disengagement, Dubi argued, such a freeze beyond the fence would signal to Palestinians that Sharon would take further steps after Gaza; it would signal that Israel was coming to see the area beyond the fence as Palestine. I had an additional thought: What if Israel adopted a Gaza-style compensation law for the areas beyond the fence, thereby encouraging settlers to move west? Surely many thousands would, again showing Israel's ultimate intentions.

Hadley rejected the deal, again on the ground that all of this had to await a final status agreement. To me it seemed a lost opportunity. In Israel, settlers in the major blocks are viewed as suburbanites, who might well live in the major cities if they could afford it. Those who live, for example, in Ma'ale Adumim, now a town of 40,000 from which it takes 15 minutes to get to downtown Jerusalem, are hardly viewed as settlers at all. Settlers beyond the fence have far less popular appeal. If we supported Sharon in dividing them, freezing beyond the fence only, I thought we would be helping Sharon build a majority for future West Bank disengagement. Instead, we made efforts to lower Kurtzer's volume and produce repeated statements of support for Sharon from the White House.

Gaza disengagement finally came to pass, beginning on August 15, 2006. Israeli police took the lead in evacuating the settlers, nearly eight thousand in Gaza and a few hundred in the West Bank, while the IDF stood guard. Settlers departed on August 15, and 16, and 17, and those who would not leave were removed forcibly. When protesters (many from Israel proper, not Gaza communities) gathered at synagogues in two Gaza settlements, the IDF stormed the synagogues and removed them too. By August 22, the last Israeli settlers were out of Gaza, and on the following day, they were out of those four West Bank settlements.

Israel's presence in Gaza was over. And so is this government, Weissglas told Rice on the phone as soldiers removed Israeli protesters. Now comes the struggle inside Likud, between Arik and Bibi. Please, he asked her, be careful what you say about settlement construction; don't treat every announcement as a *casus belli*.

Gaza up for Grabs

In Gaza, the early days after disengagement did not give much reason for hope that – as we had endlessly told the PA leaders – Gaza would be a model for the Palestinian state. Look, we had said, if you produce in Gaza a working model, some place that is peaceful and democratic, it will occur to just about all Israelis that it's time to move forward in the West Bank too; after all, what would there be to be afraid of if things are working out so well in Gaza? Make Gaza the model.

Instead, it quickly became a model of every Israeli fear, from disorder and terror to violence and misrule. The fate of the greenhouses, that experiment with benevolence and economic modernization, quickly pointed the way. Almost from the moment the Israelis pulled back, looting began. On September 13, the Associated Press reported that

Palestinians looted dozens of greenhouses on Tuesday, walking off with irrigation hoses, water pumps and plastic sheeting in a blow to fledgling efforts to reconstruct the Gaza Strip. . . . Palestinian police stood by helplessly Tuesday as looters carted off materials from greenhouses in several settlements, and commanders complained they did not have enough manpower to protect the prized assets. In some instances, there was no security and in others, police even joined the looters, witnesses said.[15]

What in retrospect was even more consequential was the beginning of the war between Hamas and the PA/Fatah forces. On September 7, Moussa Arafat, one of the most powerful Fatah officials and a cousin of Yasser Arafat, was murdered. The *Times* of London reported the event:

Internecine strife in Gaza claimed its most senior victim yesterday when militants assassinated one of the most hated security chiefs there in a brazen challenge to Mahmoud Abbas's Palestinian Authority. Witnesses told how a convoy of about twenty four-wheel-drive vehicles packed with masked gunmen arrived outside Moussa Arafat's home in Gaza City before dawn. They fought a 45-minute battle with his guards before leaving him dead in the street and kidnapping his son.[16]

This was a huge show of force against Fatah and the PA, and the PA did not respond. Although on paper it had the guns and the men to assert control of Gaza, and the timing was perfect – just as Israel left – those in charge failed to take charge. Whether one blames Abbas, or Dahlan, or the entire PA leadership, this event and the failure to respond to it sent a dire message: Control of Gaza was not certain. It was up for grabs.

Can Hamas Run?

We were watching Palestinian politics with equal attention. The postponed elections were now scheduled for January 2006. When the president had called Sharon on August 14, on the eve of the actual Gaza withdrawal, he had found Sharon voluble about the old question of Hamas and the elections. Hamas participation cannot happen, he said. In a democracy you cannot have armed organized parties participate in elections. We are totally against their participation in elections because everyone will say, "Look, Hamas participated in elections; they are democratic." It's a major mistake. Sharon then said he would refuse to help the elections take place if Hamas was in them, and he had the means to do that. Though now out of Gaza, in the West Bank, Israel could either cooperate on Election Day by making sure roads were open and mobility good for voters, poll watchers, and international observers – or if it refused to do so, elections would be far harder to pull off. In Jerusalem, Israel could allow Palestinian voters to participate in the voting or flatly forbid it. In the January 2005 presidential election, Israel had followed the precedent set in the 1996 Palestinian elections: It had permitted voting in five East Jerusalem post offices. By doing so, Israel maintained the fiction that Palestinians weren't "voting in Jerusalem" but rather mailing postal or absentee ballots from post offices there. Most Palestinians eligible to vote in PA elections did so outside Jerusalem, in the West Bank; only about 5,000 would likely vote in those post offices. Now Sharon was threatening to forbid that. That action might not reduce total voting much, but the symbolism was powerful and the PA might even call off the election entirely. It could not permit the appearance of relinquishing any part of its claim to Jerusalem, and agreeing that no Palestinian in Jerusalem was part of the Palestinian political system would be criticized as precisely such a symbolic act.

Why were not only Israelis but many Americans so strongly opposed to Hamas participation? It is worth recalling not only the terrorism Hamas practiced but also just what Hamas stood for, as embodied in the words of its Charter, adopted in 1988. Genocidal anti-Semitism and the elimination of the State of Israel are themes that permeate the document, as shown in the following:

The Hamas has been looking forward to implement Allah's promise whatever time it might take. The prophet, prayer and peace be upon him, said: The time will not come until Muslims will fight the Jews (and kill them); until the Jews hide behind rocks and trees, which will cry: O Muslim! there is a Jew hiding behind me, come on and kill him!

The Islamic Resistance Movement believes that the land of Palestine has been an Islamic Waqf throughout the generations and until the Day of Resurrection, no one can renounce it or part of it, or abandon it or part of it.

Initiatives, and so-called peaceful solutions and international conferences, are in contradiction to the principles of the Islamic Resistance Movement.

There is no solution to the Palestinian problem except by Jihad.

The enemies have been scheming for a long time.... They stood behind the French and the Communist Revolutions.... They also used the money to establish clandestine organizations which are spreading around the world, in order to destroy societies and carry out Zionist interests. Such organizations are: the Freemasons, Rotary Clubs, Lions Clubs, B'nai B'rith and the like.... They obtained the Balfour Declaration and established the League of Nations in order to rule the world by means of that organization. They also stood behind World War II, where they collected immense benefits from trading with war materials and prepared for the establishment of their state. They inspired the establishment of the United Nations and the Security Council to replace the League of Nations, in order to rule the world by their intermediary.

Their scheme has been laid out in the Protocols of the Elders of Zion.[17]

Over time, many efforts have been made to explain Hamas's conduct, but no guide is better than the Charter.

Later, in 2006 and afterward, questions were sometimes raised why Hamas did not bend in ways that might have put them in a better tactical position. But Hamas is neither a political party nor even a national liberation movement; it is a religious movement permeated by anti-Semitism that is not even disguised as anti-Zionism, and it is opposed entirely to the existence of the State of Israel. No doubt there are individuals in it whose motives are less pure, more personal, or more political and who would under pressure agree to amend its charter to eliminate the worst of the anti-Semitic filth. But when Israelis looked at the movement, they saw people who were killing Jews and explaining why it was right to do so. There was no "moderate strain" in Hamas arguing that terrorism is morally wrong, and those members who sometimes argued for a halt or reduction in terror made it clear that they sought only an armed truce and would never agree to the permanent existence of the Jewish State.

So the Israelis were opposed, all across their broad political spectrum, to allowing such groups to join in the PLC elections and run as if they were normal political parties. Sharon's view was not only the perspective of the Israeli right; the Israeli left also shared it. The left had championed the Oslo Accords, which had clearly and intentionally barred terrorist groups like Hamas from participating in elections until they disarmed. In September 2005, Yossi Beilin, a participant in Oslo and now head of the leftist Meretz Party, wrote, "There can be no doubt that participation by Hamas in elections held in the Palestinian Authority in January 2006 is a gross violation of the Israeli-Palestinian interim agreement.... That this military organization, appearing as a political party, is allowed to abuse democracy is a prize for terror and violence." This was not simply a matter of principle and of fealty to Oslo: Beilin and others on the left feared that if Hamas, PIJ, and similar extremist groups found a place in the PA political system, all hopes of future peace negotiations would be dashed. As Beilin put it, "Hamas' entrance into PA institutions is liable to cast a veto on future peace moves, without eliminating the option of violence."[18]

Sharon, long a pariah internationally, had a brief moment of popularity when he attended the UN General Assembly in mid-September 2005. He met not only with President Bush but also with dozens of foreign ministers and prime ministers who joined in congratulating him for the Gaza withdrawal. No doubt he enjoyed it, though what he thought privately of some of those now coming to pay court can only be imagined. A Quartet statement issued after it met on September 20 took into account the Israeli complaints that they never got any credit:

The Quartet recognizes and welcomes the successful conclusion of the Israeli withdrawal from Gaza and parts of the northern West Bank and the moment of opportunity that it brings to renew efforts on the Roadmap. The Quartet reiterates its belief that this brave and historic decision should open a new chapter on the path to peace in the region. It paid tribute to the political courage of Prime Minister Sharon and commends the Israeli government, its armed forces and its police for the smooth and professional execution of the operation. . . . On settlements, the Quartet welcomed the fact that, in areas covered by disengagement, Israel has gone beyond its obligations under the first phase of the Roadmap.[19]

"Diplomatic Prestidigitation"

At that same Quartet meeting, it had begun to shift its position and, more important, that of the Americans, on Hamas's participation in the elections. The Quartet statement quoted earlier also included this text:

The Quartet calls for an end to all violence and terror. While the PA leadership has condemned violence and has sought to encourage Palestinian groups who have engaged in terrorism to abandon this course and engage in the democratic process, the Quartet further urges the Palestinian Authority to maintain law and order and dismantle terrorist capabilities and infrastructure. . . . The rule of law through authorized security institutions is fundamental to democratic practice.

Yet what Secretary General Annan said to the press at the conclusion of the meeting was a bit different and went further in suggesting that Hamas might participate in elections:

The Quartet discussed armed groups and the political process. The Palestinian Authority leadership has condemned violence and has sought to encourage Palestinian groups who have engaged in terrorism to abandon this course and engage in the democratic process. Ultimately, those who want to be part of the political process should not engage in armed group or militia activities, for there is a fundamental contradiction between such activities and the building of a democratic State.[20]

This statement was the product of the usual Quartet negotiations and pre-negotiations. "Quartet envoys" – meaning David Welch and me for the United States, the EU envoy in Jerusalem, the United Nations special envoy for Middle East peace, some Russian functionary, plus assistants to all of us – would meet a day or two before the Quartet Principals met. That meeting could be anywhere: Jerusalem, Berlin, New York, Moscow, London; this was a floating crap game. We envoys would meet; then the Principals would meet and (usually) approve a statement we had drafted for them; then they would hold a press conference, where Kofi Annan would read the Quartet statement; and then the Principals would answer questions from the media. The Principals were the U.S. secretary of state, the Russian foreign minister, Kofi Annan (and later Ban Ki-moon), and a team of European officials – because Europe did not speak with one voice. Sometimes the formula seemed to be "the less influence you have, the more people you send to the meeting." But Quartet meetings did allow us to bind the Europeans to formulations and positions that were far more balanced than they would otherwise have taken, and they had the same effect for the Russians. If we were not exactly all united, at least we were not taking manifestly contradictory positions, undercutting each other and making American diplomacy that much harder. This was true most of the time; in those press conferences, it was not hard to see where the papering over differences had taken place and where apparent consensus was belied by very different underlying views. The Israelis hated the Quartet and refused to meet with it; their view was that American positions were constantly being watered down by the Quartet, and there was some truth in that.

This Quartet statement was at first glance odd: The sentence "The rule of law through authorized security institutions is fundamental to democratic practice" read like something out of a civics text. Sure, true, fine, but so what? What was the Quartet trying to say? Missing was a flat requirement that groups that "have engaged in terrorism" must stop doing so – must lay down their arms – before they can "engage in the democratic process." There had in fact been language to that effect in the draft Quartet Statement, but participants in the meeting knew that Abbas wanted Hamas to participate and believed elections would be illegitimate if they were prohibited from doing so. If the Quartet said that groups must disarm or at least announce they were abandoning terror before they could field candidates, would that not be undermining Abbas? Rice instructed David Welch to leave Kofi Annan's conference room, where we were meeting, and call Abbas. Welch reached him and got the Arabic equivalent of "Yikes" when Abbas heard the proposed wording. Don't put it in, he said, or people will think I don't want Hamas to participate.

UN Under Secretary General for the Middle East Alvaro de Soto described in his final report how Quartet principals decided to handle the touchy situation:

> [T]he Principals deliberated and, after consulting by telephone with Abu Mazen, agreed to a formula which consisted of Secretary-General Annan reading to the press . . . a sentence – not included in the written statement that was issued – in which the view was expressed that the forthcoming Palestinian legislative elections should [be] seen as a stage in Palestinian evolution toward democracy, and that the question of participation should be left to the Palestinians themselves, notwithstanding the "fundamental contradiction" between participation in elections and possession of militias. . . . Even accounting for the diplomatic prestidigitation, this was a far-reaching move by the Quartet, by which the Palestinians were given a pass on the requirement, spelled out in the first stage of the Roadmap, to disarm militias.[21]

In her memoir, Rice concludes that this equivocation had all been a mistake: "In retrospect, we should have insisted that every party disarm as a condition for participation in the vote."[22] We should have, and I wish now that I had protested more strongly back then. But at that time, in the usual postmeeting press conference, Rice went even further toward accommodating Abbas's view: "This is going to be a Palestinian process and I think we have to give the Palestinians some room for the evolution of their political process. We hope that the elections can go forward and that everyone will work to make those elections go forward."

The Israelis were getting the same message about the American view and were acquiescing to it. "In September 2005 at the UN, we had a meeting," Shalom Tourgeman explained, "Dubi and myself, and Condi, and Welch, in

New York, in which she said, 'This is the wish of the President' and we were forced to accept it. In New York we came to Sharon and we told him, 'Look, this is what was in the meeting,' and he said, 'Well, I'm not going to fight it. I mean, this is what the Americans want, and this is what the Palestinians want – I'm not going to fight it, though I think it's a mistake.'"[23]

On September 28, Secretary Rice addressed the gathering celebrating the 75th anniversary of the Woodrow Wilson School at Princeton, demanding that the Palestinian terrorist groups be disbanded, as the Roadmap required. On Hamas and the elections she said this:

There are periods of time of transition in which one has to give some space to the participants, in this case the Palestinians, to begin to come to a new national compact. But I cannot imagine, in the final analysis, a new national compact that leaves an armed resistance group within the political space. You cannot simultaneously keep an option open on politics and an option on violence. There simply isn't a case that I can think of internationally where that's been permitted to happen.... It is absolutely the case that you cannot have armed groups ultimately participating in politics with no expectation that they're going to disarm.[24]

This message gave the Palestinians a bit of room: Apparently, Hamas could participate if someone had an expectation that, in the end, they would disarm. Then one might call its participation in elections the first step in that process. The key word was "ultimately." From the Israeli perspective, this was a clear U.S. retreat because "ultimately" could mean a very long time. Rice insisted that the words had meaning: There had to be reason to believe participation was part of the process that would lead to disarmament.

A few weeks later, the Palestinians came to Washington once again, and that was the message Secretary Rice delivered to Abbas at dinner on September 19, the night before he saw the president. There are plenty of transitional cases, she said, but the group must agree to the goal; Hamas cannot participate unless there is an *expectation* they will disarm. But Abbas disagreed: Even the new Rice/Quartet position was too strong for him. No, he said; I want them in, not out. I don't want them to be martyrs who were refused any role by us. Then once they're in, and part of the political system, we'll say no one can be in politics and have guns too.

Jake Walles, then serving as consul general in Jerusalem, flew back to attend the meetings with Abbas and described them later:

He believed Hamas should participate. That they needed to be brought into the process and defeated. That if they left them out, they would be a spoiler – he didn't want them to be a spoiler. He said that once the election was over, the first thing that the new PLC will do is to ban the militias – so there will be one gun, one authority. So he said all the right things.... [P]ractically speaking, after that we had basically acquiesced in Hamas participating in this election.[25]

The notion that Hamas would win a majority of seats and could prevent such a law banning militias did not seem to enter Abbas's mind or ours. Our concern, once that decision was taken, was to prevent Hamas's participation in the government to be elected unless Hamas renounced its goal of destroying Israel, renounced terrorism, and accepted that it must disarm. There could be no coalition or unity government in which Hamas participated, in our view, unless Hamas met those conditions. In that sense, our focus was shifting from the election to the postelection period. But it is obvious that even here we fell far short and should have stated clearly *before* the election that, however the vote went, we would not engage with Hamas and would oppose its participation in the government until it disarmed. We did not do so because Abbas wished us to avoid the degree of clarity that might give Hamas an excuse for refusing to participate in the election at all.

Abbas met the president the following day, where he got another pep talk about making difficult decisions. The president was optimistic: There was a real opportunity now. Abbas spoke mostly about the elections and the Hamas role. The culture of violence had surrounded the Palestinian cause for decades, he said, but there was change. The truce had lowered the level of violence. PA police were slowly but surely enforcing a new rule against the carrying of guns in public. Municipal elections had been held successfully during 2005. Now came the PLC elections, and he did want some of the armed groups to participate. Either they were inside the system or sat outside it criticizing. If they were inside, they would be participating in accordance with their true size, not the size al Jazeera gave them. So the election gives me a chance, he said, to send a message: Everyone can participate in political life but subject to law and in their true size.

Abbas and his men made it clear again that barring Hamas participation was anathema to them because such an election would delegitimize Abbas. An election in which the main opposition is barred? The Arab Middle East had had dozens of such elections; that was the way tyrants stayed in power. Moreover, Hamas would obviously be beaten in the elections, which would greatly strengthen Abbas and Fatah and the PA. If we absolutely insisted that Hamas be barred from running candidates, the Palestinians said, it would be better to cancel the election. The United States bought the argument. Although Hamas as a party would not present candidates, people linked to them, supported by them, and known at least to be fellow travelers of Hamas would be able to run. Forced by the Palestinian logic to choose between canceling the elections entirely or allowing Hamas-linked candidates to run, we chose the latter and decided not to have a confrontation with Abbas. In retrospect, the decision was wrong both in principle and in practice.

Hamas and PIJ, whatever their thoughts about the election, gave no evidence of changing their view of terrorism. Two drive-by shooting attacks on October 16 left four Israelis dead. On October 26, a suicide bombing at a falafel stand in an outdoor market in Hadera, a town 30 miles north of Tel Aviv, killed 6 and wounded 55. The Palestinian Islamic Jihad claimed responsibility. Israel hit back the following day with air strikes in the West Bank and Gaza.

Rice returned to the Middle East in November. We went first to Bahrain on November 12, for the first meeting of the Forum for the Future that had been created at the Sea Island Summit. One American goal had been creation of the "Fund for the Future" that would promote democracy, but Arab governments refused to approve any fund that they would not control. "A U.S.-backed Mideast democracy and development summit ended in rancor," the Associated Press reported. "A draft declaration on democratic and economic principles was scuttled after Egypt insisted on language that would have given Arab governments greater control over charitable and good-government organizations."[26] For Rice, the meeting was a failure: Despite all her work, there was no final communiqué. This was not an auspicious beginning for the trip and was later called "an astonishing rebuff" and a "public relations nightmare."[27]

Gaza All-Nighter

We flew off to Israel, where the Labor Party had chosen a new leader on November 10: Trade union leader Amir Peretz had defeated veteran Labor Party official Shimon Peres. Peretz immediately threatened to pull Labor out of the Sharon coalition, so we figured Israeli politics would be high on the agenda with Sharon. It was not. Sharon merely told us there might be elections; he said he was trying to figure out whether he would stay and fight in Likud or create his own new party.

But mostly he wanted to talk about the Palestinians. The PA security forces were not fighting terror, he said; instead of fighting Hamas, Abbas wants them in the elections. He repeated his total opposition to its inclusion. Terror is the main issue, he told Rice: I want to solve the basic problem – one does not stay forever, but I cannot do it if the terror continues. This "one does not stay forever" was a rare reference to his own mortality, or at least his longevity in the prime minister position. There cannot be progress on the Roadmap if Abu Mazen does not act against terror; tell him that, he urged Rice. He holds meetings but nothing happens. Rice urged patience: His elections are coming. He is far better than the alternatives.

Sharon was not persuaded and answered at length. There was not the slightest sign that Abu Mazen would act, he said. He is doing zero now and he will not be stronger after the elections. Allowing Hamas in the elections is a major mistake. We will not interfere in the Palestinian elections, but neither will we coordinate the elections; we want Hamas treated differently. If we find Hamas guys, we will jail them immediately. Hamas must amend their covenant and stop terror. Doing that could change my position. Once they are in the elections, the EU will see Hamas as legitimate. Allowing Hamas to play a role could bring the Roadmap to an end. How can we move forward with a now-legitimate terrorist organization in the democratic political process? The Bush effort to promote democracy is very important. I could take more risks if we were surrounded by democracies, but if democracy is used by terrorist organizations, how will it work? Will international observers escort Hamas murderers? We will not interfere in the elections but we will not help them. It is a major mistake. Terrorist organizations cannot participate in elections in the EU; they can't under Oslo. They can't anywhere – and there is an attempt to impose it on us.

Rice argued for the position she and the Quartet had begun to take in September, telling Sharon that actually the Quartet view was not much different from his own. In some cases, she said, a group can disarm after the elections: That happened in Angola and Northern Ireland. We agree with you that they cannot be legitimized while armed. They have to disarm. But there is a fine line between your not helping those elections and actually interfering with them. Don't cross it. Hamas will lose the election; don't give them an excuse to avoid that, she concluded. Sharon remained unpersuaded. He simply did not believe Abu Mazen would be stronger after the elections if Hamas was then sitting in the parliament. There would be more meetings, and Abu Mazen would be sitting and talking with a group whose charter calls for eliminating the State of Israel and attacking Jews. He won't disarm anything, Sharon said. Then he'll lose our support, Rice rejoined. We will not deal with Hamas, not at all. And I can tell you, she said, the United States won't agree to a situation where terrorist organizations remain armed and part of the PA.

Rice's main goal in this part of the trip was to address the problems that had arisen after the Gaza withdrawal. It was now three months since the Israelis had left, but the expected advantages to the Palestinians were invisible. Palestinians could not easily move back and forth from Gaza to the West Bank, nor could they conduct normal export and import activity. Israel's disengagement had been unilateral, and though there had been a good deal of contacts between the two sides, they had never negotiated, or even much discussed, mechanisms for trade and mobility. This was turning into a bitter impasse rather than progress in Israeli-Palestinian relations, and it might affect the January PLC election. Rice wanted to address these issues; both sides realized something had to be done. Delaying her departure for her next stop, the Asia Pacific Economic Conference in Korea, she and all of us jumped into what turned out to be an all-night negotiating session to produce an agreement.

The Israelis had a team, the PA had a team, and we had ours, operating out of the David's Citadel Hotel, where we commandeered the ballroom floor. Javier Solana, the EU foreign minister, and James Wolfensohn were also in Jerusalem. The outcome of our efforts was two documents: an agreement on the operation of the Rafah crossing, and the Agreement on Movement and Access (AMA) that presented detailed rules for operating crossing points between Israel and Gaza and the link between Gaza and the West Bank, as well as comments on the proposed Gaza seaport and airport and on movement within the West Bank. Its level of detail was considerable: For example, here is one section of the AMA:

The new and additional scanner will be installed and fully operational by December 31. At that time, the number of export trucks per day to be processed through Karni will reach 150, and 400 by end-2006. A common management system will be adopted by both parties.... The management system that has been developed for Karni should, with suitable local variations, be adapted to the passages at Erez and Kerem Shalom. . . . Israel will allow the passage of convoys [between the West Bank and Gaza] to facilitate the movements of goods and persons. Specifically: Establish bus convoys by December 15; Establish truck convoys by January 15.

There being no goodwill on which to rely, we thought such detail was the only way to guarantee success; in the agreements were rules that each side could understand and follow. Rice told the PA to forget about an airport in Gaza; we had trouble guaranteeing the safety of our own airports, so how realistic was it for the Israelis to trust that the PA could operate an airport safely? On the seaport, the Agreement on Movement and Access said "construction . . . can commence"; the dangers were far lower.

The heart of the negotiation was about how people and goods could move safely, without adding to terrorism. How could Israel trust that arms and explosives were not moving in and out of Gaza? What inspections would be made and by whom? Who would examine Palestinians moving in and out of Gaza to stop terrorists? It is not worth elaborating further on the agreements reached because they were not implemented. Rice has been criticized for this failure: "[S]he got on a plane to Asia – and within weeks the carefully negotiated deadlines and agreements had fallen apart."[28] But Rice had taken a huge risk in diving into the negotiation as she did. Had she failed, as we nearly did, to reach any agreement, reporters would have added in the setback in Bahrain and said her trip was a terrible personal failure. Just before our arrival, on November 9, three terrorist bombings at hotels in Amman, Jordan, had killed 60 and wounded 115, so it is not hard to guess there would have been stories about how the whole region was falling apart.

Instead, Rice took the risk and banged heads. She told both sides she was absolutely determined to get a deal while she was in Jerusalem. Hour after hour, we prodded and persuaded and cajoled the Israelis and Palestinians, balancing compromises and concessions, pushing them toward an agreement. This was my first all-nighter since college. Rice departed midway through the evening, for a quick condolence and solidarity trip to Amman (less than an hour away) to see King Abdullah. We carried on in her brief absence. Toward midnight, as the sides seemed to be drifting apart, I called Weissglas. He was sitting with the entire Israeli interagency team and had me on speakerphone. After some preliminary remarks, I asked him to turn off the speakerphone. Look, I told him, Condi needs this agreement; I explained about Bahrain and the press. Tell the prime minister, I said; this is personal. This is a favor to her; she needs to have a victory here. He got the point quickly and said he'd do what he could. At least at that juncture, even with the disagreement over Hamas's possible participation in the PLC elections, relations between the Israelis and Condi were excellent. She liked Sharon and he liked her. This personal appeal would do some good, I knew.

Solana added his personal touch: He called and said he was simply available to do what we asked – a lot, nothing, a press appearance – he just wanted to be useful. Wolfensohn was another matter; he called to say he was on the way over to the David's Citadel to join the negotiating sessions. Yikes! I called Rice on her plane and received her instructions: On no account was he to be allowed to join what were extremely delicate sessions. When he arrived, we had him seated for a while on another floor, away from the teams gathered around large tables in meeting rooms. He fumed. I was sent to meet with him, to kill time until Condi returned and dealt with him. Now he added his own personal touch. I am James D. Wolfensohn, he said, and I have never ever been treated this way in my entire life. He then gave me a brief biography: his banking career, riches, contacts, the World Bank, Quartet Special Envoy for Disengagement. And now here we were, negotiating about Gaza, and we had not called on him, had not invited him, and had not sought his advice. He would not tolerate this. I was apologetic, while wondering why he was so obtuse as to ignore the obvious fact that Condi had decided to keep him out for a reason: He had nothing to contribute, his record as envoy was dismal, and his ego kept getting in the way – as it was doing right then. When Condi returned, I updated her on this session and she said to send him up to her suite; she said she had experience dealing with teenaged boys.

By morning we had a deal; both sides agreed on the language, and Rice could depart with a triumph. "Secretary of State Condoleezza Rice spent all day and night successfully brokering an accord on Tuesday on security controls at a Gaza border crossing, suddenly elevating the Bush administration's involvement in the Israeli-Palestinian conflict to a new level," the *New York Times* reported.[29] The "elevation" point was false but was a reminder of the criticism that faced Bush administration officials during and after his term: There wasn't enough involvement, Bush didn't care, didn't pay attention to this, and didn't spend enough time on it. Fixed in their minds was the Clinton ideal, of the president spending day after day at Camp David, in negotiations hour after hour. They did not seem to recall that Camp David had been a massive failure that had produced only the violence of the intifada. Later criticism of Rice because the Agreement on Movement and Access also failed suggested she should have done more, when it would have been more logical to question whether this kind of intense personal role – presidential or secretarial – produced success or highly visible disappointment.

Very shortly after we left Jerusalem, Sharon made his decision: to leave the Likud Party he had founded and to form a new party. On November 21, he announced that he was starting the Kadima Party ("kadima" means "forward" in English) and that Shimon Peres was leaving the Labor Party to join it. Sharon also called for new elections, to be held in March 2006.

The Agreement on Movement and Access began to fray soon after we left: On December 5, Palestinian Islamic Jihad perpetrated a suicide bombing in Netanya at the entrance to a shopping mall. Five people were killed and about fifty injured, and the Israelis reacted not only with air strikes and arrests but also by calling off scheduled talks with the PA over implementation of the AMA. There had been a session planned to discuss the bus convoys between the West Bank and Gaza that were to be the initial link between the two; now it was canceled.

Postpone the Election?

On holding the Palestinian election as scheduled, President Abbas remained firm throughout December. There was talk of postponement, but he was adamantly against it. He told the EU envoy Marc Otte that postponing elections "will kill me." But Otte also found that Abbas was feeling low: He reacted to European pressure on Fatah to maintain law and order and reform its governance and finances by explaining why he could not really do anything. Dahlan, for his part, was seeking a postponement. Dahlan told the Israelis – but initially did not tell us – that he had concluded the elections would be a disaster and must be delayed. The postponement would be easy to explain, he felt: Blame everything on the lack of adequate access to the polls in Jerusalem, blame the Israelis, blame Sharon. Weissglas told us he thought the Palestinians would in the end postpone the elections. Dahlan did then turn to us, telling David Welch that Fatah needed more time to get better organized. Of course, we wondered whom Dahlan was speaking for, given what Abbas was saying to the Europeans, and we certainly placed more faith in Abbas's view. Moreover, how could a postponement be defended? The Jerusalem voting problem was fixed: The same previously acceptable method of voting in post offices was arranged, Weissglas told us. So the real story would be clear: The elections were postponed because Fatah might lose. Moreover, the elections had already been postponed from the previous summer. If they were postponed again, most people would conclude, perhaps rightly, that they would simply never be held.

We could not take that approach because it would make a mockery of our support for free elections throughout the region. What the Palestinians did not fully grasp, I thought, was how much a postponement or cancellation of the election would undermine their own demand for statehood. The appeal of the Palestinian position was that Palestinians wished to move from living under occupation to living in freedom. Freedom had to mean more than getting the IDF out; the president was using Palestine, like Iraq and Lebanon, as an example of how democracy might be coming to the Arab world. A Palestine that would be ruled by Arafat's cronies forever, without elections or democracy, was hardly what President Bush was aiming for and would win little sympathy in the United States. But a free election was an indication that Palestinians were capable of and entitled to self-rule.

A large group met in Rice's conference room in December to discuss these issues, and the consensus was strong: How could we call off Palestinian elections, just days after the successful parliamentary elections in Iraq (on December 15)? Millions had gone to the polls there, despite the violence, and proudly held up their purple fingers (marked with dye to prevent voting more than once) to television cameras. Now an election would be canceled because we weren't sure of the outcome? Rob Danin, who had gone over to State with Condi when we decided I would not do so, was the sole dissenter, arguing for making Hamas pay a price for participation. Postpone briefly, he said, and extract something from them for allowing them to run. But the president had a clear view, and Secretary Rice reflected and asserted it: hold the elections. My own view, expressed at the meeting, was to go ahead; there was no reason to think Fatah would be in any better shape six months later. The Quartet did issue, on December 28, a "Statement on Upcoming Palestinian Elections," which "call[ed] on all participants to renounce violence, recognize Israel's right to exist, and disarm" and said the PA cabinet "should include no member who has not committed to the principles of Israel's right to exist in peace and security and an unequivocal end to violence and terrorism."[30]

The assumption was that Fatah would win a plurality in the PLC and would then create and lead a governing coalition, and in this statement, the Quartet was trying to establish some rules for its formation. We did not anticipate that Fatah would lose: We were hearing that from Dahlan but not from Abbas – and not from the Israelis. Their view was that the Hamas vote was increasing, but no Israeli official, not even the intelligence officials, suggested that Hamas would win. The leading Palestinian pollster, Khalil Shikaki, said the same: His final poll, taken December 29–31, 2005, predicted that Fatah would win 43% of the vote and Hamas only 25%; 19% said they were undecided. (The previous poll in December had 50% of the vote for Fatah versus 32% for Hamas, with 9% undecided, so it appeared that Fatah was losing ground but Hamas was not gaining any.) This was the consensus view: that Hamas would make a good showing but Fatah would win. The BBC, for example, reported that "the Islamist militant group is making a strong challenge to President Abbas' Fatah movement, and polls suggest it could win up to a third of the vote."[31] In the leadership ranks, Abbas and others may have been more worried – but they did not tell us this.

Tourgeman recounted the final weeks:

I remember a stormy discussion with Saeb [Erekat] in Jerusalem where he told us, "Don't interfere. Don't interfere with our internal business. We want the Hamas to participate, we will beat the hell out of them, and we will win." It started changing when Hamas decided they would participate; when they decided to participate, it was like a snowball because people then had something to choose. And then you started to see the rise of the support to Hamas in the Palestinian streets from 20–25 to 30%. And then 40, with 40 to Abu Mazen. . . . [A]nd Abu Mazen understood he was in a problem. And then he wanted to postpone the elections; he didn't know how. He knew that if he will go to the public and say, "I postpone the elections," he will be criticized. He couldn't do it because the U.S. administration said that they insisted on elections. And we saw that he's trying to put the blame on Israel. How did he try to put the blame on Israel? He hoped that Israel will not allow the elections in Jerusalem and that will be an excuse for him to postpone the elections. Abu Mazen approached us and said. "Don't allow the elections in Jerusalem." We analyzed it and said, "Look, it's your business to have the elections or not. If you have the elections, we will help you conduct them in the most proper way – in the same way that it was conducted in January 2005 including in

Jerusalem." The message to us was very clear: "Postpone the elections. We cannot do it. The Americans will not allow it, so do it by not allowing the elections in Jerusalem."[32]

The Israelis refused, and Abbas never came to us with this request – rightly so, for he would have been rebuffed.

"I Have No Doubt I Can Move Forward"

On December 14, Dubi Weissglas came to Washington and explained where Sharon thought things stood. Sharon continues to be popular, and Gaza went more smoothly than people anticipated. He has correctly judged that most Israelis want some kind of deal with the Palestinians – the Israelis do not like them or trust them, but they want a deal. Sharon wants to move forward; he wants to set the final borders. He sees a window of three more years, the time he and President Bush overlap, to bring about a more stable situation. He would prefer a signed agreement, under the Roadmap, and will try to get it throughout 2006. Only a signed, final agreement justifies the pain of pulling back, provides real compensation. He is not sure if Abu Mazen is strong enough to sign anything. If that fails, he will look to unilateral moves in 2007 and 2008. He thinks he's the only person who can do it.

Four days later, Sharon gave us all a scare when he suffered a mild stroke. He lost consciousness, but only very briefly. He was hospitalized for only two days. When he emerged, President Bush called him. I will rest for a few days and then get back to work, he told the president. The president told him to be careful: We need you healthy; don't work too hard. Keep rational hours! Watch what you eat. I want to see a slimmer Sharon! We need your leadership and your courage to get to peace. Sharon replied that the two of them could accomplish many things; I have no doubt I can move forward, he said, as long as the terror stops; Israel will not cooperate with terror. That was the last time they spoke.

On January 4, 2006, at his ranch, Sharon suffered a massive stroke from which he never recovered. His death was expected, and we in Washington laid plans for the funeral; the president intended to go. I wrote a eulogy for the president to read at the funeral and kept it with me over the next few months so it would be handy when Sharon died. But he outlasted Bush's term in office, lying in a hospital in Jerusalem in what the doctors called a persistent vegetative state for nearly five years before being moved back to his ranch in late 2010.

Did the pressure of disengagement that summer and fall, and of leaving Likud to create a new party, lead to the stroke? Not according to General Kaplinsky. In the fall of 2005, he told me, Sharon

was in his best shape. And he felt on top of the world. He would tell you about the visit in the United Nations, when the entire world stood in line in order to meet him – and you know Sharon was along his career almost isolated in most of the countries. Second, he was in his best situation under pressure. He could be tired sometimes, he would be upset sometimes, but when something happened and he has to – when he was under pressure, that was his best condition. Suddenly you'd find you met another Ariel Sharon: cool, easy, sense of humor, the ability [to] hear a lot of different opinions and maneuver between them, think three steps ahead. Only when he was under pressure.[33]

That was not a medical opinion, of course, and the doctors have long argued about whether Sharon's second stroke was inevitable or caused by the treatment he received after his first. I was actually on my way to Israel when the second stroke hit. I was at Dulles Airport in Washington and had checked my bags when news came from the White House. I called Tourgeman to see how serious this was: Was it a mild stroke like the first one? His choked voice told me all I needed to know. I went home.

For me the loss was official but also personal. I had formed a warm relationship with Sharon, and he trusted me. Sometimes when I spoke with Weissglas over the phone, Sharon could be heard asking in Hebrew "Who is that?" and, hearing it was me, would take the phone to say hello and drive home some points that were on his mind, that he thought the president needed to hear right away. Twice he invited me and my family, when on vacation in Israel, to his ranch for a Shabbat lunch, and we have photos of Sharon with all our children. He had formed a working relationship with Secretary Rice, Steve Hadley, and the president, and I believed he meant to do what Dubi told us: to use this time as prime minister to change the Israeli-Palestinian conflict. He had begun with the withdrawal from Gaza, but he had meant it when he said this would not be "Gaza only." What exactly did he intend?

We will never know. Giladi believed he intended to pull back from 42% of the West Bank, roughly the areas that under the Oslo Accords were designated Areas A and B (Area A was in theory under Palestinian security control and administration, and Area B was under Israeli military control but PA administration). Rice too was confident that he would do more after Gaza: "Oh, absolutely," she later said.[34] Kaplinsky agreed: "I believe that he planned to do more; that's what *I* felt. He was very practical, you know? Most of the people in Israel don't understand how pragmatic and practical he was. His solution was completely different than 'give them the West Bank.' He believed that we have to keep control of some key points in the West Bank . . . for example, the Jordan Valley."[35]

Weissglas shared the view that Sharon would have built on expected success in Gaza. There were no plans, but there were thoughts, he told me in a later conversation. The thoughts were of similar but not identical movements in the West Bank, trying slowly to disengage from small, isolated, and remote settlements. The next step was to copy the same compensation law that had been used for Gaza and apply it to Judea and Samaria but with one difference: to apply it without a deadline. For several years, he explained, anybody who wanted would be able to take his money and go west; the goal was to see if there was somehow a way to move the settlements and the settlers westbound, and to see if security conditions allowed the military as well to redeploy on a strip east of the security fence. It would not, he acknowledged, have constituted a political solution or reached a legal definition of disengagement. But, he concluded, when we thought "what next?," the idea was to start to shrink, push westward, continue and complete the fence, and end up with this strip east of the fence, whose dimensions of course would change as the terrain – topography – required, to have the military there, and to start tempting the settlers from small isolated settlements to move.[36]

On the Palestinian side, there were fears of exactly this approach, which might lead to a very long-term interim phase. Ghaith al-Omari, an advisor to Abbas, summarized this concern:

It was a Palestinian understanding – and fear. And fear because of two things. One thing is when he completely left Gaza, it was very clear that the next step is going to be a partial withdrawal from the West Bank, and this might become the de facto Palestinian state in half the West Bank. So that was the first grounds of fear. The second grounds, which was more political: it was very clear that once he withdrew unilaterally from Gaza, Hamas took the credit for that. Partly because of the nature of unilateralism, which some of us were warning of before it happened, and partly because of miserable political mismanagement from the Fatah side.... You know, this is the lack of strategic thinking. You are saying, "No, no, no," until they came to reality, and suddenly in the last month there was very intensive cooperation, and security, and greenhouses, and Condi coming for the Access and Movement and all of that. They had no story to tell. The Fatah crowd had no political story to tell, nor did they try. There were some half-baked attempts to talk about the economic dividend of that, but Hamas had a very vibrant campaign: "Three years of resistance beat ten years of negotiations." They had it all set. They took the credit for it and there was a sense that if we move in that direction in the West Bank, we're going to have a similar political outcome.[37]

That was not the view in Washington. Just before Sharon's stroke, we saw hope and change. Bush had been handed a disaster by President Clinton: All negotiations had failed and had produced an intifada. The levels of violence were awful. The Bush administration had worked to get those levels down in 2001 and then after 9/11 had developed a firm policy. The United States would support a Palestinian state as a key American goal, if and when change in the Palestinian leadership gave promise of producing a peaceful and democratic Palestine. This was a bold and widely criticized decision by the president, who had characteristically cut right to the heart of the problem. It was time for the Israelis to pull back and for the Palestinians to govern themselves, but that was simply impossible while the PA was led by a corrupt, despotic terrorist.

If that seems obvious now, it was far from obvious in most government palaces and foreign ministries in 2002. But Bush's view – requiring the marginalization of Arafat – steadily attracted international support and was enshrined in the Roadmap. By June 2003, after the Sharm and Aqaba summits, we had Arab and European backing. Arafat had been forced to allow creation of the prime ministerial position, and it had been filled by Mahmoud Abbas. At Aqaba, he and Sharon shook hands and talked of the way forward: an end to the militarization of the conflict and of terror, peace negotiations, Palestinian self-government, and an end to the Israeli occupation. By the end of that summer, these hopes were dashed by Arafat, who reasserted himself as the sole Palestinian leader. Negotiations were, then, impossible, so by the end of 2003 Sharon seized the initiative: He would get out of Gaza and four small (token, in the best sense) settlements in the West Bank. Then, we believed, he would begin to pull back farther in the West Bank. After Arafat's death, the Gaza withdrawal went forward successfully, and what seemed to lie ahead was either a new effort at negotiations or that Israeli pullback. Either way, the situation would be transformed. A situation that had been unchanged since the 1967 war had begun to change, with Gaza, and Bush would be able to leave office in 2009 with significant changes as well in the West Bank. The policy we were following was working, despite all the efforts to derail it. That was the way it looked to us as 2006 began, when Arik Sharon suffered his second stroke and his role in Israel's wars and its politics came to an end.

Notes

1. The President's News Conference with Prime Minister Tony Blair of the United Kingdom, 3 Pub. Papers 2693–2791 (November 12, 2004).
2. Al-Omari, interview, p. 12.
3. Giladi, interview, p. 11.
4. Meridor, interview, p. 5.
5. "Suicide and Other Bombing Attacks in Israel since the Declaration of Principles (Sept 1993)," *Israel Ministry of Foreign Affairs*, August 18, 2011, http://www.mfa.gov.il/MFA/Terrorism+Obstacle+to+Peace/Palestinian+terror+since+2000/Suicide+and+Other+Bombing+Attacks+in+Israel+Since.htm.
6. Address before a Joint Session of the Congress on the State of the Union, 1 Pub. Papers 113–121 (February 2, 2005).
7. Hefetz and Bloom, *Ariel Sharon: A Life*, 462.
8. Kessler, *The Confidante: Condoleezza Rice and the Creation of the Bush Legacy*, 134.
9. Israeli-Palestinian Interim Agreement on the West Bank and the Gaza Strip, Israel-Palestine, Sept. 25, 1995, http://www.mfa.gov.il/MFA/Peace+Process/Guide+to+the+Peace+Process/THE+ISRAELI-PALESTINIAN+INTERIM+AGREEMENT.htm.
10. Jacob Walles, interview by the author, January 26, 2010, pp. 9–10.
11. Gush Etzion lies at the south of Jerusalem and by 1948, four communities there had about 450 Jewish settlers. During the 1948 War of Independence, the kibbutz at Kfar Etzion was overrun by Arab soldiers, who killed nearly every soldier and civilian present, numbering in the hundreds. Hundreds more in the other kibbutzim were taken captive by Jordan and held prisoner for a year before their release. The area was resettled after Israel won it in the 1967 war, and about 40,000 Jews now live there.
12. The President's News Conference with President Mahmoud Abbas of the Palestinian Authority, 41 Weekly Comp. Pres. Doc. 886–891 (May 26, 2005).
13. Rice, *No Higher Honor*, 293.
14. United Nations, Alvaro de Soto, End of Mission Report (marked confidential), May 2007, 6–7.

15. Associated Press, "Looters Strip Gaza Greenhouses," *MSNBC.com*, September 13, 2005, http://www.msnbc.msn.com/id/9331863/ns/world_news-mideast_n_africa/t/looters-strip-gaza-greenhouses/#.T5B6oqtYuDU.

16. Stephen Farrell, "Militants Kill Hated Security Chief," *The Times* [of London], September 8, 2005, http://go.galegroup.com/ps/i.do?action=interpret&id=GALE%7CA135950979&v=2.1&u=nysl_me_gradctr&it=r&p=AONE&sw=w&authCount=1.

17. TheJerusalemFund.org. "The Charter of Allah: The Platform of the Islamic Resistance Movement (Hamas)," accessed April 24, 2012, http://www.thejerusalemfund.org/www.thejerusalemfund.org/carryover/documents/charter.html.

18. Yossi Beilin, "Recognizing Hamas is irresponsible," Bitterlemons.org, last modified September 26, 2005, http://www.bitterlemons.org/previous/bl260905ed35.html.

19. Middle East Quartet, "Quartet Statement," news release, September 20, 2005, New York, http://www.eu-un.europa.eu/articles/fr/article_5044_fr.htm.

20. Transcript of Press Conference on Middle East, by Secretary General Kofi Annan, Quartet Foreign Ministers, at United Nations Headquarters, 20 September 2005, http://unispal.un.org/UNISPAL.NSF/0/0076097BFAD0F17585257083004E730E.

21. De Soto, "End of Mission Report," 16.

22. Rice, *No Higher Honor*, 415.

23. Tourgeman, October interview, p. 3.

24. Aluf Benn, "Rice: Hamas Must Disarm before Entering Palestinian Politics," *Haaretz*, October 2, 2005.

25. Walles, interview, p. 3.

26. Associated Press, "Mideast Summit Ends without Key Agreement," *MSNBC*, November 12, 2005, http://www.msnbc.msn.com/id/9998770/ns/world_news-mideast_n_africa/t/mideast-summit-ends-without-key-agreement/#.T5GKwqtYuDU.

27. Kessler, *The Confidante*, 120–21.

28. Ibid., 134.

29. Steven Weisman, "For Rice, a Risky Dive Into the Mideast Storm," *New York Times*, November 16, 2005.

30. Middle East Quartet, "Quartet Statement on upcoming Palestinian elections," December 28, 2005, http://unispal.un.org/unispal.nsf/fdc5376a7a0587a4852570d000708f4b/b4b69a9ac0a2a35e852570eb00620be7?OpenDocument.

31. "Israel to 'Allow Jerusalem Vote,'" BBC News, January 10, 2006, http://news.bbc.co.uk/2/hi/middle_east/4598258.stm.

32. Tourgeman, October interview, pp. 3–5.

33. Kaplinsky, interview, p. 11.

34. Rice, interview, p. 2.

35. Kaplinsky, interview, p. 5.

36. Weissglas, interview, pp. 1, 5.

37. Al-Omari, interview, p. 15.

6

Olmert – Peace or War?

Sharon's second stroke, on January 4, was quickly understood to have wreaked irreversible harm. That night, Sharon was declared "temporarily incapable of discharging his powers," and the deputy prime minister, Ehud Olmert, became "acting prime minister." Shortly thereafter, Olmert and the cabinet announced that the elections would take place on March 28 as scheduled.

Olmert was a veteran politician. First elected to the Knesset at age 28, he had served as mayor of Jerusalem from 1993 to 2003 and over the years in several ministerial posts. His rise to the position of prime minister was accidental; he would never have reached it had he not had the ceremonial title of "deputy prime minister" when Sharon was incapacitated. He had actually sought to be finance minister under Sharon, a post that went instead to Benjamin Netanyahu, a more powerful figure in Likud. Olmert had been offered the far less powerful position of minister of industry and trade, had refused it, and had been persuaded to accept it only when given the added sweetener of the (usually meaningless) title "deputy prime minister." Olmert had been a staunch hardliner: He had voted against the Camp David Accords in 1978, but he had backed Sharon on disengagement and followed him out of Likud and into the new Kadima Party. The two men were political allies, but they were not close: Giving him the title of deputy prime minister "was a mistake," Sharon's son and adviser Gilad later wrote, because "my father did not for a moment believe that Olmert should replace him or that he was worthy of the role; nor did he intend to allow that to happen.... [H]e had no intention of bestowing that title [of deputy prime minister] on Olmert again after 2006."[1]

Olmert had many friends in the United States but no close ties to those of us handling Middle East policy in the Bush administration. The president called him soon after he became acting prime minister, and their conversation – beyond the niceties about Sharon and the need to meet after the Israeli elections – centered on the forthcoming Palestinian elections, then just weeks away. The president reiterated his view that there was an inescapable contradiction between militias and democracy. We were for a free election, he said, but he assured Olmert that if Hamas did not recognize the right of Israel to exist and disarm, we would have no contact with them whatsoever.

That was our position – the position into which we had been pushed by two forces: the president's overall policy of backing free elections and democracy on the one hand, which meant that we would not support cancellation of the PLC elections, and Abbas's insistence that Hamas be allowed to run in them. It is easy in retrospect to say that this was an impossible combination: allow the election but do not plan to respect the result if it is the "wrong" one. But as we would learn, the meaning of "respect the result" was not entirely clear then or later. The formulation toward which we had slowly been moving allowed participation in the elections with the assumption – or prayer – that the armed group, in this case Hamas, would make the requisite pledges after the election. We had not agreed with those who said an armed group may not run; we were turning instead to the view that they may run but not join in governing until they had begun the process of accommodating to democratic practices by agreeing that the state must "ultimately" have a monopoly on violence. As President Abbas kept putting it, "one gun:" Only the PA would have security forces. At the very least, the phone call from Bush alerted Olmert to the president's disinclination to see the elections canceled just weeks before they were to take place simply because Fatah was nervous about victory.

On January 16, Kadima elected Olmert as chairman, replacing Sharon, and declared that he would be the candidate for prime minister in the March 28 elections. David Welch and I were sent out on the Middle East trip that Sharon's stroke had postponed. Now we would not only deal with the Palestinian elections but also meet the new prime minister and see what he intended.

Was Disengagement Doomed?

Meeting with Israeli security officials, we heard yet again that Dahlan and others in Fatah were worried about the elections and wanted them canceled. Hamas had initially sought only a good showing, perhaps 30% of the vote, but the Israelis were now predicting it would get 35 or 40% – and maybe higher. The Israelis did not urge cancellation, however. They believed that anarchy in Gaza had been spreading since the day Israeli forces left, and cancellation – a sure sign of weakness – could produce more violence and would weaken the PA's hand further. The PA security forces were doing nothing, smuggling of weapons by Hamas was continuing, and the real challenge was not the elections: It was restoring order in Gaza.

Was disengagement doomed from the start? There is a powerful argument that we did not understand, nor did Sharon and Israel, the negative implications of the fact that Hamas claimed and was given credit for the Israeli withdrawal by the Palestinian population. The message from Hamas was simple: Terrorism, not negotiation, got the Israelis out; it was "resistance" rather than the Fatah approach that succeeded. The unilateral nature of the Israeli approach can be blamed for the success of this message, at least in part, because it denied the PA some credit it might otherwise have gained. Yet even though disengagement was a unilateral decision made by the Israelis, its implementation could still have been better coordinated with the Palestinians. This would not have destroyed the Hamas narrative but might have weakened it.

Another school of thought blames the Israelis for allowing the growth of Hamas power: Had they responded faster and more fiercely to rocket and mortar strikes from Gaza, and hit arms-smuggling tunnels more often along the Philadelphi Strip, the outcome would have been different. This analysis is flawed, however, because the struggle for power in Gaza was internal. In the fall of 2005, after the Israeli withdrawal, there were but a handful of attacks from there into Israel. And, in fact, Sharon did respond; there was an Israeli attack into Gaza after each attack from Gaza. The real problem was the failure of the PA security forces to organize and assert themselves – despite their larger numbers. The bloody Moussa Arafat execution was telling; the failure of the PA to respond to it was more so. Repeatedly, Hamas and allied groups crossed red lines, defying the PA security forces very publicly, and the public would have accepted a strong reaction. The PA could have asserted its rule. It did not act. So it was quickly apparent that Gaza would not be what we and the PA had once hoped, a model for Palestinian statehood, but not because there were pressures or constraints that prevented the PA from acting. In 2004, Weissglas had explained that testing the model, putting the PA on the spot, was one of the objectives of disengagement: It places the Palestinians under tremendous pressure, he said. They have no more excuses and the world is watching them, not Israel, and asking how they will now rule Gaza.[2]

The PA was quickly failing this test. Because of its own internal weaknesses, political and military, the PA could not get its act together. Throughout 2005, Abbas had been president and Ahmed Qurie (Abu Ala'a) had been prime minister, but they had been largely uninterested in reforming PA institutions or Fatah – before or after disengagement. They had relied, as we had and as in a sense the Israelis had, on Mohammed Dahlan, who was a Gazan, to keep order there and maintain the PA's control despite the evident strength of Hamas and other terrorist groups. It is difficult to think what the United States or Israel could have done to maintain PA control after the Israeli withdrawal if the PA itself was too inert, too corrupt, and too incompetent to act in its own defense. All of that was not yet clear in January 2006, although it would soon become far clearer when the PLC elections were held.

Welch and I then met with Olmert. I had probably shaken his hand at official gatherings before but had never really engaged with him. One difference from Sharon was age; he was of my generation and that of the president, not 20 years older; another was language, because he spoke English almost perfectly, and the occasional misunderstandings with Sharon were entirely absent. He was charming and, I later learned, inspired real loyalty in his staff, whom he treated fairly and well. What he lacked, of course, was Sharon's history as a general and as a participant in every war Israel had ever fought; Olmert was and had all his life been a politician. Later he would be indicted on several corruption charges, which ultimately brought his political career to an end, but in my dealings with him he was straightforward and, when necessary, blunt. His main political problem was that however his friends and interlocutors saw him, Israelis over time came to view him more and more as a politician who could not be trusted to govern the country well; he never recovered after the Second Lebanon War in the summer of 2006.

When Welch and I saw him in mid-January 2006, all of that was well in the future; the country was rallying behind him now, seeking unity after Sharon's shocking departure. We needed to know what Olmert believed and what he planned. He began with the Palestinian elections, telling us he knew Sharon had decided not to interfere and not to give the Palestinians any excuse to postpone them. But he was very uneasy with allowing Hamas to run and wanted us to report back home that he believed this decision was a mistake. To me, it was not surprising that although Olmert put his views on the record, he did not say he would prevent the elections or refuse to allow voting in Jerusalem if Hamas participated (which would have given the PA an excuse to cancel them). He had just become prime minister and needed to build a relationship with President Bush. Given the president's very clear views about having the election go forward, Olmert did not wish to sabotage the election and thereby sabotage his own possibilities with the president. (Ironically, I found myself in nearly the same position: I did not think Hamas should be permitted to run, but I knew where the president and Condi stood, so I had not fought that battle either.)

"A Major Move Forward"

Olmert then turned to his real subject. I want to use the coming four years [which would be his statutory term in office if Kadima won the March elections] to make a major move forward with the Palestinians, he told us. I know President Bush; I don't know who's next. I want to change things now, and I am willing to take risks. We can build on what Sharon achieved; disengagement was a start and a basis now exists to go further. This is the time to see if it can work – or, if it fails, to see what else can be done. Maybe Abu Mazen will fail the test, he said. Unilateral action is not my first choice; an agreement is, but acting unilaterally is an option. The thing is that we can't move forward in the face of terrorism; the PA has got to get control and act against the terrorist organizations.

We reported all this when we returned to Washington, and Olmert made it public soon thereafter. On January 24, his speech to the Herzliya Conference made it clear that he planned to move forward:

The existence of a Jewish majority in the State of Israel cannot be maintained with the continued control over the Palestinian population in Judea, Samaria and the Gaza Strip.... In order to ensure the existence of a Jewish national homeland, we will not be able to continue ruling over the territories in which the majority of the Palestinian population lives. We must create a clear boundary as soon as possible, one which will reflect the demographic reality on the ground. Israel will maintain control over the security zones, the Jewish settlement blocks, and those places which have supreme national importance to the Jewish people, first and foremost a united Jerusalem under Israeli sovereignty.... This is the path Prime Minister Ariel Sharon announced several years ago. We – who were his partners in its formation – worked with him in order to establish a new public movement, which will determine our path in the coming years, and which will propel Israel forward.

The existence of two nations, one Jewish and one Palestinian, is the full solution to all the national aspirations and problems of each of the peoples, including the issue of refugees who will be absorbed solely in a Palestinian state. We will not allow the entry of Palestinian refugees into the State of Israel. This is our clear stance, which is backed by the unequivocal American position expressed in the United States President's letter of April 2004, to the Prime Minister. The only way to achieve this goal is the full implementation of the Roadmap, and of President Bush's vision of June 2002.

The Roadmap is based on a simple and just idea: if the Palestinians abandon the path of terror, and stop their war against the citizens of Israel, they can receive national independence in a Palestinian state with temporary borders, even before all the complicated issues connected to a final agreement are resolved. All these issues will be resolved later during negotiations between the two countries, in the accepted manner in which countries resolve their differences.[3]

So Olmert was, or at least said he was, planning to make a move in the West Bank. He was proposing a negotiation that would leave Israel in control of the major blocks, as the president had suggested in his April 2004 letter to Sharon, but acknowledged that Israel would need to pull back elsewhere. The importance of this speech lay in its timing as well as its content: It was delivered just two months before the elections. Olmert was not hiding his intentions from the voters but rather making them a platform.

In a *Jerusalem Post* interview published on March 9, Olmert spelled out his plan:

I spoke in general about Gush Etzion, the Jerusalem envelope, Ma'ale Adumim and the Ariel region remaining part of Israel, and I spoke about the Jordan Valley as a security border.... After the elections, I intend to wait and see if the PA accepts the three [Quartet] principles.... We will wait, but I don't intend to wait forever. I am not willing to have Israel live according to a PA-set timetable any longer. If, after a reasonable time passes, it becomes clear that the PA is not willing to accept these principles, we will need to begin to act.... How much time will Israel wait? Forever? Will we be captives to a PA that is not willing to make peace? Will we sit back and deal only with terror, only react, not initiate? Or at some point do we say, "Okay, we waited. There is no way there will be a change on the other side, so let's see what we have to do in order to serve Israeli interests." We will always prefer an agreement. But if this turns out to be impossible, we will have to weigh our next steps. In the final analysis, my intention is that, within four years, we will arrive at Israel's permanent borders, according to which we will completely separate from the majority of the Palestinian population, and preserve a large and stable Jewish majority in Israel.[4]

But the Palestinian elections were first. Indeed, they were held the very day after Olmert spoke in Herzliya, on January 25. Hamas won 44% of the vote versus 41% for Fatah: 440,000 votes for the Hamas-linked party "Change and Reform" versus 410,000 for Fatah. (Several smaller parties, including Salam Fayyad's and one representing the terrorist Popular Front for the Liberation of Palestine (PFLP), split the rest of the vote.) Despite the close margin, it was a shocking victory for a terrorist group, one that had not been predicted – neither by the Israelis, Americans, Fatah leaders, nor Palestinian pollsters. Going into Election Day, we nervously anticipated that Hamas would do well – but did not believe it would win. The Palestinian electoral system provided for both proportional representation and constituency voting; each voter received two ballots, one for the national race and one for his or her local race. In the national race, Hamas prevailed by three points, but the victory was magnified by its success in the constituencies, where a disorganized Fatah had often presented two or even three candidates who then split the vote and lost to a Hamas candidate. In the end, Fatah had 45 seats in the PLC, whereas Hamas had 74. The terrorist PFLP won three seats; Salam Fayyad's moderate "Third Way" party and Mustafa Barghouti's "Independent Palestine" each won two.

"What to Do If Hamas Wins"

Fatah had been the leading element in Palestinian politics for 40 years, so this was a stunning defeat. Prime Minister Qurie (Abu Ala'a) resigned immediately. In Washington, we scrambled; this Hamas victory was unthinkable, and there were no plans for what to do next. No one had even bothered to write a planning paper on "What to Do If Hamas Wins," for no one had thought that outcome possible.

First, we had a legal problem. Hamas was a terrorist group, officially designated by the U.S. government, so we could not give it any funds or allow funds to be given to it through the U.S. financial system. Legally, we had to treat Hamas as we treated al Qaeda. Lawyers at both the Treasury and State Departments explained the impact of Hamas's victory. The PA was a parliamentary system and, in fact, a key goal of the United States in the Arafat era had been to expand the powers of the prime minister. After the election, Hamas would have a majority in the PLC and control the cabinet. Legally, that meant the whole PA was under Hamas domination and could not be given a dime. For those of us working on the policy end, that conclusion went too far. We resisted it for legal as well as policy reasons. We did not want all foreign aid, on which Palestinians depended to keep their economy afloat, to be cut off overnight. We did not want to abandon President Abbas; we wanted him to resist Hamas and keep the fight going. We wanted the Hamas government to fail unless Hamas changed its line and its conduct, but there had to be an alternative.

Abbas and other parts of the PA system not subordinate to the PLC became that alternative. The president was, after all, separately elected and under the

PA's Basic Law was not subordinate in any way to the legislature, so we could go on funding the Office of the President – and any PA body under Abbas rather than the PLC. We could fund the Presidential Guard, for example, which was one of the security forces. Mayors were separately elected, so perhaps aid going directly to cities and towns rather than the PA itself could continue. Aid going through UN bodies or providing direct assistance to the people could also continue, so long as it went around Hamas.

As time went by, we were able to tighten the financial noose on Hamas by using the financial system itself. We considered monies sent to the PA to be money sent to Hamas, a crime under U.S. law. U.S. banks were accordingly told not to forward or handle such transfers, and they did not do so. Nor did any bank operating in the United States, including Middle Eastern and even Palestinian banks. Soon enough, a financial boycott of Hamas was in place, and both we and the Israelis were surprised at the speed with which it became effective.

But the legal and financial reaction to the Hamas victory was the easy part; most of it was driven by our own counterterrorism laws. Figuring out what had happened in the elections and how to react politically were the tougher tasks. The debate over why Hamas won continues to this day, but the Bush administration immediately proffered the Fatah corruption theory. Fatah was redolent with corruption and Palestinians were tired of it. Fatah had not delivered, nor had it reformed in the year since Arafat's death. Jake Walles recalled his conversation with Secretary of State Rice, noting that it was 14 months since Arafat had died and two and a half years since the Aqaba summit had supposedly begun a new peace process:

I remember the day after the election Condi called me and said, "What happened?" I told her I thought there were three reasons: one was corruption; one was that Fatah ran a bad campaign; and third, that there was no peace process. . . . Abu Mazen and Fatah, their whole story was "We want peace." . . . They had nothing to point to to say that "This is how we can achieve it." And that's after Abu Mazen took over from Arafat, so there should be no objection from the Americans now. Arafat's gone, but there was no process.[5]

The "bad campaign" theory was widely popular; indeed, at a meeting with Abbas later that year (in September at the UN General Assembly), President Bush noted that Fatah had never had real competition until the January election and simply did not know how to campaign. This was certainly true but did not explain how Hamas had managed to master the art so quickly. Hamas had better slogans, better campaign materials, and better candidates: A good proportion of those running on the "Change and Reform" ticket were professionals – engineers or doctors, for example – who may well have looked far more attractive than Fatah careerists.

I thought there were deeper reasons for the victory, though 20–20 hindsight was of limited help. Fatah was not a democratic political party and had never been one, nor did those who ran it really seek to make it one. It had been a vehicle for Yasser Arafat, totally dominated by him, and a ruling party in the typical Arab sense: It governed but did not seek the consent of those it governed. As the months passed after Arafat's death, there was no reform in Fatah; later, as the years passed, there was still none. Palestinians noticed. It was not just that Fatah was corrupt or unfamiliar with free elections but that it was simply not a democratic political party at all.

Fatah was also a secular party, whereas Hamas was of course Islamist. For a long time people had been saying that this was a problem for Hamas because "Palestinian culture is secular," but that point of view was increasingly outmoded. Palestinian society was part of the Arab and Muslim world, where the Islamist trends were clear (and became clearer after free elections were held in 2011 in Morocco, Tunisia, and Egypt). As in Cairo and Amman or, for that matter, in Lahore or Algiers, more women covered their heads and more men attended mosques as the years passed. The rejection of Fatah was in part, I thought, far deeper than a protest against graft; it showed a desire for a society more closely guided by Islam. The Arab nationalism of Nasser and Arafat was a phenomenon of the past, while Islam's strength was growing.

Finally, there was another factor that was equally disturbing: Perhaps Palestinians *were* voting for "armed struggle." This was certainly not our public line, which focused on Palestinians' fatigue with Fatah corruption. But one very bright line between Fatah and Hamas was violence against Israelis: Abbas and Fatah had abandoned it, in principle anyway, after Aqaba, whereas Hamas was dedicated to it. Perhaps Palestinians did believe that terrorism had gotten the Israelis out of Gaza and was an essential part – even the heart – of any effort to get a state. If that was true, our long-term efforts for peace were doomed.

If we had missed all of this and for that reason had been confident of a Fatah victory, so had Fatah. Abbas later told the president (at their September 2006 meeting) that he and his associates had all believed they would win. One myth that deserves killing is that the PA/Fatah leaders never wanted elections and were forced to hold them by the United States – that these elections were the product of the Bush administration's foolish demand that elections be held everywhere at once, whatever the local conditions. It is true that we favored elections; how could we not? How else could a new and legitimate leadership, one that would be capable of taking difficult decisions for peace, be chosen after Arafat's death? But the Palestinian leadership wanted elections too and told us so; they too saw elections as the means to legitimize their own positions. They also appeared to understand that the elections were an important argument for Palestinian sovereignty: Free elections were evidence they could govern themselves and strengthened their demand that they should be allowed to do so. Free elections were a powerful argument that it was time for Israel to stop governing Palestinians. The presidential election of January 2005 suggested to them that the formula worked. The PLC elections would further strengthen their hand, they thought, because they would both entice Hamas into the political system and then defeat it. That would make it easier for them to govern and to negotiate with the Israelis. It is true that they became very nervous in the final days before the PLC elections, and some of them – it remains unclear whether this was the unified view of the PA leadership – looked for excuses to postpone the election yet again. But the claim that those elections were simply George Bush's idea, imposed on unwilling Palestinians who knew better, is false.

Beginning with the September 2005 Quartet meeting, we had been moving to a new position on Hamas's participation in the elections. Rejecting the idea of banning them, instead we had said the true test would come later and would involve their possible role in the PA government. An armed group could run but could not then participate in the government unless it made certain pledges and took certain actions to renounce violence. In a news release issued after a brief meeting in London on January 30, 2006, just five days after the Hamas victory, the Quartet expanded on this approach:

The Quartet congratulated the Palestinian people on an electoral process that was free, fair and secure. The Quartet believes that the Palestinian people have the right to expect that a new government will address their aspirations for peace and statehood, and it welcomed President Abbas' affirmation that the Palestinian Authority is committed to the Roadmap, previous agreements and obligations between the parties, and a negotiated two-state solution to the Israeli-Palestinian conflict. It is the view of the Quartet that all members of a future Palestinian government must be committed to nonviolence, recognition of Israel, and acceptance of previous agreements and obligations, including the Roadmap. We urge both parties to respect their existing agreements, including on movement and access. Mindful of the needs of the Palestinian people, the Quartet discussed the issue of assistance to the Palestinian Authority. . . . [T]he Quartet concluded that it was inevitable that future assistance to any new government would be reviewed by donors against that government's commitment to the principles of nonviolence, recognition of Israel, and acceptance of previous agreements and obligations, including the Roadmap. The Quartet calls upon the newly elected PLC to support the formation of a government committed to these Principles.[6]

This was a remarkably tough line for the Quartet – that is, the EU, and Russia, and Kofi Annan – to adopt within days of the Hamas victory. We were delighted. In plainer English, what had the Quartet just said? It had enunciated what soon became known as the three "Quartet Principles": Hamas must abandon violence and terror (in Quartet language, "be committed to nonviolence"), recognize Israel's right to exist, and accept all previous agreements between the Palestinians and Israel. If it did not do so, the statement politely threatened, it was "inevitable" that aid to the PA would be cut. The price of acceptance was not immediate disarmament, but it was very high: Hamas would have to abandon all acts of violence and terror and agree with Abbas that armed resistance was over. It would have to abandon its Charter, with its goal of eliminating Israel. It would have to accept the Oslo Accords and every agreement made since then, agreements in which Arafat and the PLO had accepted the right of Israel to exist permanently. At the press conference after the Quartet meeting, Rice and Solana made all this clear. Rice said, "[T]here are a set of obligations that have been taken by Palestinian leaders over more than a decade and those obligations are noted here. It is incumbent now on all to insist that any future Palestinian government will indeed live up to those obligations." Solana then chimed in: "What I would like to say on behalf of the European Union is that once these conditions are fulfilled, the European Union will stand ready to continue to support the Palestinian economic development and democratic stability, but it has to be compliant with all these conditions which are here." Annan answered a reporter's challenge that the Quartet was refusing to respect the election result: "I think the fact that one has indicated that these three principles or requirements has [sic] to be met doesn't mean one is walking away from Hamas. If Hamas accepts them and transforms itself from an armed movement into a political party respecting the rules of the game and representing its people, I think the international community should be able to work with them."[7]

The Quartet Principles soon achieved what may have appeared to be canonical status. Visiting Jerusalem right after the election, German chancellor Merkel told the press that the Hamas victory "means that continued cooperation will only be possible under three conditions: Hamas needs to recognize the existence of Israel; Hamas has to prove that the use of violence is out of the question; and Hamas needs to respect and accept steps in the peace process reached so far."[8] But we in the administration were under no illusions about Quartet and wider international solidarity. This Quartet Statement was a victory, but it could be undermined quickly. The Russians and some in the UN bureaucracy wanted very much to talk to Hamas despite its status as a terrorist group and before it had made the slightest gesture toward fulfilling the Quartet Principles. The UN special envoy for the Middle East, Alvaro de Soto, immediately made plans to meet with Ismail Haniyeh, the Hamas leader who was the likely PA prime minister (and did get the post). Fortunately, David Welch and I found out about de Soto's plans and immediately blocked them. Smiling photos of the UN's top official in the region meeting with terrorist leaders were not what we had in mind for keeping the pressure on Hamas.

"The Quartet Was Looking for Any Sign that Hamas Was Going to Come Over"

There is a myth that, from the day of the elections, Bush policy was to destroy any Hamas government and undo the election results. In fact, the policy was to destroy any Hamas government that remained committed to terrorism and eliminating the State of Israel, but not before testing whether Hamas could be moved away from those positions. The Russians and others sent messages to Hamas that were supposed to say, "We can work something out if you will accept the Quartet Principles" but more likely suggested to Hamas that Russia would seize on any gesture to break up the unified Quartet position toward Hamas. As Condi Rice described it, Hamas "missed an opportunity because I think early on, particularly through the Russians, the Quartet tried to send signals that if they would accept – even kind of make a feint in the way of those conditions, then there might be something for them...even an inch in that direction.... [W]e were kind of holding the fort, because the Quartet was looking for *any* sign that Hamas was going to come over."[9]

Various face-saving devices were offered to Hamas: Hamas could say it would be bound by all agreements Arafat had signed, or that it accepted the right of the PLO to negotiate a binding agreement with Israel. Hamas could have invented all sorts of ambiguous formulations, allowing those who wanted to engage with it to say, "See, this is new, let's build on it." Hamas might have dissected the principles, arguing that the three were not of equal importance: Surely the abandonment of terrorism and violence was fundamental, and the issues of "recognition" of Israel and the exact Hamas position on previous agreements were complex and could be negotiated later. But that, of course, would have required at least a commitment to abandon violence and terror once and for all, something Hamas was entirely unwilling to make. Instead, Hamas stood firm on its own principles and, as Rice said, "that really took the air out of the talk-to-Hamas movement."[10] The Quartet solidarity, especially the apparent toughness of the U.S. and European positions, was a gift to us from Hamas.

Interlocutors with the terrorist group found that its Charter reflected not the ravings of a few Hamas founders but rather the views of its top officials. Hamas had omitted its call for an end to Israel from its election manifesto but made clear that its basic views were unchanged. There would be no end to terrorism: "We will not stand against the resistance, we will not condemn any operation and will never arrest any mujahed [holy warrior]," said Khaled Meshal, a top Hamas leader. "Anyone who thinks Hamas will change is wrong."[11] Instead, Hamas said a long-term truce was possible only if Israel withdrew to 1967 borders – meaning not only all of the West Bank but also evacuating all of the Old City of Jerusalem including the Jewish Quarter – and recognized the "right of return." With this demand, Hamas rejected all three of the "Quartet Principles."

Back home after the Quartet meeting in London, we continued to elaborate a way forward. One option was to separate the executive and legislative branches of the PA government; it was not a pure parliamentary system because it had an elected president with considerable power. We could continue to support those organs that were under the presidency. Because the president was, under the PA Basic Law, commander in chief of the security forces, perhaps we could say that all the security organs were part of the executive branch and not under the PLC, to be led by Hamas once it convened. We could work with Abbas, refuse absolutely to work with Hamas, insist on the Quartet Principles, and force Hamas to make a choice. The position we were taking had full congressional support as well, and both houses of Congress adopted resolutions stating that "no United States assistance should be provided directly to the PA if any representative political party holding a majority of parliamentary seats within the PA maintains a position calling for the destruction of Israel."

Here was part of the notice that USAID put out describing what was and was not permissible:

1. Contact with PA Ministries: No contact is allowed with PA officials under the authority of the Prime Minister or any other minister. Contact with all officials in these ministries, including working-level employees, is prohibited.

2. Contact with the PA Presidency: Contact is allowed with the Palestinian Authority Presidency and agencies under his authority, including the Office of the President, Presidential Security, General Intelligence, Governors and Governorate staff, the Attorney General's Office, and the Palestine Investment Fund (PIF). This list may be updated from time to time.

3. Contact with Independent PA Entities: Contact is allowed with PA offices and officials that are independent of the Prime Minister and cabinet ministers. This includes: The Palestinian Judiciary, including the Higher Judicial Council; Members of the Palestinian Legislative Council (PLC), PLC staff, and officials under their authority who are not Designated Terrorist Organization (DTO) members or affiliates [All PLC members elected on the Hamas-affiliated ticket and their staffs are off-limits] and Independent agencies, including the Central Elections Commission; the Independent Citizens Rights Commission; the General Audit Authority/External Audit Agency; and the Palestinian Monetary Authority. This list may be updated from time to time.[12]

There is no path to statehood through violence and terror, Secretary Rice put it when we met in her conference room, so what we are doing is the only way forward toward peace. When the King of Jordan visited on February 8, the president told him that Hamas could obviously not be a partner for peace if its platform calls for the destruction of Israel. Expect a tough American line on this, he explained to the king. Our goal remains the same: peace, the two-state solution. But I can't force a peace deal if the situation is impossible, the president said, and things will move according to reality in the region, not the American political calendar. I am not going to try and force a solution to get a Nobel Peace Prize, he told Abdullah.

The following day, Tzipi Livni, who had been named Israel's foreign minister, visited the White House and the president reiterated that we would not yield with regard to Hamas. He did not think the Palestinian people would turn to the Hamas philosophy, he said, because there was such a large, secular, educated middle class. But if they do, he told her, just finish building the wall. Of one thing the president was sure: This was no time for any disagreements or tensions with Israel. Reviewing a memo we at the NSC had written about Hamas, his only comment was that, above all else, we should be sure that there is no daylight between the United States and Israel.

On February 18, the PLC convened and Hamas took over, with a clear majority of 74 of 132 seats. In the month since its election victory, it had remained true to its "principles." Those who were surprised by this misunderstood the nature of the group. Hamas was not a political party but rather an armed terrorist organization that espoused a militant and extreme Islamist view. Yet the search for "moderates" inside Hamas continued, especially by some bureaucrats from Europe and the UN. Abbas, in his speech opening the parliamentary session, was clear: The PA was bound by agreements previously signed.

By contrast to what happened in the PA, Israel's elections on March 28 were no surprise: Kadima won the most seats. The new party took 28 seats in the 120-member Knesset, meaning that Olmert would need to cobble together a coalition. Labor came in second with 20 seats and would obviously be part of that coalition. The very next day, March 29, the new PA cabinet was sworn in, under Ismail Haniyeh as prime minister. The cabinet had 24 members and Hamas provided 19 of them. Several technocrats and one Christian were added to the mix.

David Welch and I went back to the region on March 30. We had the unhappy task of telling President Abbas that the $50 million given to the PA must now be returned, if there was anything left. The way our lawyers saw it, there was no alternative. Abbas and Fayyad, who had no desire to leave money in the till for Hamas, complied – and we found that very little of the money had been spent. We told Abbas about our legal debates, which were still somewhat unsettled: Exactly which PA organs could we fund and to what extent? Actually, the debates were leaning toward funding the presidency, but we did not want to risk building up expectations we could not meet so we left it vague.

"Hitkansut"

Back in Jerusalem, Weissglas was still in the Prime Minister's Office, but he was a Sharon guy. This position would not last; once Olmert assembled his own team, Weissglas would be out. Tourgeman's fate was less clear because he was a career diplomat. Weissglas explained to us that the new Israeli cabinet would be different. Sharon had truly dominated his government; Olmert would not. There would be much more politics, with everyone wondering when the next election would come. Typically, he told us, a new prime minister governs for a year or at best two, and then enters the election cycle. Olmert was committed to withdrawals in the West Bank, said Dubi, but he would find it much harder to implement them than it would have been for Sharon. Welch and I then met at length with officials of Israel's National Security Council (a group that sometimes advised the prime minister but was more often kept quite distant from the corridors of power), and found that they had devoted tremendous efforts to studying withdrawals in the West Bank – how to sequence actions, what to do and where, how to maintain security, and what locations could not be given up at all.

As I reflected on the meetings with Israelis, it seemed to me that the Israeli right had not had a conversion to believing in Palestinian statehood. Instead, the conversion had been from believing in "Greater Israel," including the West Bank, to believing in separation from the Palestinians. Statehood was, to them, a tactic to achieve separation, and if Hamas were to be in charge of the state or even a major force within it, they would drop their support for that tactic. That would be the end of the Roadmap. But it might not be the end of separation; it might not mean staying in every place in the West Bank they then held. So while further disengagement might not produce a Palestinian state in accordance with the Roadmap, it might well produce real separation on the ground – already achieved in Gaza, next in the West Bank or major parts of it. To me, this suggested a way forward because any Israeli pullback in the West Bank, involving tens of thousands of settlers, would necessarily take years: We should continue to support Abbas against Hamas (despite all his weaknesses, Abbas was all we had), continue the pressure for Fatah reform, and try to beat Hamas in the next election and make its January victory a one-time fluke. I did not believe Hamas would change, but trying to create internal splits within Hamas was a no-lose proposition; that effort too could go ahead so long as it was Hamas that bent its principles, not the PA. Americans would have no part in that "split Hamas" effort, but Russia and other governments, including the Arabs, were going to try anyway.

Three weeks later, Welch and I traveled to London for a quiet dinner with Weissglas and Tourgeman. Weissglas spoke with great seriousness about Olmert's new approach: what Olmert had renamed *hitkansut* or "convergence," replacing Sharon's term "disengagement." The first step would be a Gaza-style compensation law for the West Bank, which would lead some significant proportion of settlers to leave – a fourth, a third, perhaps more. There were thousands who would leave now if they could, but there were no buyers for their houses, especially those in outlying settlements. This law would be implemented without any coordination with the PA, of course, said Dubi, but if there were at some point a new Palestinian government without Hamas, Israel could reengage with it. All this would take plenty of time anyway and required completion of the fence – a 9- to 18-month proposition itself. Israel could withdraw from up to 90% of the West Bank, about 12% of which was west of the fence; there could be further bargaining down the road. As to Jerusalem, Weisglass said that the municipality was too large and its borders should be adjusted; it now took in too many Arab villages and even a refugee camp at Shuafat. He did not suggest that the Old City or Holy Basin would be affected or shared with the PA.

For this withdrawal to happen, he said, the United States would need to commend Israel for such a pullback and support it, as it did in Gaza. In turn, Israel would state that a final status agreement was still needed and that everything had to be negotiated. Yet the key was the status of the major settlement blocks. As part of such a huge pullback in the West Bank, he said, we will annex these blocks and we will want U.S. support. That's the price of getting us out of the West Bank now. We are getting nothing from the Palestinians, so why do this? The only compensation is from you, the United States. We have to be able to persuade Israelis that we are getting out of 90% percent of the West Bank so that our hold on the other 10% will be better, stronger. Look, he said, Camp David would have given the Palestinians maybe 94 or 95% of the West Bank; under this approach, they will have us out of 90 or 91%. So we are arguing about 3% only. And we could say something about swaps, so some of that could even be remedied.

But Israel won't do this without you, Weisglass continued. We need coordination and we need your approval. Otherwise, we're going to be in a kind of confrontation with you, and all these moves would be without compensation. Now is the time to do it – under Sharon's shadow and while Bush is there, and before it's too late.

Welch and I did not respond because we had no authority to do so. Moreover, it was not entirely clear for whom Weissglas spoke: Was this really the Olmert plan? And even if it was, Olmert had no government yet and coalition negotiations were still continuing, so who could tell what compromises might come in the future? Finally, Weissglas was a terrific negotiator and might well be staking out some positions he planned to trade away later. I could not see the administration supporting formal Israeli annexation of the major settlement blocks, but I could see some compromises that would allow us to support the basic plan – especially if it was the only game in town.

After all, the Hamas victory had prevented the negotiations we had envisioned. After Aqaba in June 2003, it was Arafat who had prevented the expected peace negotiations between Israel and an "empowered" Palestinian prime minister. When negotiations were blocked, Sharon had moved in Gaza, unilaterally. Arafat's death and Abbas's election as president had opened the door for negotiation after Gaza disengagement, but Sharon's stroke had created a delay – and now the Hamas victory threw any chance for peace negotiations out the window once again. On April 17, there had been a terrorist attack – a suicide bombing of a falafel restaurant in central Tel Aviv that had killed 11 and injured 60 people – and Hamas, or rather someone speaking for the new Hamas-led PA government, had justified it as an act of self-defense. So once again the Israelis were proposing to make unilateral decisions, but ones that would lead in a direction we all favored. Once again, if one could not envision "peace," one could envision President Bush leaving office with the situation on the ground transformed.

The central question, then, was what Israel planned. Gen. Giladi described his sense of the moment:

Olmert gets into the prime minister office and he's elected for one single thing and this is what we used to call the convergence. He one hundred percent adopted the concept that we take the momentum created with the disengagement and move on the West Bank.... Let's shape the future unilaterally. We put up this fence – barrier, wall, whatever people call it. We pull out of Gaza.... In the next two to three years we can incentivize people to move.... [I]if you have most of the West Bank empty of Israelis, all Gaza empty of Israelis, and arrange the connections between the two, this is exactly the second phase of the Roadmap: a Palestinian state with provisional borders and attributes of sovereignty that we will recognize – and the language I used was "We will agree to a Palestinian state without an agreement." ... The basic element was the financial compensation package and then if you remember something called the ideological compensation package.... I said, "You know, we would like to have some people ready to move – even religious people, not just the secular people; not the extreme, but those that they will move if we can let them move into the big blocks. So they would say, "You know, it's hard, but we'll do Ma'ale Adumim, Gush Etzion..." So we discussed at that time can we change the formula of the understanding we have about no building in settlements.... The real goal was to create a semi-state actor for final status negotiation. There is no way we can negotiate with a bunch of militias.[13]

Like Weissglas, Giladi understood the constraints on construction in settlements but believed they would have to be lifted somewhat to make "convergence" work – if and when settlers coming from the areas beyond the fence decided to move to the major blocks. Our rule about "new construction only in already built-up areas" might have to be bent, he was arguing, if those areas could simply not accommodate the numbers of settlers who wished to move there. I advised Giladi at the time that Olmert should present this package of ideas directly to the president because I was confident he would be intrigued by them just as he had been by Sharon's proposals.

The attraction for Israel was clear: As Olmert's new chief of staff, Yoram Turbowitz, described it, "the beauty of it was really that it all depends on us.... What was appealing in the *hitkansut* and was appealing in the disengagement was that we are taking our destiny in our hands."[14] Down the road, Olmert hoped for American and perhaps European support for recognition at the United Nations that through *hitkansut* Israel had fulfilled its obligations under Resolution 242, passed after the 1967 war. It would have withdrawn from most but not all of the territories it had occupied in 1967 – from all of Gaza and perhaps 90% of the West Bank.

The Israelis recognized that the withdrawal from the West Bank was far more complicated than disengagement from Gaza (security and water issues alone guaranteed that) and perhaps had come to realize that greater cooperation with the Palestinians was in their own interest. Of course, they could not cooperate with the PA because of the Hamas election victory, but they could try to cooperate with President Abbas. In fact, if this cooperation worked well, it was possible to strengthen his role and his influence; in any event, the goal would be to ensure that Abbas and not Hamas got the "peace dividend," the credit for any Israeli withdrawal.

Olmert later described the situation to me, as he saw it when he assumed power:

At that time, I was skeptical about an agreement.... I decided to spell it out in a most explicit way before the elections, which most of my advisors said was a mistake because it would lose me votes. But I said, "I want to have a mandate, a clear mandate so that if I'm elected, I can act, no one can come with complaints and tell me they didn't know what I'm going to do." I said, "First I will try seriously and genuinely negotiations. If the negotiations will fail, then I will not hesitate to pull out on a unilateral basis."

I think that the strategic goal is separation. Now, preferably through agreement. If it doesn't work, then pulling out unilaterally, even, is still better. Look, I think that the fact that we pulled out from Gaza completely gave us the moral power and the moral support from the world to do whatever we wanted to do in Gaza. We were never criticized, not one time, not just by you, OK, but even Europe. There was no criticism. Why? Because everyone said, "What do you want from these guys? They pulled out completely and they're being attacked on a daily basis." So I still think that pulling out from the West Bank – from where we *want* to pull out – not from 100%.... I'm ready... if an agreement will not be signed.[15]

The Bush administration did not favor Israeli unilateralism because we had seen Hamas benefit from it in Gaza. There, the lack of cooperation between Israel and the PA had prevented, or at least undermined, Abbas's ability to gain credit for the Israeli withdrawal. The West Bank was both more complicated and more consequential. Condi Rice was very dubious: "I was just always uncomfortable with the unilateral withdrawal.... In the final analysis, I didn't think it would work."[16] Why not? For one thing, because the withdrawal would not be complete, as it had been in Gaza, it would be immensely complex. Palestinians and Israelis would still be living next to each other in many areas. There would be no negotiated security arrangements at all. There would be no arrangements regarding water. There would be endless arguments – including with the United States – about the exact lines of the withdrawal, which Israel could not specify for us.

Olmert Comes to Washington

On April 30, Olmert gained the support of Shas, a Sephardic-based religious party, giving him a majority in the Knesset. On May 4, his new government was approved, holding 67 of the 120 seats, with Kadima, Labor, Shas, and the new Pensioners Party making up the coalition. Three weeks later, Olmert came to Washington; the Oval Office meeting with the President was on May 23. At preliminary meetings with Secretary Rice, Steve Hadley, Welch, and me, he reiterated that he intended to move from Gaza disengagement to his "convergence" plan in the West Bank. This would reduce the Israeli presence to a minimum and thereby reduce Israeli-Palestinian friction. Rice told him that the president would push him to try negotiations first, so Olmert was ready for that message when it came. I prefer negotiations, he told Bush; if there is a chance for negotiations under the Roadmap, that's better. Start there, the president told him. Olmert agreed to meet with Abbas but expressed his doubts: He did not think Abbas was capable of delivering anything. Still, he agreed to try. Let's try to get it done in two years, the president said. Assume that Abbas can deliver, and you can move in a different way if he does not. Go the extra mile with him. OK, said Olmert, but the problem is they need to recognize Israel and put an end to terrorism. I will meet with him and do what I can for him. What we can't do is replace his determination to fight terrorist organizations.

The president invited Olmert for a lengthy talk on the Truman Balcony of the White House overlooking the South Lawn, joined only by Mrs. Olmert. It was a typically Bush-like gesture: courteous but also smart. He wanted to see how the Olmerts related to each other, how her presence changed the way Olmert acted or spoke, what her influence on him might be. Olmert reiterated his plan to move forward in the West Bank and told the president he was absolutely sincere about it. But it would not work without strong American support, he said, and he needed it. The president again pressed him to try negotiations first. He would support unilateral moves in the end, he said, but only if and when negotiations had been tried and had failed.

This session was significant not only in persuading both men that they had a common vision of the path ahead but also in cementing Bush's positive impression of Olmert. The president was well aware of the corruption accusations against Olmert that grew louder and louder during his tenure as prime minister, in the end destroying his political career. But he did not share the view of Olmert as a man without principles whose main goal was to feather his nest. During a conversation with Israeli journalists held nearly two years later, for example, they explained fully the widespread view of Olmert in Israel as a shifty politician, and I had always kept the president informed of Olmert's political situation. Week after week and month after month, especially if I had been to Israel on a trip, the president would greet my next appearance in the Oval Office with the question, "How's my buddy Olmert?" I pulled no punches, keeping him up to date on Olmert's political and legal travails and on his declining poll numbers. He would sometimes wince or shake his head, but he believed Olmert was sincere about seeking to move forward in the West Bank.

One other issue arose, for the first time, during that visit: the idea of some kind of big international conference on the Middle East. Condi was beginning to think about it. At that point it was not at all clear why she wanted it because Palestinian politics were still entirely unsettled, and the new Olmert government was providing a way ahead now in the West Bank. Olmert was entirely against such a conference: Whatever was done with the Palestinians would be unilateral or at best bilateral. He saw no role for Europe and the Arab states at that point. Yet Condi's intentions were serious enough for her to take Olmert aside in a one-on-one conversation, following a larger meeting we all had at Blair House where Olmert was staying. She asked Olmert about the possibility of having a big conference on the Middle East in December. Olmert reacted negatively:

And I then said, "I don't know what you need this international conference for.... I'm not going to negotiate with 20 Arab countries at the same time, there is no way that I am going to do it. I am ready to sit with Abu Mazen; until now he turned down all my attempts to meet with him. So, if he needs some kind of an international umbrella to help him get into touch with me, that's fine." And, so she said, "OK, we'll talk about it." But then, you know, Lebanon came, and everything's changed.[17]

Actually, everything changed even before the Second Lebanon War. Within six weeks, the hopes that existed after Olmert's visit to Washington were largely gone. I was increasingly coming to understand the view that David Welch and many others in the Near East Bureau at State took. Some people there were simply anti-Israel, and the notion that there was an old "Arabist" school in NEA was certainly true. But Welch's view was different: Although he did not believe anything the Israelis said, he also did not believe anything the Arabs said or anything that was pledged and promised and predicted because he had been burned too many times. Even when people spoke in good faith, their ability to control events was suspect; predicting and even controlling the future seemed a lot more likely in Washington than in the Middle East. When people assured you of the many good things they would soon do, the biblical term "soothsayer" came more and more frequently to mind. In just six months, we had seen hopes dashed when Sharon had a stroke, raised again when Olmert pledged to move forward, dashed when Hamas won its election victory, and then raised by the prospect of movement despite Hamas, whether through unilateral Israeli movement or through negotiations over the West Bank. Now in a matter of weeks came more Israeli-Palestinian violence, a Hamas-Fatah unity government, and then war.

Among the Palestinian factions, there was "progress" toward a political agreement and a national unity government in May. Palestinian prisoners from Hamas, Islamic Jihad, Fatah, the PFLP, and the DFLP who were together in Israeli jails overcame factional differences and produced on May 11 a "Document of National Accord." They strongly urged cooperation of all factions in a new unity government that would move toward Palestinian statehood, including "all the territories occupied in 1967" and "the right of the refugees to return." The document also asserted the "right of the Palestinian people to resistance; adhering to the option of resistance through various means," which appeared to include terrorism. The "use of weapons" was banned when it came to internal struggles only, and only "shedding Palestinian blood" was called "inadmissible." On June 27, Hamas, Fatah, and other groups backed this document. Later, in August, President Abbas said the prime minister, Ismail Haniyeh of Hamas, would talk with Fatah leaders with the goal of creating a national unity government. But the terms of all these moves clearly did not meet the Quartet Principles; Hamas was not being required to say the magic words. We told Abbas, and leaders of Arab states, repeatedly throughout this period that nothing good could come of this effort. Our financial boycott of the Hamas-led PA government would not end and, indeed, the establishment of the unity government could come to ruin our relationship with Abbas and Fatah. It would end any prospect of negotiations with Israel.

In addition, while the political negotiations among Fatah and Hamas leaders were underway, their followers were beginning to fight each other. For the first time since the elections in January, there had been a serious clash, which occurred on May 8 in southern Gaza, killing 3 and wounding 11; while the prisoners were cooperating, those out of prison were shooting at each other. Throughout May and June, each side reacted by trying to strengthen its own forces.

On June 10 came the end of the 16-month partial truce between Hamas and Israel. An explosion on a Gaza beach on June 9 killed eight civilians and wounded dozens of others. Hamas claimed that the explosion was caused by Israeli shelling; an Israeli investigation denied responsibility, saying it might have been caused by a Palestinian land mine or the explosion of shells that had landed on the beach earlier and been covered by sand. No matter: Hamas responded by formally ending the truce and firing Qassam missiles into Israel. This would not necessarily have had a huge impact without the events of June 25. On that day, Hamas forces tunneled from Gaza into Israel, killed two soldiers, and kidnapped a third, Corporal Gilad Shalit. Between the Israeli withdrawal in the summer of 2005 and late June 2006, Hamas had fired more than 750 rockets and mortars into Israel (with the pace quickening in 2006), but Israel had responded only with artillery and from the air.[18] The kidnapping of Shalit, and the killing of two other soldiers, was the last straw, and Israel responded with "Operation Summer Rains," its first major ground operation in Gaza since disengagement. We now faced an Israel at war with Hamas while Hamas and Fatah negotiated over a unity government. As part of "Summer Rains," Israeli forces seized 64 Hamas officials, including PLC members and cabinet ministers.

The recent talk of peace negotiations suddenly seemed far away. Yet what no one anticipated was another war that would largely destroy Olmert's political position – and Rice's own relationship with and faith in him and in Israel's political and military leadership. The Bush policy that had been formulated in June 2002 would become another casualty of the Second Lebanon War of 2006.

Notes

1. Sharon, *Sharon*, 545.
2. Ari Shavit, "The Big Freeze," *Haaretz*, October 8, 2004, http://jewishpolitic alchronicle.org/nov04/Big%20freeze.pdf.
3. Ehud Olmert, "Address by Acting PM Ehud Olmert to the 6th Herzliya Confer- ence," *Israel Ministry of Foreign Affairs*, January 24, 2006, http://www.mfa.gov. il/MFA/Government/Speeches+by+Israeli+leaders/2006/Address+by+Acting+PM+ Ehud+Olmert+to+the+6th+Herzliya+Conference+24-Jan-2006.htm.
4. Herb Keinon, Gil Hoffman, and Etgar Lefkovits, "Olmert: We Will Separate within Four Years," *Jerusalem Post*, March 9, 2006, http://www.jpost.com/Home/Article. aspx?id=15613.
5. Walles, interview, p. 17.
6. Middle East Quartet, "Quartet Statement," news release, January 30, 2006, http://www.consilium.europa.eu/uedocs/cms_data/docs/pressdata/en/declarations/ 88201.pdf.

7. Ibid.
8. "Israel Seeks World Support over Hamas," CNN, January 29, 2006, http://www.cnn.com/2006/WORLD/meast/01/29/mideast/.
9. Rice, interview, p. 8.
10. Ibid.
11. Tim Butcher, "Hamas Offers Deal if Israel Pulls Out," *Daily Telegraph*, February 9, 2006, http://www.telegraph.co.uk/news/worldnews/middleeast/israel/1510074/Hamas-offers-deal-if-Israel-pulls-out.html.
12. Roy Plucknett, "Contact Policy for the Palestinian Authority," USAID, April 26, 2006, http://www.usaid.gov/wbg/misc/2006-WBG-17.pdf.
13. Giladi, interview, pp. 12–13, 2, 14.
14. Yoram Turbowitz, interview by the author, January 31, 2010, pp. 3–4.
15. Ehud Olmert, interview by the author, June 25, 2009, pp. 2–3.
16. Rice, interview, p. 2.
17. Olmert, interview, p. 8.
18. "The Hamas Terror War against Israel," *Israel Ministry of Foreign Affairs*, March 2011, http://www.mfa.gov.il/MFA/Terrorism+Obstacle+to+Peace/Palestinian+terror+since+2000/Missile+fire+from+Gaza+on+Israeli+civilian+targets+Aug+2007.htm.

7

War in Lebanon – and Condi

On July 12, 2006, Hizballah attacked Israel with rockets and mortars, and Hizballah terrorists stormed across the Israel-Lebanon border, attacking a squad of Israeli soldiers. They killed eight soldiers and kidnapped two, although whether either was by then alive or how long those two stayed alive remained unclear. This action started the Lebanon War, which is worth describing briefly, because though it did not affect Israeli-Palestinian issues directly, it had an enormous impact on U.S.-Israel relations, especially on Condi Rice's view of and relations with Israeli officials and on Olmert's political fate. On July 13, Israel struck back at Hizballah, with air and artillery; Hizballah raised the ante with rocket attacks on Israeli villages and towns, including Haifa, averaging about 100 rockets a day. Israel's air strikes and artillery were soon joined by ground operations, and the targets included not only Hizballah leadership, weapons caches, and rocket launch sites but also parts of the Lebanese infrastructure that Hizballah used. Hizballah continued its rocket fire at Israeli towns, and soon hundreds of thousands of Israelis were either living in bomb shelters or had evacuated toward the south; similarly, hundreds of thousands of Lebanese fled the fighting, moving north. During the war, 157 Israelis and roughly 1,000 Lebanese were killed. The fighting lasted for a month, ending with UN Security Council Resolution 1701, passed on August 11 and accepted by Israel on August 13. The text demanded an end to the fighting and an Israeli withdrawal from Lebanon. To prevent a recurrence, the resolution called for an enlargement of the UN's force in southern Lebanon, UNIFIL, to 15,000 and the deployment of 15,000 Lebanese Army troops in the same area, with the goal of ending Hizballah's control there. Resolution 1701 also required that no outside power rearm Hizballah; arms could go only to the Lebanese Army. Finally, it demanded the release of the two kidnapped Israeli soldiers (whose bodies were finally exchanged with Israel in July 2008).

"Hizballah Had to Lose"

When the fighting began, it was crystal clear to everyone – not just in Israel and in Washington but also in Arab capitals – that Hizballah had started it. Given that Hizballah was a Shia group armed by and allied with Iran, it elicited no sympathy from the Arabs, who looked forward to seeing Israel thrash it – and told us so. Condi's clearly stated view when the war began, which was shared by Hadley and the president, was that Hizballah had to lose.

In the early days, we assumed this outcome would happen, as it seems did everyone else: the Israelis, Europeans, and Arabs. That assessment under-rated Hizballah's strength and organizational skills, but later Israeli analyses tended to the conclusion that Israel's effort had been poorly organized. The official report (from the Winograd Commission) concluded that the government did not decide between the two options: "a short, painful, strong and unexpected blow on Hezbollah, primarily through standoff fire-power" and "a large ground operation, including a temporary occupation of the South of Lebanon." During the early weeks of the war, there was "equivocation" between these approaches, causing "a very long delay in the deployment nec-essary for an extensive ground offensive." The report concluded, "As a result, Israel did not stop after its early military achievements, and was 'dragged' into a ground operation only after the political and diplomatic timetable prevented its effective completion."[1]

I do not recall any analysis predicting this outcome, and we did not anticipate it. We were concerned mostly with the thousands of American citizens caught up by the war. We chartered commercial ships and used U.S. Navy vessels to help them escape from Lebanon. We also began talking early on about an international force in Lebanon that – assuming Hizballah would be weakened by this war – could step into the south and prevent Hizballah from reconquering territory near the Israeli border.

But as the weeks dragged on, we and the Europeans began to split from Israel over the desired consequences for Lebanon. We and the French, with the rest of the EU following, had built a strongly supportive relationship with Fouad Siniora, the prime minister who had assumed office after the Syrian departure and the May–June 2005 elections. While Rafik Hariri's son Saad led the Sunni community and the preeminent Future Party, it was widely agreed that an older and more experienced figure should lead the cabinet. Siniora had been a successful finance minister and was a skilled technocrat, and he had worked for Rafik Hariri in the past. In Washington, we viewed him as a talented official dedicated to Lebanese independence; only as time went by did I come to see the depths of his Arab nationalist beliefs and his deep hostility to Israel.

The difference between the United States and Israel was that we wanted to protect Siniora and his government; we did not want them, too, to be casualties of the war. Over time, the survival of Siniora and his government became the central European war aim and an increasingly important one of ours. But not so for the Israelis. When we visited the region in mid-July, Livni said to me flatly that "[s]aving Siniora is not an Israeli goal. He is too weak. We don't care to save him." Olmert told us that the main goals were clear: to hit Hizballah, to reduce their firepower, and to reduce the missile threat substantially. Saving Siniora was not on the list. Meanwhile, the conflict in Gaza continued: Israel was fighting on two fronts.

The Arab leaders had hoped for a quick knockout of Hizballah; now they were torn. "Lebanon is being destroyed," one top Arab official told us glumly, but he had no advice to offer; his government did not want Hizballah to win. The president's view in late July was clear: This war was an Iranian move, using its surrogate Hizballah just as it was using surrogates in Iraq. We all agreed that a victory for Siniora and for Lebanon was vital, and the way to get it was through victory by the IDF. In the end, we needed a more effective international force in the south of Lebanon and a more effective Lebanese Army, sharing the job of constraining Hizballah. We need shooters, not school-crossing guards, the president told visitors. A ceasefire today is a win for Hizballah, so we would oppose it. It was clear to him and to Rice that the European (and in public, at least, the Arab) demand for an immediate ceasefire was a mistake and that it would only benefit Hizballah. Give the IDF time to pound them. Then, at some point a bit down the road, organize a bridging force and then a permanent international force in south Lebanon. That would give the Israelis an excuse to stop fighting and would result in a long-term change on the ground.

On August 2, Olmert had told a reporter that "Israel will stop fighting when the international force will be present in the south of Lebanon." He continued, "We can't stop before because if there will not be a presence of a very effective and robust military international force, Hezbollah will be there and we will have achieved nothing."[2] But securing that international force would not be easy. I recall a conversation, one of many, between Rice and Prince Bandar, the long-time Saudi ambassador. She described our goals, and he asked why Hizballah would ever agree to them. International pressure, she answered. "Don't count on it," Bandar replied.

A big international conference on the war in Lebanon was called for July 26 in Rome. On July 21, Rice held a press conference announcing her travel plans and said that "a ceasefire would be a false promise if it simply returns us to the status quo, allowing terrorists to launch attacks at the time and terms of their choosing and to threaten innocent people, Arab and Israeli, throughout the region. That would be a guarantee of future violence."[3] In preparation for the conference, we flew first to Beirut to see Siniora; the war was now in its third week. It was not safe to use the airport in Beirut, so Rice's plane landed in Cyprus and we jumped over to Beirut in a helicopter. The ancient military craft was deafeningly loud and leaked oil all over us, ruining suits, dresses, and hairdos as we flew the 125 miles. We rigged up plastic sheeting over Rice to protect her from the steady dripping. On the ground, Rice's motorcade rushed through the city at high and unsafe speeds, seeking to avoid possible ambushes or bombs.

"Why Do I Have to Ask for the Force?"

At his beautiful offices in downtown Beirut, built by Rafik Hariri, Rice told Prime Minister Siniora that we opposed any return to the status quo ante and thus opposed an immediate ceasefire. No one has confidence in UNIFIL, she added; the UN force in southern Lebanon had never actually constrained Hizballah, and a "UNIFIL Plus" would be no better – she would not support it. We need a bridging force that is serious, allowing a ceasefire to hold, and then a really capable force from NATO or the EU to put into southern Lebanon and along the Syria–Lebanon border (to block arms shipments going to Hizballah). Turkey, Jordan, and Egypt might be invited to join. If Siniora said yes, she would get a yes from Olmert at her next stop, the Rome conference could endorse the plan, and then we would go to New York to get it put into a Security Council resolution. All of that could be done in a week, Rice told him. The war would then be over. How do we start? You ask for this international force, she told Siniora.

He balked. Why do I have to ask for the force, he said; the Security Council should just impose it. Rice was startled; did he not want to take the lead in asserting Lebanese sovereignty? Siniora gulped. No force, no ceasefire? That's right, Rice replied. No one can protect South Lebanon without an international force now. The humanitarian situation will get worse. You could have a major accident by the IDF, she said. So, what you should do now is agree that the government of Lebanon is prepared to accept a robust but temporary humanitarian stabilization force of several thousand. I am going to Israel tomorrow and then to Rome. I want to be able to say some elements are agreed. The alternative is that the whole Rome conference goes nowhere. You need to do two things: Demand that Hizballah leave the border area and ask for this robust force.

It was quickly evident that Siniora would do no such thing. He was more afraid of Hizballah and of Syria than of Israel and the war. In the coming weeks, his refusal to assert Lebanon's rights as a state would make our task far harder: How could we keep insisting on conditions for the protection of Lebanese sovereignty if its own government hung back? How could we demand the stationing of European or other troops on the Lebanese borders with Syria and Israel if its prime minister was mumbling? In fact, he was mumbling about everything except Israel, which he denounced in propaganda terms that Israel's actual conduct of the war belied. The Beirut International Airport was closed, but Israel was careful not to damage it beyond making a runway temporarily unusable; it reopened within a week of the passage of Security Council Resolution 1701. Same for the port. Same for downtown Beirut. Driving near the port, we had seen a lighthouse whose beacon was shot out by an Israeli missile. But the missile had been guided to hit only the beacon, leaving the entire structure intact and obviously capable of quick restoration. Only the Dahiye neighborhood of Beirut, a southern suburb that is Hizballah's headquarters, was badly damaged.

This was not the war Siniora's speeches described – while he carefully elided any criticism of Syria or Hizballah and refused to make the demands that the world needed to hear if real sovereignty was to be gained. Siniora was an honest man and a patriot, beleaguered on all sides; in that sense, he was an attractive figure, but his tendency to shrink from making any demands of Hizballah or Syria and to mouth instead the oldest lines about Israel ("Lebanon will be the last Arab country to make peace with Israel" was an example) eventually lost him my sympathy.

He and Rice then argued about Sheba'a Farms, eight square miles close to the Syria–Lebanon–Israel tri-border area that Siniora insisted was Lebanese and had to be mentioned in any agreement. Rice resisted, replying that the UN maintains that this area is not part of Lebanon but rather of the Syrian Golan; the UN says Israel got entirely out of Lebanese territory in 2000. This is not the time to fight over that. Any progress now is likely to be credited to Hizballah and the war, not to you, she told him. Siniora was insistent and prepared to discuss the subject endlessly. It was as if this issue relieved him of the need to face the forces that were really tearing Lebanon apart; it provided a lawyerly refuge from reality. Rice's resistance was slowly eroded, partly because she was having trouble inducing Siniora to agree to anything at all. In this visit, she agreed to throw Sheba'a into the pot, and over time she became a strong advocate of pushing Israel to give the area to Lebanon – later adding another bone of contention with Olmert and the Israelis. She summed up the situation for Siniora: If you do what I ask, you get a ceasefire, you have asserted your sovereignty, and you get some mention of Sheba'a.

We then flew to Israel, on the way working on a plan for ending the conflict. The ingredients: a prohibition on the importation of weapons by anyone but the Lebanese Army; a prohibition on militias, including Hizballah, starting near the Israeli border and over time working farther north; a new military force on the ground, with a UN mandate; a humanitarian program for Lebanon's south; and something about Sheba'a Farms. Rice was now fully on board with the inclusion of Sheba'a.

In Jerusalem, she told Olmert we did not want Lebanon to become yet another failed state. We need a big humanitarian program and an international force on the ground; it would not be a NATO force but would be really capable. The EU was not on board yet but we were working on that; Rice believed she could move the Europeans when she saw them in Rome, but this proved to be an illusion. In fact, despite efforts by Tony Blair to round up a force, EU nations were saying they would perhaps participate – but only *after* a ceasefire had been put in place. The fire brigade might arrive some day, it seemed, but not while there was an actual fire. NATO officials were saying they did not have the ability to help, and the United States would not participate in any force lest our troops become a Hizballah target, as they had been in the past. But the highest priority now is to strengthen the government of Lebanon so that it is not a failed state, Rice told the Israelis, and they need something about Sheba'a. A long argument about Sheba'a ensued, with the secretary buying and now trying to sell in Jerusalem the Siniora line that including it was essential if we wished to weaken Hizballah. Olmert and his team bought the rest of the plan but said no on Sheba'a.

"We Want a Durable Ceasefire"

Off to Rome. We had a preliminary session with Massimo D'Alema, a former prime minister (and former communist) who had become foreign minister in April. The Arabs want an immediate ceasefire, he told Rice. Let's call on Israel to stop bombing, particularly in the south, in the border area. Rice was tough: Don't try to direct Israel's military operations. She reminded D'Alema what the G-8 had done on July 16, just 10 days earlier, when it was meeting in St. Petersburg: It had issued a statement blaming Hizballah for starting the war and had *not* called for an immediate ceasefire.

In the conference room, Rice faced a terrible problem: Emotionally, most delegations simply wanted the fighting to end. They did not care about political and military considerations and avoiding the status quo ante. Siniora himself gave a tearful presentation about how Lebanon was being completely destroyed, which was false but moving. Everyone seemed to be demanding an immediate ceasefire, an end to the violence, an Israeli withdrawal. Rice was isolated – but she did not abandon or weaken the American position. She alone stopped the conference from giving in to Siniora's tears, with one brief moment of solidarity from the British Foreign Secretary Margaret Beckett – Tony Blair's last foreign minister and the first woman to hold the post. Either Beckett was reflecting Blair's pragmatic and pro-American positions, or she was simply offering some sisterly solidarity to the lonely Rice. Rice told the delegates that we need immediate humanitarian aid and a big donor's conference to rebuild Lebanon. But this time, she said, we need real peace, not a failed ceasefire. This time we want a durable ceasefire, and that depends on Lebanese sovereignty in all its territory. We do not want to be back here in six months for the same thing. We want an "urgent" end to the violence, but one that lasts.

We returned to Israel. On July 27, the day after the Rome conference, Olmert told us he wanted 10 more days of bombing and the insertion of a real international force, a fighting force, and then the war would end. Lebanon should ask for the force, he said, and we will agree to it; I want Secretary Rice to have something to deliver. But it has to be real; something has to change on the ground. We need and you need to emerge with a sense of achievement. This is just a chapter in confronting Iran and they must not win this test, he told us – sounding just like the president. Putting in a security force will take 10 days anyway; then I will be ready. Then came a long argument over the fate of Sheba'a: Olmert and Livni told Rice that leaving Sheba'a, or even agreeing to leave Sheba'a, or saying anything at all about Sheba'a, would be a victory for Hizballah. Sheba'a was not central, I thought, but this was the first real, prolonged argument between the Israelis and Rice on a policy matter.

At dinner on July 29, Rice and Olmert covered mostly humanitarian issues. Humanitarian corridors had been established, but Rice said they were not working. Olmert replied that Israel had no war with the government of Lebanon or the Lebanese people and was showing restraint, but errors are made – it is war. Yes, but you cannot win a solely military victory, she argued: Look at Iraq and Afghanistan. You can win militarily and lose politically; we did in Vietnam. The Israelis quoted Rice's recent speeches about Lebanon back at her: Hizballah must be defeated. After dinner, Rice and Olmert met alone. Olmert had reiterated that the IDF needed another week or 10 days; it believes it is really hurting Hizballah now. Of course, we felt that would be a good thing – if it were true – but we had no way of knowing that. Rice had replied that another week or 10 days of war was not sustainable without diplomacy, and diplomacy was not sustainable without some moves on Sheba'a. Olmert had given her three thousand reasons why that was not possible, she later told us. She had told Olmert that if Israel would not make any move on Sheba'a, we would: The United States could announce something, and we could give it to Lebanon.

I was startled by her report of her private meeting with Olmert: The tough and determined Rice of the Rome conference was now not only buying Siniora's Sheba'a argument lock, stock, and barrel but also telling the Israelis we would go forward on it with or without them. I thought an American move on Sheba'a would be a victory for Hizballah, won by starting a war. We could offer no other explanation for such a change in U.S. policy. It was also clear that the tone of the meeting with Olmert had not been positive – something else that was beginning to happen now. After all our meetings, I called home near midnight on a secure phone to report to the White House that slowly but surely our line was shifting. The president had been firm about dealing a defeat to Hizballah and Iran, but now we seemed to be seeking an accommodation. Perhaps the isolation at the Rome conference had taken a larger toll on Condi than I had thought – with everyone calling for an immediate end to the war, shedding tears for the Lebanese, and Condi standing almost alone for what we called "no status quo ante" but everyone else saw as "keep the war going." Whatever the reason, she was now looking less for ways to win than for ways to get the thing over with. I urged that the president call Condi with a pep talk, lest we continue to drift away from the line he had taken.

The following day Rice met with Livni and again pressed on the Sheba'a issue. On the timing of an Israeli end to operations, we were not so far apart because organizing a new force and getting the Security Council to approve it would probably take a week anyway. But Rice told Livni that it was increasingly hard to sustain the war; for us to arrange a decent finish we needed Siniora, and for that we needed something on Sheba'a. You're not thinking creatively, she told Livni, about strengthening the moderate Arabs. The United States cannot stay in its current position; we will have to move. If Israel cannot speak about Sheba'a, the United States will do so, in our own words.

Again, I was amazed by the way this marginal issue, a flimsy excuse that Hizballah proffered for its need to maintain an army, was taking center stage. If we took this position on Sheba'a, I thought, Hizballah would claim victory for its "resistance" and note that we all now acknowledged it had been right all along. And then it would find other excuses for its arms: There would be other villages it claimed were "really" Lebanese, not Israeli or Syrian.

Nevertheless, Sheba'a or no Sheba'a, Rice was working hard to get Olmert and Siniora to commit to one piece of paper – a piece of paper that could become a Security Council resolution. There was progress; the basic elements were coming together in our minds. Our plan was to go to Beirut and get Siniora on board, then return to Jerusalem for Olmert's agreement, and then head for New York. With this resolution, the war would end. It would be quite an achievement not only for the United States but also, of course, for Rice herself. She had been secretary of state for a year and a half and securing a good ceasefire – one with elements that might change the situation on the ground in southern Lebanon – would be a tremendous feat. The arguments with the Israelis would go away, understood as a matter of wartime tension; Lebanon would be better off with Hizballah constrained; and Rice's own role would be celebrated.

We were not quite there yet. Our plan included deployment of the Lebanese Army in the south, plus an international peacekeeping force and a demand by the UN and the Lebanese government that Hizballah disarm. Then a ceasefire could be declared, and Israel would address the Sheba'a issue. Yet neither Lebanon nor Israel was fully on board. The Israelis were saying no on Sheba'a. The Lebanese Cabinet approved strengthening UNIFIL and deploying the Lebanese Army in the south but no international force. And the sequence was not yet agreed: Did the ceasefire come first or would it come only after these deployments? As potential troop contributors balked, it was increasingly clear that such a quick deployment was simply not going to happen. Still, we were getting close; compromises and bridging proposals should still be possible.

Qana and After: Things Fall Apart

Everything fell apart on the night of July 29–30. Shortly after midnight, Israeli jets bombed a three-story house in Qana, a village in South Lebanon from which Israel claimed there had been rockets fired into Israel repeatedly during the war. Hiding inside the house were civilians who were fleeing the combat. Twenty-eight people were killed, half of them children, although initial media reports suggested twice those numbers. I recalled Condi saying to Siniora a week before that "you might have a major accident by the IDF." Now it had happened. We were on the phones throughout the morning hours, first trying to determine what had happened. We urged the Israelis to declare a bombing pause, at least while it investigated the incident; the following day, they announced a pause for 48 hours. The Lebanese called the bombing a deliberate assault, saying the Israelis must have known there were women and children hiding in the house;

it was a massacre and a war crime. The IDF claimed then and later that it thought the building was empty of civilians and was being used by Hizballah fighters. But the early versions varied: At one point, the Israelis were claiming they had hit the house eight hours before it collapsed on those hiding inside. This did not inspire confidence; it was the usual fog of war.

But the main effect was that Siniora canceled our visit to Beirut; we were not welcome. Siniora gave a televised address, saying, "There is no place on this sad morning for any discussion other than an immediate and unconditional cease-fire as well as an international investigation into the Israeli massacres." He added that Israel's leaders were "war criminals." Once again, I wondered why he thought he could outbid Hizballah in the rhetoric department. Rice decided to do one more round of talks with the Israelis and then head home overnight.

Unsurprisingly, these were the worst talks we had ever had with Israelis. Olmert described his impression later: "I got the message that Condi wanted to meet me immediately. She was absolutely angry at the event in Qana. It was two o'clock in the afternoon. I advised my staff to set the meeting for 7 pm. Time will cool off the atmosphere, I thought."[4]

The frost was evident immediately when we entered his office: Olmert addressed her formally as "Madam Secretary," not the usual "Condi," and as I recall it, they did not even shake hands. The discussion began with an argument about leaks. Rice complained that matters she had brought up with him in private ended up in the newspapers. He responded with the same complaint about the U.S. side: Someone had told the papers that she was going to have a very tough talk with him about Sheba'a, and that someone was not an Israeli.

Having established that each was deeply irritated with the other, they moved on. Rice pressed Olmert for compromises; give me something to work with, she told him. He responded that the Israeli view had not changed: This is not the moment to retreat or all will have been lost; a ceasefire now would make the whole effort useless; we will issue an apology but we cannot stop now or the whole effort is lost. Olmert also told her that the cabinet rejected the idea of giving up Sheba'a; even the Labor Party people said the message would be that kidnapping pays. You must keep that out of the UN resolution, or the whole world will be sending that message. He said Israel had apologized for Qana and would now investigate the incident. Rice brushed that aside. This is a new situation; pressures have been building for 18 days now (the duration of the war) and this pushes it over. After their nasty exchange over leaks, Rice warned Olmert that you said you needed 10 days; now we don't have 10 days. We will be in the Security Council this week. You have shown perseverance and strength, Olmert replied, and I see why you're angry and how difficult it is for the United States. But you know that we are right. We live here and cannot give up everything because of this one event. The ceasefire you now have in mind will not work; it will be like all the ceasefires with the Palestinians and last three days.

Rice shot back that she hadn't been standing with Israel for 18 days but for 5 years. I am analyzing this situation and we have to make some moves. We need to avoid a damaging UN resolution that says "immediate and unconditional ceasefire." You and we will need to announce a "suspension of hostilities." But what about the international force, Olmert asked. We all agreed it had to be in place before Israel would stop fighting. There will be no international force, Rice said; the circumstances have changed. The potential contributors have pulled back. Olmert speculated about an Israeli ground operation, using the limited time that remained to gain more territory, but Rice pushed back; she was trying to end this war. Olmert talked of the gains that could be achieved in a few more days on the ground, the damage Hizballah could suffer, but Rice replied that perhaps if she believed Israel could achieve this . . . but she did not. There is no political context and political sensitivity. Today puts you in a bad position. The damage is done. We cannot undo it, she told the prime minister. I need 10 more days, Olmert answered; we will hit them hard. Hizballah must get no benefit from this war.

In separate meetings, aides to Olmert told us that he would not survive politically if the war ended this way. That would mean Israel had lost the war and Iran had won: It would be a victory for Hizballah, and worse yet under U.S. pressure. This would be the first time since 9/11, Turbowitz said to me, that the United States was taking a stand against Israel after a terrorist attack.

In fact, Olmert and Rice's timetables were not so far apart because action in the UN did not come until August 11, just over 10 days later. But Olmert was arguing for the original U.S. and Israeli conditions: full deployment of an international force before a ceasefire. To Rice, this was simply unrealistic: There was going to be no such force, no matter what Israel or the United States did. So other grounds for the ceasefire would have to be found, or the war would go on forever. The minute any new forces start to deploy, you must stop, she told Olmert. I cannot hold the line against calls for an immediate ceasefire any more. There will be a gap between that call and deployment. You need to announce some sort of pause in action today, and we will shoot for the best resolution we can. We will not veto a resolution because it has "immediate ceasefire" language. Don't put us in a different position from that of the United States, Olmert pleaded – a position where the resolution passes, you say stop, and we won't stop. But Rice had said her piece: If we can establish the conditions, we are for a ceasefire and we will vote for it, she told him as the meeting ended. Accept the resolution when it passes and start implementing it. It may not be 10 days from today but it will likely be 10 days from the first time you told me you just needed 10 more days.

After the meeting, Rice told us that we could now say something like this: "We believe the elements now exist for ceasefire and if adopted by the Security Council would create a ceasefire." We will have some separation from Israel, once the resolution passes, she said; this may be good especially if there is a ground offensive this week. Let's go to the Security Council this week and set out as much as we can in the draft text. We drove to Ben Gurion Airport and took off for Washington. Rice's biographers called Lebanon her "worst crisis as Secretary of State" and said she "headed home exhausted and battered,"[5] "shaken and drained."[6]

"From Then on It Was Just Downhill"

Security Council Resolution 1701 was adopted unanimously on Friday, August 11, accepted unanimously by the Lebanese cabinet on the following day, and accepted unanimously by the Israeli cabinet the day after that. The Lebanon War of 2006 was over. Ten days of vigorous diplomacy after we returned from Israel had produced the best resolution we could get but one that did nothing to change the status quo ante. The text called for full control of Lebanese territory by the government of Lebanon and the Lebanese Army, but after the war Hizballah controlled more territory, and more firmly, than before. The text called for Hizballah to be disarmed, but it was soon rebuilding and became far stronger than before. The text said there must be no supply of arms except with the authorization of the government of Lebanon, but Hizballah subsequently received thousands of rockets and missiles from Iran and Syria. The resolution did expand the size of UNIFIL, but UNIFIL became no stronger or better able (or willing) to resist Hizballah.

During those days of diplomatic wrangling, tensions between us and the Israelis mounted even further. Hadley spoke daily with Turbowitz, but those conversations did not smooth things out. Both lawyers, the two would debate textual points endlessly, but agreement was made even harder because they were not looking at the same drafts: Somehow Israel never got the latest draft from the State Department. Relations between the two men were fine, but at bottom there was a growing gap between our position and that of Israel. They were clinging to demands they had made from the day the war started, but we had concluded that those demands simply could not be met. They reflected Israel's war aims but not the actual military situation on the ground, much less the situation at the Security Council.

Israel could not win at the UN what it had failed to achieve on the battlefield: It had not crushed Hizballah on the ground and, having failed to achieve its military goals, could not achieve its diplomatic goals. Hizballah remained the dominant force within Lebanon, though in another way it lost a good deal in the war: So much damage was done to Hizballah and to the Shiite population who supported it that Hizballah has kept the border mostly quiet since the summer of 2006. There have been incidents but no conflagrations; Israel's deterrence was restored by the war. Thus, if Israel did not "win," it also did not "lose," despite many verdicts to that effect in 2006.

Yet Israel's Second Lebanon War was a turning point not only in Olmert's political life but also in Condi Rice's attitude toward Israel and her personal relations with Israeli officials. Olmert never recovered from the widespread view that he had botched this conflict. The failure of the IDF to do more damage to Hizballah in the 34 days of war was blamed in part on its chief of staff, who was forced to resign, and in part on the defense minister, a trade union and Labor Party official with no military experience, but mostly on Olmert. After all, it was not obvious that the only possible response to the July 12 kidnappings was war – as opposed, for example, to a wave of air strikes. Going to war was his decision. The loss of public confidence was soon deepened by the next rounds of corruption accusations, but the corner was turned in Lebanon – and that loss of confidence soon affected not only Olmert's conduct of military affairs but also his conduct of relations with the Palestinians. How did Israel move from the "convergence" plan – taking control of its own fate, acting unilaterally if bilateral negotiations failed, and rejecting any big international conferences – to the great international festival at Annapolis in 2007? Gen. Giladi explained how in an interview years later:

The second war in Lebanon. If you ask me, this is a major factor. And after the war, an Israeli prime minister that launches a war – let's face it, we launched a war. Nasrallah defined the date, but we could respond locally, we could respond in three, four days; we decided to go for a war. You cannot launch a war and be found not prepared.... An Israeli prime minister that launches a war and doesn't win it cannot survive. Maybe survive, cannot recover. And I felt that Olmert cannot recover to the level of leadership necessary to lead a strategic plan. And I told him, "The Israeli people didn't change their mind. They want to stay in the West Bank because of Lebanon? Forget it. What the Israeli people have at the moment – they don't believe they have the necessary leadership to lead such a step." And this is why he lost it.[7]

Olmert lost both the Israeli public's belief in his strength, something that had been critical to Sharon's power as prime minister, and its confidence in his stewardship. And on the latter, he lost not only the Israelis but also Condi Rice. The meeting with Olmert had been not so much "tense" as overtly hostile. She did not trust him to make wise decisions, and she had also lost her faith in the abilities of the IDF. The comments in her memoir that during the Second Lebanon War Israel "laid waste to Lebanon's infrastructure" and "the IDF...was destroying the country" are suggestive of how her opinion changed.[8] Years later I asked Danny Ayalon, sitting in his Knesset office as deputy foreign minister, when Rice's warm relationship with Israel began to sour:

I'll tell you. I'll tell you exactly when. I was then still in Washington so I wasn't here, but Condi came here and she talked to Tzipi and Olmert. And then she was going to Lebanon to try to get an agreement. Then, Qana.... And from then on it was just...downhill.[9]

This was my perspective as well – and Rice's own staff agreed. Her counselor at State, Eliot Cohen, was not involved in Israeli-Palestinian matters but watched closely from his ringside seat:

The Lebanon war was a traumatic experience. It colored a lot of things thereafter...and there were a couple of elements to it. One was her own sense of having extended herself to defend the Israelis as they bumbled along in Lebanon. Another was a profound sense of Israeli incompetence at managing their own security affairs. And the third element was a personal distrust of Olmert – quite different from her view of Sharon.[10]

Rice may have understood far faster than most Israelis or other Americans what the Second Lebanon War meant for Israeli-Palestinian matters. Once again, our path forward had been blocked – first by Arafat, once by Sharon's stroke, and now by the war and its effect on Olmert. Whatever his intentions, he would not be able to carry out the convergence plan. He made one misguided effort to suggest that Lebanon proved how essential convergence would be, but it backfired badly: Families living in the West Bank immediately shot back that their sons were not fighting in Lebanon so they could allow Olmert to throw them out of their homes, and some Army reservists said they would refuse to fight in Lebanon if the convergence plan were the real goal.[11] Shalom Tourgeman explained that "there was a terrible backlash politically. . . . [T]hat gave a political blow to the plan, and it lost momentum. I can't tell you the exact date it was put off the table, but it was being put off the table for all practical purposes."[12]

Moreover, withdrawal from the West Bank would inevitably be far more complicated than Gaza, and Israelis now lacked the trust in Olmert that he would need to carry it out to the end. The vision we had once had of how things would look by January 20, 2009 – Israel out of Gaza and a significant part of the West Bank, the first significant change there since 1967 and likely due to unilateral Israeli moves – once again looked increasingly unrealistic.

This put the focus back on negotiations, and Rice had a view of how to move them forward: Simply cajoling the two negotiating teams would not be enough, so broader international support would now be needed. Whether it could work was a different question, but Rice's new "international conference" approach covered two bases. First, she believed it was the most likely foundation of any successful negotiation because Abbas would need Arab cover to make difficult compromises. Olmert too – now more than ever – would need some form of compensation for his compromises, and it could come in the form of some Arab moves toward Israel. But it seemed to me later that Rice also had another idea in mind – something closer to what had led Sharon to propose "disengagement" in Gaza to begin with. There was a vacuum, and something had to fill it with hopes of peace or at least of forward movement. An international conference might help lead to peace – or at least fill the space if no movement were possible.

"She Didn't Want to Just Kind of Manage the Store for the Last Two Years"

The timing was significant for Rice because she was soon approaching the halfway mark in her tenure as secretary. The Agreement on Movement and Access of November 2005 had long since fallen apart. She had been close to brokering a peace in the Second Lebanon War, but Qana had blown that

up. What was there to show for two years as secretary of state? Eliot Cohen
summed up the moment this way: "She didn't want to just kind of manage the
store for the last two years. She wanted some large accomplishments and I think
inevitably somebody in that position wants – they're thinking about history,
but I think she was also thinking she doesn't want to just be a caretaker for the
last two years."[13]

Soon the news stories pontificating about a major effort in the Middle East
would start appearing, so it is not surprising that making such an effort seemed
increasingly worthwhile to her – as it had to so many predecessors. As for the
president, 2006 was turning into a disastrous year. Iraq was bitter and bloody
and appeared hopeless; the "surge" that changed that situation would come
only in 2007. In Lebanon, there was war. In Congress, we were heading toward
a terrible defeat that gave the Democrats control over both houses for the first
time in 12 years and made the president seem even more like a lame duck.
So a diplomatic initiative for Middle East peace must have seemed to Rice an
awfully attractive effort – for her, for the president, and for the country. What
is more, it would be *her* initiative. For better or worse, she was not in charge of
the major issue occupying the country and consuming the president's time: the
Iraq War. That was primarily a Defense Department issue, with a large NSC
staff component deeply involved on a day-to-day basis; State was clearly in a
secondary role. In a Middle East peace initiative, she could be the leader. Other
agencies would be marginal.

There were other influences as well, all pushing in this same direction. One
was the press. As a State Department veteran described the way the media
affected top officials, "These guys read the press about themselves and they've
got advisors who read the press and give it to them.... And so they start
reacting to the press rather than driving it – they would deny this, I'm sure, but
I saw it firsthand – they start reacting to it. And so if something starts to get
you positive stories in the press, it's another motivator for just getting sucked
along there."[14]

There was the influence of foreign officials as well, always a far greater
factor in the State Department than in the White House. In the West Wing,
Rice had been surrounded by Americans. Foreign leaders visited, to be sure,
but Rice made very few foreign trips during her four years as national security
advisor. Now she was traveling constantly, and the milieu in which she existed
consisted of foreign heads of state and their foreign ministers and of events at
the UN, not White House staff meetings where the Bush team discussed the
economy, the Congress, and everything from what the state governors wanted
to the latest opinion polls. Rice was now seeing more of Kofi Annan than of
Karl Rove or White House chief of staff Josh Bolten.

And she was doing so in a period where most foreign officials thought the
war in Iraq was lost and Bush was of declining importance. John Hannah of
the vice president's office described how these perceptions strengthened Rice's
decision to put together a major Middle East initiative:

I'm sure she was under a lot of pressure from a lot of people that she dealt with on foreign policy on her trips to do it. . . . I think it's what everybody else wants to do, internationally. . . . I think at a point in time by the second term when the administration is certainly beginning day-by-day to feel politically weakened, it becomes much harder for it to resist that kind of pressure from the rest of the international community – when it's constantly being raised that this is what they want to do. . . . It becomes much harder to resist those arguments, given that . . . the sense of our international position and standing and dominance begin to recede just naturally as the administration gets closer and closer to the end. . . . [T]here's a sense that we're weaker and you may have to pay more to get other people to do some of the things you want to do, and invariably the Israeli-Palestinian thing becomes an easy thing to grab onto to say, "[H]ere, we're really going to make an effort."[15]

Ironically, one of those foreign officials who must have influenced Rice, and who certainly influenced the president, was Ehud Olmert. Whether this influence was despite of or due to the corruption allegations increasingly surrounding him; whether it was due to his perception of having a shortened time horizon in office after the Second Lebanon War and his desire to make his historic mark; or whether he genuinely believed he could achieve a peace settlement quickly are questions about Olmert that Israelis continue to debate. Polls taken after the Second Lebanon War showed that Olmert never recovered significant popularity, but he was determined to undertake major steps as prime minister. Already in August 2006, there was discussion of a new effort to negotiate with Syria over the Golan.[16] By early 2007, Israel was engaged with the Turks, exchanging notes that led in the following year to indirect negotiations. Throughout 2007 and 2008, Olmert would tell American officials that a breakthrough with the Palestinians was entirely possible and that he was determined to achieve it. Whatever her own doubts about what could be done, Rice must have seen Olmert's view as an additional source of optimism.

Rice was also influenced by the personnel and mechanisms of the State Department itself. Like Powell, Rice had come to State with no background in the Middle East (her academic field had been Russia), though she had arrived with four years of experience as national security advisor. In those four years, however, she had spent hours each day with President Bush; now that influence was diminished as her day was spent among the career diplomats at State and the foreign officials she met there and when traveling. As she notes in her memoir, when he was secretary of state, George Shultz has made sure that more than half the regional assistant secretaries of state were political appointees loyal to him and to President Reagan; indeed, I had been one of those appointees. But Condi "wanted to make career appointments to those positions whenever possible. . . . In the final analysis, five of the six regional assistant secretaries came from the career ranks."[17] So the State Department officials who had spent careers in the region were the experts on whom she now relied – primarily David Welch and several ambassadors in the field, in Egypt, Jordan, Lebanon, and in Jerusalem, where our consul general was actually our ambassador to the Palestinians. To put the point more sharply, her Middle East hand at the NSC had been me; now she was getting information and advice from officials whose entire careers had been spent in the Arab world. Now Rice's advice came from officials of the Near East bureau, at home and in the field.

Ironically, our closeness to the Israelis at this time created a huge disadvantage for them. We in the administration, in the White House and the State Department, were in constant contact with Israeli officials. Rice, Hadley, and I spoke with some combination of Olmert, Turbowitz, Tourgeman, Foreign Minister Livni, Defense Minister Barak, and many others almost daily. We were getting the Israeli view directly. But because we knew that their job was not only to inform us but also to spin us we discounted that view to some extent. If Israeli officials said, "Olmert must have *this*, and by Friday," we wondered why they were saying so, what percentage of *this* he really needed, how precisely they were trying to move us. Missing was any evaluation from our man in the field, the U.S. ambassador, confirming the truth of the Israeli assertions and giving us his view that we should indeed take them very seriously.

Yet when it came to the Arabs, our ambassadors were key interlocutors, and their cables were read avidly. Whatever the comments of Arab officials being reported, their validation by an American officer made them far more compelling. On-the-ground reporting, even if duplicative to a large extent of facts we already knew, could confirm impressions or give more positive perspectives. The Near Eastern Affairs (NEA) bureau told the secretary what the Arabs thought, or too often what the Arabs wanted her to think they thought, and often passed on their views with an imprimatur of approval. Of course, sometimes the reporting cables would contradict the message the Arab officials wanted delivered, but this was still greatly advantageous to the Arabs on balance. What we were hearing from the Israelis was always discounted to some extent at State as an effort to spin us, because we were hearing it from them directly: The medium undercut the message. In contrast, on the Arab side, those messages from our ambassadors rightly influenced Rice; the imbalance existed because our system of direct contact with the Israelis meant there were few such messages and analyses from Embassy Tel Aviv. And given the number of Arab states, NEA officials in Washington were rarely equipped to provide what was missing: They had all served in Arab capitals, but few had ever served one day in Israel.

Shalom Tourgeman gave the Israeli view, which over time was one of increasing frustration with Rice and her NEA advisors:

I think that person who is heading the State Department, from my experience his input on Middle Eastern issues is very little. This is my analysis. Because you have so many experts that are telling you, "We lived there; we know. We know what will be their reaction." Take the Lebanon war, when she told us, "Look. The Arab world will go up in flames this Friday if you will not stop. I spoke with the Emirates and the Lebanese, with the Saudis." Now, nothing happened; we got other impressions from them – because no one wanted us to stop the fighting in Lebanon. So this is what she got from the ambassadors, and without any filters, and she continued, or forwarded, or threw the ball immediately to us. This is what she heard; this is what she's stating. Which was a mistake; I mean, take it, analyze it. See what are the pros and cons. See what the broader picture of the war is; see what really matters.[18]

Nor was there much leavening from noncareer appointees when it came to this issue: Rice chose as her deputy secretary Robert Zoellick, whose main interests lay outside the Middle East and who played little role in policy making for the region. When he left in July 2006, he was followed eventually (February 2007) by John Negroponte, a career foreign service officer who similarly focused elsewhere. Whatever biases might inhere in NEA officers, career diplomats in general had one obvious *deformation professionelle*: They believed in diplomacy and conferences and meetings, even when an outsider might wonder whether the moment was right. As Eliot Cohen put it, "At the end of any administration more and more of the career people come to the fore. She had very good relationships with those folks – and her high opinion of them was reciprocated. They really liked her and the ethos at the top was a kind of professional diplomat ethos."[19] If Rice had any inclination to a big international conference on the Middle East, she was certainly going to get nothing but reinforcement from the career service. They remembered the Madrid Conference of 1991 and the Camp David negotiations of 2000 as highlights of American diplomacy, not as failed efforts at Israeli-Palestinian peace.

As we returned home from Israel on July 30, Rice told us what she was thinking. We gathered in her cabin in the plane, an 8 x 15 foot space where her State Department staff and I sat on and around the sofa, spilling onto the floor. First, get the Security Council resolution passed and get the combat to stop. Get the Lebanese Army to deploy south, or at least start the motions. Get some additional forces in there. Tell the Israelis that as soon as the Lebanese Army begins to move, they must simply stop. Organize Russian and French and UK support for our new text. Tomorrow was July 31, a Thursday. We could vote on Monday, August 4, the Lebanese deploy on Wednesday the 6th, and the Israelis stop on the 7th. They will have had the 10 days Olmert wanted. In fact, things took one week longer, but Rice organized this diplomacy in her mind and with her team – and then told us her thinking about what would come next.

"People Are Lost Now in the Middle East"

People are lost now in the Middle East and we need to act, she said; we need to make a big proposal. We need to think about a comprehensive Middle East settlement. Maybe the president should propose it in his UN General Assembly speech. The pieces are all there – from Gaza disengagement to convergence and some of the Palestinian proposals; she said she was agnostic about whether to try for an Israeli-Syria settlement at the same time or to pressure the Syrians by leaving them out for a while. Maybe we couldn't solve everything between the Israelis and Palestinians, maybe we couldn't solve Jerusalem, but we could describe the borders, say there would be some land swaps, say there would be no right of return, and call for establishing a Palestinian state now, with provisional borders. The Arabs were all worried about Iran, so maybe we could get them to support this – strongly. The sequence would be a big speech by the president and then an international conference. We would invite the key Arab states, the Europeans, and Russia. After the speech and the conference, we would produce a framework for diplomatic action. That would be the legacy we'd leave; we blew up the Middle East and now we need to show how we are going to resolve all these problems. It has to be ambitious. We'll shove the Quartet aside and bring on our Arab partners; leaving them out was Clinton's mistake and we won't repeat it. The only condition we impose on the Palestinians is that they accept Israel.

This was the outline of what became the Annapolis Conference 15 months later. I was opposed to it immediately and remained opposed throughout the period when Condi tried to persuade the president to buy in – which he finally did only in July 2007. There in her cabin I argued – softly – that this new Palestinian state would be a terrorist state, a Hamas state; who would keep order there? What had happened to all the preconditions the president had mentioned in his June 24, 2002, speech and his April 14, 2004, letter to Sharon? And as to the Golan, how could we possibly include it and reward Assad, who was Iran's ally? At the least, must not a Syrian shift away from Iran be a precondition for any movement on the Golan? During the Second Lebanon War, I had thought Condi was shifting away from the line the president had taken (though I also knew she talked with him constantly, far more often than I did, and might be reflecting a change in his view). But that shift might have reflected the intense pressures she was under as the war dragged on week after week and Israel failed to achieve the kind of military victory that would have been needed to secure all its diplomatic goals. I now had that feeling again. What had happened that justified such a great change in U.S. policy toward the Palestinians?

A week later, before the Lebanon resolution was even passed in the Security Council, Condi gathered her advisors in her apartment for a "skull" session on the Middle East. As usual, I was the only person there who was *not* in her employ at the State Department. During this August 6 meeting, she outlined what I described to Hadley in a reporting memo as an extremely expansive view of what the president should say in his UN General Assembly speech in September. Moreover, this was not just musing; David Welch had prepared a paper, which was handed around. One quick read showed me that all democracy and human rights issues were now to be skipped over; let the Palestinians handle all that once they get statehood, the paper suggested. And what about maintaining security in the West Bank? Put a U.S. National Guard division in there, Welch was suggesting. This statement was taken seriously, though the wisdom of setting such an American target in front of Hamas eluded me entirely – and the domestic politics involved would, I thought, kill such a proposal in seconds. Was it possible that Rice had discussed that with the president, I wondered. But there was more: The UN speech should announce that we were calling a major international conference, to be held in Williamsburg. But it would not need to negotiate borders for the Palestinian state: Those would be set by the president in his UN speech. When Condi explained that she had just had dinner with Brent Scowcroft and also spoken with Jim Baker, asking them about how they organized the 1991 Madrid Conference, there was no doubt left in my mind. Whatever this approach was, it was not the policy that President Bush had outlined in his 2002 speech and his April 14, 2004, letter to Sharon. Scowcroft and Baker had dealt uncomplainingly with Arafat and had never had the slightest sympathy for the president's focus on democracy – or, for that matter, his deep appreciation for Israel.

Condi addressed this concern: She claimed there was no great policy change. The only real change since the April 14 letter, she said, is that there we said "fix the internal parts of the Palestinian state first, then do the peace negotiation"; now we would be saying to "do them in parallel." We can't wait forever, she said; we need to get the Palestinian state now. As I told Hadley in my report, she would in the end move forward, even if the political and security conditions were not there. My memo suggested that this would abandon the president's insistence that he would never create a terrorist state. Rice's plan was also Clintonian in its timing: a desperate effort as the administration entered its final two years.

Behind this remarkable change in Rice's approach were, I thought, the Second Lebanon War and her apparent loss of faith in the Israelis' ability to handle their own affairs. But she was also adopting a new – or perhaps more accurately, a very old – view of the relationship between the Israeli-Palestinian issue and other Middle East matters. Once she had said that we cannot want peace more than the parties did, and they would need to be in the lead. Now she was arguing that our national security interests required a peace settlement, whatever the views and interests of the parties. Moreover, it seemed to me this was buying the view – long a staple of the State Department and especially the NEA outlook – that our relationship with Israel was undermining all our interests in the region. Condi's long-time colleague and friend Philip Zelikow, whom she had named counselor at the State Department, spelled out this approach in a September speech about "the task of building security in the broader Middle East," which concluded "by discussing Israel and its neighbors":

The significance of the Arab-Israeli dispute across these problems is, I think, obvious to all of you. What I would want to emphasize is, if you see the threats in a way something like the way I've just described them, think then about what is the coalition you need to amass in order to combat those threats. Who are the key members of that coalition? You can imagine the United States, key European allies, the state of Israel, and the Arab moderates – Arabs who seek a peaceful future. You could call it the coalition of the builders, not just a coalition of the willing. The coalition of the builders as opposed to the coalition of the destroyers.

What would bind that coalition and help keep them together is a sense that the Arab-Israeli issues are being addressed, that they see a common determination to sustain an active policy that tries to deal with the problems of Israel and the Palestinians....

For the Arab moderates and for the Europeans, some sense of progress and momentum on the Arab-Israeli dispute is just a sine qua non for their ability to cooperate actively with the United States on a lot of other things that we care about. We can rail against that belief; we can find it completely justifiable, but it's fact. That means an active policy on the Arab-Israeli dispute is an essential ingredient to forging a coalition that deals with the most dangerous problems.[20]

After his remarks, he and I engaged in a poison-pen email exchange because I thought what he said in the speech was very far from the president's policy. Using only a very slightly arcane diplomatic vocabulary, Zelikow had articulated what it seemed Condi was now thinking: We need the Arabs, for Iraq and other matters, so we need to push the Israelis into some peace deal. You didn't need a decoder ring to see where this was headed. There was no evidence for this assertion, of course; no Arab leader had said, "I will change my policy on Iraq or Iran or Afghanistan if you muscle the Israelis." The Arab leaders were pursuing their national interests – or at least their own interests, the interests of unelected regimes whose goal above all else was regime survival. To believe, for example, that the Saudis, who did not wish to see a democratic Shia-led government in Iraq because they took dim views of both democracy and Shias, would change that view if Israelis and Palestinians were negotiating peace seemed downright silly to me.

"The Balance of Forces in the Administration as a Whole Shifted in the State Department's Direction"

But Rice was pressing forward: On September 5, Prince Bandar met with Rice, Hadley, and me in Hadley's White House corner office, and he told us how pleased the king was with the proposed UN speech and the idea of a big international conference. Clearly, the secretary had been discussing these ideas with Bandar, without – I thought, or at least hoped – approval from the president. Bandar said the Saudis proposed a vague UN speech that nevertheless demanded immediate final status talks. I argued to Bandar that this approach would not work, any more than it had in the past; the security conditions needed to underlie successful final status talks did not yet exist. When Hadley said he agreed with me, the question of where the president stood on all of this remained a mystery to me.

The late Peter Rodman, a brilliant analyst of foreign policy and an official in several Republican administrations, wrote in his last book of the problem I was increasingly seeing from my Middle East policy vantage point. In the first term, Powell had been the odd man out in the administration. After 9/11, he and the president did not see the world in the same way, and I thought Powell had never aligned his views to those of the president. He had signed on as secretary of state to a new president with no foreign policy experience; Powell would be tutor, representative, analyst, policy maker. After 9/11, George Bush took over foreign policy, along with Vice President Cheney and Defense Secretary Rumsfeld. Powell became marginalized, and State was often seen as out of tune with what the president wanted. In his memoir, President Bush writes, "I admired Colin, but sometimes it seemed like the State Department he led wasn't fully on board with my philosophy and politics."[21] Having the president's closest advisor, Condi Rice, take over State, Rodman had written, "was thought to solve the problem; she had been more attuned than anyone else to Bush's thinking." Yet it did not work: "Over time however, the role of the career service reasserted itself in the department, and State's policy drifted in that direction" – back toward the traditional approaches of the Foreign Service. And that trend became stronger over time: "Especially with the departure of Rumsfeld, the balance of forces in the administration as a whole shifted in the State Department's direction. Hadley often acted as Rice's partner."[22]

My own experience suggested the truth of what Rodman had described. The president had never said anything about a major policy change or a shift in his relationship with Israel. Yet every meeting Rice had with the Israelis after the Second Lebanon War was strained and difficult. As time passed, and especially in 2007 and 2008, I would often write memos to Hadley expressing that we were deviating from stated policy, taking positions that put all of the pressure on Israel and nearly none on the Palestinians and forgetting the major insights that had constituted the Bush approach. At times I would discuss the problem with the vice president or with White House chief of staff Josh Bolten, never suggesting that I knew what to do about it but wanting to ensure that they were at least aware of it. The vice president was a skeptic about the kind of diplomatic maneuvers the State Department and our EU friends found so alluring, preferring to rely on the sinews of power to protect the United States and our friends in Israel. While he maintained his close ties to the Saudis and other Arab rulers, he was an unwavering voice of support for the Jewish State.

Whether he and Josh raised these matters with the president was something I never knew, for rightly they kept their private conversations with him private; nor did I know what Hadley told him when they were alone. I had certainly seen the president express disagreement with Rice, contradict her words, and rein in her actions. But she was still his closest advisor on foreign affairs, far more influential than Hadley – who in any event did not like to take her on. His own foreign policy judgment was often, I thought, better than hers, not least on Israeli-Palestinian issues, but he did not consider a battle with Condi in his job description. In that, he was right: The president had left the Rice/Hadley team in place for the second term because it worked smoothly, and he surely did not want a bureaucratic war. But I thought Hadley took this policy of avoiding conflict too far; I thought the president should have heard more about the policy changes now being discussed, and heard them not as explanations from Condi why what she was doing was natural and sensible, but as real debates.

On some issues this debate happened, certainly on matters like the surge in Iraq; later, our internal discussions of what to do about the al-Kibar nuclear reactor discovered in Syria were models of debating options heatedly before the president so he could choose one. Yet such discussion did not occur often when it came to Condi's transformation of our Middle East policy after the Second Lebanon War. Vice President Cheney notes in his memoirs the same failure to present "crisply drawn options for the president" and "clear choices" rather than "policy recommendations that split the difference" as a means of "managing conflicting views."[23]

The very next day after the Bandar meeting came more evidence that something important had changed: We had one of the worst meetings ever with the Israelis. Turbowitz and Tourgeman, along with Israeli Ambassador Danny Ayalon, joined Rice, Hadley, and me in Hadley's office. It was three weeks after the end of the Second Lebanon War and just before the UN General Assembly would meet. Rice told the Israelis that when we destroyed the regime in Iraq, we destroyed the old Middle East, and the radicals are gaining. Iran is the greatest strategic challenge since the Cold War. This administration has two years left and we need to move forward fast to implement the two-state vision. Turbowitz replied there was now very little support for Olmert's convergence plan because after withdrawing from south Lebanon and Gaza, Israel was being attacked from both. Nor was Olmert strong enough to overcome that resistance. As for negotiations, the Palestinians were not ready or able: Ismail Haniyeh was prime minister, and they did not have a government that accepted the three Quartet Principles, so there was really no one to negotiate with. True, said Hadley, but that's just analysis; I don't see a strategy. There are no shortcuts, Turbowitz said; we want to move forward, but don't see any plan that allows it.

"We Have a Strategic Imperative"

This comment by Turbowitz brought Rice into the conversation. There is always a way; she said; if there is no solution, we will lose the bigger strategic game with Iran. Either reflecting Zelikow's advice or presaging what she would tell him to say, Rice told the Israelis that the United States could not put in place the alliance we need with the Arabs. We need Arab allies willing to confront Iran, but the moderate Arabs are saying they cannot confront Iran without movement on the Israeli-Palestinian issue. We have a strategic imperative to find an Israeli-Palestinian solution. You need a policy now and don't have the luxury of saying there is no solution, she lectured Tourgeman and Turbowitz. I had heard this line many times before from State Department officials, going back to my days in the Reagan administration; we were always going to lose the Arabs unless we pushed the Israelis harder – except we never lost them. This was a theory for which no persuasive evidence was ever adduced. I wondered how

Rice could believe that the Arabs, who opposed Iran for their own religious, political, and security reasons, would cut their own throats out of concern for the Palestinians. She was buying the NEA line.

We had a policy, Turbowitz argued – the Roadmap, disengagement, and then convergence, which we lost in the Lebanon War; now we are thinking anew but there are grave risks. We have to have a solution, Rice shot back; we don't have the luxury of not having one. Given our investment in Iraq, with 3,000 dead, the Middle East is now our fight. We need a new approach. All this was said to the Israelis not in a soothing manner designed to sugarcoat the message, but with language (and body language) reflecting her new mood. A worried Turbowitz asked whether the former plans and principles were now being jettisoned; what about the Roadmap? It may be an impediment, Rice said, or at least the detailed sequencing may be. The Palestinians do have to fight terror, of course, but now we may want to do things in parallel, not in sequence. But the whole crux was to stop terror, said Turbowitz. No, it was the *effort* to stop terror, Rice pushed back. No, said Turbowitz, the real criterion is results; we should not forfeit our conditions because the Palestinians cannot meet them. They can't stop terror, Rice replied; we can't either, in Iraq or Afghanistan.

Now an angry Tourgeman jumped in and, in fact, his own relationship with Rice never recovered from their exchanges in this meeting. What you are now saying is exactly what was tried in the Clinton administration, and it failed totally and it produced the intifada. Doing it simultaneously, demanding negotiations while the terror continues, is just what Clinton did, he told Rice. She did not appreciate the remark, and said no, we must simultaneously create a positive vision and space, a political alternative while fighting terrorism. Tourgeman shot back that this was the Rabin/Clinton approach, and we got negotiations in the morning and terrorism at night. Then you carried it out wrong, said Rice, but we have a strategic imperative and must have an answer. Her response struck me as mumbo-jumbo; "strategic imperative" is the kind of term that academics and Foreign Service gurus throw around, a Zelikow special, I thought, but it has no real intrinsic meaning. It means whatever you say it does.

Now Hadley told the Israelis about the forthcoming UN speech: there is great pressure for the president to talk about the Middle East at the General Assembly. He has to, Rice interjected, seeming to me to be arguing with Hadley more than the Israelis. Hadley continued, saying that the president wants to be knit up with Israel and with Olmert and, of course, true to his principles. Turbowitz was aghast: The General Assembly is only two weeks away. Don't surprise us. This is very alarming. What about the Roadmap and the Quartet Principles? To say you have an imperative is one thing, but how do we work out the details in two weeks? There are so many dangers here: enormous risks, things could deteriorate into violence easily. No, said Rice; we can't say we have a strategic imperative but can't meet it; we simply must meet it. In two weeks? Turbowitz asked again. Time is too short. No, it isn't, replied Rice; it isn't a big departure; all we're saying is that discussing borders and discussing terrorism must go together. And the United States might state our basic views on issues like borders and the major blocks and the right of return. Wait a minute, said Turbowitz, now you're talking about jumping past Phases I and II of the Roadmap and starting to negotiate final status issues. Well, forget the sequence, there's no sequence now, said Rice; when you got out of Gaza you jumbled the sequence. Whoa, I thought: Now we are *punishing* the Israelis for getting out of Gaza, telling them they abandoned the sequence of the Roadmap?

I walked the Israelis out to the White House gates on Pennsylvania Avenue. Tourgeman was fuming, too angry to say much. Turbowitz was pale; what just happened there? he asked me. The 2002 speech is gone, the 2004 letters with Sharon are gone, the Roadmap is gone, Hamas won the election, there is a Hamas prime minister – and you have a strategic imperative to make us forget it all and start negotiating final status issues? All of a sudden Condi was saying final status issues should be discussed, right now; as she put it, we would "build the house" but not let the Palestinians move into the house until terror had ended. There was not much I could say. Condi's forcefulness, her tone of impatience and near hostility, had stunned me too. I suggested that Turbo, as everyone called him, discuss it with the prime minister and then maybe ask for another conversation with Hadley for him to explain where we were heading.

Turbo called Hadley three days later. The prime minister is very worried, Turbo said, and he just spoke to Condi; she told him not to worry because these were just her initial thoughts. What he told her, Turbo continued, was that there are no shortcuts, and he cannot change course now in a way that seems to reward terror. The basic element in disengagement, he had told Rice, was the April 14 letter, which had flatly said "the United States remains committed to my vision and to its implementation as described in the roadmap. The United States will do its utmost to prevent any attempt by anyone to impose any other plan." The Roadmap is not a principle, it lays out a plan – a series of steps in order. All of a sudden you consider a new order. Turbo went on: Condi had confirmed to Olmert that the "principles" of the Roadmap were alive but not the sequence. The prime minister said he could not agree to that; he could not tolerate it. But listen, Hadley answered, the president needs to say something about all this at the UN, and he's going to. He needs to show leadership. There will be no new Middle East peace plan, but there will be something – a down payment.

A few days later, the president spoke at the 100th anniversary dinner of the American Jewish Historical Society, which I attended. As soon as his remarks were over, I left and was out front on the street as he got into his limo. Seeing me, he invited me in for the ride back to the White House. The president asked me how the Jewish community is feeling. Nervous, I replied. Nervous? Why? They are nervous about Condi, I said. What they hear when they meet with her now, and frankly what they must be hearing from the Israelis, unsettles them. They don't know how far it is going, where it's leading, whether we are looking for new tactics or a whole new policy. They can see that there is a serious new tension between her and the Israelis. The president took it in and did not comment.

The president delivered his address to the UN General Assembly on September 19, and Condi lost her battle for including a major new Middle East initiative in the speech. Inside the White House there was no support for this, and instead the president covered Iran, Lebanon, Darfur, Afghanistan, Syria, and Iraq, as well as the Israeli-Palestinian conflict. What she got instead of a new initiative was a personal endorsement from the president, or perhaps what in the bureaucracy is called a "tasking":

I believe peace can be achieved, and that a democratic Palestinian state is possible. I hear from leaders in the region who want to help. I've directed Secretary of State Rice to lead a diplomatic effort to engage moderate leaders across the region, to help the Palestinians reform their security services, and support Israeli and Palestinian leaders in their efforts to come together to resolve their differences. Prime Minister Blair has indicated that his country will work with partners in Europe to help strengthen the governing institutions of the Palestinian administration. We welcome his initiative. Countries like Saudi Arabia and Jordan and Egypt have made clear they're willing to contribute the diplomatic and financial assistance necessary to help these efforts succeed. I'm optimistic that by supporting the forces of democracy and moderation, we can help Israelis and Palestinians build a more hopeful future and achieve the peace in a Holy Land we all want.

"A Political Horizon"

Rice did not win a call for a great new international conference, but behind the scenes she was getting her way on significant policy changes. What so agitated Tourgeman and Turbowitz – whom the president and everyone else now called "T and T" – was an accurate take on these changes: The "sequence of the Roadmap," which had been a holy grail for Sharon, was now being given a different meaning. This sequence had been understood by all of us, Americans as well as Israelis, as meaning "beat terrorism first; no negotiations while terrorism continues." Now we had revised that to mean "no *implementation* until terrorism is beaten, but negotiations should be underway." As I explained it to the Israelis – indeed, as I explained it to myself – we were still absolutely opposed to moving into Phase III of the Roadmap, a Palestinian state, until we had gone through the earlier phases and terrorist organizations had been "dismantled" as the Roadmap said. But why couldn't we *talk* about Phase III? In fact, maybe talk about Phase III would provide the Palestinians with the "political horizon" they needed to act against terror.

This "political horizon" theory became a mantra, especially for Rice. I was one of those who helped formulate the new Roadmap lingo, trying to help persuade the Israelis not to get into a huge fight with Condi over it. But the "political horizon" theory left me cold; I thought it was absurd. Ariel Sharon had called for a Palestinian state at Aqaba in 2003 and had in 2005 left Gaza – and had won an election with this policy. After Sharon's stroke, Olmert had committed himself to leaving parts of the West Bank and had won an election with that proposal. That a "political horizon" existed was obvious; it was Palestinian statehood, and the vast majority of Israelis were now in favor of it. The old dreams of a "Greater Israel" held fewer and fewer Israelis in their spell because a wide majority now wanted separation from the Palestinians. What more did Palestinians need than this, which was the clear horizon? Under this horizon, I thought, the main effort should be on the ground in the West Bank and Gaza, building the institutions of self-government from the bottom up.

Why did the president endorse this change in the U.S. approach on the Roadmap? As I interviewed top Israeli officials years later, one of them gave me his thoughtful assessment off the record:

I thought that President Bush worked within a framework that the endgame should be two states; that this and peace with security can be based only on true leadership, total renunciation of terror, proven end to terror and on the basis of two democracies living side-by-side.... [S]o the endgame is clear. At the same time, no shortcuts in the road to this endgame. And this I thought was what served him to support Israel in fighting terror, not wanting to deal with Arafat, supporting the idea that first no terror and *then* political negotiations and the like....

What I sensed happened during 2006 ... was that he was convinced that we were in a deadlock, that only working bottom-up will not do the trick, and that there needs to be this horizon or this agreement on the endgame in order to gain enough momentum for the bottom-up to work. I think that he had to be satisfied for himself with the security issue and the terror issue, and this is why he bought into the notion that there is no *implementation* until there is full implementation of the Roadmap – and thus he wouldn't put Israel's security in jeopardy and thus he wouldn't betray any of his core principles. So once he was presented with the notion that the current no-movement situation ... is dangerous and there is a way to go about it that would not betray the values, would not put Israel's security in danger, because there would be no implementation until such conditions are created, he bought into the notion that you can change the sequence of the Roadmap, not only implementation but on the process itself.

I felt that this was largely cultivated by Condi and I wasn't sure, let's say until the middle of '06, where the president stood; I wasn't sure whether Condi was reflecting Bush's views at the time. I reached a conclusion at a certain point that Bush crossed a certain line.... He basically said to us, "Tell my friend Olmert, what is your strategy? Where do you think this is going to go? Why not try this?" So Condi was not freelancing. And at that point I felt that the president after struggling with the issue got convinced that this is something he should try. I don't know what would've been his reaction had Olmert said no. Maybe it was a trial balloon, maybe he was testing the water, but it was then clear to me that either he himself or Condi had been able to construct for him a structure which would suggest starting political negotiations without making him violate his core principles with regard to democracy, terror, or the security of Israel – because the sequence of *implementation* will be guaranteed. So I felt there was a change in 2006 in terms of moving into parallel tracks which was very different from the vision of the roadmap – which basically suggested political negotiations at the later stage. And I thought that he was gradually accepting it, I thought that there was a point by which, at least he presented to us, a position that he did accept it, challenging us, 'What's your alternative?' And I thought that it was constructed for him brilliantly in a way that he could lead with in terms of his own values and principles.[24]

This assessment seems right to me. The president believed he was both breaking through a stalemate and remaining true to his policies and his support for Israel's security. Talking about final status issues was OK so long as implementation was delayed – or anyway that was the theory. It fit with our actions in the fall of 2006, but only because Condi had not yet won her battle for a big international conference that would try to leap to a final status agreement. The notion that such an agreement could be signed but not implemented for years and years, until the PA "dismantled" all terrorist groups, always seemed ridiculous to me. Was it not obvious that once a deal had been signed, implementation would have to begin? I thought it clear that Palestinians would start pushing for implementation literally before the signatures were dry on any treaty, and in this they would have the full support of the Arab world and of the EU. Israel's objections – the Palestinians haven't done this yet or that yet; they haven't fulfilled provision A and amendment B – would fall on deaf ears. The pressure for implementation would grow inexorably and irresistibly.

None of this policy change would have happened without some support in Jerusalem. Tzipi Livni bought into this approach, more or less. On certain issues she was as tough as nails – no Hamas participation in the elections, the need to build the security fence, the absolute insistence that the number of Palestinian "refugees" who would "return" to Israel was zero. But on this matter of "the sequence of the Roadmap," she worked closely with Rice. As to Olmert, he never said no, for his own reasons. Once he perceived that this was the Bush view, he did not want to fight with the president over it. There was also his rivalry with Livni, which made him wish to play down the Livni-Rice channel and to take up negotiations himself.

Above all, there was his own desire to achieve peace and prove that he was a consequential historical figure, not an accidental prime minister who had failed in Lebanon and was mired in corruption charges. As time went by, these latter considerations would lead Olmert to make offers to Abbas that I thought could not get through his own cabinet or the Knesset, and whose rejection by them would have harmed Israel greatly. Olmert was always torn. He understood Israel's security requirements and was getting tough-minded advice from advisors like "T and T" and from the security organizations themselves – the IDF and the Shin Bet, Israel's internal security service. Sometimes he stood firm on this advice and he had a series of difficult meetings with Rice, from 2006 to the end of the administration. But he could not resist casting himself as a hero of peace, which was not coincidentally how he wished his own family – not one member of which was supportive of the positions he had taken throughout his career in Likud – to see him. Olmert wanted to vindicate his life and his career in politics with a peace breakthrough, and this worried not only his closest advisers but also a number of us on the American side. If he leapt farther than Israel's politics allowed, his government would collapse and from its ruins would come not peace but a collapse of the negotiations and perhaps more violence.

But in the fall of 2006, we were far more worried about Palestinian than Israeli politics. On September 11, President Abbas announced the formation of a Fatah-Hamas national unity government. The private message from our Palestinian interlocutors was "hold off on the criticism, see how it goes; don't denounce us." President Chirac of France expressed EU opinion when he immediately issued a congratulatory statement. The Palestinian announcement was so vague that we could not immediately tell what had been agreed; had Hamas blinked, and said things tantamount to abandoning terror and recognizing both Israel and all previous agreements with her, thereby meeting the Quartet principles? Fatah officials were making that claim. We asked the Israelis, who told us they did not know if that were true; their immediate reaction was guarded but positive: "If that were to happen, we would have a re-energized peace process and new momentum in the Israeli-Palestinian dialogue," their spokesman said.[25] On September 13, Livni was in Washington to see Rice, and at their joint press conference Rice spoke carefully:

I think that the outcome of the process is not clear. It's an ongoing process and our purpose has been to be very clear that we do believe that the Quartet principles represent the consensus of the international community about the way forward between Israel and the Palestinians. It goes without saying that it's hard to have a partner for peace if you don't accept the right of the other partner to exist. It goes without saying that it's hard to have a process for peace if you do not renounce violence. And so we will see what the outcome is here.[26]

A week later on September 20, while the president was in New York for the General Assembly, he met with President Abbas and the discussion of the national unity government continued. The president reiterated his support for a Palestinian state and said it was a key objective of his administration. The question is how to get to the point where you and Olmert can negotiate and get it done and conclude a satisfactory arrangement, he said. A national unity government has to be judged from that perspective, the president told Abbas: It is a useless exercise unless it leads to a state. You cannot put the Israelis or the United States in a position where we are negotiating with people who want to destroy Israel. A unity government does not help me if it does not make it easier to negotiate a state, the president reiterated. Here again, the mythology about American policy is shown to be false because the president did not sabotage or denounce Abbas's efforts to form a unity government or demand that they cease. Instead, he explained our perspective and urged Abbas to be sure that any unity government pulled us all in the right direction and not farther away from peace negotiations.

But within two weeks, the Fatah-Hamas coalition government was blown apart by bloodshed. On October 1 and 2, nearly a dozen people were killed and about 100 wounded in fighting between Hamas and Fatah. How could

there be a unity government, we wondered – or was this the way Hamas negotiated for better terms? Throughout October, Arab leaders made mediation
attempts aimed at ending the Fatah-Hamas confrontation. Egypt and Qatar
sent their foreign ministers to meet with both parties. There were even mediation efforts by other, smaller Palestinian terrorist groups such as Islamic Jihad
and the Popular Front for the Liberation of Palestine. At the end of the month,
Israel launched another large incursion into Gaza to stop rocket and mortar
attacks still being launched from there into Israel; this was "Operation Autumn
Clouds" and lasted from November 1 to 7.

"You Don't Have to Pay Them off in Israeli-Palestinian Currency"

While Israelis and Palestinian terror groups fought in Gaza, Welch and I visited
Israel and the West Bank in early November to discuss once again Condi's idea
of an international conference and to see where the Palestinian "national unity
government" efforts stood. She had scaled back her idea and was thinking not
of a new Madrid Conference but a smaller one – with just the Quartet, Israelis
and Palestinians, Egypt and Jordan (which had peace treaties and diplomatic
relations with Israel), and perhaps the Gulf countries under the umbrella of the
Gulf Cooperation Council. Israel had at times had trade links and face-to-face
talks with Qatar, the Emirates, Bahrain, and Oman, so their participation was
not impossible. This would not be a major international conference but just a
regional meeting.

Welch and I met with Olmert, but he was not buying even this more limited
conference. I have told Condi repeatedly, he said, that whatever you want from
the moderate Arabs for Afghanistan and Iraq you can get because of Iran; you
don't have to pay them off in Israeli-Palestinian currency. And look, he said,
Abbas is doing nothing. He should not be rewarded by a huge drama where
Kofi and Javier Solana will want to come. And anyway, a long emotional appeal
on the misery of the Palestinians, supposedly all caused by Israel, will not lead
Abbas to act. Why does such a meeting encourage him? It sets expectations too
high, and then they'll be devastated. Why should Abbas deal with Olmert and
the Israelis privately when a huge conference like this allows him an out, and
kills the Roadmap?

Olmert then pulled back a bit and said he was not saying no to the conference
but was just laying out his concerns. I share the view that we need to do
something, he said, and I realize the advantage of getting the Arabs involved.
But is this the only possible way? He warned us: What if there are more
Qassams, and more terrorism, and we react, and it is worse in Gaza, and then
the Arabs cancel? So let's analyze it first, let's be careful, don't spread the idea. I
am thinking of ways to move forward and will explain them next time I see the
president. The chances of progress without a powerful disciplined Palestinian
partner are slim, he said, and we don't have one. And right now, unilateralism
is not politically realistic. My position is the same – Israel must pull out from
most of the West Bank and create a Palestinian state. What I'm thinking about,

Olmert said, is what is the process if it is no longer "convergence?" I told Olmert we could address some of the problems in the outcome document for the conference and made the old argument: We need to fill the vacuum, and there is a danger of doing nothing. I agreed with Olmert, not with Condi, but my job during this trip was to advance the goal she had apparently sold to the president: get some international meeting.

I get it, said Olmert, but if Abbas does zero and gets the conference, he will continue to do zero. Anyway, what you are talking about is not really a regional meeting, Israeli and Arab; there will be too many attending from the international community and then it becomes an international conference. Let me think about it and we'll discuss it more when I come to Washington. Olmert did send "T and T" to Washington soon thereafter, and Hadley told them our thinking now was a meeting in Amman of the United States, Israel, the PA, Jordan, Egypt, and some Gulf countries. We're surprised you're so negative, Hadley told them; this isn't some great international conference. You want to avoid "Madrid II," and so do we. The Israelis remembered this among many conversations where they were promised a small meeting – not the Annapolis Conference we later held.

On November 6, Welch and I then traveled from Jerusalem to Ramallah to see Abbas. He said to us that after the national unity government failed, I told Hamas I want a government of independent technocrats based on certain principles. We have been discussing those principles – and today is the deadline for Hamas to name three independents, and I will then choose one of them to be a prime minister. It has to be a moderate who accepts my letter designating him as prime minister, so he will be acceptable to the international community. All the ministers will be independents, not party members, nominated by Hamas or Fatah. Welch replied that, remember, we need a government we can work with, which means it must endorse the Quartet principles. It has to be clear, no loopholes. Well, said Abbas, my letter won't mention the Quartet principles but it will refer to my UN Security Council speech, which did. Then the prime minister will accept my designation letter and will form a government accordingly. The new prime minister will not be a Hamas member. Abbas got to his bottom line: Will you lift the siege (meaning, end the financial boycott) if there is a technocratic government? Welch gave the obvious reply: Yes, if the new government accepts the three Quartet principles.

We were fully aware of Abbas's plan from our own diplomatic reporting. After efforts to reach a coalition government under Ismail Haniyeh broke down in September, there had been almost constant Hamas-Fatah violence in October. Eight had been killed on October 1 and several more in the days that followed; then on October 11, 20 were killed and more than 100 injured. A truce was brokered and broke down on October 20. The rivalry between Hamas and Fatah was visible in Ramallah in endless political machinations and the tug of war between Prime Minister Haniyeh and his cabinet versus President Abbas and the PA organs under him. But in Gaza, the rivalry was producing daily gunfights.

The new Abbas proposal was to have a nonparty government, a government of technocrats who were "fellow travelers," some of whom were Hamas and others from Fatah. As Abbas had explained, Haniyeh would propose three names for prime minister and Abbas would choose one. Haniyeh himself would not be among the names, making it far easier for the Quartet and the United States to accept the new cabinet. Fatah and Hamas would divide the cabinet posts and we assumed Fayyad would be finance minister again – if Fayyad agreed to participate in this new game. As Abbas had explained to us, he would issue a letter to the new prime minister he was appointing, who would formally accept this charge. November 6 was the last day for Hamas to respond to the proposal. Welch and I pressed Abbas and his advisors again, reminding them that no confusion, no loopholes were possible. We could not accept the new government if we could not say it was operating under the three Quartet Principles. In fact, we had worked with both Israel and the PA vetting names for prime minister and believed there were a couple of men who would be acceptable. Welch was in frequent touch with Abbas's advisors as they worked through lists of names. Far from seeking to sabotage Abbas's plans, we were quietly working to see if they could be implemented. But we also asked Abbas what he would do if Hamas said no. He would give a speech a week or two later, he said, and might declare a state of emergency and appoint some kind of caretaker government. Then he would call for new elections.

In fact, no deal was concluded despite weeks more of work. In the second week of November, after the supposed deadline had passed, the PA was still floating names past us, and we were still trying to help them make Abbas's plan succeed. But the division of ministries between Fatah and Hamas was never agreed: Who would get which of the important posts such as interior (which meant security), finance, and foreign affairs? The text of Abbas's letter to a new prime minister was also never agreed: Would the letter demand that Hamas *honor* previous agreements, or *respect* them, or *comply with* them? The exact formulation was critical. But on November 14, Hamas stated again that it would never recognize Israel, making further negotiations senseless.

At the end of November, we were on the road again with Secretary Rice. We have two years left, Condi told the king of Jordan, so it is increasingly unlikely that we can go all the way to a final status agreement. Is an interim agreement possible? We can go part of the way if not the whole way in two years; will the Palestinians accept that? In her meeting with Abbas, he told her the idea of a national unity government was dead. The door is closed; the dialogue with Hamas is over. Condi told Israelis and Palestinians she would come back to the region again in January, six weeks from then, to take stock.

On December 16, Abbas said he would call early elections, for both the PLC and his own presidential post. With political agreement impossible, the gunfights escalated once again. There was significant violence from December 11–22, with scores wounded and several killed in battles almost every day and with Fatah and Hamas capturing each other's security men and executing them. The violence picked up again on January 1 and continued through January into February: Fatah and Hamas gunmen were killing each other almost every day, attacking each other's strongholds and offices, ambushing motorcades, agreeing to truces, and then breaking them within hours.

We did not think this violence marked the end of any chance for Israeli-Palestinian progress; in fact, the contrary might be true. It was clear that Olmert could not go forward with unilateral withdrawals on the West Bank because there was little public support for such a move after the Second Lebanon War and the corruption allegations against him. But that did not rule out negotiations and, in fact, Olmert and Abbas met – for the first time since June – on December 24, 2006, amidst the Hamas-Fatah violence. The day before, Olmert had made several gestures of support for the PA: Israel would hand over to the PA about $100 million in tax revenues it had collected for the PA but had previously refused to disgorge, and it would remove some checkpoints in the West Bank. Shortly after the meeting, the Israelis authorized Egypt to supply lethal weapons to PA/Fatah forces in Gaza.

One way ahead seemed open: for Abbas to dismiss the Hamas government and appoint a new one. Asserting himself against Hamas would gain him additional credibility in Israel as well as with us, and we would then try to broker new rounds of peace talks between Olmert and the new Palestinian government – which would have no one from Hamas in it. A cold-blooded assessment showed that the more Fatah fought Hamas, the more Israelis would think it worth engaging in talks with Fatah and Abbas, and would think it smart to support the PA – which surely would emerge victorious from these confrontations. Condi Rice believed the negotiations could be advanced by some sort of international meeting that would include Arab states as well as the Israelis and Palestinians, and had been pressing that idea at least since the end of the Lebanon conflict the previous summer. I was unpersuaded about the need for such a conference but did agree that Israeli-Palestinian negotiations were possible as Fatah took on Hamas. We made plans for another Rice trip to the Middle East, in February, to see how we could move the ball forward.

Notes

1. "English Summary of the Winograd Commission Report," *New York Times*, January 30, 2008, http://www.nytimes.com/2008/01/30/world/middleeast/31winograd-web.html?_r=1&pagewanted=all.
2. Ehud Olmert, interview with Associated Press, August 2, 2006.
3. U.S. Department of State, "Special Briefing on Travel to the Middle East and Europe," press release, July 21, 2006, http://merln.ndu.edu/archivepdf/syria/State/69331.pdf.
4. Olmert, interview, pp. 6–7.
5. Bumiller, *Condoleezza Rice*, 291, 295.
6. Kessler, *Confidante*, 225.
7. Giladi, interview, p. 13.
8. Rice, *No Higher Honor*, 480.
9. Ayalon, interview, p. 20.

10. Cohen, interview, pp. 2–3.
11. Yechiel Spira and Ezra HaLevi, "Olmert Says War Will Advance Realignment, Refusals Result," *Israel National News*, August 3, 2006, http://www.israelnationalnews.com/News/News.aspx/109044#.T5DUPY7S6gM.
12. Turbowitz, interview, p. 4.
13. Cohen, interview, p. 2.
14. Interview with State Department officer, November 30, 2009 (name withheld by request).
15. Hannah, interview, p. 11.
16. Aaron Klein, "'Desperate' Olmert Resorting to Radical Moves; Cairo Report Blasts Israeli PM for Calls to Negotiate with Syria," *World Net Daily*, August 23, 2006, http://www.wnd.com/news/article.asp?ARTICLE_ID=51646.
17. Rice, *No Higher Honor*, 310.
18. Tourgeman, October interview, p. 22.
19. Cohen, interview, p. 4.
20. Philip Zelikow, "Building Security in the Broader Middle East" (Keynote Address, Weinberg Founders Conference, Washington, DC, September 15, 2006).
21. Bush, *Decision Points*, 90.
22. Peter W. Rodman, *Presidential Command: Power, Leadership, and the Making of Foreign Policy from Richard Nixon to George W. Bush* (New York: Vintage Books, 2009), 270.
23. Cheney, *In My Time*, 449.
24. Interview with Israeli official, October 2009 (name withheld by request).
25. "Hamas, Fatah Agree to Unity Government," *PBS NewsHour*, September 11, 2006, http://www.pbs.org/newshour/updates/middle_east/july-dec06/mideast_09–11.html.
26. Israel Ministry of Foreign Affairs, "Joint Press Conference by FM Livni & Secy of State Rice," press release, September 13, 2006, http://www.mfa.gov.il/MFA/Government/Speeches+by+Israeli+leaders/2006/Joint+press+conference+by+FM+Livni+and+Secy+of+State+Rice+13-Sep-2006.htm.

8

From Mecca to Annapolis

Intense fighting between Hamas and Fatah continued during January 2007, and there were especially heavy clashes in the first four days of February. Each side set up roadblocks, kidnapped people from the other party, attacked the other's strong points, and executed people whom they captured. There were occasional truces, which were soon violated as more murders followed a few hours of calm. Arab television viewers were still seeing plenty of violence in Gaza and some in the West Bank, but it was not Israeli-Palestinian violence; the bloodshed they were now seeing was Palestinian on Palestinian. The Israelis were spectators to this fighting and no doubt turned a blind eye when Fatah forces in Gaza were sent additional weapons or ammunition from the West Bank. Fatah and Hamas seemed evenly matched, or at least neither side appeared to have much of an upper hand; perhaps we and the Israelis should have been more startled by this because on paper, Hamas was greatly outnumbered. Such fighting certainly met any test the Israelis put to the PA on whether it was fighting terrorism and seeking to dismantle terrorist groups, as the Roadmap required. Whatever its motivation, the PA was acting.

This action laid a foundation for possible negotiations, though the Israelis and we – and the Quartet, at least in principle – were still nervous about the prospect of a Palestinian national unity government that might follow a truce. But Abbas had assured us that negotiations with Hamas were finished, and the violence we saw suggested such hostility that a coalition government was increasingly unthinkable.

Shortly after New Year's, Secretary Rice traveled to the region again. Rice thought the timing was right to continue her push for final status negotiations between Israel and the PA, though they were described as discussions of Phase III of the Roadmap while implementation would be delayed until the key condition of Phase I – an end to terrorism – was fulfilled. The Israelis resisted – a pattern that would repeat itself over the next two years. Tourgeman and Turbowitz were especially tough, but Olmert was less so. In part, this difference reflected the simple fact that they were behind-the-scenes advisors while he was an elected political leader trying to hold onto a relationship with Rice and Bush. In part, it reflected their real positions because as we would see very clearly in 2008, Olmert was willing to contemplate concessions that his advisors did not support. In these January 2007 discussions, we laid out a plan for simultaneous work on Phase I and discussion of Phase III. To the Israelis, this was an abandonment of the Roadmap and a demand that they negotiate while terrorism continued.

"Like Riding a Bike"

The Israelis were not shocked by this plan – I knew this was coming, said Turbo – but they were totally opposed to it. Tourgeman took up the argument: Discussing the status of Jerusalem and the return of refugees will bring about the next intifada because the discussion will fail and that failure will harm Abbas. What can we offer him? Shalom asked. The most he can get from any Israeli government is something like 90% of the West Bank, no right of return, and something on Jerusalem – and if he offers that to the Palestinians, he will fail. Hamas will say they want the 1967 borders, and a right of return, and all of Jerusalem like they had before 1967. We cannot have adventures, and we cannot go forward in the dark; this is an adventure.

We had often told the Israelis that this process was like riding a bike: You could not stop or you would fall off, so you had to keep moving forward. It is true that you will fall off a bike if it is not moving forward, Shalom acerbically told us, but it is better to fall off when you stop the bike than to fall off it at 100 km speed. We don't want to see what happened to Clinton now happen to Bush: actions that are counterproductive and an end result that is a setback. Final status talks now will fail because agreement cannot be reached on Jerusalem, refugees, and the borders. This failure could harm Abbas, who is too weak to lead his people to accept what Israel can offer now. And anyway, the Israelis argued, to move forward now is to abandon the Roadmap because the Roadmap requires serious action on security first.

These arguments left Condi cold, but I agreed with them on the whole. I did not see how such negotiations could help Abbas, especially because we were all talking about a "shelf agreement." That is, we all agreed with the Israelis that a final status agreement could not be implemented at this time. Condi's idea was nevertheless to negotiate such an agreement to give the Palestinians a "political horizon" but then to put it on the shelf for some years until the preconditions were met. To me, it seemed this formula would be disastrous to both the Israelis and the PA. For Abbas, it meant that whatever concessions he made – which were bound, as Tourgeman had said, to be attacked by Hamas and other extremist groups as treason – he would be unable to show anything but an Israeli promise that someday, down the road, at a date the Israelis would judge appropriate, there would be a state. How could such a situation benefit Abbas? I also believed, as noted before, that there would be immense and irresistible pressure on the Israelis to shorten the wait and to move to the implementation phase even if the conditions were not right. So I thought that the wait, the time "on the shelf," would be long enough to undermine Abbas but not long enough to ensure that all the sensible preconditions were met. A perfect storm.

Yet that was our policy, and while I fought it internally, I supported it in meetings with the parties. It did not seem to me this policy could work, and I believed that the Israelis and Palestinians would come to the same analysis I did – regardless of what they said to U.S. officials – and would never accept a shelf agreement. So I stayed in the game, pushing what I thought was a more realistic path: keep some negotiations going while building up the PA's security forces so that they could successfully fight terror. Under Gen. Keith Dayton, who had replaced Gen. Ward, U.S. training efforts were beginning in earnest. Initially, Ward and then Dayton had no budget but that was remedied over time, and Dayton arranged to use a training center in Jordan. An initially ragged effort gradually picked up steam, training not a PA army but a decent police force, more along the lines of a gendarmerie on the European model. President Bush had once asked Abbas, during an Oval Office visit, whether he was able to send forces anywhere; if he picked up the phone, would anything happen? No, Abbas had acknowledged. We aimed to change that – to give the PA a professional force that could jump into nasty situations, could be deployed in particular cities or towns to keep order, could gradually show real professionalism and gain the respect of Palestinians. Dayton's main problems, initially, were a lack of funds and a lack of a decent interlocutor on the PA side. Who was really in charge and dedicated to developing a professional force and would ensure that the force was not tainted by politics and corruption?

The meeting Welch and I had with Turbo and Tourgeman found us entirely at odds. We concluded by telling them the theme for the secretary's trip was how to accelerate completion of the Roadmap and "contemplate the establishment of a Palestinian state." With our bicycle metaphor, we argued the need for progress and the impossibility of standing still but, as noted, Tourgeman argued that falling off was inevitable and you would at least not get hurt if you were not speeding when you did fall. We tried another metaphor: The Palestinians needed to see where this was going. We would "build the house" by describing the Palestinian state but tell them they could not "move in" until their obligations had been met. The Europeans liked this metaphor and talked enthusiastically about building the house, furnishing it, painting it, and preparing it. But "T and T" were not buying this one either; they asked if we could not see what happens to an unoccupied house. It can collapse or attract squatters; it is dangerous. You are destroying the Roadmap to save it, Shalom concluded. Why is a Palestinian state a success if it is a failed state, a terrorist state? His arguments seemed to me far stronger than ours.

In Rice's meeting with Olmert, she had a new agenda item: her own role. She was firmly pressing now for trilateral meetings in which she would join Abbas and Olmert. Olmert did not care for the idea, if I was any judge of body language, but he was not prepared then to fight it. I did not then see how trilaterals could advance the negotiating process, and later did see with my own eyes that in fact they slowed it down. Rice told Olmert she would be back in February, and March, and as often as was needed; she would tell the press that the United States was deepening its involvement and beginning now to engage the bigger issues. The Roadmap was central, but broader issues would be on the table as well. Whatever Olmert's private view, at that point he did not push back.

In Rice's meetings with the Palestinians, the message was the same. We would discuss how to complete the Roadmap, and though we would not use the term "final status," we would "contemplate the establishment of a Palestinian state." When, she asked the Palestinians, could the informal talks they were having with the Israelis be transformed into more formal negotiations? At that point, the United States could do more; we could say we were launching a formal negotiation and could get the Quartet or the Security Council or the key Arab states to bless this effort. The Palestinians thought about it and said perhaps the informal talks could continue for the rest of 2007; they were far more focused on the Fatah-Hamas fighting than on negotiations with the Israelis. Moreover, I thought this was proof I had it right: They were happy with informal talks that showed the "peace process" was still alive but scared of formal negotiations where their concessions would have to be made and then revealed. To the secretary, waiting until 2008 to go beyond informal talks was too long; she told them something would have to move well before the end of the year.

We then flew off to Kuwait where Rice met again with Arab leaders in the format that we were calling the GCC +2: the Gulf countries (organized in the Gulf Cooperation Council) plus Jordan and Egypt. I broke through, she told them, and we will indeed be talking about the future phases even as we implement Phase I. It's a start, and the United States will be deepening our involvement as we engage these broader issues. As we flew home to Washington, Rice told us that in her private talks with Olmert he had said six months was about right: He could move to formal negotiations in the summer. The question, she mused, was when to bring the president into this picture. In her discussions with the team en route, she was moving into the fundamental final status issues and seemed to me very clearly to intend reaching a full final status agreement in 2008. I felt that this approach ignored the signals we had gotten from the Palestinians, who were immersed in internal politics. Their focus was Hamas, not Israel. But Rice had been correct in what she told the Arabs in Kuwait: The fundamental breakthrough had been achieved. We could talk and they would talk about the final status issues of Phase III of the Roadmap even as we worked on implementing Phase I. Our metaphors had been destroyed, but our plan was intact.

On January 30, Rice had dinner alone with Sallai Meridor, the new Israeli ambassador who had arrived in November. Danny Ayalon had returned home with a plan to jump into politics, which he was able to do successfully: In the next elections, he got a seat in the Knesset and became deputy foreign minister.

Meridor had been head of the Jewish Agency and the World Zionist Organization, so his contacts throughout the Jewish world and in Israeli politics were very good. He was also a deeply humane and thoughtful man, highly intelligent and with a very ready sense of humor, and we had quickly become good friends. Meridor used the dinner to express his worries to Condi because he thought the distinction between a broad political horizon and actual final status talks had to be maintained. Moreover, he could not see serious negotiations occurring while Abbas was struggling for control over the Palestinian territories. The six months or so of preliminary talks were a critical period, he said, for Abbas to gain a strong position against Hamas.

More Daylight Every Day

A few days later, on February 5, Welch and I met with "T and T" in London to see where things stood. The Israelis' first message was that security remained their top priority: For the first time in months there was a suicide bombing, on January 29 at a bakery in Eilat, and people had been killed. It was the first-ever attack in Eilat. So, they said, they were clinging fast to the Roadmap with its prioritization of security matters. Their question for us was whether we had in effect abandoned the Roadmap and decided instead to push Israel into final status negotiations even if there was no progress against terrorism. They reiterated their view that seeing whether there is "a basis for negotiations," a formula we had used a few times, and actually "commencing negotiations" are the same thing. Welch replied that we want to discuss all three phases without necessarily moving into Phases II and III. Turbo said this approach is a big change; discussions about final status issues are final status negotiations, so starting them now means having final status negotiations without security performance. How does this differ from what Clinton did, they asked – and not for the first time. Welch told them that we did in fact want to launch final status negotiations, if not in 2007 then in 2008. Tourgeman said David had answered their question: Yes, we were abandoning the Roadmap, which the April 14 letter had promised we would not do.

I described the scene for Hadley in a memo, telling him the Israelis' real problem is not the difficulty of final status negotiations, tough as those might be – especially when the issue of Jerusalem arose. Tougher for them was the sense that we were abandoning their security struggle and were now willing to push for final status negotiations even without a security situation that would truly permit them to live in peace. They believed there had been a fundamental change in U.S. policy.

There had been. A day or two after Welch and I were in London, Hadley met with the Egyptian foreign minister and confirmed to him that Condi would push for final status negotiations as soon as she felt them to be possible. On February 7, I wrote a memo to Hadley saying that although the president had said he wanted no daylight between us and the Israelis, there was more every day. Moreover, I told him, there was a growing gap between us and the Palestinians. We seemed to want negotiations leading to a final status agreement, whereupon Abbas would hold an election and beat Hamas, but he seemed to want a national unity government with Hamas. It was clear to me that we were not listening carefully any more to what the Israelis and Palestinians were saying, nor were we noting what was really on the mind of Abbas and his advisors – their internal struggles. As recently as February 2, 20 people had been killed in factional fighting in Gaza, and more people died on February 3 and 4. This bloodshed was all over the Arab TV networks, and this war was far more significant to the Palestinians than our diplomatic moves.

The TV coverage turned out to be of great significance because one of the Arab television viewers was the king of Saudi Arabia. I had been to several of his palaces and had seen the banks of TV screens that surrounded him almost everywhere. At his favorite retreat, his horse farm, the set-up in the giant dining room (at most dinners I could count about 100 people) placed a huge screen, probably six feet square and tuned to Saudi-backed Al-Arabiya, right in front of the king. Much affected (it was explained to us later) by the intra-Palestinian violence, he acted. He summoned both parties to Mecca, Islam's holiest city, to arrange a truce. Neither could refuse the summons even if they had wished to, given the prestige of the king and the wide support for this effort to stop the bloodshed (and on the PA side, the fact that the Saudis were a key source of financial backing). We in Washington made our views crystal clear to the Saudis: The three Quartet Principles remained our guide. Anything they did beyond a truce had to meet that standard. Any kind of coalition government that did not require Hamas to renounce terrorism, recognize Israel's right to exist, and accept past Israeli-Palestinian agreements would be a tremendous setback. In fact, the Saudi meetings were in themselves a huge setback because the Saudi government was treating Hamas and the PA as equals. The Israelis could not be expected to negotiate with a government half made up of people who wanted to destroy their state and who engaged in terror against it, and we would not ask them to do so. Therefore, as we urged the Saudis, stopping the violence – sure; national unity government – disaster.

But it was a national unity government for which they pressed, for reasons never explained to us. They simply ignored our advice. Perhaps they thought we were too pro-Israel; perhaps Saudi officials were following an order from the king that permitted no consideration of American doubts; perhaps their confidence in us was a casualty of Iraq, where we seemed to them to be fighting hard to establish a Shia-led government that per se they viewed as a disaster. Whatever the reason, they forged ahead and the Palestinians went along.

Mecca

The Mecca Agreement was announced on February 8. It was very short, declaring four principles. "First: to ban the shedding of the Palestinian blood . . . and to stress the importance of national unity. . . . Second: Final agreement to form

a Palestinian national unity government.... Third: to move ahead in measures
to activate and reform the Palestine Liberation Organization.... Fourth: to
stress on the principle of political partnership [and] political pluralism."[1] The
"reform the PLO" language was a huge victory for Hamas: It meant letting
Hamas into the PLO, which we believed it had a long-term plan to penetrate
and take over. Formally, it was the PLO that negotiated with Israel, not the
PA, and it was the PLO that sat as an observer in the United Nations. Now
the Mecca Agreement was advancing Hamas's goals in the PLO as well. More
important, it threw the Quartet Principles out the window. Olmert may have
been ready to negotiate with Abbas and the PA, but after Mecca it was hard to
see how such negotiations could take place: by signing the Mecca Agreement,
Abbas was deliberately fudging the distinctions between Hamas and the PA.
Even more, he had specifically told both American and Israeli officials that the
national unity government idea was dead and that he opposed it. So much for
his credibility.

On February 15, Abbas dissolved the PA government and authorized
Haniyeh to organize a new one. After several weeks of negotiations, a new
government was agreed on March 15. On March 17, the PLC approved it,
with Haniyeh remaining prime minister. The new national unity government
met none of the Quartet conditions. When asked how he could possibly have
agreed to it, Abbas would smile nervously and say he really had no choice once
the king had asked him to do it.

Reactions to Mecca revealed the stresses within the Quartet, for while
we viewed it negatively, others were delighted. We saw to it that the initial
Quartet statement in response was cautious and reaffirmed the three principles, but separately the EU expressed support for the Mecca deal. Worse, the
EU language now suggested that the new unity government could "reflect"
rather than adhere to the Quartet Principles, vague terminology that could
mean almost anything. The Europeans were all over the lot and viewed the
American approach as too rigid. Russia actually called for a lifting of international sanctions; Norway was bubbling with enthusiasm for Mecca and the
new unity government.[2] We pulled our punches a bit, trying not to say anything
that would kill Secretary Rice's next trip to the region and waiting to see if the
unity government actually came into being.

The impact of the Mecca Agreement was considerable, as summed up years
later by Condi Rice:

I thought there was some chance that you might be able to negotiate. Now, of course
what killed that – any hope of that – was Mecca and then we spent a year trying
to recover from Mecca. And really Annapolis was a way to get things back on track
that Mecca knocked off balance.... I was supposed to meet with Abbas and Olmert
in February and I was scheduled to go to the Middle East to meet with them; it was
going to be a trilateral. Mecca happens [February 8, 2007]... and there is a question
of whether or not I even ought to go because it's not clear they'll talk to each other at
that point.... Olmert is ready to go, we set up for me to... go and kick off negotiations
between the two of them, and then Mecca happens.[3]

Rice had been pressing for an international conference as early as the summer of 2006, after the Second Lebanon War, so it was certainly not Mecca that gave birth to that idea. It may, however, have persuaded Rice that an international conference was inevitable. After the Second Lebanon War, she had nearly managed to bring the parties back to the negotiating track over a period of six months, but now Abbas, or perhaps more fairly one should say the king of Saudi Arabia, had acted to blow up that possibility. In Rice's view, something dramatic was once again needed.

"A Little Nervous about Condi"

At the White House, the president read news bulletins about the announce-ment of the Mecca Agreement and asked Hadley and me if it met the Quartet Principles. We told him it clearly did not and that Haniyeh, from Hamas, remained as prime minister. Let it play out then, the president said. We need to insist on the Quartet Principles. Let's see what the new government says and does. The Israelis took a dimmer view, saying that Mecca had wrecked any chance of negotiations and that we should all now shun the PA. Our core assumptions about the PA have been challenged, Sallai Meridor told Hadley; we thought Abbas and the PA were confronting Hamas, not making deals with them. The administration told the Israelis we were equally upset but would have a different contact policy: We would stay in touch with Abbas and Fayyad.

The president spoke with Olmert on February 16, and their differences were evident. An angry Olmert said Abbas had betrayed all of us by agreeing to a unity government with Hamas. A far more relaxed Bush said our best bet was to let it play out; he did not think this unity government could last. It will change or it will collapse, so let it run, he advised Olmert. But there was a second subject of this call: Condi. We were to travel again very soon, and Condi was pushing Olmert for a trilateral meeting: She wanted to get Olmert and Abbas together. He was resisting, still angry over Mecca, and his tone made his concern evident. It sounds to me like you're a little nervous about Condi, the president told Olmert. I feel how important this meeting is to her, Olmert said; she does not want me to spoil the party.

This brief exchange was the first, but far from the last time, in which Olmert attempted to place himself between Condi and the president. With the exception of the administration's final UN Security Council vote in January 2009, for which Olmert (and others) did persuade the president to move from Condi's desired "yes" to an abstention, these efforts by Olmert had one principal effect: They angered Rice. They did not succeed in changing U.S. policy directly, though they may have slowed Rice down from time to time; certainly, she knew that the president liked Olmert. It remains unclear how much the president or Hadley told Rice privately about such statements by Olmert, although it was not long before the president referred to them directly in larger meetings where both were present.

The secretary's party then traveled again to the Middle East. The main subject raised with Abbas was the national unity government, which he now defended as the only alternative to a combination of violence and new elections. However, when we told him we could not recognize or deal with the new government and would take a "wait and see" attitude, he actually appeared relieved. The meeting with him was fine: relaxed, without tension, friendly. We were now in the pattern that had begun after the Second Lebanon War and would prevail to the end of the administration: There was never a bad meeting with the Palestinians and never a good one with the Israelis. Perhaps it was just personal chemistry, but it seemed to me there was more: a combination of Rice's drive for negotiations and her assumption that very little could actually be expected from Abbas (so concessions would have to come from the Israelis). The phrase that rung in my head was Bush's: "the soft bigotry of low expectations."

When we met with Olmert, sparks flew – despite the fact that Olmert, moved by our pressure, had decided he would continue to meet with Abbas. I told the president that the Palestinians betrayed us and deceived us, Olmert said to Rice. Abu Mazen said he needed weapons and money to fight Hamas, and now he is in a national unity government with them. I will not close the door to him, but let me tell you – now I know better who he is. Then he told her he had spoken with the president and that the president thinks the national unity government will not work – we should not do anything abrupt; we should wait. OK, but we must be more careful and more realistic, Olmert concluded. This reference to the president set Rice off: I know exactly what the president thinks, she responded. He thinks it is important to keep open a path for the Palestinians. Now Olmert shot back: I don't remember this phrasing. I can show you the transcript of the call, Rice replied. This was not an auspicious way for the post-Mecca cooperation to begin.

Tourgeman and others soon explained to me just why Olmert was pugnacious: He thought Rice was building a relationship with Foreign Minister Livni that went beyond their diplomatic business and looked more like Rice trying to pick his successor. Olmert continued to be battered by the corruption charges and had never recovered from Lebanon (his popularity level was in single digits in all the polls), and he resented the news stories about how close Rice and Livni were becoming. Olmert also wondered just where Rice was heading; he did not understand where she thought the trilaterals would take him and Israel, and the Egyptians and Jordanians were telling the Israelis about excellent conversations they were having with Rice covering final status talks. All this made him nervous and out of sorts and, in addition, he was about to do something he did not want to do: join Rice and Abbas in the trilateral. In the end, he decided not to say "no" to Rice.

The trilateral meeting took place on February 19. Olmert used it to complain face to face to Abbas: You promised there would be no national unity government; you especially promised there would be no new government formed without the release of Corporal Gilad Shalit in Gaza; now you are kissing

Khaled Meshal. Abbas was not apologetic. The reality is, he replied, that the United States forced us to hold an election and Hamas won, and they now have four years to govern. So what do we do? Do we leave them to govern alone? We just went close to having a civil war in Gaza, and we need more time to build our strength.

Rice told them both that a "political horizon" was needed. Rice's thinking at that point was that there would have to be an election and that for Abbas and Fatah to win it, we would all have to outline that "political horizon" more clearly. That was the only product Abbas could sell. There was some truth to this view – the only thing he could sell was the prospect of peace and an avoidance of endless confrontations with Israel – but negotiations also posed an obvious danger for Abbas. The more details were spelled out, the easier it would be for Hamas to accuse Abbas and Fatah of selling out. Statehood, independence, an end to Israeli occupation, an end to violence – those were all fine. But as soon as Abbas gave the slightest detail about the compromises he was planning to make, Hamas would brand him as a traitor: giving up pieces of holy Jerusalem, abandoning the refugees, and so on. Rice's pressure to outline a "political horizon" was, then, a formula for endless arguments with the Israelis, who said we were pushing them to final status negotiations despite the unity government with Hamas; it was also a risk for Abbas the moment the "horizon" gained any definite content.

The statement put out after the trilateral meeting was anodyne:

U.S. Secretary of State Condoleezza Rice, Palestinian President Mahmoud Abbas, and Israeli Prime Minister Ehud Olmert met today, February 19. It was a useful and productive meeting. The leaders affirmed their commitment to a two-state solution, agreed that a Palestinian state cannot be born of violence and terror, and reiterated their acceptance of previous agreements and obligations, including the Roadmap. The President and the Prime Minister discussed how to move forward on mutual obligations in the Roadmap in regard to the implementation of Phase I. The participants called for respecting the ceasefire declared in November. The President and the Prime Minister also discussed issues arising from the agreement for a Palestinian national unity government, and the position of the Quartet that any Palestinian Authority government must be committed to non-violence, recognition of Israel, and acceptance of previous agreements and obligations, including regarding the Roadmap. The President and the Prime Minister discussed their views of the diplomatic and political horizon and how it might unfold toward the two state vision of President Bush. The President and the Prime Minister agreed that they would meet together again soon. They reiterated their desire for American participation and leadership in facilitating efforts to overcome obstacles, rally regional and international support, and move forward toward peace. In that vein, Secretary Rice expects to return soon.[4]

No doubt Olmert had agreed to the final two sentences with gritted teeth.

We then traveled to Berlin where a Quartet meeting turned into a squabble between Rice and the Russian foreign minister, Sergei Lavrov. Rice explained our view: We hoped for an election in a few months that would lead to a Hamas defeat; the Palestinian people needed to choose between the vision

Hamas was presenting and the one Abbas was presenting. Once they did, and a new government was in place, peace negotiations could resume in earnest. Lavrov was not buying that approach: Russia wants the Mecca process to continue, he said; stop interfering in Palestinian politics.

A month later, during the last week of March, we were back in Jerusalem once again; Rice was now coming there every four to five weeks. In Ramallah we met with Abbas, who again defended the Mecca Agreement as a way of stopping the bloodshed by bringing all the factions into the government. I realize it does not meet the Quartet Principles, he said, but it is still an important step forward. Rice told him she did think a political horizon was necessary but explained that Mecca and the national unity government made things far harder for Olmert. We will just keep busy, she said, being very active in our diplomacy; that was the theme of her press conference alongside Abbas as well. To me this sounded like substituting motion for progress: There was a peace process because Rice was there. We would keep coming back, keep insisting on meetings, to create the appearance that something positive was happening. In fact, we were stuck because however many meetings took place, there would be no serious negotiating with Abbas while he was in a unity government with Hamas. To the Israelis, Abbas was now entirely compromised; he was leading the Palestinians nowhere. He was neither fighting Hamas on the ground nor in elections.

Rice then met with Olmert for another sour and tense session. She pressed hard not only for Olmert and Livni to continue talks with the Palestinians but also to allow her to participate in them. Olmert pushed back: He wanted bilateral talks, and he did not want final status negotiations. He thought the "political horizon" idea was foolish. I am ready to leave most of the West Bank and do a deal on Jerusalem, he said to Rice; why do you need more? I need to know more, more detail, she answered. Which are the major blocks, and what are the borders for each? This is just for me; I will not tell the Palestinians your positions. But we do need to structure a process; let's start the discussion to create a sense of movement and progress. Tell them what the vision looks like now, as an inducement. Help them strengthen their forces, which did not perform very well against Hamas in Gaza. Help them improve the economy, so Abbas can really argue that life is getting better. If there is no change, we have four years of Hamas.

The main argument was about the role of the United States – or, more specifically, of Rice herself. Turbo proposed very frequent Olmert-Abbas meetings to show there was a process. Meetings with Abbas are a very good idea, Rice countered, but let's see if we cannot find a way for the United States to play a role. When our talks continued the next day, Rice pushed again. We need to structure the American role so it does not supplant the bilateral path but rather can supplement it. There are issues I want to raise. Anyway, the Arabs won't trust a purely bilateral process. The American role gives it greater seriousness and prevents a final status negotiation prematurely. She proposed that they tell the press that the Israelis and Palestinians have agreed to work together and meet every two weeks, and she would return periodically and work in parallel, to try to find a common approach to enable moving forward in the context of the Roadmap to a Palestinian state. This is not shuttle diplomacy, she told Olmert; publicly I want to say I can join your bilaterals periodically for a trilateral.

Finally, Olmert agreed. He did not seem to me to be persuaded because the Israelis were extremely dubious about Rice's approach. Tourgeman explained their concern: We are worried that we will end up negotiating with the U.S. government on final status issues. But Olmert may have concluded that he did not have the ability to resist and get into a public fight with Rice with his own popularity so low. This was late March, and he knew the final report of the commission investigating his stewardship of the Second Lebanon War was due in April – and would surely worsen his political standing. Perhaps he felt that a continuing series of sessions with Abbas and with Rice would lift his poll results or, in any event, change the subject from war to peace. Confusing his own interests with those of Israel was getting easier for him, and many of the people I spoke to in Israel – officials and former officials, journalists, academics – increasingly said they worried that Olmert was now simply looking out for Olmert.

I summarized all these discussions in a series of memos to Hadley in March and April. I saw little benefit from trilaterals where both sides talked to us rather than negotiating with each other. I did not believe any good would come from negotiations over the "political horizon" that were simply preliminary final status negotiations. I thought this idea of a shelf agreement was still wrong because it would force both sides into making politically damaging concessions without giving them the rewards of final status. The moment we crossed into specifics, it seemed to me, Abbas would be harmed, and his enemies would attack any concessions he appeared to be ready to make. I told Hadley this diplomatic process was simply becoming untethered to reality: Abbas was in a coalition with Hamas, while Olmert's own popularity was in single digits and he too was extremely weak. Yet State's NEA bureau had developed for Rice a draft timetable that has the president making a major speech on the Middle East in May and launching final status negotiations in June, thereby dragging him into a diplomatic process that may fail at high cost. And all of this activity was increasing tension and distance between us and the Israelis, despite the president's wish that we avoid it. On April 25, Sallai Meridor came in to see Hadley and told him there was increasing "daylight" between the United States and Israel. The core of the difference between us is the risk-opportunity calculus, Meridor told us – the risk of moving fast versus the opportunity to reach a deal now. You deprecate the risk and see a great opportunity. We see the opposite: huge risks and little opportunity now.

On April 30, the Winograd Commission on Lebanon issued its preliminary report. Its criticism of Olmert was even harsher than expected and produced in May a good deal of Kadima Party infighting. Olmert and his team felt that Livni was jockeying to force him out and replace him. In Washington, NEA pushed on; in a May 8 meeting, David Welch told me that Secretary Rice planned another trilateral in Jerusalem in June and was still thinking about what exact role the president should play. It seemed that June was too early to pull him in; perhaps the president could host an international meeting. We had to explore all this, and the goal is to "launch negotiations" for a final status agreement. We needed to work on a timetable and participants list. I told him I disagreed with this approach for many reasons, including this one: There was barely a functioning government of Israel right then, after the Winograd report. This grandiose international conference idea would not work.

"Off the Record Is a Completely Meaningless Phrase in Washington"

On May 9 I spoke to a group of Jewish staffers on Capitol Hill, at the invitation of Eric Cantor, the Republican congressman from Richmond, Virginia. Cantor, already rising in the Republican leadership (and later to be House Majority Leader) and a committed Jew and supporter of very strong U.S.-Israel relations himself, chaired periodic sessions of this group. This was one of many conversations I was having in those weeks with Jewish leaders, seeking to calm them down and assure them that the president's views of Israel and the "peace process" had not changed. When they met with Israeli leaders, they were hearing about arguments and difficult meetings, and they knew relations with Israel now contained a tension that had previously been absent.

The Cantor meeting was entirely off the record, a completely meaningless phrase in Washington. The Jewish newspaper *The Forward* carried on May 11 an account of some of my "private" remarks that day and several days before:

As Secretary of State Condoleezza Rice presses Israelis and Palestinians to meet a new set of policy benchmarks, the White House is reassuring Jewish groups and conservatives that the president has no plans to pressure Jerusalem. Deputy National Security Advisor Elliott Abrams told a group of Jewish communal leaders last week that the president would ensure that the process does not lead to Israel being pushed into an agreement with which it is uncomfortable. Also last week, at a regular gathering of Jewish Republicans, sources said, Abrams described President Bush as an "emergency brake" who would prevent Israel from being pressed into a deal; during the breakfast gathering, the White House official also said that a lot of what is done during Rice's frequent trips to the region is "just process" – steps needed in order to keep the Europeans and moderate Arab countries "on the team" and to make sure they feel that the United States is promoting peace in the Middle East.[5]

The article was largely accurate. I did not believe the president would permit relations with Israel to be driven into a path of endlessly growing tension, nor did I believe he would ever press the Israelis to do anything that risked their security. I knew that Olmert had made the president aware of tensions with Rice, and I had myself told him (and, separately, told chief of staff Josh Bolten) of the nervousness of Jewish leaders.

Rice spoke with Hadley that morning and then with me; she was angry and let us know it. This policy is the president's policy, she said, and I speak for the president on foreign policy. She and the president were as closely linked up on it, and on all foreign policy matters, as it is possible to be. Fully linked up. Period. Elliott is not secretary of state and he knows it. Cantor called her to say the story was not entirely accurate and that I had done a good job reassuring nervous Jewish staffers to trust the president and relax; what I had done was useful to the administration, he said. The silent message was also there: Elliott has lots and lots of friends in the Republican Party and in the Jewish community, and they trust him, so leave him alone. When Rice vented at Hadley, he had asked her if she wanted me fired; it isn't clear to me what would have happened had she said "yes, absolutely," but she did not. Our personal relations, from the four years I had worked for her at the NSC, had always remained very good, and she did also understand I was the person many conservative Republicans and Jewish leaders turned to constantly for reassurance about where our Middle East policy was heading. What I had said to the Cantor group was in fact such reassurance: Yes, the Israelis are nervous and perhaps rightly so, and so am I, but the president is the president and you can trust him.

The gap between the president's apparent views and feelings, and what Rice was doing in pressuring the Israelis, was apparent to me, as it was to many outside the administration. I could not see that the president was restraining Condi, although if he were, I would not necessarily see it anyway: Any such messages from him would be delivered to her alone. His reaction to those who claimed or even intimated that she was "freelancing" was to contradict the assertion and assure the speaker that she was not: The administration spoke with one voice, and she was his agent, faithfully expressing his views. I thought it was more complicated than that, at least after she went over to State. His faith in her was enormous though not total; she could err, and he trusted himself and his own relations with world leaders more than he trusted anyone else's. So I believed what I was telling Jewish leaders. The tension could not be denied, but if we ever got to the edge of the cliff, he would pull us – pull her – back. We were not there yet.

And as was happening with increasing frequency, my own ability to get the president to see things my way was counteracted by Olmert. It did no good for him to express nervousness about Condi, and it was counterproductive for him to express resentment or hostility. He needed to make policy arguments and to stick to them. As the months passed, I often found myself giving an opinion or analysis to the president that showed I was dubious about our policy, especially about the chances that Olmert and Abbas would reach any peace agreement, only to hear the president reply, "You may be right but Olmert thinks otherwise – and he's prime minister of Israel." He was indeed but was increasingly a discredited and isolated prime minister without the ability to make commitments that would get through his own cabinet and the Knesset. He had one great asset now as prime minister, I thought: George W. Bush. The president still liked Olmert and viewed him as someone who could and would do a peace deal if any serious opportunity presented itself.

As to Condi, her post-Mecca actions may also have a personal element: asserting her own leadership as a world statesman in an area (unlike Iraq or Afghanistan) where her stewardship was clear. But she was also trying to hold together thin and strained threads in the Middle East, trying to show the Arabs and Europeans – as I had said to the Cantor group – that there was a peace process. One can caricature this activity as reminiscent of Peter Pan: The peace process was like Tinkerbelle, in that if we all just believed in it firmly enough it really would survive. But as Sharon had said in explaining his Gaza disengagement initiative, vacuums can be dangerous in the Middle East. She was trying to prevent one and to a large extent using the best tool she had: herself, her own presence in American diplomatic activity in holding meeting after meeting and making trip after trip to Jerusalem and Ramallah. I did not think this effort would result in any peace agreement, and on this Condi and I disagreed all along. But the least one can say for her approach is that she did prevent any Arab or EU initiative, directly or through the UN, that would have made matters worse, such as by legitimizing the Hamas role in the PA. UN envoy de Soto, who had astonished Welch and me by announcing after the 2006 Palestinian election that he planned to meet with Hamas officials, continued to press Kofi Annan for permission to do so.[6] Rice's activities helped prevent such moves toward Hamas, no small gain under the circumstances (which included continuing Russian contacts with Hamas).

Long before my "off the record" remarks on Capitol Hill, Condi was well aware that, increasingly, I did not see eye to eye with her on policy matters and did not believe this tension with the Israelis was productive for us. She was acute enough to see it even had I not expressed it, usually to Hadley and to the president, but not to her directly. I worked for Hadley and the president, not for her and the State Department, so it seemed to me doubts and objections should go up my chain. It is also true that I did not believe repeated objections would have gotten me anywhere with Condi, who achieved so much in life and in government because she was a determined and formidable figure once she had made up her mind. The two people who could change her mind were Hadley and the president, so I made my complaints and addressed my arguments to them. Condi never let any of this affect our personal relations; usually, she was as friendly and warm as she had been during the first term when I had been her chief assistant in pushing the president's line on Middle East policy.

Two other matters worth noting occurred in May 2007. First, the ceasefires between Israel and Hamas, and between Hamas and Fatah, were being blown away. Rocket and mortar attacks on Israel from Gaza were increasing and by May running at 30 a day. Beginning on May 16, air attacks by Israel returned fire on terrorists in Gaza. On May 18, Israeli retaliatory strikes killed seven Palestinians in Gaza. Israelis were killed by Qassam rocket fire from Gaza on May 21 and May 27, in the city of Sderot near the Gaza/Israel border. Often, responsibility for the attacks was claimed by smaller Palestinian terrorist groups rather than Hamas, but it seemed clear that Hamas was either behind them or at least not acting to prevent them. In addition to the Israeli-Palestinian violence, violence between the PA and Fatah on the one hand and Hamas on the other was returning. Severe fighting erupted on May 15, and roughly 50 Palestinians were killed in the factional bloodshed that lasted about three weeks. Despite whatever was going on at the political level where a national unity government was theoretically in place, in the streets these rivals were fighting it out for control of Gaza. On May 23, less than two months after the national unity government was sworn in, Abbas and Haniyeh met to discuss how to stop the escalation of violence between Fatah and Hamas. Their efforts showed no success.

Second, in mid-May, we received an urgent request to receive Mossad chief Meir Dagan at the White House. Olmert asked that he be allowed to show some material to the president, but we headed that off with a suggestion that he show whatever he had to Hadley and me first. The vice president joined us in Hadley's office for Dagan's show-and-tell. What Dagan had was astonishing and explosive: He showed us intelligence demonstrating that Syria was constructing a nuclear reactor whose design was supplied by North Korea – and doing so with North Korean technical assistance. Dagan left us with one stark message: The bottom line was clear to all Israeli policy makers who knew about this, and it was that the reactor had to go away.[7]

There then began a four-month process of extremely close cooperation with Israel about this reactor. As soon as our own intelligence had confirmed the Israeli information and we all agreed on what we were dealing with, Hadley established a process for gathering further information, considering our options, and sharing our thinking with Israel. This process was run entirely out of the White House, with extremely limited participation to maintain secrecy. The effort at secrecy succeeded and there were no leaks, an amazing feat in Washington – especially when the information being held so tightly is as startling and sexy as this was. Initially, there were doubts that Syrian president Assad could be so stupid as to try this stunt of building a nuclear reactor with North Korean help. Did he really think he would get away with it – that Israel would permit it? But he nearly did; had the reactor been activated, striking it militarily could have strewn radioactive material into the wind and into the Euphrates, along which it lay and which was its source for the water the reactor needed for cooling. When we found out about the reactor, it was at an advanced construction stage, just a few months from being "hot."

The consideration of what to do about the reactor continued alongside the tense Rice-Israel diplomatic meetings, but the two did not collide. For the most part, this was because different personnel were involved: military and intelligence personnel uninvolved in peace negotiations were the key interlocutors for Israel in considering the al-Kibar reactor, as were individuals on the vice president's staff, sympathetic to Israel's position. The work on al-Kibar was a model both of U.S.-Israel collaboration and of interagency cooperation without leaks. Papers I circulated to the group were returned to me when meetings ended or were kept under lock and key; secretaries and executive assistants were kept out of the loop; meetings were called under vague names like "the study group."

Hamas Takes Gaza

What to do about the al-Kibar reactor lurked in the background as, in the foreground, intra-Palestinian violence continued and escalated into June. The International Red Cross estimated that between June 8 and 15, 550 people were wounded and at least 155 killed.[8] Fighting had burst out again, especially after June 10; on that day, Hamas forces threw a Fatah official off the top of a 15-story building. Fatah fighters attacked Ismail Haniyeh's house that day, and the following day his house and Abbas's Gaza residence were hit. Hamas began more systematic assaults on Fatah strong points on June 12, and position after position fell; on June 13, the headquarters of the National Security Forces, one of the PA security organizations and therefore Fatah-controlled, was occupied. On June 13, one of the key offices of the Preventive Security Organization (PSO), another PA force and one directly controlled by Mohammed Dahlan, fell to Hamas. On June 14, Hamas occupied the PSO's main office in Gaza, taking control of all the arms, ammunition, and vehicles stored there. Hamas was steadily rolling over the Fatah forces that on paper greatly outnumbered its own, and by June 14, the battles were over. On that day President Abbas formally dissolved the national unity government. Hamas controlled Gaza, Fatah controlled the West Bank, and a state of emergency was declared in both. A new government was appointed on June 17, with Salam Fayyad as prime minister. The government of Egypt denounced the Hamas takeover in Gaza as a "coup against legitimacy"[9] and publicly accused Iran of fomenting the violence: The Egyptian foreign minister said, "Iran's policies encouraged Hamas to do what it has done in Gaza."[10] I remembered ruefully Omar Soliman's confident assurances to Hadley and me that Egypt would never permit a Hamas takeover of Gaza; that Egyptian bluster had proved to consist of words without any real-world content.

Why had Hamas acted? Why had the continuing Fatah-Hamas violence led this time to an escalating confrontation and finally a Hamas takeover? There were accusations by Hamas and its supporters that it was self-defense because the Americans were arming Fatah/PA forces to crush Hamas. That we were arming them was not true because all our aid was nonlethal, but that we were seeking to enlarge and professionalize the PA security forces was, of course, true. That had been the task of Gen. Ward and Gen. Dayton. Dayton told a congressional committee in May, just weeks before the Hamas takeover, that "[t]he situation has gotten to be quite dire in Gaza; we have a situation of lawlessness and outright chaos. This chaotic situation is why the [US] is focused on [helping] the legal, legitimate security forces in our effort to reestablish law and order."[11] From our perspective, we had made the demand of professionalization since 2002, when Arafat was in control of the 13 rival gangs he called security forces. Moreover, the Roadmap had clearly spelled out the need to eliminate terrorist organizations and all "militias" so that the PA government had a monopoly on arms. This was the "one gun" phrase President Abbas used so often. In theory, had the Dayton program continued on year after year while Hamas forces grew no stronger, we might have reached the point where PA forces could defeat Hamas. Ward and Dayton had faced the great frustration of having to achieve a task, professionalization of the PA forces, without any resources to work with; they were forced to be all talk until the fall of 2007, months after the Hamas action, when the first funds arrived. The first PA forces did not arrive for training at the Jordan International Police Training Center until January 2008. From that point on, their progress was remarkable. It was unfortunate that these Palestinian police were sometimes referred to as "the Dayton forces," but it was also a tribute to the work Gen. Dayton was leading.

In fact, it was ironically Hamas that made Gen. Dayton operational because he could not work with the national unity government. Once Hamas acted in Gaza and President Abbas dissolved that government, the way was finally clear for serious efforts to train PA security forces. Meanwhile, Hamas forces had steadily grown stronger because of the aid they were receiving from Iran. In earlier years, there had been a debate as to whether there existed or could possibly exist close ties between Iran and Hamas, given that Hamas was a Sunni Islamist group that was part of the Muslim Brotherhood whereas Iran was Shia. That question was answered clearly by Iran's pouring of money and weaponry into Gaza for Hamas, once the Israelis left the Philadelphi Strip separating Gaza from Egypt. By June 2007, we saw, Hamas was well organized and well armed, a tribute to the outside help it was getting but even more to its superior organization and dedication. Once again, Dahlan had proved to be better at padding the payroll than taking risks or inspiring his troops.

For Hamas, then, this may have been the optimal moment to act – with Iranian support available and after it had concluded there was a conspiracy to crush it, but before the balance of forces began shifting due to any actual American training of PA security forces. The pattern of unity meetings and even unity governments, then more Fatah-Hamas violence, and then more unity efforts was now broken. When I later asked Jake Walles, who had been our ambassador to the Palestinians as consul general, for his explanation of the Hamas coup, he wondered about what could have been the Hamas view of the world that month:

I think that Hamas really did believe that we were conspiring with Dahlan to bring them down. I don't think we were in the sense that they believed we were, but . . . all that spring before it happened, there were repeated clashes in Gaza between Fatah guys, meaning Dahlan's people, and Hamas. They were battling over who was in charge. . . . And we were meeting with Dahlan. . . . It wasn't a secret that I would meet with Dahlan, and that you guys would come out and we'd meet with Dahlan, and when Abu Mazen had meetings with the Secretary, Dahlan was there. So, I think Hamas put all of this stuff together, and I think they felt that there was a risk that this "conspiracy" would topple them – this nonexistent conspiracy. So rather than wait for it to happen, they just pulled the plug. . . . I always felt that their priority was control of Gaza and control of a piece of territory. And that's important to them as a movement, and also to the Muslim Brotherhood more generally. And so I think it appealed to them to take over Gaza. And when they saw that they could do it, they didn't hesitate.[12]

It can also be argued that the Hamas takeover was the inevitable result of Israel's withdrawal. One version of that theory even suggests that Sharon foresaw this happening and welcomed it as a way of forestalling movement to Palestinian statehood, but most criticism simply suggests that Gaza disengagement was a terrible error for Israel. Far from allowing Israel to "disengage" from Gaza, the removal of all IDF forces led to thousands of rockets and mortars, the kidnapping of Gilad Shalit, the Hamas takeover, and ultimately the "Gaza War" of December 2008 and January 2009. Neither at the time, in June 2007, nor later did it seem to me inevitable that Hamas would conquer Gaza. Tougher action by Egypt and the PA from the time of disengagement in the summer of 2005 onward might have avoided it; so could have Israel, which tolerated attacks from Gaza far longer than anyone had anticipated.

In retrospect, the turning point that led to the Hamas takeover was not the 2005 disengagement but perhaps the PLC election of 2006 and the Mecca Agreement of February 2007 – just four months before the fighting that led to the Hamas victory. There were three possible paths after that. Taking one path, Hamas could change or appear to change, suggesting that it might accept some of the Quartet Principles or using ambiguous language to that effect. Doing so would have quickly undone Quartet unity, and the Russians, some in Europe, and many in the UN bureaucracy would have strongly backed Palestinian unity governments. This outcome was very likely had Hamas shown any ideological flexibility or greater tactical agility in dealing with Western diplomats. Or, following a second path, we could have given up on the Quartet Principles and simply accepted Hamas as it was – a terrorist group, but one with which we simply had to negotiate. In the absence of compromises by Hamas, we would have had to compromise. However, that outcome was unacceptable to the president, not least because we were involved in a global war on terror. The implications of such an ideological collapse would have undermined efforts far removed from the Palestinian territories. Such an outcome was also unacceptable to the Israelis, who were not going to negotiate with an Islamist group dedicated to destroying their state through constant acts of terror.

Or, third, either Hamas or the PA/Fatah forces might simply prevail over the other. That the PA would prevail had been our goal since 2002 and was clearly stated in the Roadmap, which after all had broad international support. Terrorist organizations would be dismantled, and the PA would develop the professional security forces it would need to become a peaceful independent state. That Hamas might win this battle by taking over both Gaza and the West Bank was inconceivable while Israel was in control of both, and both we and the Israelis also believed Hamas was not strong enough to succeed when the PA took over. As time passed, especially in 2008 and later, the Fatah gangs were increasingly turning into genuine PA government security forces – a tribute to the work of Gen. Dayton and to Salam Fayyad's leadership. But in 2007, it was still essentially Fatah versus Hamas, rival Palestinian factions, with Fatah holding the upper hand in the West Bank and with the IDF and Shin Bet active there to prevent any increase in Hamas strength.

In Gaza, however, the Israelis had by June 2007 been out for nearly two years. There, the third path was available for Hamas: military victory over Fatah. From the Hamas perspective, unless it believed a national unity government would truly work – which was impossible given Hamas's absolute refusal to compromise on its beliefs in terrorism and denial of Israel's right to exist – there was no reason to delay. Intra-Palestinian truces came and went but the confrontation between Fatah and Hamas was endless, and time might bring greater strength for what Hamas saw as Fatah and we saw as the legitimate PA national security forces. In that sense, it is right to argue that a violent confrontation between Fatah and Hamas was inevitable and that Israel, Egypt, the United States, and the PA/Fatah leaders themselves should have acted sooner to ensure that Hamas could not win it. There is plenty of blame to share, precisely because – it is worth repeating – the Hamas victory was *not* inevitable; more action sooner could have prevented it. Egypt could have blocked arms moving into Gaza; Israel could have permitted the training of PA forces sooner and the United States could have undertaken this work sooner and more intensively; Israel could have hit back with greater impact on Hamas whenever attacked from Gaza; and, of course, the PA leadership could have acted to organize and motivate its men under arms. All this happened later, in 2008 and 2009, but only after Hamas had acted first, in June 2007.

A final note on Sharon's Gaza disengagement strategy: Those who malign it must ask how Israel would have fared had it still been in Gaza in 2007, with all the settlers and settlements to defend and thousands of IDF troops stationed there to provide that defense. First, the considerable international support that Israel in the end received for pulling out of Gaza would never have materialized, and instead there would have been intense pressure on other fronts to make concessions to the Palestinians. The vacuum that Sharon saw and filled with disengagement would have been filled some other way. Second, the IDF would have been engaged in a deadly daily war with Hamas in Gaza throughout 2006, 2007, and after, with far more casualties among settlers and soldiers than Israel suffered from Hamas rockets after disengagement. How would Israel have dealt with the situation of its soldiers and settlers in Gaza the day after Hamas won the January 2006 elections? How would it have dealt with their safety during the Second Lebanon War in the summer of 2006 or during the war between Hamas and Fatah in 2007? Sharon made a military judgment that the cost of defending the settlements and settlers was not worth paying, and those who criticize that judgment must also realize that the cost might well have risen as Iran's support to Hamas increased. By the summer of 2007, Israel might have had eight thousand settlers surrounded entirely by Hamas.

How Far Would Olmert Go?

On June 14, the very day of the Hamas victory in Gaza, the president met with a group of Jewish leaders organized by the Conference of Presidents of Major American Jewish Organizations. I see no other solution for the Palestinians and Israel but a Palestinian state, he told them, for demographic reasons among others. The Gaza withdrawal was a brilliant move, a clarifying move, he said; it forced the world to see that elements of Palestinian society were rejectionists and terrorists. We will not ask Israel to deal with Hamas unless it adheres to the three Quartet Principles. As I listened, I wondered how he would break out of the box that we and the Israelis were now in: OK, the threat from Hamas was more widely understood, but how do you beat them? What now? We present a competing vision, he told the Jewish leaders: We support the development of democracy in Lebanon and Iraq; we help moderates in Egypt and Saudi Arabia build more decent societies. In the long run, he was still arguing, the moderates and democrats would beat the terrorists and radicals.

The president then let the Jewish leaders in on some of the debate continuing inside the administration. Secretary Rice had been pressing hard for the president to commemorate the fifth anniversary of his June 24, 2002, speech with a new one setting forth the next big effort – a big international conference. Condi later wrote that "the pieces were falling into place for a big push toward a resolution of the Israeli-Palestinian conflict."[13] I was opposed to such a conference and the inevitable pressures it would place on us and on Israel, and I now had a stronger argument against it: Matters in the region were in so much flux after the Hamas takeover of Gaza. How could the president possibly respond to that argument? How could calling a peace conference 10 days after the Hamas victory be sensible? Peace with whom? Had not Abbas and the PA just shown they were in no position to deliver peace? The timing seemed preposterous to me.

I have not decided yet on a speech, the president told the Jewish leaders, but if I do give it, I won't push Israel to deal with terrorists. Remember, Abbas does recognize Israel. The question is, can he lead? Obviously, not in Gaza. Does Olmert still believe in a Palestinian state and in withdrawals in the West Bank? Yes, but he may think now is not the time, the president said. That was a hell of an understatement, I thought: How could Olmert possibly speak about withdrawals from the West Bank just as Israelis were seeing what withdrawal from Gaza had wrought? In fact, the president did not give a speech on June 24; the "anniversary" went by in silence. I had won that round, although nine days later, Welch was showing me a speech text for something the president "might" say. Condi was not giving up.

On June 18, the day after President Abbas appointed an emergency government by decree, the president called him to express support. Abbas's response was to say he needed to get into negotiations with the Israelis, to show the people he was still leading and to give them hope. The call to Abbas was in part an effort to show balance because Olmert was in Washington then for a previously planned visit. At dinner that night with Rice, Hadley, Welch, and me, Olmert interposed no objection to negotiating. On the contrary, he said, I am ready to show them a political horizon and surprise Abu Mazen at our next meeting. I am ready to discuss everything with him, Olmert added. The Winograd report was coming soon, I recalled as I listened to Olmert, and Olmert's popularity ratings were in the cellar, so I wondered about his willingness to negotiate. The weaker he became politically, the more Olmert seemed willing to risk. This was perhaps logical as a matter of individual psychology, but where would it lead Israel? How far would he go – and, more to the point, would anyone go there with him?

Rice asked if Olmert were willing to say that the time had come to prepare for final status negotiations. Yes, but look at the circumstances facing Abu Mazen, Olmert replied; he faces real limits. No, Rice answered; that is not what the president heard from him when they spoke today. On the contrary, his legitimacy comes from the link to statehood, and without that he loses his strongest card. It is time to say there will be a state and you will negotiate it with Abu Mazen, in a reasonable time – and to work toward an international meeting. I do not want a big international conference with 25 countries, Olmert replied; this had always been the Israeli position. Right, Rice agreed, we do not want another Madrid either. I just mean the Arab Quartet, Olmert said, referring to Jordan, Egypt, Saudi Arabia, and the United Arab Emirates, a group Rice had been promoting since March as responsible states interested in stability in the region. OK, Rice, said, the Arab Quartet; maybe Morocco also. Good, said Olmert; we certainly don't need Spain and Italy. Now Rice demurred: Well, you need Portugal, which will be the rotating head of the EU starting July 1, and you need Tony Blair (who had recently resigned as prime minister and taken up a new task as the Quartet's envoy); we'll see. I knew that she did not want the Arab Quartet plus Morocco but in fact wanted a larger list – more Arab states, perhaps more Muslim states from outside the region. The goal was positive – to ensure that Abbas would have Arab and Muslim support for any compromises to which he agreed in negotiations with Israel. But she did not make that clear to Olmert, and she did not make it clear that she intended a big "conference," not a "meeting." The Israelis insisted on the latter term because it sounded smaller and did not arouse memories of huge conferences like Madrid. The United States agreed to call whatever happened a "meeting," but we never kept that promise nor, I think, did we intend to.

On June 19, Olmert met the president. You said you were prepared to unilaterally create a state when we first met, the president said. I am still ready, Olmert answered; if I cannot negotiate a state, I will move forward alone. That would be a big risk, the president said, but Olmert replied that he had ideas on how to keep stability in that situation; for example, by getting Jordanian help. It is in the interest of Israel to clear out from the major part of the territories –

but not all of them, Olmert went on. I will do what I told you, he said to the president: I am going to make a genuine effort to lay the groundwork, but it will take some time to negotiate a Palestinian state.

Precisely what Olmert was saying was not clear to me. What did "lay the groundwork" mean? What did "prepare" for final status negotiations mean as well? What threshold had to be passed before you were actually *in* final status negotiations? The lack of clarity was fine from Secretary Rice's point of view but not from mine. It seemed to me that a final status negotiation between Abbas – who had just lost Gaza, who had lost an election to Hamas, whose hold on the West Bank was tenuous without the IDF and Shin Bet being active there – and Olmert, whose own political situation was dismal, was a mistake. Olmert might make far-reaching compromises given his personal situation, but those would be illegitimate in the eyes of most Israelis; I thought that Abbas was in a position where no compromises were possible.

The discussions in the Oval Office left a very bad taste for another reason. The agreement on military aid to Israel, negotiated in January 2001 by the Clinton administration after Camp David, soon needed to be addressed. Under that agreement, we were providing more military aid – $2.4 billion per year – and eliminating economic aid. Olmert now proposed to the president that we announce a new 10-year deal increasing military aid to $3 billion annually. There was no pressing military reason to make the announcement just then, but there were political reasons. There was grumbling about increased U.S. pressure on Israel, and this announcement would help end it; there was concern about the Hamas threat from Gaza now that it ruled there, and this would address it; and the announcement would greatly help the beleaguered Olmert. It would show that, whatever his troubles, his relations with Bush and America remained a real asset to Israel. The president was willing. He and Olmert had been chatting alone in the Oval and called me in. Work this out, the president said to me. I spoke immediately with the budget director, OMB chief (and now Senator from Ohio) Rob Portman, who interposed no objection. This would come in the "out years," anyway (beginning with the 2011 budget), when Bush was gone, making the commitment easier for a budget director to approve; Portman also noted that Congress would be not only agreeable but also enthusiastic. We could get this done. Hadley and chief of staff Josh Bolten were on board as well.

Unfortunately, Secretary Rice was not. The argument she proffered was budgetary: That increase of $600 million might crowd out other military assistance we needed, for example, for Pakistan. We had to think about it. We had to take more soundings on the Hill. Let's reflect some more, study it, work this through. That was not, I believed, the real problem, because Congress could be persuaded to keep the accounts whole while increasing aid to Israel. To me it seemed this objection was more visceral: She was annoyed at Olmert and struggling with him, their chemistry was now bad and getting worse, and she did not want him to get this victory. She blocked an immediate announcement of an increase in aid, though of course the president could have brushed the objections aside had he felt strongly enough about it. Very soon, Israel got the $3 billion; Olmert announced the aid increase in Jerusalem on July 29 and said the decision had been made when he had met with Bush on June 19.[14] But Olmert got very little credit for it, especially when compared with the personal victory this would have meant for him had he been able to announce it in Washington. I was annoyed that the president had let Condi delay it and was annoyed at her for trying to do so; I could not see how this would help bilateral relations or make Olmert more likely to work more easily with Condi and David Welch.

That night Olmert dined with the vice president and repeated that he was ready for a serious effort to move forward – though without inflated expectations. Abu Mazen let us down by signing the Mecca Agreement and setting up a national unity government with Hamas, he said. Condi believes that a political horizon would add the missing ingredient, giving a big boost to Abu Mazen to do what he has never done. I am ready for risks, he continued. The political risk is, how many times can I try with nothing in return? In his heart, Abu Mazen knows he cannot make serious decisions. We will cooperate and not look for excuses, but do not create expectations now – that would be dangerous, Olmert concluded.

This discussion left even more ground in doubt. If Olmert really believed Abu Mazen "cannot make serious decisions," what was he himself doing? Trying to prove to Bush that he had tried, so that he could then go ahead unilaterally? But he could not do that, I thought; there would be no support in Israel for unilateral withdrawals in the West Bank just after Gaza had fallen to Hamas, and especially not when the unilateral decisions were being taken by such a discredited government. Did Olmert not see this – or did he not care? Was he just trying to act, to assert leadership, thereby defying the political obituaries and trying to recover lost ground? Did he think boldness would win him wider public support and the backing of the key newspapers and (mostly left-wing) reporters who were now jumping all over him?

The Syrian Nuclear Reactor

After Olmert left town, the argument about a major presidential speech was joined again. Within it was the battle over the great international conference, which I also opposed. And this argument was happening against the background of our deliberations over the Syrian reactor. Round after round of analyses had been refined, describing all the realistic options we and the Israelis had. The debates were vigorous in our secret meetings in the White House Situation Room; at my level, when the Principals met in Hadley's office; and, ultimately, before the president when we met secretly in the Residence wing of the White House to escape attention. In the Situation Room, individuals expressed their own views and those of their boss – which did not always match. But our role was not to decide what was to be done about the reactor; it was merely to be sure every issue had been thoroughly debated and was covered

in the memos we drafted for Principals and for the president. The Principals –
Hadley and Rice, Defense Secretary Gates, CIA Director Hayden, Director of
National Intelligence McConnell, Joint Chiefs of Staff Chairman Peter Pace,
and Vice President Cheney – debated at length and repeatedly. Again, this was
an excellent example of how policy should be made; several of us noted that
when all the memos were declassified, this ought to be a model, studied by
schools of government. Several times Principals trooped over to the president's
living room in the Residence to have it out before him, answer his questions,
and see what more information he sought. I attended all these meetings as note
taker, and the notes are under lock and key at the National Archives. The day
I left those notes on the floor under my chair in the president's living room
and, discovered when back at the NSC that I no longer had them, remains
locked in my mind. These were among the most sensitive notes then existing
in the U.S. government, amazing precautions for secrecy had been taken, and
I had left them on the floor. Pale and drenched with sweat I ran back to the
Residence, where the butler graciously let me back in and accompanied me to
the Yellow Oval Room where we had met. There was my portfolio, under the
chair, untouched. Well, I thought, if the butler keeps his mouth shut, I may
actually not be shot after all.

The facts about al-Kibar were soon clear, and about them there was no
debate: It was a nuclear reactor that was almost an exact copy of the Yongbyon
reactor in North Korea, and North Koreans had been involved with Syria's
development of the site. Given its location and its lack of connection to any
electrical grid, it was evident that this reactor was part of a nuclear weapons
program rather than created to produce electric power. The options were clear
as well: overt or covert, Israel or United States, military or diplomatic. The
United States and Israel both had a clear military option: Bomb the site and
destroy the reactor. This was not much of a military challenge, General Pace
assured the president. Whether anything short of a military strike could destroy
the reactor was another question, and the difficulties with such an option
were obvious: Just how would you get the needed explosives to the site except
through a military attack? It was soon agreed that a covert option did not exist,
and military options were quickly designed to make the reactor disappear; as
Dagan had said when he first visited us, the Israelis clearly believed it had
to go away. We developed elaborate scenarios for U.S. and Israeli military
action addressing these issues: Who would you inform when, what would you
announce and what keep secret, and what if anything would you say to the
Syrians?

But a diplomatic option existed as well and we did draw up elaborate
scenarios for it as well. We would begin by informing the International Atomic
Energy Agency (IAEA) of the facts and making them public in a dramatic
session before the IAEA Board of Governors in Vienna. We would demand
immediate inspections and that Syria halt work on the reactor. If it refused,
we would go to the UN Security Council and demand action. If there was no
action, the military option in theory remained open.

However, this diplomatic option seemed faintly ridiculous to me. For one thing, it would never be acceptable to Israel, whose experience with the United Nations was uniformly bad. It would never trust its national security to the UN. For another, it would not work; Syria's friends in the UN, especially Russia, would protect it. At the IAEA, we had plenty of experience with Director General Mohammed el-Baradei, who was an Egyptian. He was redefining the director general's role from that of inspector and cop to that of peacemaker and diplomat; he would seek a deal with Syria rather than concerted action against it. Moreover, taking the reactor issue to the UN and the IAEA meant handing it over to the State Department, and I thought an issue of this importance should be handled right in the White House.

Finally, the argument that there would always remain a military option as a last resort was misleading at best. Once we made public our knowledge of the site, Syria could put a kindergarten right next to it or take some similar move using human shields. Military action required secrecy, and once we made our announcement, that option would be gone.

The vice president thought we should bomb the site. Given our troubles in Iraq and the growing confrontation with Iran, this would be a useful assertion of power and would help restore our credibility. As he later wrote, "I made the case for U.S. military action against the reactor. Not only would it make the region and the world safer, but it would also demonstrate our seriousness with respect to non-proliferation.... But I was a lone voice. After I finished, the president asked 'Does anyone here agree with the vice president?' Not a single hand went up around the room."[15]

My hand did not go up (and as we left the president's living room that day, June 17, I apologized to the vice president for leaving him isolated) because I thought the Israelis should bomb the reactor, restoring their credibility after the Second Lebanon War and the Hamas takeover of Gaza. It seemed to me that Israel would suffer if we bombed it because analysts would point out that Israel had acted against the Osirak reactor in Iraq in 1981 but was now paralyzed. Such an analysis might embolden Iran and Hamas, a development that would be greatly against American interests. Moreover, hostile reactions in the Islamic world against the bombing strike might hurt us at a time when we were fighting in Afghanistan and Iraq, another argument for letting Israel do the job. (I did not think there would be any such reactions, but this was an argument worth deploying in our internal debate.)

Secretaries Gates and Rice argued strenuously for the diplomatic option. Gates also argued for preventing Israel from bombing the reactor and urged putting the whole relationship between the United States and Israel on the line; his language recalled the "agonizing reappraisal" of relations John Foster Dulles had once threatened for Europe. I thought I understood why Gates did not want the United States to bomb Syria: As a steward of wars in two Islamic countries already, striking a third one seemed terribly unattractive to him. Why he was almost equally insistent that we prevent Israel from bombing it was never comprehensible to me, nor was Rice's similar position. It seemed clear to me that if we could not prevent Syria from undertaking a nuclear weapons program, our entire position in the Middle East would be weakened, just as it was being weakened by our inability to stop the Iranian program. If there were too many risks and potential complications from striking Syria ourselves, we should not only allow but encourage Israel to do it; a Syrian nuclear program in addition to Iran's should be flatly unacceptable to the United States.

I tried to think my way through Rice's reasoning but came up with only one theory. As with her opposition to announcing a new and increased program of military aid to Israel, she had an underlying strategy: She did not want Israel feeling stronger, but rather she wanted it and especially Olmert feeling more dependent on the United States. That way she would be able to push forward with plans for a conference and for final status talks. I hoped this was not her intention because it seemed to me sure to fail. An Israel that was facing Hamas in Gaza and now *two* hostile nuclear programs, in Iran and just across the border in Syria, would never take the risks she was asking it to take. I thought we had learned that lesson with Sharon as Clinton had learned it with Rabin: Wrap your arms around Israel if you want it to take more risks, so it feels more secure, not less.

The arguments for going to the IAEA and UN seemed so flimsy to me, despite the length and detail of the planning memos and scenarios to which they gave rise, that I did not much worry about them. Who could believe these organizations would act effectively? Who could believe we would not be sitting there five years later entangled in the same diplomatic dance over the Syrian program that we were in when it came to Iran?

But in the end, our near-perfect policy process produced the wrong result. At a final session with the president in the gracious Yellow Oval Room over at the Residence, he came down on Rice's side. We would go to Vienna, to the IAEA; he would call Olmert and tell him what the decision was. I was astounded and realized I had underestimated Rice's influence – even after all this time. The president had gone with Condi in the end. Soon he would tell Olmert.

I tried to figure this one out and could not. Perhaps it was the same worry that Gates had about making another American military strike in the Islamic world. The president had decided, despite some very powerful moral arguments for action, not to bomb Sudan's tiny air force to stop mass murder in Darfur. He did not lose sleep over decisions made in past years, and that decision not to bomb Sudan was one of the very few I had ever heard him doubt. But that would not explain why he bought the IAEA/UN strategy lock, stock, and barrel; instead, he could have said, "Let the Israelis do what they want; let's just tell them we will not do it." Years later I asked him if he thought he had been wrong; he said no. Yet I could not figure it out then or later. In his memoir, he explains one key consideration: The CIA told him it had "high confidence" that the facility in Syria was a nuclear reactor but "low confidence" that Syria had a nuclear weapons program because it could not locate the other components of the program. The president thought that "low confidence" judgment would leak, as it surely would have, and the United States would have been attacked for conducting the bombing raid despite the "low confidence" report. That is a reasonable argument, but it explains only why we did not bomb – not why he urged the Israelis not to do so.

On July 10, I gave Hadley a memo explaining my views on where we stood with the Israelis. First, we were on the verge of telling the Israelis that we considered which of us should act against the reactor and decided that neither of us should use force. Moreover, we would pressure them not to do so even if they disagreed. Hamas had just taken over Gaza, Hizballah was back fully rearmed in Lebanon despite all those UN Security Council resolutions we told the Israelis would work, Iran was moving toward a nuclear capability, and now Syria was building a reactor that could only be part of a nuclear weapons program – and we were telling the Israelis not to act. Second was the forthcoming international conference. It looked as if we would soon be telling them we are about to call for an international meeting on the Palestinians that they do not want and that in fact they fear – and we will be doing so in a presidential speech that talks about negotiations for Palestinian statehood "soon" – that word was in the NEA drafts. How could the president deliver that speech three days before delivering his al-Kibar statement (which under some of the scenarios was planned for July 13), announcing what we knew and calling for IAEA action as if there were no relationship between the two speeches and the two issues?

The editorial comment from our friends on the right, I told Hadley, will be that we have taken leave of our senses: Hamas takes over Gaza, Syria and Iran build nukes, and we are handing things over to the UN and then pushing final status talks? I still did not think there was a need for any speech, but if there is to be one, it should be sober about the situation and supportive of Fayyad, I concluded. At that point, he had been prime minister for about a month, and already the PA was changing. It now had a serious, talented, incorruptible executive at the top of the government. This had never been tried before. The least we could do was to back him, firmly and fully, and not spend all our political capital on great conferences. Every time we pushed the Israelis into some concession related to the conference, we were wasting an asset we could have used to help Fayyad in the real world – or, better put, to help Fayyad improve how Palestinians were actually living in the West Bank. If we wanted Palestinians to see that in Gaza there was disaster while in the West Bank there was progress, practical matters and not conferences were the way to do so.

It was, as I recall it, a terrific memo, well written and well reasoned, yet like all the wonderful memos about the Syrian reactor, it had no impact whatsoever. On July 16, the speech that Condi had wanted to be delivered on June 24 was given. "Bush Calls for Middle East Peace Conference," the headlines read. In his remarks, the president first reviewed the past and then spoke of the next steps:

More than five years ago, I became the first American President to call for the creation of a Palestinian state.... Since then, many changes have come – some hopeful, some dispiriting. Israel has taken difficult actions, including withdrawal from Gaza and parts of the West Bank. Palestinians have held free elections, and chosen a president committed to peace.... Confronted with the prospect of peace, extremists have responded with acts of aggression and terror. In Gaza, Hamas radicals betrayed the Palestinian people with a lawless and violent takeover.... This is a moment of clarity for all Palestinians. And now comes a moment of choice. The alternatives before the Palestinian people are stark. There is the vision of Hamas, which the world saw in Gaza – with murderers in black masks, and summary executions, and men thrown to their death from rooftops. By following this path, the Palestinian people would guarantee chaos, and suffering, and the endless perpetuation of grievance. They would surrender their future to Hamas's foreign sponsors in Syria and Iran. And they would crush the possibility of a Palestinian state. There's another option, and that's a hopeful option. It is the vision of President Abbas and Prime Minister Fayyad; it's the vision of their government; it's the vision of a peaceful state called Palestine as a homeland for the Palestinian people.... By following this path, Palestinians can reclaim their dignity and their future – and establish a state of their own.

Only the Palestinians can decide which of these courses to pursue. Yet all responsible nations have a duty to help clarify the way forward.... So in consultation with our partners in the Quartet – the European Union, Russia, and the United Nations – the United States is taking a series of steps to strengthen the forces of moderation and peace among the Palestinian people. First, we are strengthening our financial commitment. This year, we will provide the Palestinians with more than $190 million in American assistance – including funds for humanitarian relief in Gaza. Today, I announce our intention to make a direct contribution of $80 million to help Palestinians reform their security services – a vital effort they're undertaking with the guidance of American General Keith Dayton.... Second, we're strengthening our political and diplomatic commitment. Again today, President Abbas and Prime Minister Olmert sat down together to discuss priorities and resolve issues. Secretary Rice and I have strongly supported these meetings, and she has worked with both parties to sketch out a "political horizon" for a Palestinian state. Now we will intensify these efforts, with the goal of increasing the confidence of all parties in a two-state solution.... Third, we're strengthening our commitment to helping build the institutions of a Palestinian state. Last month, former Prime Minister – British Prime Minister Tony Blair agreed to take on a new role as Quartet representative....

The world can do more to build the conditions for peace. So I will call together an international meeting this fall of representatives from nations that support a two-state solution, reject violence, recognize Israel's right to exist, and commit to all previous agreements between the parties. The key participants in this meeting will be the Israelis, the Palestinians, and their neighbors in the region. Secretary Rice will chair the meeting. She and her counterparts will review the progress that has been made toward building Palestinian institutions. They will look for innovative and effective ways to support further reform. And they will provide diplomatic support for the parties in their bilateral discussions and negotiations, so that we can move forward on a successful path to a Palestinian state.[16]

The $80 million was truly consequential; for the first time, the effort to build PA security forces would be funded. Once Congress appropriated those funds, Gen. Dayton was off and running. Additional funds followed, and finally the idea became a reality: Serious, trained PA police were hitting the streets. After 18 months without a cent, Dayton was able to move and proved that his claims and promises were absolutely reliable: He did the job and many of the doubters – not least those in the IDF and Shin Bet – became his greatest fans.

Aside from this announcement of aid, the speech reflected the tensions and contradictions in our policy all too well. The language presented a tough challenge to the Palestinians: "This is a moment of clarity for all Palestinians. And now comes a moment of choice." But, in fact, there was no "moment of choice" for Palestinians and no demands were placed on them; instead, we asked for concession after concession from the Israelis. The speech suggested that support for Fayyad's real-world actions would now be central in our policy, but instead we held a conference. The institution-building took a back seat. Armed with the president's endorsement, Secretary Rice and State took off; soon the "meeting" – the weaker term Israel had demanded and that the president had used – became an international conference and the attendance list expanded ultimately to 40 nations.

What did the president think of all this diplomatic activity, so reminiscent of the late Clinton administration? In his memoir the president writes, "At first I was skeptical . . . but I came to like the idea."[17] He thought it was worth a try, as Josh Bolten explained:

The president was always skeptical. Condi basically had to drag him into Annapolis and follow-on activities. Drag is too strong; she had the burden of proof to overcome and the president was always skeptical, though I never saw him entirely negative. I think he was realistic, probably figuring there was a one-in-three chance. But when he ran for president, he was one-in-six to become the president of the United States – by my calculation. He had a one-in-two chance of winning the Republican nomination and a one-in-three chance the Republican nominee would win the election. So he was one-in-six, but he went into that. If you're going to be in that kind of position, you take your shots. So it could easily have been one-in-three, but if you asked him he would have thought that "one-in-three, one-in-four is absolutely worth a try." One-in-fifty, maybe not.[18]

Not mentioned in the July 16 speech had been reform of the Fatah Party, but that never left the president's mind. He was, after all, a politician, unlike almost everyone else dealing with Middle East peace except Tony Blair, with whom he discussed the subject often and intimately. Just before the July 16 speech, they went over once again the need to reform Fatah or get someone to start a new party; they both felt new blood and new leaders were needed but never succeeded in figuring out how to move the idea forward in Palestinian politics. Bush reflected on it again in a chat with Ban ki-Moon, Kofi Annan's successor at the UN, the day after the speech. We need young Palestinians to get into politics, Bush said; too many of the old guys have one hand in the till while the other is shaking your hand. This was July 2007, and after the Hamas victory in January 2006, the Palestinians never again held an election while Bush was president or for years afterward. The old politicians learned a different lesson than did Bush: He saw the need for change and reform, whereas they saw the need simply to avoid putting themselves to an electoral test again.

The greater problem, I thought then and saw played out in the ensuing months both before and after the "meeting" that became the Annapolis Conference, was that we did not have our eye on the ball. Fatah might be unreformable, but the PA was not. In fact, it was being reformed before our eyes. Fayyad did not need our lessons about good governance. He had a long list of things the Israelis could do to make success more likely, but those requests were low on our list; we were focused on the conference. Because the PLO was the organization charged with negotiations with Israel, another way of saying it is that we were focused on helping Abbas and the PLO, not Fayyad and the PA.

At the end of July, we returned to the region. In Saudi Arabia, the king used the meeting with us to complain about Abbas as well as Hamas, for they had all come to Mecca and sworn an oath not to fight each other again – and almost immediately broken the pledge. Rice defended Abbas; what was he to do when Hamas attacked? But the king blamed them equally, an attitude that helped explain his lack of enthusiasm (and cash) for the PA in future months and years. Rice palliated him by saying we hoped for real progress toward the establishment of a Palestinian state by January 2009. This, of course, went beyond what the president had said in his July 16 speech but did not surprise me. It seemed we were going Clintonian now: The great rush for a Middle East deal in the 18 months we had left was clear.

Notes

1. Associated French Press, "Text of Palestinians' Mecca Agreement," *Khaleej Times*, February 9, 2007, http://www.khaleejtimes.com/DisplayArticleNew.asp? xfile=data/middleeast/2007/February/middleeast_February141.xml&section= middleeast&col.
2. International Crisis Group Middle East Report, *After Mecca: Engaging Hamas* (Amman: International Crisis Group, 2007), 21–22.
3. Rice, interview, p. 3.
4. United Nations Information System on the Question of Palestine, "Statement with Palestinian President Mahmoud Abbas and Israeli Prime Minister Ehud Olmert after Their Meeting," news release, February 19, 2007, http://unispal .un.org/unispal.nsf/eed216406b50bf6485256ce10072f637/ 3905e9beobco8ef2852572880050df79?OpenDocument.
5. Nathan Guttman, "Top Bush Adviser Says Rice's Push for Mideast Peace Is 'Just Process,'" *The Forward*, May 11, 2007.

6. United Nations, Alvaro de Soto, End of Mission Report (marked confidential), May 2007, 34–37.

7. David E. Sanger, *The Inheritance: The World Obama Confronts and the Challenges to American Power* (New York: Harmony Books, 2009), 271.

8. International Committee of the Red Cross, "Gaza-Westbank – ICRC Bulletin No. 22 / 2007," news release, June 15, 2007, http://www.alertnet.org/thenews/fromthefield/220224/025f24b73a37ef712ad576eb84b22e84.htm.

9. Alaa Shahine, "Angry Egypt Says Hamas' Gaza Takeover Was a Coup against Legitimacy," *Reuters*, June 23, 2007, http://www.reuters.com/article/idUSL23637408.

10. Carolynne Wheeler, "Egypt Threatened by Iranian Support for Hamas," *Daily Telegraph*, June 22, 2007, http://www.telegraph.co.uk/news/worldnews/1555373/Egypt-threatened-by-Iranian-support-for-Hamas.html.

11. Dan Murphy and Joshua Mitnick, "Israel, US, and Egypt Back Fatah's fight against Hamas," *Christian Science Monitor*, May 25, 2007, http://www.csmonitor.com/2007/0525/p07s02-wome.html.

12. Walles, interview, p. 11.

13. Rice, *No Higher Honor*, 582.

14. "Israeli PM Announces 30 Billion US Dollar US Defence Aid," *Thomson Financial*, July 29, 2007, http://www.forbes.com/feeds/afx/2007/07/29/afx3963706.html.

15. Cheney, *In My Time*, 471.

16. Remarks on the Middle East, 29 Weekly Comp. Pres. Doc. 966–969 (July 16, 2007).

17. Bush, *Decision Points*, 408.

18. Joshua Bolten, interview by the author, November 9, 2009, pp. 4–5.

9

The "Meeting" at Annapolis

On August 1 we were in Israel again, and the meetings once again struck me as miserable. First Rice met with Barak, who cautioned wisely that despite our desire to help Abbas and Fayyad succeed against Hamas, we should recognize our limits. We cannot pretend we can decide the internal struggle for power and legitimacy among the Palestinians, he told Rice and our party. Crossing some subtle lines would hurt them – they would seem to sit on our bayonets. Abu Mazen and Fayyad hold pens; we need people ready to kill and be killed. Dahlan had five times the number of fighters, but Hamas was ready to fight and shoot and die.

All this seemed sensible to me, but it set Rice off. Over time, I became at least as frustrated with Barak as she did because it became clear that he was thoughtful but completely indecisive about the West Bank. Whatever move we asked for, such as removing a roadblock here or a checkpoint there to allow the Palestinians additional mobility, would always be taken under careful consideration, reviewed, studied seriously – and never done. But this meeting was held just weeks after the Hamas coup and the announcement of the coming international conference, and Barak's advice seemed interesting and correct to me. Condi saw it as immobilism. This is the best Palestinian government you will have in your generation, she told Barak. Palestinian political life is radicalizing, and if you don't help these guys succeed, it will not be Hamas you are facing but Al Qaeda. The window is closing for those Palestinians who believe in the two-state solution. If there is no way out, it will radicalize. This is just what was happening under segregation in Alabama when I was growing up, she said; if the moderates cannot pull it off, the radicals will move in. So you must think bigger with this government.

Barak listened impassively and replied that you are accurate but I am afraid this is a Greek tragedy between us and the Palestinian people. They had so many opportunities and it gets worse in every round, he added. He then turned to the coming international "meeting" and said the problem is this: It can produce the appearance of a diplomatic process that will be perceived by Israelis and the Palestinian people as unreal. The process will be happening in diplomatic salons in Europe but not on the ground. It will have no gravitas unless there are real players on the ground. Rice bridled at this criticism of the conference. It is hard to do on the ground if there is no hope of a Palestinian independent state, she rejoined. The need for permits to travel on certain roads is the kind of thing that just made me angry as a child in segregated Alabama.

Israelis as Bull Connor

This comparison was new. Never before had I heard Condi cast the Israelis as Bull Connor and the Palestinians as the civil rights movement. It was a dreadful sign of just how far she had moved away from sympathy with the Israeli position and of just how much antagonism was developing. Condi's 2010 memoir, *Extraordinary, Ordinary People: A Memoir of Family*, describes in searing fashion the insults and the harm inflicted on her own family and their community in the years before and during the civil rights struggle, making it even clearer how her emotions about Israel were changing profoundly. And on the Israeli side, such comments elicited a sense that she simply did not understand the world of the Middle East. Olmert, years after leaving power, recalled the issue:

I once told her something which I don't think anyone ever said to her. I said to her, in four-eyes [a one-on-one meeting], I said, "Condi, you know, I think that I can understand, why you feel so much empathy for the Palestinians." I said, "You don't understand something. You're talking to a nation whose ethos is of liquidation, of massacre, of losing millions of people in the most brutal way, and therefore, you are not aware enough, I mean, of what it means for us that after all this, we have to go to the street and see that a bus was being exploded and the bodies of tens of people are torn to pieces, spread over 200 meters in the middle of town."[1]

Nor could I see how Condi was ignoring the racially mixed character of Israeli society, for everywhere we went we saw soldiers and police who were black – reminders of the rescue of Ethiopian Jews, which was ongoing. The Israelis, perhaps wisely, never raised this with the secretary, but every time we saw a baby carriage with a little black Jewish infant or encountered a few young black Israeli kids, I wondered whether Condi was not seeing what I was. At any rate, her civil rights references were a measure of the tensions between her and the Israelis in 2007 and 2008. For she was at bottom deeply sympathetic to Israel's situation and the threats it faced, and she had no illusions about the Arabs. She enjoyed visiting Israel and the Christian and Jewish religious sites there. Moreover, she was fully aware of the standing of women (and, indeed, of the role of skin color) in most Arab societies and had little tolerance for these mores: She would wear a head covering when visiting the Pope but not when visiting the king of Saudi Arabia. I did not view the comparison to segregation as an expression of her fundamental view of Israel or of the Arab-Israel conflict but rather as the product of growing frustration.

Later that same day, on August 1, we met with Olmert, and the discussion focused on the "meeting" the president had announced. I will make a statement saying that I'm ready to deal with the president of the Palestinian Authority on fundamental issues that will lead us into negotiations on the establishment of a Palestinian state soon or as soon as possible, he told us. This commitment should have improved Condi's mood because Olmert was going as far as he possibly could. Using this language – fundamental issues, Palestinian state, as soon as possible – was more than I thought the traffic in Israel could bear. Either I was wrong in judging Israeli politics, which was quite possible, or Olmert was simply ignoring politics – spurred by an ambition to make history, a dedication to peace, or the calculation that his political fate could only be rescued by a dramatic peace move.

When we returned to Washington, Condi called a meeting on August 13 to discuss the Middle East. There was a lot on the agenda – from training Palestinian police, to getting the Israelis to remove some obstacles to mobility in the West Bank, to financial support for the PA. And then there was the international "meeting." But as I complained to Hadley in a memo the next day, the real world had not been allowed to intrude. The session had focused solely on plans for the "meeting." Where would it be? Williamsburg? Annapolis? On exactly which dates? Could the invitation list be expanded? American diplomacy in the Middle East was now about that meeting and little else.

The Bombing of Al-Kibar

But there was a real world out there, as the events of September 6 reminded us: On that day, Israel bombed the al-Kibar nuclear reactor in Syria.[2] The turn of events after our final session with the president on this topic had been dramatic. On July 13, he had called Prime Minister Olmert from his desk in the Oval Office and explained his view. I have gone over this in great detail, he explained on the secure phone to the Israeli prime minister, looking at every possible scenario and its likely aftermath. We have looked at overt and covert options, and I have made a decision. We are not going to take the military path; we are instead going to the UN. Bush recounts in his memoir that he told Olmert, "I cannot justify an attack on a sovereign nation unless my intelligence agencies stand up and say it's a weapons program" and that "I had decided on the diplomatic option backed by the threat of force."[3] We will announce this approach soon, he said, and we will then launch a major diplomatic campaign, starting at the IAEA and then the UN Security Council. And, of course, a military option always remains available down the line.

I wondered how Olmert would react and believed I could predict his response: He would say wait, give me some time to think about this, to consult my team, to reflect, and I will call you tomorrow. I was quite wrong. He reacted immediately and forcefully: George, he said, this leaves me surprised and disappointed. And I cannot accept it. We told you from the first day, when Dagan came to Washington, and I've told you since then whenever we discussed it, that the reactor had to go away. Israel cannot live with a Syrian nuclear reactor; we will not accept it. It would change the entire region and our national security cannot accept it. You are telling me you will not act; so, we will act. The timing is another matter, Olmert said, and we will not do anything precipitous.

This is not the account President Bush gives in his memoir, in which he writes that Prime Minister Olmert initially said, "George, I'm asking you to bomb the compound."[4] Some day transcripts of their conversation will be available, but that is not my recollection. I believe the Israelis and we studied the information we had and looked at all the options, though Dagan had made clear from the start that the Israelis believed the reactor had to be destroyed. How to destroy it was a matter of examination and debate.

After that conversation, the delay from July 13 to September 6 had been filled with Israeli military calculations – watching the weather and Syrian movements on the ground – with the aim of being sure that Israel could act before the reactor went "critical" or "hot." We knew the Israelis would strike sooner or later. They acted, in the end, when a leak was imminent and Syria might then have gotten notice that Israel knew of the reactor. That would have given President Assad time to put civilians or nuclear fuel near the site. The Israelis did not seek nor did they get a green or red light from us; "no stoplights" had been our agreement. Nor did they announce their timing in advance; they told us as they were blowing up the site.

In the Oval Office, I had sat across the room from the president on July 13 listening to his conversation with Olmert and had heard Olmert push back immediately. I wondered how the president would react to the Israeli action. With anger? Or more pressure? None of it. He listened calmly to Olmert and acknowledged that Israel had a right to protect its national security. After hanging up, the president said something like "that guy has guts." It was said admiringly and the incident was over; the differences over al-Kibar would obviously not affect his relationship with Olmert or his view of Israel. So quickly did he accept the Olmert decision that I wondered then, and do still, if the president did not at some level anticipate and desire this result. He had sided with Condi and shown that she was still in charge of Middle East policy, but her "take it to the UN" plan had been blown up along with the reactor. He did not seem very regretful. What is more, he instructed us all to abandon the diplomatic plans and maintain absolute silence, ensuring that Israel could carry out its plan.

The Israeli assessment of Syria's likely reactions was correct. The Israelis believed that if they and we spoke about the strike, Assad might be forced to react to this humiliation by trying to attack Israel. If, however, we all shut up, he might do nothing – nothing at all. He might try to hide the fact that anything had happened. And with every day that passed, the possibility that he would acknowledge the event and fight back diminished. That was the Israelis' theory, and they knew their man. We maintained silence and so did Israel – no leaks. As the weeks went by, the chances of an Israeli-Syrian confrontation grew slim and then disappeared. Syria has never admitted that there was a reactor at the site, continuing to stonewall IAEA requests to examine it carefully. Soon after the bombing, the Syrians bulldozed the reactor site, but the only way they could be sure their lies about it were not contradicted was to prevent a full examination. When a 2008 site visit by IAEA inspectors found some uranium traces, Syria made sure never to permit a return visit.[5]

Two final points on the Syrian reaction to being bombed in September 2007 are worth noting. First, in May 2008, Turkish-mediated peace talks between Israel and Syria were publicly announced in Istanbul. The discussions had begun secretly in February 2007, soon after Olmert became prime minister, and obviously had continued after the Israeli strike on al-Kibar. That strike seems to have made the Syrians more, not less, desirous of talking to the Israelis because it made them afraid of Israeli power. But it also made them less afraid of American power, the second point. The Israeli strike was on September 6, and a very well-placed Arab diplomat later told us that it had left President Assad deeply worried as to what was coming next. Assad had turned Syria into the main transit route for jihadis going to Iraq to kill American soldiers. From Libya or Indonesia, Pakistan or Egypt, they would fly to Damascus International Airport and be shepherded into Iraq. Assad was afraid that on the heels of the Israeli strike would come American action to punish him for all this involvement. But just weeks later, he received his invitation to send a Syrian delegation to Annapolis, and as he told this Arab envoy, he relaxed immediately; he knew he would be OK. I had not wanted Syria invited to Annapolis because of its involvement in killing Americans in Iraq, but Condi had wanted complete Arab representation as a sign that comprehensive peace might be possible. It was only years later that I learned that Assad had instead interpreted the invitation just as I had: as a sign that the United States would not seriously threaten or punish him for what Syria was doing in Iraq.

It Was All Annapolis Now

Watching carefully to see what Syria was doing – or not doing – in reaction to the strike, we turned back to planning for the "meeting." On September 12, I shared my doubts with Hadley. The meeting would be held almost exactly two years after the Agreement on Movement and Access. That "agreement" turned out to have little reality to it; it existed on paper only. And here we were, doing it again, I argued. This diplomacy will not work unless and until the security situation improves, yet we were concentrating not on that issue but on the location, the banners, and the program for our conference. In the background, I added, there is zero Fatah reform. In fact, there was a hilarious moment at one of our lunches in Ramallah, in the Muqata, with the Palestinian team. Someone raised Fatah reform with President Abbas and he replied, oh yes, very important, absolutely – and then said Abu Ala'a is in charge of that, and turned to him to give a progress report. As he began to tell us how much progress was being made, I looked over at our consul general Jake Walles, and we made a determined effort not to laugh out loud. Putting Abu Ala'a in charge of reform of Fatah was like putting Arafat in charge of an anticorruption fight. Yet on we marched toward Annapolis.

Olmert was worried about Annapolis, fearing both unduly high expectations and pressure on Israel to make further concessions. On September 18, the president called him, at Condi's request, to soften him up. People are desperate for peace, the president said, and you won the election because you presented a vision of how to get there. Let's make an effort to get Palestinian buy-in, and if we really cannot get it, you can try your unilateral route while I am still president. Olmert replied that he was ready to do a lot, more than anyone before him, but let's not at this stage build inflated expectations. What we hope for may not come true.

The Palestinians were equally worried. At one session, Abbas had told the president that he wanted any agreements reached with Olmert kept secret. That was impossible, but his motivation was clear: He was unwilling to make compromises that would be unpopular and that Hamas could attack. Fayyad and others with whom we spoke were also worried about building unreasonable expectations, and they were urging that we deemphasize the meeting, saying it was just the start of a long process. There was simply no enthusiasm for Annapolis on either side, I told Hadley at the end of September, but we are not listening – not just to the Israelis but not even to the Palestinians.

Abbas and Olmert met on October 1, and we were told by both sides that they had a good and candid discussion. (The Israelis reported through me, and the Palestinians through Walles or Welch: As had been true for decades, the State Department was closer to the Arabs and the White House to the Israelis.) They told their staffs to try and draft a joint statement for Annapolis. The tension was clear, not between the two men but rather between the need for some meat in the statement while avoiding details that could arouse criticism and opposition. The staffs did indeed meet in the following weeks to work on terminology that appeared specific enough – but not too specific. What they all wanted out of Annapolis was, it seemed, to avoid damage.

We meanwhile decided that Hadley and I would return to the region. There was plenty to discuss with both sides, from the beginning of Gen. Dayton's practical training efforts, to the West Bank economy, the PA's role in Gaza, Fatah reform, the Abbas-Olmert meetings, to where we were on the Roadmap, Olmert's political situation, Syria and al-Kibar – the list was long. But in our preparatory meetings, held not coincidentally in Condi's conference room at State, there had been only one subject: Annapolis. Period. I told Hadley this was a mistake. The whole purpose of our trip had changed. We were not going there to have deep discussions of the sort we had had with Sharon but instead to pressure the Israelis for concessions. We were asking them to release 1,500 more Palestinian prisoners, to allow Egypt to place soldiers near the Gaza border despite the Israeli-Egyptian peace treaty terms that forbade that, and to stop settlement construction. They were also being told that we insisted on using the term "comprehensive peace" to describe the goal at Annapolis (a term that included peace with Syria) when we knew they wanted to discuss only Israeli-Palestinian matters; we were also asking for a timetable for negotiations. Meanwhile, zero was being asked of the Palestinians: no political reform, no additional action against terrorism. Moreover, we were asking nothing of the Arab states except the great honor of accepting our invitation to Annapolis. They were not being asked to provide additional funds for the PA or to close off all arms smuggling into Gaza. So every meeting with the Palestinians was nice and friendly, and every meeting with the Israelis was testy and difficult. It was all Annapolis now – and the road to Annapolis was to be paved with Israeli concessions.

In late October, Hadley and I made our visit. President Abbas told us he had had six meetings with Olmert and had begun to discuss final status issues with him. There are six issues, he said: Jerusalem, borders, security, refugees, the economy, and water. I do not say we reached agreement on any of them, he told us, but we discussed them. What I want in Annapolis is to launch final status negotiations, and our goal is a final status agreement while Bush is still in office, he continued. So we'll start at Annapolis, try to reach an agreement, and then I would present it to a referendum or to the Palestine National Council – the PLO's "legislative" body.

My objections notwithstanding, Hadley asked the Israelis for steps that he said would help make Annapolis succeed: the release of thousands of prisoners, a settlement construction freeze for a while, and some changes in the route of the security fence. Foreign Minister Livni pushed back: We will enter the negotiating game with the Palestinians after Annapolis, so why take these political risks now to get small gains at Annapolis?

Olmert was unhappy with our pressure as well. Look, he said, I want an agreement while Bush is president and I have told him that. Under your pressure I changed the Roadmap by accepting the idea of a political horizon, so we agreed to discuss Phases II and III even though we are still in Phase I. OK – but I do not want to find myself like an idiot with the Palestinians pressuring to put more and more things into effect immediately. They are going to be saying "The final picture is known, so why not do it now?" I have to avoid that and I am going to resist it, he told us. Implementation according to the sequencing of the Roadmap is more important now because we are talking about Phases II and III. You are going to tell me that we will not get anyone better than Abu Mazen, said Olmert, and I know it, but he is capable of delivering nothing now. He is weak. I am not going into this with false illusions. I am ready to take risks, including political risks, but I do not want to go to Annapolis as Barak went to Camp David, Olmert concluded.

In fact, the political ground had moved under Ehud Barak's feet while he negotiated at Camp David in 2000. As rumors of the concessions he was proposing circulated back in Israel, political allies deserted him and his poll ratings plummeted. And Olmert was not starting from a base of firm popularity; since Lebanon, his own ratings had been dismal.

I will say at Annapolis that we are ready to launch negotiations to continue until all issues are resolved, Olmert told us. We will talk until we have agreement on all issues; implementation will be subject to the phases and sequence of the Roadmap unless that is changed in the agreement. We can say we will have "continuous negotiations" but no timetables. Listen, Olmert concluded, I would like to do this with Abu Mazen, Fayyad, and Bush. You don't need to pressure me for that.

I thought Olmert had gone very far, and farther than I had initially anticipated. He had agreed to discuss the later phases of the Roadmap, including all final status issues, even though the Palestinians had not dismantled terrorist groups and indeed one of them was now in control of Gaza and had a majority in the PLC. He was agreeing to a larger "meeting" than we had initially discussed, one that was morphing into a huge international conference. He had, to my surprise, agreed to say we were "launching" final status negotiations at Annapolis. I knew he must have seen some personal political advantage to all of this, but he was nevertheless acting for the State of Israel and coming very far. It did not seem to me that our response should be to pocket all of this and demand more and more. I took this view not because of some deep personal anguish about the political risk to Olmert, because I got along fine with Livni and it would have made little difference to me personally if he had resigned one day and she had become prime minister the next. My problem was that I thought all our efforts and all the concessions we were demanding were aimed in the wrong direction – toward a successful conference rather than pragmatic movement toward building a Palestinian state. Condi believed the conference was a critical step in that direction; I believed the conference mania was a mistake. It would fill a vacuum after the Hamas coup in Gaza, as she believed, but it would teach that despite that coup there was hope for peace negotiations. I was sure, however, that the negotiations could not succeed and was worried that their collapse would leave us worse off.

I was not worried about violence, about a new intifada, if Annapolis led nowhere. The intifada had not sprung up spontaneously from the souls of Palestinians in 2000 and 2001. It was the creation of Yasser Arafat and his cronies. Now there was a Palestinian leadership that did not espouse violence and would try to prevent it. What worried me was losing the momentum we could build in the West Bank by playing all our cards with the Israelis in ways irrelevant to most Palestinians and to a real start to building the institutions they would need for statehood.

Birthday Dinner

The best example of what I was afraid of came very soon, in the run-up to Annapolis. The Israelis sent a delegation to Washington to work out final details, and Condi hosted a dinner at a restaurant in the Watergate on November 14. It was two weeks to Annapolis, and it was her birthday. She wore a gorgeous red dress and was going off to a birthday party in her honor after our early meal. Hadley and I and David Welch joined her, and the Israeli side included "T and T"; Ambassador Sallai Meridor; Gen. Ido Nehustan, who was head of planning at the IDF and later head of Israel's air force; and Livni's top aide, the director general of the Foreign Ministry, Aaron Abramowitz. A career civil servant, Aaron had been Livni's top aide when she was minister of justice as well and was a careful, thoughtful, highly competent professional. Most of the talk was about settlements, and Condi pressed the Israelis to announce soon that there would be an absolute construction freeze during the negotiations that would commence after Annapolis. This will help set the mood for Annapolis, she said. The Israelis pushed back and were determined to stick to the previous understanding: build up and in, but not out. As Livni had told us, they wanted to save any concessions for bargaining with the Palestinians when negotiations began, not to give them away to create a better mood for this conference.

Having failed on settlements, Condi then turned to another idea: The Israelis should return the bodies of Palestinians who had been killed by the IDF and buried in Israel. This was presented as a concession to the PA, but I could not imagine how it would help Abbas. These were likely to be the bodies of either criminals or terrorists, many from Hamas and Islamic Jihad. How did their return help the PA, Fatah, or Abbas himself? Who had even suggested this, I wondered, for I had never heard Abbas demand it.

Finally, Condi pressed for the release of 1,500 Palestinian prisoners. This would really help establish the right tone in advance of Annapolis. Turbo replied that that was impossible. It is not impossible, said Condi; you have around ten thousand Palestinians under detention. She and David Welch then started proposing who might be released. Release those with short sentences. Release the youngest. Release the oldest. Finally, Condi suggested releasing those who had been in jail longest. To this demand, Aaron Abramowitz responded. Look, he said, we do not have the death penalty in Israel, except for Nazi war criminals. So those who have been in jail the longest are murderers, and in fact murderers who committed aggravated acts – like murdering children or murdering with extreme cruelty. What is the moral basis for this demand that we release such people?

As I now recall it, a dead silence around the table followed. Not long after this exchange, Condi left for her party, telling Tourgeman as she departed that "you ruined my birthday." This small, private dinner was emblematic to me, both of Condi's deteriorated relationship with the Israelis and of the role Annapolis played in it. The concessions for which she had pushed made no sense to the Israelis and were refused; the only impact they had was to chill relations further. I thought it a squandered opportunity because we might instead have pushed the Israelis hard for moves that would be felt by average Palestinians and would improve their lives quickly. Remove this checkpoint or that road barrier, or allow Israeli Arabs to shop in the West Bank and perk up its commercial sector, for example. These actions were finally taken by Israel, under Prime Minister Netanyahu in 2009. They would not have been impossible in 2007 and 2008, had we focused on such practical acts and put the symbolic moves aside – and put aside the idea that our main goal was a successful conference.

On November 27, just after Thanksgiving, the Annapolis Conference took place in a spectacular setting at the U.S. Naval Academy. The very word "conference" annoyed the Israelis, for they had repeatedly been promised it would be a "meeting." In the end, invitees included the UN, EU, World Bank, IMF, Arab League, and about 40 countries. Using the term "meeting" or "conference" was a small difference, to be sure, but symbolized for the Israelis the ways in which U.S. policy was drifting away from them. The events at the conference itself were an anticlimax; the fact of everyone coming together to celebrate this launching of peace negotiations was the real news. Saudi Foreign Minister Prince Saud sat in the room when Olmert spoke; much was made of this as a great breakthrough. Olmert, Abbas, and the president made very good speeches. At the halfway point during the day, I got up to wander around for a moment. An Arab foreign minister came over to say hello, bored with listening to speeches all day. As we shook hands, he told me this was a beautiful place and a very well-organized conference. I agreed. But you know nothing will come of this, don't you, he said with a thin smile. I smiled back, because I agreed. I did not see how the negotiations being launched that day could possibly lead to a final status agreement in the year we had left in office.

The more significant events took place off stage, in the meetings the president held with Abbas and Olmert. The day before the conference, on November 26, he met with both men and their delegations separately at the White House. At Annapolis he met them again, together, and then we repeated the separate meetings the day after.

An Exercise in Futility or Can it Work?

At the White House on November 26, we began with Olmert. After the pleasantries, the president tried to reassure Olmert and the Israelis. The real issue is whether this whole thing is an exercise in futility or can work, and that's up to you and the Palestinians. After all, he reminded Olmert, if you had not convinced me that a Palestinian state is possible, we would not be here. I am not here to force you and the Palestinians to do something. I won't cram it down your throat. I understand your concern that this is just a big trap, but I think we have an opportunity that will enhance Israel's security.

The following moments left many in the Oval Office squirming. The president once again said he would not cram anything down the Israelis' throats and said he knew "T and T" were rebellious. This was probably a reference to things I had told him: Turbo and Tourgeman were deeply anxious about the conference for two reasons. They were worried about the pressure that might be brought on Israel, and in my view they were also worried about Olmert. Might the international setting and the possibility of widespread praise, so different from the terrible pressures and attacks he faced back home, lead Olmert to make concessions they would both view as excessive? Olmert responded graciously to the president, saying he was grateful for the very hard work and dedication both the president and Secretary Rice had put in. Your leadership and Condi's were essential.

So you're not mad at her? the president asked with a smile. Although no one could have been surprised that he was aware of the tensions between Condi and the Israelis, there was something close to shock that he was bringing them to the surface – right there in the Oval Office and in front of the full U.S. and Israeli delegations. No, said Olmert, with a stiff smile, but I can argue with her.

They would return to the subject of Condi in the post-Annapolis meeting, but then the president continued on the topic of the conference, saying its purpose is to lay out a vision, and then it will be up to you and Abbas to negotiate what a Palestinian state would look like. That is exactly right, I thought to myself; this conference is about some grand vision and not about the actual on-the-ground work we should be doing in the West Bank. The president went on and once again showed his awareness of the tensions between us and the Israelis. Anyway, calling it a meeting or a conference, who cares, he said to Olmert.

Olmert replied stiffly that we had all agreed on the term "meeting," and the agreement was the point. It's important there are no more misunderstandings on the way, he said. He then turned to Gaza and terrorism, which was safer ground, and told us that Israel would act freely to protect Israeli citizens. We won't ask anyone, he said. We will do all we can to complete these new negotiations next year, but we will not give up our opportunity to defend ourselves. That raises the issue of Gaza and just what commitments the Palestinians have met. While Gaza is in terrorist hands, they have not met their Roadmap commitments about terrorism. He then warned us, as he and Barak repeatedly did throughout 2007 and 2008, that Israel might well launch an operation into Gaza if the rocket and mortar attacks from there did not cease.

This warning did not faze the president and he returned to his basic point: The Palestinians need a clear vision of a state, although it was obvious that implementation of any agreement could not happen while he was president and could, he added, take as long as a decade. They need a vision of a state; the state may take a while, he said. Perhaps Abbas was not the man who could lead them to a state but he could negotiate the vision.

At his meeting with the president, Abbas reiterated his desire to launch negotiations immediately and conclude an agreement the following year, while President Bush was still in office. This is a historic moment that can alter the balance between hope and despair, the president replied. You and the Israelis must get to the definition of a state. But, he added, the Roadmap is vital; peace cannot be achieved if we do not follow the Roadmap. But the vision is vital; it changes everything. This is how the president is squaring the circle in his own mind, I thought as I listened. On the one hand, he has the Roadmap and the Israeli insistence on following its sequence, and on the other he has Condi

saying we need to jump to talks on Phase III and talk about a Palestinian state.
So he wants both.

Why are we having this conference? the president then asked. There are
three or four reasons to have a big meeting like this. First, it makes Rice feel
good. Second, it is important for the Arab world to be involved so that when
you finally reach an agreement with Israel, they are on board. Third, it gives
Israel confidence that the agreement with you helps them with the Arab world.
Fourth, the donors are watching, and we want them present so it is easier to
get a "yes" when we knock on the door. Otherwise, we could have just held a
three-man meeting, with you, me, and Olmert.

I knew the president had long felt very strongly about Arab involvement,
wanting broad representation at Sharm el-Sheik in 2003, at Sea Island in 2004,
and now at Annapolis. In Olmert's first visit to the White House, in May 2006,
the president had told him ruefully that the error Clinton made was not to
line up the Arabs. They wouldn't even take his call in the end, Bush said,
and it was clear that he would work to avoid any such outcome on his own
watch.

Abbas had only one substantive request: that the president not talk about
Israel as a "Jewish State." The goal here is to reach a Palestinian state, he said;
we are not here to define the character of the state that is next door to us. They
can define themselves any way they want. The President shook his head. I can't
do that, he answered, because I have already said it and I have to say it again.
You're about four speeches too late. Four years too late, Rice added.

"I'm Not a Timetable Guy but the Timetable Is Me Leaving Office"

At Annapolis the next morning, on November 27, the president arrived by
helicopter from the White House and the three men held a trilateral meeting.
It was a presidential pep talk, but the president also used it to define his role
as he saw it. If you want me to negotiate the deal, he said, I won't do it. The
American position is clear: We want you two to solve the problem, but I will
be as engaged as you want me to be. I am a phone call away, so call me. The
goal is an agreement on the definition of a state. If you think it is important,
now is the time to get it done. Do not waste this opportunity; do not let it slip
through your fingers. Now is the time; there's no telling what the next group
will do. I'm not a timetable guy, but the timetable is me leaving office.

With considerable difficulty, we finally got the "Annapolis Declaration," a
text that both Israelis and Palestinians could live with. Its key parts reaffirmed
the launching of final status negotiations, the deadline of December 2008, the
two tracks (Abbas-Olmert and a "steering committee"), and the American role
in judging who was implementing the Roadmap and who was not. We actually
set up a mechanism to judge compliance, under a three-star Air Force general,
Will Fraser, who provided reliable information – though little was done with
it in the remaining year. The Israelis won, in the final paragraph, the language

they wanted about implementation of any peace treaty agreed to by the parties: It would be subject to the sequence of the Roadmap:

In furtherance of the goal of two states, Israel and Palestine, living side by side in peace and security, we agree to immediately launch good-faith bilateral negotiations in order to conclude a peace treaty, resolving all outstanding issues, including all core issues without exception, as specified in previous agreements.

We agree to engage in vigorous, ongoing and continuous negotiations, and shall make every effort to conclude an agreement before the end of 2008. For this purpose, a steering committee, led jointly by the head of the delegation of each party, will meet continuously, as agreed.

The steering committee will develop a joint work plan and establish and oversee the work of negotiations teams to address all issues, to be headed by one lead representative from each party. The first session of the steering committee will be held on 12 December 2007.

President Abbas and Prime Minister Olmert will continue to meet on a biweekly basis to follow up the negotiations in order to offer all necessary assistance for their advancement.

The parties also commit to immediately implement their respective obligations under the performance-based road map to a permanent two-state solution to the Israel-Palestinian conflict, issued by the Quartet on 30 April 2003 – this is called the road map – and agree to form an American, Palestinian and Israeli mechanism, led by the United States, to follow up on the implementation of the road map.

The parties further commit to continue the implementation of the ongoing obligations of the road map until they reach a peace treaty. The United States will monitor and judge the fulfillment of the commitment of both sides of the road map. Unless otherwise agreed by the parties, implementation of the future peace treaty will be subject to the implementation of the road map, as judged by the United States.[6]

The president used the meeting with Abbas the following day, November 28, to deliver two messages. I hope one myth I dispelled yesterday was that I won't spend time on the issue, he said. I will, and I will travel to the Middle East. The number of trips is not an indication of desire, anyway, he added. I will work hard and so will Condi. She doesn't go out there and freelance. I will tell Olmert the same thing; I won't let it happen that Bush means this but Rice means that, the president said. Why the president felt it necessary to deliver either message was not at all clear to me, especially not at that moment. But the issue of Condi arose again, more dramatically, at the Olmert meeting later that day.

Olmert began his account of the Annapolis conference by saying he admired the efforts of Dr. Rice. No you don't, she pisses you off, the president replied. There was no squirming among all the members of the U.S. and Israeli delegations now; jaws seemed to hang open. Well, sometimes, Olmert said, but we work together – and we remain friends, Condi added, in a very smart effort to end this particular discussion. But Olmert did not take the hint and added that whatever his good relationship with Rice, he would never hesitate to talk to Bush directly. There is no difference between us; don't try to drive a wedge between us, the president pushed back, adding that he had just told Abbas the same thing. Now that Olmert saw the subject was on the table, he reiterated his position: Condi and I will work together, but if we disagree, I will present the disagreement to you. This made Rice mad and she shot back: You will get the same answer. When you say something is wrong, I tell the president. Olmert objected: But I need the freedom to call the president so I can explain why a position you hold may seem so wrong to me. I don't freelance, Rice replied, and the president and I are never apart on these issues. The stiff smiles were all gone now.

I understand that, Olmert now explained at some length. But I have an obligation to my people. I have an obligation to the State of Israel and to the Jewish people. It is so different, the history of our people. I am the prime minister of a society that throughout history has lived through the constant threat of annihilation. When you hear Ahmadinejad raving, you aren't worried about it; you can wipe him out in one minute. I am the prime minister of six million Jews who were thrown out of their countries. The most powerful experience in their lives comes to me as prime minister when Ahmadinejad says "annihilate." It is not a game; it is a reality. So when I argue with you, this is on issues of life and death. I would betray my responsibility if I stop because I cannot convince Condi Rice. I must go to the president. That is the lesson of recent experience, some of it not happy. We have to define in the most accurate way the red lines that are essential for us. I don't want to surprise you or to be surprised. I don't want the slightest misunderstanding between the prime minister of Israel and the president of the United States.

The rest of the meeting was calmer, but that exchange was as remarkable as any I heard in eight years working at the White House. Like the conversation with the president about al-Kibar, here was Olmert at his best, explaining that he had a responsibility for the security of a state whose security was always on the line – and for a people who had learned from history what happens to Jews without security. Israelis knew of neither conversation, and many – most, according to polls – saw Olmert as a cynical politician. That side of him existed, but so did this one.

It has to be added that this tactic – going around Condi to the president – was never a successful one. Dubi Weissglas explained the problem in a conversation we had several years later: Olmert seriously believed that if he was having any problems with Condi Rice, he did not have a real reason to be worried because at the end of day his close friend would take his position. He seriously believed that Bush was his close friend. And during the very short period I was still there [in the Prime Minister's Office after Sharon's stroke] I told him, "Don't be mistaken; you might be dear to him, I don't know. But nothing is even close to his relationship with Condi. And don't be that stupid to try to end up between them – because you're going to break your head. We [under Sharon], we never ever ever did it," Dubi had concluded.

Weissglas was right; Olmert almost always made a mistake when he sought to go around Rice to the president. He would have been better off having Turbowitz or Tourgeman contacting Hadley or me, explaining their views fully and asking that we reconsider. We had the chance in an internal process to change Condi's mind, something Hadley could try to do just through force of argument, or to bring decisions to the president. However, in a head-on dispute between Condi and a foreign leader, the president was never going to undercut his secretary of state.

The tensions were, in any event, out on the table now and would remain there throughout 2007 and 2008; they would spike again in January 2009 in the final days of the Bush administration. But Annapolis was now behind us and Condi had not only gotten the international conference she had wanted but also had gotten negotiations started. However Olmert described it, he had agreed to jump to Phase III of the Roadmap and start negotiating final status issues. The debate about "parallelism versus sequentialism," about whether Phase I had to be entirely completed before negotiations could start, was over.

The Three Generals

I did not think those negotiations could succeed, but the argument for trying was strong. First, what else positive was going on after the Hamas takeover of Gaza? This was the "vacuum theory," that something hopeful needed to be provided for Israelis and Palestinians, and for the Europeans and Arab states as well: Some sign was needed that progress was possible. It was never entirely clear how optimistic the president or Olmert was, and that may well have changed over time. Neither one had an alternative to what Condi was proposing, and both ended up as enthusiastic supporters and participants in this negotiating track.

In fact, there were now to be two tracks because Olmert would be negotiating with Abbas while Livni would be meeting with Abu Ala'a and the veteran PLO negotiator Saeb Erekat. Both of these Palestinians were smart and charming in a certain cloying way, and both were extremely knowledgeable about the details of past negotiations. But there was a downside to this team. Abu Ala'a (Ahmed Qurie) stood for everything we did not like in Palestinian politics and the Palestinian state to be created, from corruption to the hopeless Fatah Party. Erekat was an inveterate leaker whose participation meant that the substance of the talks was unlikely to remain secret, and he was also famous among the Israelis for lies he had told in previous years, such as his accounts of the "Jenin Massacre" in 2002. Nevertheless, both were fully capable of negotiating seriously on all the issues that would arise, large and small. If the idea was to fill the vacuum with a real negotiation, these were the best negotiators the PLO had to offer, and both had immense networks of contacts throughout the Arab world. They and Livni aimed for a concrete agreement, not just a statement of general principles.

The second argument for trying was that the process might itself engender forward movement. As one Palestinian who had been involved in the 2003 talks at Sharm and Aqaba later described it,

I've always believed and I still believe that if you launch a process, it creates its own dynamic. You launch it thinking we're going to get into a shelf agreement.... [A]t worst, what it can do is create a framework for things on the ground to work, because at that point I became also a strong believer on things happening on the ground. But I also believe that once you start negotiations... neither side really would want a shelf agreement. Actually both sides realized that it might be better to go for a real agreement. My sense, and this continues to be my sense now, is: sit, negotiate, and you start covering areas of commonalities. Then, more areas of commonalities – and you both come to have a stake in the success of the process you're invested in. And in some ways, politically this is what happened for Olmert and Abu Mazen.... It was a useful event. It did create a very unexpected, in my view, period of chemistry among Palestinians and Israelis.[7]

So there were good arguments for trying – but there were costs for going this route. We had chosen to maximize the hoopla. We had put a gigantic spotlight on the talks at Annapolis, and Condi's nearly monthly trips kept the process very much in the news. I wondered if this was the path to progress. Given the political difficulties that compromise presented to both sides, perhaps a bit more quiet would have produced a bit more progress. The greater cost was the loss of a pragmatic focus. We were betting on the top-down approach, but I thought going bottom-up had a better chance to succeed. These negotiations might well fail – as they finally did – and leave behind zero progress or embittered relations. One great advantage of the bottom-up approach, of focusing on actual progress in building the bases of a Palestinian state in the West Bank, was that every step forward was real and permanent. Negotiations were all or nothing; in contrast, on the ground, if you did not train 1,000 new policemen, you might hit 750; if you did not remove five checkpoints, you might remove three; if you did not build 10 new schools, you would build 2 or 4 or 6. So as the talks began in late 2007 and continued until late 2008, my skepticism about them led me to champion doing more, and pressing the Arabs to do more, to assist the efforts Salam Fayyad was making to strengthen the core elements of what might someday be the Palestinian state.

While the Israelis and Palestinians now had their two tracks, we had our three generals. Gen. Dayton continued his work on building the PA security forces; Gen. Fraser was now to monitor Roadmap implementation; and we soon added Gen. Jones (later President Obama's first national security advisor) as SEMERS. That was shorthand for his odd title – Special Envoy for Middle East Regional Security; although his task was not entirely clear, it appeared to be to work on the security issues that would someday – very soon, if the ambitions of Annapolis were realized – become part of a final status agreement. A good deal of work was done by Jones's staff and it made the Israelis extremely nervous because they believed they should negotiate those issues with the

Palestinians, not the United States. They particularly objected to the idea of a "Jones Report" that might make judgments about security claims Israel was making, and they fought against any formal conclusion to Jones's work. Although they respected Jones as a former Marine commandant and NATO commander, they did not think he understood their own situation nor had any real insight into the Middle East.

Shortly after Annapolis, on December 5, 2007, it was announced that President Bush would visit the region in January – his first visit to Israel as president. The first round of new peace talks began on December 12 and nearly failed immediately. Israel had announced a plan to build several hundred new homes in the Har Homa neighborhood of Jerusalem, and that plan was immediately denounced by the PA, the EU, and Secretary Rice. As far as the Israelis were concerned, they had agreed to build no new settlements or expand settlements physically in the West Bank. And they had agreed there would be no incentives for people to move to the West Bank. But this was Jerusalem; here, they would build, and nothing on Jerusalem was included in the settlement deal we had reached with Weissglas and Sharon. Olmert did move to assert greater control over the permitting process, to be sure the Prime Minister's Office would not be caught napping as other ministries approved plans for construction in sensitive areas and announced them at sensitive moments. Despite the arguments over Har Homa, Olmert and Abbas met on December 27 to get the ball rolling for the new year and in preparation for the Bush visit. Meanwhile, the violence continued; on December 26, there had been six rockets shot from Gaza into Israel, for example, and IDF attacks had killed six terrorists in Gaza that week.[8]

To me, the end of the year brought not only immense amounts of work preparing for the president's trip but also a clear sense that time had already run out for these peace negotiations. Annapolis had taken place less than a year before the 2008 elections, when the president would officially become a lame duck. More charges against Olmert were brewing. Gaza was in the hands of Hamas, rockets were flying, and at every meeting the Israelis told us it was only a matter of time before a massive intervention into Gaza took place. The year 2008 seemed more likely to bring war than to bring peace.

Notes

1. Olmert, interview, p. 7.
2. Yukiya Amano, "Implementation of the NPT Safeguards Agreement in the Syrian Arab Republic" (Vienna: International Atomic Energy Agency, 2010), 1; see also "Background Briefing with Senior U.S. Officials on Syria's Covert Nuclear Reactor and North Korea's Involvement," U.S. Office of the Director of National Intelligence, April 24, 2008, www.dni.gov/interviews/20080424_interview.pdf.
3. Bush, *Decision Points*, 421.
4. Ibid.

5. Fredrik Dahl, Sylvia Westall, and Andrew Roche, "Syria Stonewalling Threatens Nuclear Probe: IAEA," *Reuters*, September 6, 2010, http://www.reuters.com/article/2010/09/06/us-nuclear-syria-idUSTRE6852YF20100906.
6. Israeli Ministry of Foreign Affairs, "Annapolis Conference, Joint Understanding on Negotiations," news release, November 27, 2007, http://www.mfa.gov.il/MFA/History/Modern+History/Historic+Events/The+Annapolis+Conference+27-Nov-2007.htm#statements.
7. al-Omari, interview, p. 18.
8. Ilene Prusher, "Mideast Talks Already Tangled a Month after Annapolis Summit," *Christian Science Monitor*, December 27, 2007.

10

Two Trips to Jerusalem

The president's January trip took us to Jerusalem and then Kuwait, Bahrain, Abu Dhabi, and finally Saudi Arabia; we were on the road for more than a week. We began in Israel with a visit to President Shimon Peres, and President Bush clearly had a message on his mind. The squabbling and lack of progress since Annapolis made him wonder if he was wasting his time on the Middle East "peace process" during his precious final year in office. He told Peres it was not at all clear that Israel was ready to make the tough choices that peace would require. His purpose in talking to Israeli leaders, he said, was to determine if they were serious; if a deal is not possible, I have other things to do.

"We Survive Here Not Because We Can Quote Isaiah but Because We Have a Gun"

That same day, January 9, President Bush met with Olmert, Foreign Minister Livni, and Defense Minister Barak. First there was a thorough discussion of the refugee issue, with Livni making a forceful presentation. The president asked her if any "refugees" would be let into Israel or was her number really zero. Zero, she replied. Our goal is to end the conflict through the creation of a Palestinian state, a Palestinian homeland. Israel absorbed Jews from Europe and the Arab states; that was the raison d'être of Israel. Two states for two peoples – the creation of a Palestinian state is the solution for the Palestinians. People ask "Why not take some?," she continued. I'll explain why: To say yes means this conflict remains open for the future. First, how would we ever choose who comes back? The argument about which ones get to come to Israel would never end. And the delegitimization of Israel would continue. To give up part of our land, to divide the land between two peoples, provides an answer to their national aspirations. They cannot establish a Palestinian state and then say some should come to Israel. This affects the legitimacy of Israel. We cannot stop the process of their dreaming about replacing Israel unless we just stop any discussion of Palestinians coming here in the future.

The president was, it seemed to me, persuaded by Livni's argument. He then asked if she thought the conflict was between two peoples or two ideologies. He thought it was between two ideologies, one of which sustains terrorism and murder. If it is a conflict between two peoples, a solution may be impossible. Not at all, she rejoined. It is a conflict between two peoples, and that conflict can be solved. You have proposed the solution: two states for two peoples. A religious or ideological conflict will never be solved. Now Barak jumped in: We all share that vision of two states. But we are entering our 60th year and have had seven wars. We survive here not because we can quote Isaiah but because we have a gun. It is a tough neighborhood. He then turned to security matters and the conditions Israel would need to withdraw the IDF from the West Bank and allow a Palestinian state there. There are eight points, he said, and laid them out: They were both familiar and far-reaching, from demilitarization of the new state to control of the air space and the electromagnetic spectrum to control of the hills overlooking Ben Gurion Airport.

The president reviewed the list but said he could not agree right then on the eight points. Then he explained himself, giving for the only time in my experience a shorthand recapitulation of seven years of Middle East policy and answering the critics who suggested he should have marched into peace negotiations on January 20, 2001. I understand power and the use of power, he said, and I understand your security problems. I am pressing the issue now because I don't see a solution to your security problems except the two-state solution. My purpose in this visit is to look you all in the eye and see if you really want the two-state solution. Then I will figure out the proper role for the president of the United States. Why didn't I come sooner? he asked rhetorically. When I started in office, we faced the intifada. Mostly I blame Arafat for that. Then we had Afghanistan and Iraq. Then, Arafat had to be out. Then Sharon got sick two years ago. Then you had the Lebanon War. There is the European view – go and dictate a solution – but that is not my view. There is a danger that the Arabs will force Abu Mazen to negotiate with Hamas, but at this point they will not. Mecca was a naïve spontaneous reaction to the violence and it set us back. We got things back on track and did Annapolis. The question is where you want to go now: Are you serious?

He posed that question to the entire Israeli cabinet the following night at a dinner in Olmert's residence. I was reminded of a remark Dubi Weissglas had made about the one Israeli cabinet meeting Rice had attended: Dubi had acerbically noted to Condi that he was the only Israeli in the room *not* running for prime minister. Look, Israel has had no better friend than me, the president said flatly, and I recognize the existential threat: The threat to you is the same one that killed 3,000 people in the United States. I believe it helps your security to have a Palestinian state at some future time on your border, and I believe it's the only way you can be secure as a Jewish State. The goal now is to lay out a vision of a state, not to move to a state right now, but the alternatives seem to me to be a Palestinian state or Israeli occupation forever. I understand the security side too, but here is the question. From my point of view, we need

strong leaders. So the question is, to be frank, if the Olmert government doesn't
survive when he does hard things, it is not worth the time. We are fixing to
do a lot of hard work and make tough choices. I do not want to spend my
country's capital if it's a ruse. I do not want a political game, with people lying
in the weeds to throw him out of office. I need to know the ground won't shift
halfway through.

What the Israelis thought of this speech was not clear to me because so much
of it was in the kind of language they might not quite catch. Did they know what
a ruse was or what "lying in the weeds" meant? The president spoke the same
way to all audiences and interlocutors, on the stump or in the Oval Office; he
did not employ a separate official vocabulary for foreign officials. But I figured
they got the gist of it, which was 100% political support for Olmert. And that
seemed to me a mistake, a message the president should not have delivered. For
one thing, Olmert was so unpopular and his future so uncertain that hitching the
peace wagon to him was itself an error. He might be gone in weeks or months as
corruption charges mounted. President Bush was immensely popular in Israel,
probably more popular there in fact than in any other country on earth. If
there were ever a peace deal, his support for it would mean a great deal to
Israelis, but he should be supporting the two-state approach, I thought, not
Ehud Olmert. That kind of intervention in Israeli politics was simply unwise.
Soon there might come a point when Olmert, under the weight of the final
Winograd Commission report on Lebanon and the corruption charges, would
need to resign. Israelis – in the government and out, in his Kadima Party and
the other parties in the coalition – would need to decide when that point was
reached and Olmert must go. George Bush should not have intervened.

Olmert's response to the president was thoughtful and solid. I am absolutely
determined to carry on, he said, because it is good for Israel. The choice we
may have sooner or later is a two-state solution or one state for two peoples.
I have believed all my life in a "Greater Israel" and still do, he went on, but
either we share sovereignty or we share territory, and I prefer sharing territory.
I am dead serious about this process. To my colleagues, he continued, you
heard this man, the president of the United States, who is committed to Israel
as no one else. Is it not smarter to make an agreement now, under him? It can
be done in a year and a half or two years, but it is better to do it with him, so I
will make every effort. In this process, we will have discussions and arguments
with Condi, but we know how to deal with them. Every now and then I will
call you and I will be nervous, he said to the president. But in the end we will
achieve something. It does not mean a state in the near future, but we can
describe what a Palestinian state means, and then can go do it over time.

That was as good a summary of the Olmert approach as I had ever heard.
Of course, he had a personal agenda here too: The unspoken message was that
he had a special relationship with Bush and time was running out, so he should
be left in office to continue this work. It did not seem to me, looking around
that dinner table, that the others were buying Olmert's appeal – at least not
the personal aspect. Few of them cared at that point if he fell, and some no

doubt favored it because they saw a chance for advancing their own political interests. The president had appealed to them in essence to put politics and personality aside, but which politicians in which countries ever do that? We had achieved a moment of complete national unity after 9/11, but as we sat there in January 2008, the presidential campaign was underway and attacks on the president were vicious. Indeed, we had endured several years of such smears, and the time when politics stopped at the water's edge was clearly long gone. Similarly in Israel, complete unity could be achieved briefly during a war, but party politics and personal ambition returned quickly when the combat ended. Israel was in a sense always at war, anyway, and had been since the day it declared independence in 1948. It could not suspend politics year after year. The president's message and Olmert's might have done more good had the cabinet members been told to go ahead and pursue politics and their ambitions but to be sure they did not spoil the American effort – the Bush effort – to seek a deal with Abbas and the Palestinians.

"Probably We Will End up in a Ground Operation"

We were still on the road, in the Gulf States, when violence in Gaza reared up again. Qassams and mortars continued to rain on Israeli towns near the Gaza border, and on January 15, the Israelis struck back again, killing about 20. On January 18, they closed all border crossings in response to further Palestinian attacks. It is worth noting the total numbers of rocket and mortar attacks from Gaza into Israel: 165 in November 2007, 213 in December, 377 in January 2008, and then 485 in February. On January 23, after we had returned home, Hamas destroyed part of a wall the Egyptians had built to separate Gaza from Sinai and tens of thousands of Palestinian rushed across. While Israel was fighting with Hamas, our own efforts to improve the PA security forces were moving forward concretely: On January 24, the first battalion of PA security officers crossed into Jordan for training. On February 12, Imad Mughniyah, a top Hizballah military commander and one of the world's bloodiest and most effective terrorist masterminds, was killed by a car bomb in Damascus that everyone attributed to Israel.

But the meetings between Israeli and Palestinian leaders continued. In February, three months after Annapolis, one thing was becoming as clear as I had feared: Our attention was focused on those meetings and far too little on the real world in the West Bank. We heard this from no less a source than Salam Fayyad, who said it to the president. During a visit on February 1, Fayyad reminded us, as he put it, that Annapolis was supposed to do two things, not just one. It relaunched negotiations, and everyone understands that. The other has been forgotten or shoved aside with the excessive preoccupation with negotiations – that is, life on the ground. We must now prepare for statehood, he said, but that critical undertaking is simply being put at the margins. Of course, I agreed fully and wondered how hearing such a comment from Fayyad, who was so widely admired in Washington, would change things.

Not much, as it turned out. But there was a bright spot: security reform. Battalions were being trained in Jordan – 500 men each, one class after another – now that Gen. Dayton had some funds at his disposal. The Ministry of the Interior was being reorganized. A security infrastructure was being created – police stations, a training college, and operational bases. Dayton was also setting up a training program for senior police officials. And this was not all theoretical; men were in the field, making the streets safer for ordinary Palestinians and less safe for Hamas and Islamic Jihad. As one account put it, after June 2007, "[a]s armed men disappeared from the streets, public order was reestablished in the main population centres. This has been lauded by virtually all, irrespective of political affiliation. . . . From Jenin to Hebron, Palestinians praise their security forces for 'confronting criminals and thugs' and enabling 'ordinary families to walk outside after dark.'"[1]

That was the good news. But the PA was still living from hand to mouth, and the promised political reforms in Fatah were not happening. As to improving the Palestinian economy, many of the steps Israel could have taken were still being deferred by Barak and largely ignored by the United States. I had learned when working for George Shultz that what counts is not only what a secretary of state asks for but also what impression is left as to his or her priorities. Shultz was always careful to put human rights at the top of his list with the Soviets, at the start of every meeting, so they could never conclude or even be permitted to hope that he did not care about that issue very much. Human rights were first on the list. But because negotiations were at the top of our list, the requests we made on West Bank matters came much later in our meetings, often hurriedly noted as a meeting rushed to a conclusion. The Israelis surely took that on board and knew what our priorities were after Annapolis. When I raised the lack of attention to practical concerns, using as ammunition Fayyad's own comments, I was of course assured that we wanted both – progress in the talks and progress on the ground. But the priorities remained fixed.

On February 20, Olmert and Abbas met again, and both men were now paying more attention to the violence between Hamas and Israel. According to the Israelis, Abbas sought information about Israeli assessments and intensions, but did not pressure them to stop attacking Hamas. This was unsurprising; Hamas was now his enemy and Fatah's, so his concern would be civilian casualties and not slowing Israel's actions against the terrorists in Gaza. Abbas complained about construction in Jerusalem, but Olmert said he could not stop it for political reasons: His coalition would simply fall apart if he tried. Within days, the violence in Gaza intensified again: Hamas rockets killed a civilian in Israel, and an Israeli air strike killed five members of Hamas in Gaza. When Defense Minister Barak came to Washington at the end of February, he gave us a warning. Rockets with the ability to reach Ashkelon mean that 120,000 people more are now in range, and there are air-raid warnings every day. Our patience is at an end, he said, and we are going to strike back more forcefully. You must assume that we are entering a period of more violence that can easily deteriorate quickly into a major ground operation into Gaza. We have told this to Mubarak, Lavrov, Blair, Condi Rice, and other leaders. Hadley asked if they had decided on a ground operation and if so when. No, said Barak, we are still just reacting now, but what I am telling you is that probably we will end up in a ground operation. Barak also told us its scope was unclear; this could be a one- or two-day raid or a major operation with heavy divisions.

The U.S. focus now seemed to me doubly odd. While our energies went into the talks, we were paying too little attention not only to Fayyad's pleas for more help in building the institutions of a state in the West Bank but also to the Israeli warnings that sooner or later another Gaza war was coming. Clashes between Israel and Hamas were more frequent, and the mortars and rockets from Gaza were increasing as well: 165 in November 2007, 213 in December, 377 in January 2008 (more than 10 a day on average), and 485 in February. It was clear that the Israelis would continue to react to those numbers and sooner or later try to stop the attacks. On February 27, Hamas and other groups fired 40 Qassams into southern Israel. Israel hit back on that day and the next with missile attacks on the Interior Ministry building in Gaza and a police station in Gaza City. The IDF acknowledged killing at least 23 terrorists, though Palestinians said many civilians were also killed. On February 29, the IDF attacks increased, on the ground as well as in the air. And all these lines, military and diplomatic, did indeed intersect: Abbas accused the Israelis of "international terrorism," and on March 2, two days after our session with Barak, Abbas said he was suspending the peace talks because of the mounting civilian deaths in Gaza. The death toll that day was 54, more than in any day since the intifada in 2000. The EU condemned Israel for the disproportionate use of force and collective punishment, terms that would circulate again when the larger Gaza conflict erupted at the end of 2008, and there were protests throughout the Arab world.[2] The following day, March 3, most Israeli troops and tanks pulled out of Gaza again.

On March 4 and 5, the Rice group was back in Jerusalem. In our traveling party, optimism reigned. Welch told us Abbas would push for an agreement by May; Rice thought that was a possible achievement. The president had accepted the Israeli invitation to return to Israel to celebrate its 60th birthday in May, so perhaps he would have an agreement to celebrate. This speculation seemed to me detached from reality; the two sides were not even at the negotiating table, much less close to a breakthrough. When we met with Abbas on March 4, he explained that he had had to suspend the talks in view of the number of Palestinians being killed and was also asking for a UN Security Council resolution condemning the Israeli attacks. Rice replied that we needed to get the negotiations started again right away and to focus again on the Annapolis process. Annapolis had now morphed from a meeting, to a conference, to a process. Barak threw some cold water on the more extravagant hopes when we saw him on March 5 by telling Rice what he had told Hadley: A Gaza incursion was coming.

An Agreement in August?

On March 5, Condi met with the two Palestinian negotiators, Erekat and Abu Ala'a. She told them to resume negotiations as soon as possible and tone down their rhetoric. Otherwise, she said, you are in effect letting Hamas determine whether and when there can be negotiations. As to the initiative to seek a UN resolution condemning Israel, she was tough: The president and I are killing ourselves for you, and now you put us in a position where we will have to veto some resolution and be attacked by the whole Arab world. I'm angry about it, she said; do not do that to us. Abu Ala'a was, as always, the master of excuses for why things could not be done. We had an executive committee meeting of the PLO this week, he replied, and everyone said stop the negotiations. So we did. Now we need a decision of the executive committee to start negotiations again. So have a meeting and decide to go back to the table, Rice demanded. When can you get that done? Hmmm, maybe in the coming days, said Abu Ala'a with something less than the precision she was seeking.

Look, said an annoyed Rice, you are getting ready to run a state. You cannot run it by the executive committee of the PLO! We are trying to give you $150 million in aid and now there is a hold on it in Congress because you won't negotiate. The story must be that negotiations are starting again, or you will lose us. When can you get back to the table? We need a week more, Abu Ala'a answered, but Condi was not satisfied and told him that was too long. Announce right now that the negotiators will resume contacts, and then hold your meeting next week. Now Abu Ala'a switched excuses and said he could not go back to the negotiating table because there was settlement construction in the West Bank. Rice again dismissed the excuse; I need a negotiating meeting next week, she said. You do not understand that support is disappearing on the Hill. Abu Ala'a shook his head and answered: I need to keep our credibility. We need to see West Bank settlement developments, he added, meaning that he wanted to see if Israel was announcing more construction. No, said Rice. You need to take risks. You need to move now.

That had been a rare difficult meeting with the Palestinians. Now we moved back to the Israelis, where our difficult meetings were frequent and predictable. Rice and Livni argued at some length, after Rice pushed for Israel to stop acting in Gaza. As Rice explained, she was worried about leaving town and then having more Israeli attacks in Gaza, then a UN resolution we would have to veto, and then seeing more IDF action in Gaza. Everyone would say the United States was backing the Israeli actions and opening the door for more. Livni firmly rejected the pressure. What we do depends on Hamas actions, she said. Israel will defend itself, and if there are more rockets and mortars, we will again attack Hamas.

The very next day, March 6, a terrorist killed eight students at a Jerusalem seminary: A Palestinian gunman had fired hundreds of rounds from automatic weapons in the deadliest attack on Israelis in two years. The president called Olmert with condolences. You have my deepest sympathies, he told the prime minister; this is a sympathy and friendship call. There was no pressure from the top to stop acting in Gaza, and the difference between what they heard from Condi and what they heard from the president must have impressed the Israelis. The president understood that showing absolute solidarity with

Israel in security matters was the best way to get progress on the negotiating track.

Two weeks later, on March 21, he and Olmert spoke again, this time mostly about the talks. Olmert brought the president up to date and said he thought they might get a deal by August. However, they had not reached agreement on anything yet, and Olmert said that Abbas's demands – that Israel retain just 2% of the West Bank and accept 100,000 Palestinian refugees – were impossible. Why, in that case, Olmert thought an August agreement possible was beyond me.

Olmert and the president also discussed Syria because the Israelis knew we had decided to make much of what we knew about the reactor at al-Kibar available to the Congress and the public. Olmert was concerned that the announcements might blow up his ongoing talks with Syria. However, we knew that leaks were inevitable and were in fact coming soon, and that we would be better off giving the information before they occurred. Moreover, we did not share Olmert's enthusiasm for those talks with Syria. Olmert kept telling us this was the way to get Syria to break with Iran, but we considered this notion fanciful – and the president said so to Olmert. Olmert was planning on being in Washington in June for the annual AIPAC convention and told the president he would like to see him then and brief him fully about Syria. The president worried also that this venture with Syria meant there would be less attention and commitment to progress on the Palestinian track, but Olmert assured him it was not so – and that he would say this if and when he announced the talks with Syria publicly. The discussion of Syria brought the president to ask Olmert to consider some gesture about Sheba'a Farms, a topic I had thought dead. Olmert pushed back pretty hard: The UN has formally recognized Sheba'a as Syrian, not Lebanese, he said. We are acting in accordance with a formal UN position. It seemed to me that the president was unlikely to have had Sheba'a Farms on his mind at breakfast that morning, so Condi must have asked him to push it with Olmert.

As the Israelis had predicted, in March and April, fierce fighting in Gaza continued. In March, 299 rockets and mortars from Gaza rained down on Israel, and 518 – the highest number yet recorded – fell in April. On April 9, four Hamas fighters infiltrated Israel and hit a fuel terminal where oil was stored before being shipped into Gaza. Two Israeli civilian workers were killed. Israel struck back, with tanks on the ground and air strikes. Eighteen Palestinians and three IDF soldiers were killed on April 16. On April 19, Hamas fighters sneaked into Israel again and hit a cargo terminal; 3 from Hamas were killed and 13 IDF soldiers were wounded in the firefight.

"The Closer We Get, the More They Withdraw"

Hadley and I were in Israel on April 15 and 16, when this fighting was occurring. We met at length with Yuval Diskin, the head of Israel's General Security Service, the Shin Bet. Somewhat to my surprise, Diskin focused on the political side of things. Fatah is a big problem, he told us. You are building the security forces, but no one is building Fatah. Those police units will be trained, but they will not be backed by a political movement and will not be ideologically motivated. Hamas is defeating Fatah because it provides not just guns but an ideology too.

When we saw Olmert, he reiterated to us his desire to reach an agreement with the Palestinians in August and said he was working on maps to show Abbas. He also repeated what he had told the president on the phone: If Abbas was really insisting that Israel keep only 1.2% of the West Bank (he had told the president 2%, so had Abbas reduced this amount?), that is impossible; it's not serious. And Abbas said we need to take 10,000 refugees a year for 10 years, Olmert told us, and that is impossible. Again I wondered why Olmert thought an agreement by August or in August was remotely likely. I was struck by Ehud Barak's comment when we met with him: After decades, he told us, I am still not clear on the true position of the Palestinian leaders. It seems that the closer we get, the more they withdraw. Are they ready for painful decisions?

In our meetings on the Palestinian side, the Fatah problem that Diskin had raised with us earlier arose again. If elections were held that day, we were told in some private sessions, Fatah would simply have nothing to run on. Only Fatah could beat Hamas, but Fatah viewed the PA as a rival and did not embrace the government – even when it did things that were popular. If Fatah continued to view the government as an enemy and continued to resist reform, how could it ever build a platform that people would support? Abu Mazen is not interested in Fatah reform, we were told; Abu Ala'a is interested all right, but he is against it. As to the negotiations, so far they had gone nowhere. A deal in 2008 or even 2009 seemed far-fetched.

Yet the negotiations continued, despite all the violence. While Israel had often said it would not negotiate under fire, the fire was of course coming from Hamas and not the PA. The Abbas-Olmert and the Livni-Erekat-Abu Ala'a tracks were alive, if not alive and well. The atmosphere at most meetings, we were told by both sides, was good. When Abbas and Olmert had met on April 7, they had agreed that a final status agreement in 2008 was probably unreachable, and if a document were needed, it could only be some sort of framework agreement stating general principles. Whether such a document would do any good or actually hurt both sides – arousing opposition and criticism, but little support – was much on the minds of both teams. Abbas and Olmert had met alone for 40 minutes and their own relationship remained good, but there seemed to me to be no real progress. I had the impression each man used these meetings to explain to the other his own internal political problems – useful and perhaps conducive to trust, but not bringing an agreement any closer. I continued to think these talks were not going anywhere.

Olmert and Abbas met again on April 14, just before Abbas set off on his travels that would include Washington. We were told that Abbas had said Israel could retain 2% of the West Bank at most (with one-to-one swaps) and the Israelis had said that number was a nonstarter. There was a longer discussion of what to do about Gaza, with Abbas favoring the introduction of Arab forces as part of a deal with Hamas there. The Israelis took that on board, but in truth had no idea what to do about Gaza. It seemed they were locked in a perpetual cycle of tit-for-tat exchanges with Hamas. They could try some sort of truce directly with Hamas, but such a deal could undercut Abbas and the PA. The Israelis told us that Egypt was trying to broker some kind of truce or ceasefire. It was a delicate dance, involving both the political status of Hamas and Fatah and the Egyptian role in stopping – or not stopping – arms smuggling into Gaza.

On April 24, the administration made public most of what we knew about the al-Kibar reactor, releasing not only statements but also photos that showed the reactor was a copy of the North Korean facility at Yongbyon.[3] The Israelis maintained silence, officially. Syria denied everything: There was no reactor and never had been one. As mentioned earlier, Olmert and his team had one concern about this release of information: They were engaging in secret negotiations with Syria via Turkey and did not want this disclosure to torpedo those talks.

That same day, President Abbas visited President Bush at the White House, five months after Annapolis and still with no real progress in the negotiations. The president was philosophical. Can we do this, he wondered? He told Abbas that his wife had asked him why he thought he could solve a hundred-year-old conflict. We are racing against the clock to solve it in 2008, Abbas replied, and we need a solution we can sell to the Palestinian people. Hamas is waiting for us to fail. I tell Olmert I am prepared to meet his needs but nothing more; I have to win a referendum on this. He then gave the president some information about Fatah reform that seemed to me made up out of whole cloth, but they soon got back to whether a deal could be done with Israel. Do it this year, the president urged. Now is the time to move; a new president won't get to this in his first year; maybe my trip to the region in May will help push things forward. I will do all I can to help, he continued, and Olmert wants to do a deal. When I was there in January, I told his cabinet to back him, the president reported to Abbas.

That evening, Rice and Hadley hosted a dinner for Abbas and his team in which the focus was on what sort of agreement with Israel might be possible. A full final status agreement? How can you close the gaps? Abu Ala'a replied, telling Rice that they were working against 100 years of enmity. It had taken Fatah and Arafat 30 years, from 1965 to 1995, to persuade Palestinians to accept the need for a two-state solution. It was only in 1988 that the PNC, the PLO's legislative body, accepted it. Backchannel work had led to Oslo, but then there had been no progress; Netanyahu's government had focused on a deal with Syria instead. After the interlude of Camp David, there had been years of intifada. So negotiations are hard and there is great mistrust. I cannot see how we solve Jerusalem, he added, and then there is the refugee issue; they cannot imagine any "right of return" and we cannot imagine an agreement without it. Territory is the easiest issue. What we ought to do now is not seek a framework agreement or a final status agreement but an agreement on a number, a percent of territory. Yasser Abed Rabbo, who usually seemed to me the sharpest member of their team, reminded us that the Geneva Initiative (of which he had been a prime Palestinian mover) called for 2% or 2.3% of the West Bank for Israel, with one-to-one swaps, and said the built-up areas of the major blocks actually only take up 2% of the West Bank. And, Abbas chimed in, a link between Gaza and the West Bank can count for some of that percentage.

They then started talking about maps they would soon show the Israeli team and the chance to set borders, but Abu Ala'a returned to the topic of Jerusalem. There are modalities for security and for the holy places, he said, that we should negotiate; we can agree on taxes, municipal government, security arrangements – everything but sovereignty. Rice told the Palestinians she could not see how they would reach agreement now on Jerusalem; that just seemed to her impossible. Your goal for now should be to set up your state, she said; Jerusalem is too hard for now, so put it off. Do not delay setting up a state now because you cannot reach an agreement about the holy sites in Jerusalem. Ambiguity may be the best outcome for that. The debate continued: Erekat said they could not defeat Hamas and al Qaeda without something on Jerusalem. You are telling us Israel cannot give the Arabs sovereignty over Jerusalem now? Right, said Rice; they cannot. If you insist on it as part of a deal, we're through. Sovereignty in the Old City is the only zero-sum part of your negotiations with the Israelis, so delay it. They went back and forth on Jerusalem for a while, and I wondered: These people are on the verge of a breakthrough? Rice was talking with Livni and Barak and Olmert, I knew, about the president's May visit and wanted to see if some deal – however vague – could be closed then. That trip was three weeks way, and the goal seemed completely unreachable to me.

Abbas and Olmert met one more time after this Abbas visit to Washington and before President Bush arrived in Jerusalem again, and discussed the Egyptian efforts to arrange a truce in Gaza. The PA was most afraid of a direct Israeli-Hamas agreement that would make the PA seem marginal. In their one-on-one meeting, Olmert had again told Abbas that a deal based on Israel retaining 2% of the West Bank was unworkable, and he proposed 8%; Olmert suggested that Livni and Abu Ala'a chew on those numbers in their channel. The talks were still alive, it seemed from the accounts I received, but progress was hard to discern. Olmert spoke with Rice and was far more optimistic. He told her the Palestinians had been very responsive to his proposals and that it would be possible to close some deal in May, during the president's visit. In her memoir, Condi discusses an offer Olmert explained to her – one that seemed to her a breakthrough. But it does not seem that Olmert actually made his proposal to the Palestinians until much later in the year, in fact in September or October, when his own political fate was even clearer – and his demise nearer – than when he explained his thoughts to Condi in April.

Olmert's and Condi's optimism was balanced by certain realities on the ground as well: The PA was broke again. As we used our diplomatic clout to advance negotiations, we were not using it to lean on the Arab oil producers to provide more support of the PA budget. Fayyad told us that he was out of cash and could not pay June salaries unless more Arab money came in.

While we were working on the preparations for the president's trip, the notion that Olmert could lead Israel into a final deal took another blow: Yet more corruption charges surfaced. This time he was accused of taking bribes from an American businessman; Olmert denied the charges but said he would resign if indicted.[4] The pressures on him were building, and politicians were calling on him to step aside, arguing that the many investigations took up too much of his time and Israel needed a trustworthy, full-time prime minister. In the days leading up to our trip, the Israeli press was full of corruption stories – and stories about machinations inside Kadima as rivals positioned themselves for the post-Olmert period. The president had once described the Knesset as a shark tank, and as Olmert slowly but steadily sank, all Israeli politics took on that likeness.

Independence Day

The president's trip began in Israel on May 14, and its highlight, for me, was his powerful speech to the Knesset the following day. It struck me as one of the greatest speeches in Israel's history and in the history of Zionism. Bush placed Israel's independence in the context of all of Jewish history and God's promise to the ancient Hebrews, rooting Israel in five thousand years of history and not just in the context of the Holocaust. He reasserted America's relationship with Israel firmly:

The United States was proud to be the first nation to recognize Israel's independence. And on this landmark anniversary, America is proud to be Israel's closest ally and best friend in the world.... Earlier today, I visited Masada, an inspiring monument to courage and sacrifice. At this historic site, Israeli soldiers swear an oath: "Masada shall never fall again." Citizens of Israel: Masada shall never fall again, and America will be at your side.... [W]e insist that the people of Israel have the right to a decent, normal and peaceful life, just like the citizens of every other nation.... [W]e condemn anti-Semitism in all forms – whether by those who openly question Israel's right to exist or by others who quietly excuse them. We believe that free people should strive and sacrifice for peace. So we applaud the courageous choices Israeli's leaders have made. We also believe that nations have a right to defend themselves and that no nation should ever be forced to negotiate with killers pledged to its destruction. We believe that targeting innocent lives to achieve political objectives is always and everywhere wrong. So we stand together against terror and extremism, and we will never let down our guard or lose our resolve.

Some people suggest if the United States would just break ties with Israel, all our problems in the Middle East would go away. This is a tired argument that buys into the propaganda of the enemies of peace, and America utterly rejects it. Israel's population may be just over 7 million. But when you confront terror and evil, you are 307 million strong, because the United States of America stands with you.... Over the past six decades, the Jewish people have established ... a modern society in the Promised Land, a light unto the nations that preserves the legacy of Abraham and Isaac and Jacob. And you have built a mighty democracy that will endure forever and can always count on the United States of America to be at your side.[5]

The Israelis were deeply impressed by this display of friendship and commitment to their state. Used to decades of withering criticism from abroad and endless attacks on their conduct and their very right to exist, this emotional expression by the American president was a tonic. Bush's popularity, high in Israel since early in his presidency, soared even more.

For the core team of negotiators in the Prime Minister's Office and the Defense and Foreign Ministries, the difference in tone between this speech and the meetings with Condi must have been startling. People close to Rice denied that there was the slightest hostility to Israel in her position, then or ever. As one put it, "If you look at like UN resolutions and things like that, she always tried to weigh in and protect the Israelis up there. I frankly think it came down to this: she wanted to get this [the peace negotiations after Annapolis] done and trying to get it done just led to being brusque and tough and pushing both sides; it was just trying to knock heads on both sides. She would get unhappy with the Israelis at times, but it was always a reaction to things getting in the way of the process." In that analysis, there was a good cop–bad cop element to the Rice–Bush relationship with the Israelis: she pressured, he cajoled and supported. I thought there was more to it than this because Rice's desire for an agreement was deeper than Bush's. He was already comfortable, in 2008, with his place in history, which he knew would revolve mostly around 9/11, the war on terror, and Iraq. She was still trying to make her mark and time was running out, so a Middle East peace agreement was an important goal.

In private meetings during his trip, Bush wondered if a deal would be possible in 2008. It's too early to tell, Foreign Minister Livni told him. She was, I thought, negotiating seriously; she had concluded that mutual recognition by the Arab states and Israel would be an important strategic victory for Israel. Even if it took years for the Palestinian state to come into being, agreement on a two-state solution would mean all talk of the one-state solution would be dead, and Israel could begin to build a relationship with Arab states beyond Jordan and Egypt. The president was focused on the Olmert-Abbas channel, however, not on Livni's talks with Erekat and Abu Ala'a. Given my own opinion of both channels, I thought his focus was correct; whatever Livni's intentions, that channel would not reach an agreement. The president met with Tony Blair while in Jerusalem and told him that Olmert would likely go for the long ball, bypassing all the negotiators and pulling Abbas along into a deal.

We met with Abbas in Egypt; the Israelis had asked that this visit, meant to commemorate their 60th birthday as a state, not include travel to the West Bank. Abbas confirmed that Olmert was serious: He claimed Olmert had proposed retaining 7.3% of the West Bank and giving in exchange territory equal to 5% from Israeli territory, plus the link between the West Bank and Gaza.

This is the first time he has been so specific, Abbas went on, so that's progress. We also talked about Jerusalem, and that is a real problem for us because it is not a Palestinian issue; it is an Islamic issue. But, he told us, the Palestinians could not accept that Israel would keep the settlement blocks of Ariel, or Ma'ale Adumim, or Givat Ze'ev. If that was true, no deal was in sight – not in 2008 and not ever, I thought. Ma'ale Adumim, just east of Jerusalem, was the very definition of the major block that Israel would keep and was now home to nearly 40,000 Israelis. Abbas too was worried about failure. The road is not paved with roses, he told the president, and Iran and Hamas want us to fail. I can't help but remember Camp David, he said, because the outcome was terrifying; we lived through seven years of terror and destruction because of that failed effort.

The president told the king of Jordan, whom we also saw on this trip, that he thought a deal could be done. I did not see how. Whenever Olmert met with Abbas, two problems were lurking in the background. The first was the corruption accusations against Olmert, which seemed likely to shorten his time in office and undermined his legitimacy. Any deal he offered Abbas would be seen by many Israelis as designed to rescue his prime ministership, or at least his reputation, and might well be rejected by his own cabinet and the Knesset. Such a chain of events would be a disaster for Israel. I knew that some of Olmert's most intimate advisers shared this worry that he would go too far and had told him so, informing him that they would resign if they came to the conclusion that he was acting to salvage his reputation and had lost his moorings. I passed this concern on to the president through Steve Hadley. Hadley reported back that the president had commented that if any staff member ever said that to him, his reply would be, "No, if that's your attitude, you just resigned." Right, I told Hadley; and what does it tell you about Olmert and his own situation that his reaction to such warnings from his staff was apparently to swallow glumly? Olmert's situation was one huge problem; the other one was Gaza. What would happen to the negotiations if there were a major Israeli incursion? The talks had survived significant Israeli attacks, but the kind of ground action Israeli officials told us might be coming would certainly be the end of them.

The president was more optimistic. We need to try to get this done before the end of my presidency, he told Fayyad. Meeting with Fayyad was always a tonic even if he brought somber news because his very sobriety was evidence that the PA now had serious and dedicated leadership. I think we are approaching the point where the culture of violence is being broken, Fayyad told the president, but we still do not see enough change on the ground. People need more freedom to move around, and the IDF has to hold back more and let our guys do the job. Their morale is getting better and better and so is their capability. As they do more and more, Palestinians will be taking responsibility for themselves – and that is the backbone for a state. We say to people, persevere; Israel was not established in 1948. It was *announced* in 1948. I say create institutions now, Fayyad told us, and that is what I tell our people: don't sit and wait for the occupation to end; build a state despite the occupation.

As usual, it seemed to me Fayyad's approach was far more realistic. That occupation was not ending soon, even if a deal were reached – something I still thought far-fetched. The work of creating a state could and must be carried on, not delayed. There was a great and sad irony here because we were often accused of just plain loving Fayyad in Washington, where he was said to be far more popular than among Palestinians. And yet we were focusing our efforts on Abbas and the negotiations still; although we were helping Fayyad's efforts for sure, we were not making them central to our approach. Fayyad was paying the price for being an American ally or favorite without getting any of the benefits such a position might have been expected to bring.

On May 21, just a week after we returned to Washington, Israel and Syria finally announced that their secret peace talks had been going on. No one in the Bush administration, or at least the White House, could figure out what Olmert was doing. The president told him so when they spoke on the phone on June 4. You are giving freebies to Assad, the president said, a view with which I agreed entirely. We had a policy of isolating Syria for several reasons – its role in Iraq, its vicious repression internally, its support for terrorist groups like Hamas and Hizballah – and the policy had met with some success; for long periods, we were able to keep European foreign ministers from even visiting Damascus. All that was gone now, we knew; if Israel was negotiating with Syria, how could we persuade others to keep it isolated? We saw what Syria was getting out of the talks then but could not see that Israel had gained anything at all. Olmert claimed this was the way to break Syria off from Iran, a worthy goal that we shared. We just did not see how these talks would achieve it. But the president did not push Olmert too hard in that conversation because Olmert also explained to him how bad the Israeli political situation had become for him. It was unclear how long he would last in office, he admitted for the first time. Tourgeman and I reflected on this sad conversation, and he told me politics was now the only thing on the mind of most Israeli leaders. It seemed to me increasingly that their government was incapable of making decisions, except for one: If the missiles from Gaza did not stop, there would be a consensus to go in there.

"I Cannot Afford Progress on the Borders without Progress on Security"

In June, Secretary Rice traveled back to Jerusalem once again. The president's May trip had, of course, come and gone without a peace deal, and now it was a month later – and seven months after Annapolis and only six to our own elections. Rice had another very difficult meeting with the Israelis, this time with Livni. Livni reported on her talks with Abu Ala'a and Erekat; they were discussing borders, security, and refugees, not Jerusalem, but had reached agreement on precisely nothing. As we had heard from Olmert, she told us the Palestinians were now saying that Ma'ale Adumim, Ariel, and Givat Ze'ev had to go. Perhaps this was their negotiating position because they wanted to use them as bargaining chips to give away later, I thought; surely, they could not think Ma'ale Adumim or Givat Ze'ev – the latter a town of 10,000 just northwest of Jerusalem – was really up for discussion. Ariel was in a different situation geographically, for though it was large, it was in an isolated spot 25 miles due east of Tel Aviv and required dedicated and protected roads to allow commuting to the coast. Here, the PA might put up a fight, but I knew that abandoning a city of 18,000 was more than the traffic would bear in Israel.

Livni then discussed the territorial percentages. Olmert had offered that we would keep 7.3% and give them 5% in a swap; this gap is breachable, she told us. The Palestinians are still saying they will not go above 1.9% in Israeli hands, but if they want a state, I cannot see why they would not accept our offer. What about security matters? we asked. Nothing; they had not even been discussed. Everyone expects a Palestinian state, Livni told us, and uses words like contiguous, independent, and sovereign, but Israel's security needs will affect what those words mean. The Palestinians understand that Israel has security needs but there is nothing concrete. We have those eight points that Barak gave the president but the Palestinians just keep saying "we'll bring in international forces" as if that solved every issue. I cannot afford progress on the borders without progress on security, she told us; to reach a border agreement without any steps on security is negligence of my responsibilities to the Israeli people.

Even to me this pessimistic report was a little surprising. The constant repetition by Olmert that a deal was close, or could come in May, or was coming by August had given me the sense that there must be some progress on security issues. Rice told Livni the lack of progress was a problem, and the Palestinians were promised a map. The president feels strongly about it, she added, playing the Bush card with the Israelis – unsuccessfully, as usual, because they made their own judgments about which matters the president really cared about and which he probably saw as a detail. Not possible, Livni replied. They want a map where we show the 5% of the West Bank we will keep, while they are telling us the maximum is 1.9%. Why should I do that? There is no progress on security, she said again, and when I suggested I would give them a map, I thought we would be farther advanced on security. Nor did they accept the proposal that we would keep 7.3% and give them 5% back from Israeli territory, and we can't keep offering more and more and showing more and more on maps. I can't show them parts of Israel that would be in a Palestinian state if they won't move. If these negotiations fail, I cannot have a map like that left on the table, Livni concluded.

In our meeting with Abbas, Rice urged him to continue the negotiations and try to narrow the gaps. But she also pushed for her own role. We would like to intensify the trilateral engagement, she said, to see if the United States can help with final status negotiations. The bilateral track is working, but I think I can be helpful, Rice said. During the trip, we did have one trilateral, with Abu Ala'a and Livni, but it seemed to me that this experiment proved that trilaterals were counterproductive. We got nowhere and, in fact, Livni and Abu Ala'a got into an argument that would have been avoided had we not been there. Both of them played to the U.S. audience; there was no negotiating, and it was clear to me that there never would be while we were in the room. At this session, Abu Ala'a repeated that the Palestinian side could never accept Ma'ale Adumim, Givat Ze'ev, and Ariel, and Livni said they were not on the same page about basic matters when it came to security. They disagreed about everything, it seemed, with one exception: When Condi pushed for another trilateral, both resisted, Livni with considerable energy. This was the only issue on which the Israelis and Palestinians truly saw eye to eye.

On June 19, the efforts of Egypt to stop the violence between Israel and Hamas succeeded, and a sort of truce was declared. Though it began to fray in November and fell apart in December, the figures on rockets and mortars showed that while it lasted, it did work: 245 rockets and mortars were fired in June before the truce was declared compared to 9 in July, 11 in August, 4 in September, and 2 in October.

In the summer, the biggest news was about Olmert. There was a new and devastating accusation against him: that he had engaged in double billing during foreign travel, charging both the government and charitable groups for the same expenses and pocketing the surplus. This came on top of the previous accusations, including that an American businessman named Morris Talansky had delivered hundreds of thousands of dollars in cash to Olmert while he was the minister of industry.[6] After the July 11 announcement by the Israeli police and the Ministry of Justice about the new investigation of Olmert, it was hard to see how he could survive; the issue became more and more how and when his time as prime minister would end. Israelis whom I consulted privately said he might hang on for months, but his popularity and his legitimacy were gone.

To me this meant the pressure to complete negotiations in the "Annapolis Process" was increasingly untethered to reality. Olmert was in no position to bind Israel to anything, and I thought he should not be trying to do so. Kadima had to elect a leader in September, and it was impossible to believe he could run or win. In fact, he came to the same conclusion: On July 30, he announced his resignation – sort of. He said he would not run in the Kadima primary in September, but it was not clear when he would actually vacate the office of prime minister. This announcement did not have any legal impact: He remained prime minister, not in the caretaker role he would later have and that, under Israeli law, did formally limit his ability to act.

Yet our focus remained on the negotiating track, and we continued to pay far too little attention to events in the West Bank. On the very same day that Olmert acknowledged for the first time that he would have to go, July 30, the PA announced it was going broke. "Palestinian Prime Minister Salam Fayyad has appealed to the World Bank to help him secure emergency financing to bridge a shortfall in donor funds and pay public workers," Reuters reported. "Fayyad is seeking a so-called comfort letter from the Washington-based international lending agency to obtain short-term private bank funding, the sources said, speaking on condition of anonymity. The unusual appeal underscores the extent of the Palestinian Authority's budget crisis."[7] Once again, it struck me how skewed our priorities were and had been since Annapolis. And once again when I raised this problem, there were reassurances that we would proceed on all tracks simultaneously – but we did not.

"I May Be the Last Person on the Planet Who Thinks an Agreement Is Still Possible"

In late August, Secretary Rice visited Jerusalem again. Now we had an Israeli prime minister who was under investigation and had admitted he was on the way out, and we were just two months away from the U.S. elections that would make President Bush a lame duck. Still, Condi pressed forward. We met with the Palestinians first, and Abu Ala'a said he continued to aim for a full agreement. Rice told him she continued to believe we could finish one this year. We then met with Livni who poured some cold water on this hope, repeating that she was unwilling to move forward on border negotiations without equal progress on the issues of refugees and security – issues on which, she said, there was no progress at all. As to security, the Palestinians were saying they would not accept one single Israeli soldier on their territory, but the Israelis were opposed to having international forces there because they believed such forces would never seriously fight terrorism and would get in the way of Israeli efforts to do so. The answer, of course, was for Palestinian security forces to do the job, but they were simply not ready to do so in 2008.

Once again, Rice asked for and held a trilateral meeting, and once again there was no progress despite a pep talk from our side. You are running out of time and need to start closing these gaps, Condi urged them; you are closer than ever and you can't miss this opportunity. Rice realized that a final status agreement was impossible now because time had run out, but she believed that some sort of agreement was still possible. You cannot do a full agreement by the end of the year but you can do a framework agreement, she told them, and you should put as much into it as you are able. Abu Ala'a demurred. We do not want a framework agreement, he answered; we want a full agreement that can immediately be implemented. It should cover everything, including Jerusalem. Livni was completely allergic to mentioning Jerusalem because she was in a very tight race with former Defense Minister Shaul Mofaz for the leadership of Kadima, and if she won, then she would be competing with Benjamin Netanyahu of Likud in Israel's next election. If you start talking about Jerusalem, she told the Palestinians, this meeting will end in two minutes. In fact, that is just what happened. There was a blow-up and the meeting soon ended, the two sides probably farther apart than when we began.

We did go to see President Abbas on August 26, and the discussion showed how his thinking had evolved. We may well not reach any agreement this year, he told us, and we need to figure out how to protect the process as we go forward. It seemed clear to me that he had no hope of reaching any agreement and simply wanted to keep negotiations going while Israel and the United States held elections; he wanted to avoid a collapse of negotiations that might spark a crisis or bring violence. Condi was not giving up: Let's think about "protecting the process" in December, not now, she told him. He said he was worried that December would be too late to achieve that, but Rice had not given up on getting a document. I may be the last person on the planet who thinks an agreement is still possible, but I do, she told Abbas with a smile; the question is how to use the next few months to get to an agreement; I still think you can.

But when we all turned to substance, it became apparent that an agreement was not near. We cannot discuss Jerusalem now, Rice told the Palestinians. Abu Ala'a rejoined that he was unwilling to give in on the major settlement blocks; Ma'ale Adumim and Ariel could not be part of any deal and could not remain in Israeli hands. Rice knew this was simply unrealistic and told him so. Keep your eye on Palestinian statehood, she told them. When the April 14, 2004, Bush letter said new realities on the ground, it *meant* Ma'ale Adumim and Ariel. The issue is how to provide contiguity despite them. No Israeli prime minister can cede Ariel and Ma'ale Adumim, she concluded.

What was unclear to me was whether the president still remained optimistic and still thought – with our own election so close and Olmert on the way out – that a deal could be done. Olmert later told me he thought not; he believed that by the fall of 2008, the president had come to the conclusion that nothing would happen but that there was no downside to Condi's continuing efforts. Olmert summed up his own view of the president's approach: "He decided to play the game because that's what Condi wanted and Condi was his Foreign Minister. And there was no alternative; what was the alternative? What was the option other than to try and bring us together? And he also thought probably that, you know; as long as we talk, we don't fight.... I think that he just decided that this was the least dangerous strategy."[8]

Notes

1. International Crisis Group Middle East Report, *Squaring the Circle: Palestinian Security Reform under Occupation* (Ramallah: International Crisis Group, 2007), 8.
2. Associated Press, "EU Condemns 'Disproportionate' Use of Force by Israel," *USA Today*, March 2, 2008, http://www.usatoday.com/news/world/2008–03–02-eu-israel_N.htm.
3. Interview with intelligence officer, "Background Briefing with Senior U.S. Officials on Syria's Covert Nuclear Reactor and North Korea's Involvement," Office of Director of National Intelligence, April 24, 2008, www.dni.gov/interviews/20080424_interview.pdf.
4. "Israeli PM Denies Taking Bribes," *BBC News*, May 9, 2008, http://news.bbc.co.uk/2/hi/middle_east/7391414.stm.
5. Remarks to Members of the Knesset in Jerusalem, 19 Weekly Comp. Pres. Doc. 705–708 (May 14, 2008).

6. "Olmert Corruption Probe Widened," *BBC News*, July 11, 2008, http://news.bbc
.co.uk/2/hi/middle_east/7501281.stm.
7. Reuters, "Fayyad Appeals for World Bank Aid to Pay PA Public Sector Wages,"
Haaretz, July 30, 2008, http://www.haaretz.com/news/fayyad-appeals-for-world-
bank-aid-to-pay-pa-public-sector-wages-1.250790.
8. Olmert, interview, p. 5.

11

Final Days in Gaza and Turtle Bay

I was now telling the president, whenever we discussed the situation or whenever I reported on a trip we had made to Jerusalem, that time had run out. On September 15, the president met with Tony Blair, with whom he had kept up a running dialogue over Middle East peace through video conferences between the White House and Number 10 Downing Street and through notes Blair would intermittently send. Blair had left office in July 2007 but had remained involved as the new Quartet envoy, spending perhaps one week per month in Jerusalem. Now he told the president there would be no deal in 2008. For one thing, he said, Livni had no incentive at all to get anything done during the campaign period; she would not want any deal done until she was prime minister. So Blair urged that more attention be paid in the coming months to conditions on the ground in the West Bank, in essence, helping Fayyad move forward on the economy and on political and security reforms. When the president asked about Gen. Jones's security efforts, Blair was pragmatic: All his work should be geared to Palestinian life on the ground now, not a grand security plan. Building Palestinian capabilities is key. We should push ahead and not put all our eggs into the basket of diplomacy. Look, he concluded, reality on the ground will shape an agreement, not vice versa. I agree with that, the president replied.

Oh boy, I thought. "Reality on the ground will shape an agreement, not vice versa." Blair had summed up the error of our policy quite neatly. As he had put it, all our eggs were in the basket of diplomacy. If the president did agree with that assessment, I had to wonder why he had allowed that situation to occur; no satisfactory theory was ever put forward except his desire to allow Condi to lead in this policy area – and the fact that Olmert was pushing in the same direction as his own troubles mounted. Again I recalled the times I had told the president I did not think Condi would be able to get an agreement, despite the optimism she projected to him. Well, he had said several times, I know you think that, but Olmert thinks it's possible too and he's the prime minister of Israel. With both Rice and Olmert saying it was doable and wanting to continue on the negotiations path, my grim forecasts did not carry the day. That did not matter, but having put too many "eggs in the basket of diplomacy" did because it meant that we had not done all we could to bring progress on the ground.

With an Israeli prime minister anxious for a peace agreement, it would have been wrong for the president or the United States to express only doubts and never enthusiasm. And, in fact, Olmert got extraordinary support from the United States, even when his own situation in Israeli politics was eroding fast. My goal had not been to sow doubts but to suggest what Blair was saying: Reality on the ground must shape the diplomacy. The safety net for negotiations should be not words but real change on the ground in the West Bank. We needed to pay as much or more attention to jobs and roads and police as to conferences. We did not.

Rice and Hadley

And for that I blamed Hadley, at least in part. Some of the criticism of his tenure as national security advisor claimed he would never engage in real fights, but that was wrong. The development of the surge in Iraq proved it wrong, for there he had tenaciously fought against strong opposition in the Pentagon. But there was one exception: He would not fight Condi. Their relationship was too close and his deference to her too great. On the issue of Middle East policy, this meant that he would counsel her, but when her mind was made up, he would go along with her. I had never seen him say to the president, "Condi is wrong and you must stop her," but that was not surprising: That kind of remark should be made in a one-on-one meeting only. I had the impression, however, that he would never say this even in private, viewing it as disloyal to Condi. Of course, there were many things going on among the president, Rice, and Hadley that I did not see, meetings I did not attend, phone calls I was not on. But my impression was not idiosyncratic because everyone in the White House shared it: Steve would not fight Condi.

For the president, that was a loss because it meant that he was not getting the alternative views to which every president is entitled – and should demand. At least after Rumsfeld was gone, Rice was clearly the leading figure on foreign policy matters; she did not face what she had in the first term, where she was not only contending with Cheney, Powell, and Rumsfeld but also in their eyes held a position subordinate to theirs. Especially in 2007 and 2008, after Rumsfeld's departure, with Cheney's effectiveness hurt due to the departure of his invaluable top aide Scooter Libby and, of course, with her own former deputy at the top of the NSC, Rice had achieved almost complete supremacy on foreign policy issues. The president occasionally expressed annoyance with one action or another taken by State or by Rice; I was present once when he was informed by Chancellor Merkel of some decision Rice had taken without first seeking his approval. He then angrily called Rice to say the decision was his, and he had not made up his mind. But he appeared fundamentally satisfied by the system in place, one in which too many decisions were in my view made at the Principals' level rather than being brought to him.

His satisfaction with this system was odd because President Bush was extremely decisive. He enjoyed making decisions and did not delay facing them. So the system he put in place, or allowed to be created, remains a mystery to me: one where options were most often debated among Principals who ironed out disagreements and reached a consensus that was then reported to the president for his approval, rather than one in which disagreements were fully exposed and debated before him. Peter Rodman summed it up in *Presidential Command*:

Like Ronald Reagan, George W. Bush presents the paradox of a leader capable of great decisiveness but who set up or tolerated a system that impeded his exercise of it.... At Principals or Deputies meetings, Rice and her deputy Stephen Hadley repeatedly conveyed the President's injunction to reconcile disagreements, to "merge" or "blend" or "bridge" competing proposals, to split the differences, to come up with compromises.[1]

On Middle East policy, in any event, formal Principals meetings or NSC meetings (with the president present) were almost never held. By my own count, there were three such Principals meetings in the entire second term and no NSC meetings. Policy making was handled less formally, in meetings held in Rice's conference room or Hadley's office, and discussions with the president were equally informal: held before or after phone calls with leaders in the region or visits from them, standing around the Oval Office. It was hard to make an organized argument in such a setting, but sitting down would not have made a difference. The president was letting Olmert and Rice see what they could do in the few remaining months. Bush may have shared my skepticism or at least had his own optimism tempered by it, but he was going to let Condi run with the ball.

Olmert "Resigns" – Sort Of

Olmert's official "resignation" came on September 21, after Livni won the leadership of Kadima. She now had 42 days to form a government, or new elections would be held. This formal "resignation" meant Olmert was now a caretaker heading an interim government, a status that further reduced the legitimacy of any last-minute efforts on his part to broker a far-reaching peace deal.

Yet he kept on trying. His chief of staff Yoram Turbowitz later speculated about what drove him during this time:

Olmert was highly confident that he had a good chance of striking a deal with Abu Mazen. They had numerous meetings, most of which were one on one, and Olmert had a feeling that they could reach an understanding. For Olmert as with any politician there were a variety of motivations, but Olmert believed there was a historic opportunity to bring an end to the conflict. He thought we were running out of time for the two-state solution and he would be able to make a real mark in the history of Jewish people.

He genuinely believed the Israeli public would overwhelmingly endorse a reasonable settlement. He knew he would not run for prime minister again and he was not confident who his successor would be and if he would continue forward with the peace process.

Oddly enough, Abu Mazen avoided the opportunity Olmert offered him, and did not seriously respond to the suggestion put forward. Abu Mazen, and his team, only wanted the offer in writing. At the time the feeling was that the request to receive the offer in writing was merely a Palestinian wish to record the offer, so that it will serve as a point of departure for future negotiations. Olmert was right in not giving it to them in writing.

The reason for Abu Mazen's refusal to reach an agreement will probably remain a mystery. One may say he never wanted to strike a deal, as he was interested in the process that served his "regime's" interests. Another may say, that at the relevant time there was a perception that both parties did not have enough time to conclude a timely legitimate deal. It may well have been the case that if Olmert was firm on his seat for a while longer, an agreement may have been accomplished. It will probably remain unresolved forever.[2]

As Israeli politicians maneuvered for power, we went off to our eighth and last UN General Assembly. I had first attended the UN General Assembly in 1981 at the start of the Reagan administration, accompanying Secretary of State Alexander Haig and UN Ambassador Jeane Kirkpatrick to see Secretary General Kurt Waldheim. Now, 27 years later, this was presumably my last, a fact leading to little sadness on my part. The unreal world of the UN, where Israel had long been under vicious assault, held no attraction. This was the place that had voted that "Zionism is a form of racism" in 1975 and where president after president had had to veto unbalanced and unfair resolutions about the Middle East. If the UN had done any good in the region, it was hard to discern because whatever positive efforts one could find were outweighed by activities that simply made peace and justice harder to attain.

The president met again with Abbas in New York and took an entirely realistic tone, perhaps moved by the announcement Olmert had made so recently. There was no deal coming, he told Abbas; he knew that. But they should keep negotiating anyway, he said, to keep hope alive and hand something positive over to the new administration. Abbas did not argue with this; he said he thought Olmert was serious about the negotiations but lacked now in the credibility to pull them off. He then told us something remarkable: that many people in the Israeli government were encouraging him to break off with Olmert. We had heard this rumor – that people purporting to represent Livni had urged the Palestinians to stop now and to wait for her to become prime minister before negotiating again – but were not sure whether to believe it, and now Abbas was confirming it. On reflection, this was not all that shocking: Why would Livni want Olmert to lock her into conditions and promises she did not support or could not meet?

The president did not think Olmert could negotiate an agreement in the time left to him and told Abbas he also worried that any deal Olmert negotiated would be dead simply because he was its sponsor. The goal, he said, was to get things set so the next Israeli government will be ready to negotiate. Erekat replied that this probably suggested continuing to meet with Olmert to keep the ball rolling, but he said they just weren't sure about this approach. Olmert wanted to keep on negotiating, but other Israelis were saying it wasn't appropriate to negotiate with a caretaker. The Palestinians had a dilemma. I offered my own opinion: Don't conclude a deal with Olmert because any such deal is going to be rejected in Israel. Hadley agreed: Keep meeting and working, but do not expect to reach a final deal. We will keep saying we are making a push for a deal by the end of the year, to keep hope alive, but let's be realistic. The president agreed and said he would push even at the last minute if he thought a deal possible – but it did not seem to be. So the question would be whether the next Israeli leader and Abbas would be ready to make some very hard decisions. Will Livni be able to deliver? She has been a negotiator; soon she will be prime minister and that is a different role.

Of course, Livni never did become prime minister, though that outcome seemed very likely back in September 2008. At the meeting, it was agreed to keep things on track: The Palestinians would keep on talking with the Israelis right to the end, and the president would try to hand things off to his successor without a loss of momentum.

"We All Know What's in the Security Paper and It Can Be Written in 15 Minutes"

In a meeting the next day with Secretary Rice, Abbas told us he would deal with Olmert until the very day he left office although – he repeated – many Israelis are telling us not to. Rice urged that negotiations continue. We know what we want, she said: an agreement this year, or one early next year, that we can hand off. We know you have made more progress than people know. Keep trying to nail things down, she urged them. The final big decisions will have to await a new prime minister, but this work should go on. We won't start again at zero and the work is not wasted. We all know what's in the security paper and it can be written in 15 minutes.

It was reasonable to keep teams at work, I thought, but it was simply wrong that a security paper could be written in 15 minutes and not at all clear it could be written in 15 days or 15 weeks. It was not clear what Condi meant by "final big decisions," but she appeared to think something could still be signed before January 20. After all, if Livni got a coalition put together fast and became prime minister in October, that still left almost three months. That was the theory. And the negotiations did continue: In the middle of October, Abbas came to Jerusalem and to the sukkah at Olmert's residence, and they continued to talk about the terms of a possible deal. On October 24, the NATO Secretary General visited the White House, and the president told him privately that they were likely to get a peace deal by the end of December. This could only have come from Condi and seemed to me completely unrealistic – and also now becoming dangerous. The discredited Olmert, now officially an interim leader, should not be egged on to sign a last-minute deal with Abbas. But the president's optimism waxed and waned; on November 13, he told the Saudi king that he thought a deal would have been reached if Olmert had not been caught up in the scandals and forced to resign. Obama had been elected on November 4, and this was the last meeting the president and King Abdallah would have. He regretted leaving office without an agreement in place, the president told the king, suggesting that either Condi's own optimism had diminished or that he no longer believed what he was hearing from her.

In the background something else was changing as well: The truce between Israel and Hamas was eroding. In October, the sum total of rockets and mortars fired into Israel had been two. In November, the total began to rise: the total was 193 for the month, a number the Israelis would never tolerate. On November 14, six Grad rockets were fired at the port of Ashkelon, a serious escalation; this was a new weapon imported from Iran. Whereas the Qassam could travel 2 or 3 miles, the Grad was a truck-launched rocket with a range of 10 to 15 miles. Tourgeman told me the cabinet was debating how to respond – and there would be a response.

Olmert nevertheless continued pushing the PA for a deal. On November 17, he met with Abbas again. The PA tried to cancel the meeting, but Olmert persuaded Abbas to go through with it. Look, Olmert had argued, forget Livni; the only possible new coalition will be of the right and led by Likud. But whatever you conclude with me will pass the Knesset, so let's do it. Abbas was not exactly running away from Olmert now, but was, I thought, simply humoring him. We would act if we could, Abbas told him; we would not wait – but you and we both have internal problems, after all. Still, Olmert pressed on: He told our new and extremely able ambassador to Israel, Jim Cunningham, that in the one-on-one meeting with Abbas they had agreed that Erekat and Tourgeman would continue to meet and seek an agreement. I could see Abbas agreeing to this happily, for it got him off center stage and let Erekat take some heat – or play out the clock.

Olmert's Offer

Olmert came to Washington, for the last time as prime minister, on November 24, 2008. At a breakfast with our team, he was all optimism. There can still be an agreement, he told us, and everyone is wrong who says "Israeli politics" makes it impossible. Olmert told us he had made a proposal to Abbas, including Jerusalem; Israel would keep 6.5% of the West Bank and give the Palestinians land equal to 5.8%; the 0.7% difference was the link to Gaza. Negotiations are going to continue, he said. Now it was Condi's turn to be the voice of reason, and she told Olmert that it was very difficult for Abbas to close on an agreement. There were disputes and rivalries within Fatah and, of course, between Fatah and Hamas. How could Abbas sign, no matter what is on the table? That may be, Olmert replied, but let's be clear: The problem should not be attributed to "Israeli politics." We have acted. The political crisis in Israel did not stop us. There is an offer on the table.

What exactly was that offer? Olmert described it in interviews in 2010.[3] The percentages were pretty much what he had told us in 2008: Abbas was offered just under 94% of the West Bank with land swaps to make up the 6% – less about 1% "credit" for the West Bank–Gaza link. The PA capital would be in east Jerusalem, and the Old City would be governed jointly by Israel, the Palestinians, Jordan, Saudi Arabia, and the United States. There would be no "right of return," but Israel would acknowledge the suffering of Palestinian refugees and for humanitarian reasons agree to resettle in Israel something like 3,000–4,000 refugees a year for five years. According to Olmert, he made this offer on September 13, 2008, more than a month after his initial announcement that he intended to resign had made him a lame duck. (This contradicts the suggestion in Rice's memoir that the proposal was actually put to Abbas in May.[4] And Saeb Erekat's recollection, noted later, is also that this Olmert proposal came only in November.) He claimed to have shown the Palestinians detailed maps of what would be the Palestinian state, including the location of the link between Gaza and the West Bank, and to have described in detail the arrangements in Jerusalem, specifying roads, tunnels, and bridges. He also claimed that the United States had agreed to accept 100,000 Palestinian refugees to help swing the deal.

Many of these claims seemed to me greatly overstated. At the time, I recall no Israeli statement or information suggesting that such details had been conveyed; on the contrary, the Palestinians were complaining precisely about the lack of such detail. As to the 100,000 refugees the United States agreed to accept, that claim was I thought very near to false. No doubt we were willing, if peace came, to help organize an international effort to provide compensation to some refugees or their descendants and to encourage many countries to take some of them – and we would do our part. When a Palestinian state was created, other Arab states would start pressuring Palestinian residents to get out and move to Palestine. Because that new state could hardly absorb all of them, offering them opportunities elsewhere would help the new state in its formative years. But no one in the administration "agreed" to accept 100,000 Palestinian refugees, nor could we have – because Congress and not the executive branch makes immigration policy, an immensely sensitive subject at any time.

In my own conversations with Olmert after he left office, he cited figures close to but slightly different from what he had told us in Washington in November 2008. He told me that he had proposed to Abbas that Israel would retain 6.3% of the West Bank, a figure that included the settlements near Jerusalem as well. He would do a one-to-one swap of Israeli territory equal to 5.8%, leaving 0.5% to be accounted for by the Gaza–West Bank link. As Olmert put it to me,

Now you tell me; 5.8 is only a half a percent less than 6.3. Add to it a safe passage from Gaza to the West Bank and this is 1-on-1. And then I said, the Arab neighborhoods in Jerusalem would be yours, the Jewish neighborhoods will be ours, and the Old City will be administered by five nations, a consortium of five nations: the Saudis, Jordan, Palestinians, America, and Israel. I say, "If Saudi Arabia will agree to be part of this five-nations administrative committee, then basically the Saudis will recognize the State of Israel, which is a major breakthrough. Which is the beginning of, you know, opening up for the moderate Arab world." Afterwards, you know, if Saudis can sit with Israel, governing Jerusalem, then why not the Emirates and why not the others and so on and so forth.... And then I said, "But, I will agree to have X number of people every year on an individual humanitarian basis." When Abu Mazen asked me how many, I said from day one: a thousand a year for five years.... Now, between you and me, had Abu Mazen accepted to make a deal, 15,000 – 3,000 a year for five years – I'd have made the agreement, OK? You know, that we could tolerate. And, end of conflict and no more claims. And there will be an international force, maybe NATO intervention force on the Jordanian side to protect the border between the Palestinian state and Jordan. And that in between the international force, there will be non-uniformed Israelis in key positions to look into the Israeli interests and make sure that wrong things are not done, OK? This is what I proposed. Had I had more time, maybe we could reach an agreement.... I don't know. If not, I would have gone for a unilateral pullout.[5]

Abbas Says No

From what I knew then and later, these descriptions give an accurate picture of what Olmert had offered. What had been the response? In 2010, Erekat said Olmert's account was roughly accurate. Erekat told the press that "the Palestinians made a counter-offer, depositing their own map with the U.S. president three months later. He would not give details." But, in fact, the details were missing because Erekat's story was wrong; we were never told of any counteroffer nor was any such map "deposited with the U.S. president" at the end of Bush's term. Erekat was perhaps more candid when speaking on Al Jazeera in March 2009:

The Palestinian negotiators could have given in in 1994, 1998, or 2000, and two months ago, brother Abu Mazen could have accepted a proposal that talked about Jerusalem and almost 100% of the West Bank.... Let me recount two historical events, even if I am revealing a secret. On July 23, 2000, at his meeting with President Arafat in Camp David, President Clinton said: "You will be the first president of a Palestinian state, within the 1967 borders – give or take, considering the land swap – and East Jerusalem will be the capital of the Palestinian state, but we want you, as a religious man, to acknowledge that the Temple of Solomon is located underneath the Haram Al-Sharif." Yasser Arafat said to Clinton defiantly: "I will not be a traitor. Someone will come to liberate it after 10, 50, or 100 years. Jerusalem will be nothing but the capital of the Palestinian state, and there is nothing underneath or above the Haram Al-Sharif except for Allah." That is why Yasser Arafat was besieged, and that is why he was killed unjustly.

In November 2008 ... Olmert offered the 1967 borders, but said: "We will take 6.5% of the West Bank, and give in return 5.8% from the 1948 lands, and the 0.7% will constitute the safe passage, and East Jerusalem will be the capital, but there is a problem with the Haram and with what they called the Holy Basin." Abu Mazen too answered with defiance, saying: "I am not in a marketplace or a bazaar. I came to demarcate the borders of Palestine – the June 4, 1967 borders – without detracting a single inch, and without detracting a single stone from Jerusalem, or from the holy Christian and Muslim places." This is why the Palestinian negotiators did not sign.[6]

Erekat's accounts varied somewhat according to the audience he was addressing, but the basic facts do seem clear: Olmert made an offer that would have reduced Palestinian territory by 0.7% from the 1949 armistice lines or "1967 borders" and included taking back thousands of refugees and ending Israeli sovereignty over the Old City of Jerusalem – and the Palestinians had not responded. They had not even bargained for better terms – making up the 0.7% or getting Israel to resettle a higher number of refugees as part of the "humanitarian" return of refugees, for example – or put a rival proposal on the table.

Abbas later tried to rewrite history, claiming late in 2010 that an agreement had been reached on security and borders. On borders, "the basis for peace would be an [Israeli] withdrawal to the 1967 borders, with an option for certain border corrections, as long as the [overall size of] the West Bank territories remained the same." As to security, they "reached a full understanding that this [task] would be entrusted to a third party.... We spoke to Bush, and he agreed that the third party would be NATO."[7] There is no basis for these claims in the record or the memory of other participants. As Olmert's chief of staff, Yoram Turbowitz, recalled, the immensely complicated security issues were barely addressed, and Israel never agreed to abandon the eight-item list of security demands that Barak had given to Bush earlier that year when he visited Israel. In reaction to the Abbas claims, Turbowitz said,

They never agreed to anything. Clearly the security list was not acceptable to them. NATO forces were never seriously discussed, as it was never an option we considered, nor did it seem a plausible avenue. The same is true regarding the borders. There was Olmert's suggestion which was not met by their consent or their qualified consent. They were only interested in getting Olmert's proposal in writing, so they will be able in the future to use it as a benchmark. It was never given to them in writing nor was there any exchange of maps. It was all in an un-solidified phase.

Tourgeman has a similar recollection:

There was no agreement on the land swap and where it will be, no agreement of the worth of the Gaza–West Bank passage and in principle on the size of land Israel will keep. We said the major blocks are at least 6.3 percent, if not more, and they said not more than 1.9 percent. On foreign forces I don't recall that it was ever an option; in all our talks we said it cannot be an option, not NATO and not other forces. Our claim was always that an international force will be only observers and it will prevent the Palestinians from doing what they are obliged to do. We had the 8 points [of which Barak had spoken to President Bush] and didn't want to desert them.[8]

No one will ever know the exact words of the exchanges Olmert had with Abbas at that time, but their practice was that immediately after each session

Erekat and Tourgeman were called in and briefed on what had transpired and told what follow-up was needed. It therefore seems highly unlikely that the exchanges Abbas reports (which in any event he does not claim were in one-on-one meetings with Olmert) transpired and that any genuine understanding was reached. In this, Erekat's March 2009 version may be closer to the truth. The Palestinian leadership did not agree to Olmert's offer.

Why not? First, who was Olmert to be making these offers? What was the point of a deal with him? Whom would it bind? Even if these offers seemed generous in Israeli terms, they would be attacked by many Palestinians; for example, many would say that Abbas had sold out the refugees if he signed an agreement that returned even as many as 15,000 of them to Israel but abandoned the others. Why take that risk, why expose yourself to such criticism, by signing an agreement with a lame-duck "caretaker" prime minister whose legal power to sign any agreement was quite unclear? You might take all the criticism and find that in the end you had no binding agreement at all.

Second, there were from the Palestinian point of view too many lacunae in this deal, too many key points where there was actually no meeting of the minds at all. Security was the most important point, and Olmert's own descriptions of what he offered are blank as to security conditions. The Palestinians knew that Israel had many detailed demands, so what would be their status if the PLO signed an agreement? And although Olmert was offering specific percentages, it was not clear to the Palestinians what territory he was proposing to offer them in swaps. Olmert showed Abbas a map, but Livni also showed a map. The problem was not that they looked different but that they looked very much the same, which caused confusion because Olmert claimed to be saying he would take only 6.3% (or, in some versions, 6.5%) of the West Bank while Livni said the number had to be 8 or 10%. So how could the maps be so similar? This kind of doubt also argued against agreeing to anything.

Third, the Palestinians were actually being told by some Israelis not to sign. Messages were coming to Erekat from people who claimed to speak for Livni, saying they should wait for her to become prime minister and then sign with her, not Olmert. Waiting might not only improve relations with her if she became prime minister but might also result in better terms being offered – or at least in a deal that an existing Israeli government could support.

The Palestinians did not believe they were missing an irreplaceable opportunity. Although they were told they would never again see this combination of Israeli prime minister and American president so keen on a deal, they had heard that before. In 2001, the American negotiator Dennis Ross said precisely the same thing to Arafat about the Barak government and Clinton: "I cannot tell you how many times I would say to him: 'You're never going to have a government like this. You are never going to have another American President like this. If you don't do it now, and you lose the opportunity, you've lost it.'"[9] Yet Arafat had let the deal pass, Abbas had watched him do so, and now Abbas took the same action: inaction.

The Palestinians did not wish to sign but also wished to escape being blamed for saying no. They therefore said neither yes nor no, despite Erekat's later accounts on al Jazeera of their bravery: Instead, they played out the clock. They asked a few questions at their last meeting with Olmert and then claimed they never heard back from him, while he claimed that Abbas never gave him an answer to his proposal. As Condi Rice accurately concluded, "In the end, the Palestinians walked away from the negotiations."[10]

I thought then and still believe Abbas will never sign any deal. Ross had explained why in his view Arafat refused to sign in 2001:

I do, personally, feel that it is too hard for him to redefine himself. It is too hard for him to give up what had been the mythologies that had guided him. It is too hard, as a revolutionary – and that is what he is – to give up struggle, to give up claims, to give up grievance, because they have been the animating factors of his life. Arafat, in my judgment, is someone who was capable of launching this process, and maybe nobody else could have from the Palestinian side, but I do not believe he is capable of concluding the process.[11]

President Bush had often wondered whether Abbas could conclude the process, and we learned the answer the hard way. I did not think Abbas was a self-defined revolutionary, but I thought that like Arafat, he would not be brave enough to abandon the pose of "resistance." He knew he would be accused of treason; he knew he would face physical risks; he knew he would be sowing the whirlwind if he signed. He was a nice and mild man and not a hero, I thought, and he would not lead Palestinians to their promised land. He might be Aaron, but he was neither Moses nor Joshua.

In his memoir, President Bush discusses briefly a scenario with which I was not familiar. After Olmert had made his offer to Abbas, the president writes that "[w]e devised a process to turn the private offer into a public agreement. Olmert would travel to Washington and deposit his proposal with me. Abbas would announce that the plan was in line with Palestinian interests. I would call the leaders together to finalize the deal." The plan failed, Bush continued, because Olmert "was forced to announce his resignation in September. Abbas didn't want to make an agreement with a prime minister on his way out of office."[12]

That account suggests that this process was discussed prior to Olmert's August announcement that he intended to resign. Perhaps he was to "deposit" his proposal with Bush in September around the time of the UN General Assembly. That Olmert wanted to continue trying to close a deal even after announcing his resignation, and even after resigning, is not a surprise. But Israeli officials tell me they knew of no such "deposit" plan, which was in a sense entirely superfluous: If Abbas was willing to agree to Olmert's proposals, he could simply have said "yes" without the further drama. And there was a danger here for the Israelis. Olmert's proposals were secret back then and remained secret until he revealed them months after leaving office, by which time they clearly did not bind the successor government in Israel. Had he "deposited" them with the White House, they would have had a more official and more lasting character, despite his own status as a caretaker when they were made and despite their refusal by Abbas.

In any event, Abbas refused to go along; he never said yes to anything Olmert proposed. The Palestinian strategy may have saved Abbas from some criticism, but it was a huge strategic blunder that saved Israel from endless criticism. Had Abbas accepted the terms that Olmert proposed, Olmert would have had to present them to his cabinet and then the Knesset. Legally, it might have been ruled that he had no right to sign such an important agreement or present such terms to Abbas or to the Americans. This ruling might have made them null and void constitutionally in Israel but would itself have brought enormous criticism on Israel for saying no to peace. Worse yet from this perspective, the cabinet or Knesset might well have rejected the agreement because Olmert was extremely unpopular and the conditions themselves might not have passed muster. Livni, for example, despite messages that may have been telling the Palestinians they would get some sort of deal from her, actually opposed the return of a single refugee; on this, she had a far tougher position than Olmert. Could she have voted for the Olmert deal? And what of security? How could Israeli politicians vote for a deal that had absolutely no security content, in which they were giving up the West Bank without a single guarantee? Could the IDF itself have said it supported such a deal?

Consider the situation had Israel rejected the deal: It would have been said throughout the world that Israel rejected peace, that its own prime minister (for Olmert would be lionized far and wide across the globe as a visionary) had offered or signed an agreement only to find that Israelis preferred territory and conflict. The political and public relations disaster would have been very great, which was why I had all along feared that Olmert's efforts for a deal were increasing as his legitimacy and time left in office steadily diminished. A last-minute deal would, I thought, not bring peace closer. The proposals did not even seem to mention the word "Gaza" and proposed no way of dealing with the Hamas sheikdom there. They would be met with a few weeks of self-congratulation and then break down because they could not be implemented. And another failed agreement was the last thing we needed.

Olmert's Last Visit

All this was on my mind and that of at least some of those near the top of the Israeli government that day in November when Olmert made his last visit to the White House. It was three days before the last Thanksgiving of the Bush administration and a year since the Annapolis Conference. This final session between Bush and Olmert ended up as the final blow-up between Rice and Olmert.

I continue to seek an agreement this year, Olmert began. I am not campaigning for anything so I am free to keep trying. The president was supportive but skeptical: I'd love to see you hit the long ball, he replied, but why would

Abbas negotiate with you? You'll be out soon, just like me. You will, Olmert responded, and the security concerns we have in any agreement are very serious. That's why I have asked Condi that you not give the new administration any document on our security that we haven't seen.

This was a clear reference to the "Jones Report," the document the Israelis had feared for months. They still worried that Gen. Jones would compile American assessments of Israel's security needs that would be very far from Israel's own and that these would guide the new Obama team. The president asked what document Olmert was talking about: Was this just Jones reporting to Condi about what he's done? Yes, Olmert said, it's about the recommendations Jones will make. We don't even know if he'll make any recommendations, Condi now said, and if he does, they are just for me.

I don't remember agreeing to this, the president commented, and then asked when he had. Wow, I thought; this was dangerous for Rice. Would the president really now side with Olmert and say that he wanted no such document to be created? Hadley too saw the danger and jumped in to save her, telling the president that this document was part of a long dialogue with Israelis about assurances related to the negotiating process; Hadley's language was vague and bureaucratic and meant to be reassuring. But Rice was angry and said Jones's recommendations to her need not be negotiated with the State of Israel. In principle, I will not negotiate his recommendations with you, she told Olmert, and I will or won't pass them on as I decide.

Olmert now turned from Condi to the president and said the two of them had explicitly agreed there would be no such document assessing all of Israel's security arguments. I don't remember that, the president told Olmert, but anyway what's the big deal? What's the worry? Jones does some work and makes recommendations.

Now Olmert was worked up too. What if there is no agreement with the Palestinians, he said, and what is left as the legacy of your administration on Israeli security is a document that has not even been discussed with us? Well, it has been discussed with you, Rice shot back, and in multiple sessions. Jones works for me, and he has worked with Barak. No, Olmert replied, Barak does not know Jones's views. That is simply not true, Rice answered. I thought to myself, how often has this happened in the Oval Office – a secretary of state tells a foreign leader, in his presence and that of the president, that what he is saying is simply not true? Jones has no conclusions yet, Rice continued, but in principle he cannot negotiate his conclusions with you. Look, Olmert now said, you want an agreement; the ability of the next government to get an agreement will depend on this, on whether there are disputes between you and us on the key security issues. The legacy of this administration on security issues shouldn't be a dispute between the United States and Israel. The president now closed off the argument, saying he knew nothing about this Jones document. I had no clue about this argument, he said, and I don't want him to write something I don't agree with. I have your eight points (the ones he had gotten from Barak when visiting Israel) and I have agreed to them.

This was the only time I recalled the president saying he agreed to the eight points, but in this argument, both Olmert and Rice were right. Olmert was correct in worrying about a report in the very last days of the Bush administration that might reflect Jones's views but not those of the president and might become a source of argument between the United States and Israel. Rice was correct in insisting that she would not negotiate an internal document like that, a report from a subordinate to her, with the Israelis. Where she was wrong was in letting this argument drag on and then having it out in the Oval Office. The scene was nevertheless fitting: It exposed all the tensions that had existed since the Second Lebanon War at the very last opportunity to do so. The final Oval Office meeting was perfect, I thought: Olmert and Rice snarling at each other, Hadley trying to bridge the gap, the president basically siding with the Israelis.

Gaza Again

While the discussion on November 24 turned on what would be passed on to the next administration two months later, the ceasefire between Hamas and Israel was coming to an end in just weeks – on December 18. On December 19, Hamas declared the truce or "tahdiya" over, and rocket fire out of Gaza was intensified on December 24 – 88 rockets were fired into Israel. On Christmas Day, they fired 44 more. Beginning December 27, the Israelis struck back with "Operation Cast Lead."

The numbers of rockets and mortar fire from Gaza into Israel tell the tale of a provocation no Israeli government could allow: After only 2 incidents in October, Hamas and its allies fired 193 rockets and mortars in November – and then 602 in December. Nor was this increase only due to the ending of the truce: There was an intensification of rocket fire before that date. The Israelis had been warning us for a year that a war in Gaza was coming; now it was here. Perhaps Hamas calculated that the intensification of rocket fire before the end of the truce would force Israel into renewing it on better terms; perhaps they preferred fighting because they were, after all, a "resistance" organization and believed that they had little to gain from living endlessly under the Israeli- and Egyptian-imposed closed-border regime.

"Cast Lead" began with air strikes, which were followed by a ground incursion on January 3. By the middle of January, Israeli air strikes and ground operations in Gaza had killed hundreds of fighters from Hamas and other terrorist groups and caused large-scale damage to infrastructure and civilian life. Although roughly 750 rockets and mortars were fired into Israel during the war, Israeli battle casualties were light. The war lasted until January 17, when Israel declared a unilateral ceasefire; the following day, Hamas declared a one-week ceasefire, which became permanent when Israeli forces completed their withdrawal from Gaza on January 21, the day after George W. Bush left office.

The war exacerbated the tensions between Rice and Israel. Shortly after "Cast Lead" began, the secretary began to talk with Livni about it and the tone of the conversations was negative; the downward spiral was continuing. On the last day of the year, Rice told Livni she was working with the Arab League on a statement criticizing "illegal trade" to Gaza, which would help both Egyptian and Israeli efforts to stop arms smuggling. We are doing this for you, Rice said; you asked for this help. I did not, Livni answered. Well, Tourgeman asked for it, Rice said, which as far as I knew was simply inaccurate. Anyway, Rice had continued, you need to say something positive about the Arab League. Livni's back was now up, and she replied that she did not "need to"; she would if it was in Israel's interest and she would make that decision. Rice was now angry as well and said Livni could harm U.S.-Israel relations if there were no positive response. Livni was shocked by the threat and immediately called Olmert to report it and figure out how to protect U.S.-Israel relations during the conflict. The conversation between Rice and Livni shows not only the unfortunate tone of the contacts by that point but also that newspaper accounts of the sweet, sisterly relationship between Rice and Livni – who were said to have "bonded" – were off the mark.

The central issue between Rice and the Israelis was the possible role of the United Nations in bringing the Gaza war to an end. Rice favored its involvement; Olmert resisted. On January 1, Tourgeman called me to say that Olmert remained firm; the Security Council was not an acceptable forum. The Israelis had heard from Rice that time was running out and they had only a few days, at most a week, more before the Security Council would demand a halt to fighting in Gaza. Olmert bristled: Lebanon was at least a country! Now the UN will tell us not to fight a terrorist group! There was a 50-minute call between Rice and Olmert at 3:00 am Israeli time, in which Olmert told her he would not accept a resolution demanding a halt to Israeli action in Gaza. Well, it's going to happen, Rice replied. So veto it, Olmert told her. We can't, Rice answered; we are fighting terror in the whole region, and we have the Iraqi elections coming. The latter was a particularly weak argument because those elections were scheduled for October, 10 months away. Olmert suggested the war on terror worked the other way: A defeat for Hamas strengthens moderates and weakens radicals in the whole region. No, Rice said; one mistake like Qana and the whole region will be turned upside down. Qana again, I thought as Tourgeman recounted the conversation; Rice had been as deeply burned by that day as I thought.

"The President Has Clear Views"

The following day, January 2, Tourgeman and Hadley spoke, and Olmert picked up an extension and joined the call. Israel will not accept a Security Council resolution that puts Israel and a terrorist organization on the same level, he told Hadley. You are at the end of the administration; this is the last Security Council resolution of your eight years, and it should not rescue Hamas. We are fighting terror and I can't comprehend that the United States, through the secretary of state, would stop me. Hadley responded that this entire conversation was strange to him. I am surprised, he told Olmert; I thought we all agreed to stay out of the UN. Unless something has changed, we are trying to keep this *out* of the Security Council. The president has clear views.

This was a reasonably shocking conversation for me because it seemed the president had expressed those "clear views" to Hadley, but the secretary was pursuing a different policy. Hanging up the phone, Hadley told me the president does not want a deal at the United Nations. The president is comfortable with a veto, he said, though he added that Condi was not. Condi then called in, to affirm that she did *not* want to be forced into a veto. I'm not anxious to go to the Security Council at all, she said, but we are going to be dragged there. I need to manage the Security Council, she continued, and the United States can't stand between the Israelis and the Council. Hadley told her the president is comfortable vetoing if necessary. But that will weaken our Arab allies, Rice replied; I will explain it to him.

This was a classic conversation in several ways. It showed first that Hadley and I had been kept out of the loop as to what Rice and State were doing in the UN; our information came from the Israelis, not from our own diplomats. Hadley had thought we were all opposed to action at the UN and had candidly told the Israelis that. Second was Rice's matter-of-fact statement that we could not stand between the Security Council and the Israelis. We certainly could – and we did, every time we vetoed a resolution. It was a matter of will, and although Bush had not lost his, Condi's was weakening. Put another way, Bush was perfectly happy to leave office vetoing a resolution against Israel, while Rice was not and sought an agreement with the Europeans and Arab states. Finally, Rice's statement that a veto would "weaken the moderate Arabs" was a rote repetition of the line NEA had been peddling for years. Why would an Israeli defeat of Hamas weaken moderate Arabs, after all, when Hamas was their enemy?

The next few days brought an intricate series of negotiations among us, the French, the Israelis, and the Egyptians. Our discussions centered on actions that Egypt might take to prevent smuggling of weapons into Gaza. If Egypt would establish a credible mechanism to stop the arms smuggling, Israel would have a basis to stop the war. French President Sarkozy inserted himself into the negotiations by visiting Egypt and Israel, and he then told us he thought he could get a deal between Egypt and Israel. Even if a deal were not yet done, if there was a serious negotiation, Sarkozy would act to prevent the Security Council from meeting. The presidency of the Security Council rotates, and France held it in January 2009.

Moral Equivalency

Exactly what Sarkozy was doing was never clear to us because the French gave different versions to everyone with whom they spoke. Bush's own views were clear: On January 6, he spoke again to Chancellor Merkel and repeated the argument Olmert had used with Hadley. Israel has a right to defend herself, he told her, and the entire war on terror would be harmed if the UN were to adopt a resolution that expressed moral equivalency between a member state and a terrorist group. But, he told her, Israel could stop fighting if we could get a good agreement on smuggling, and that's what we are trying to do with the Egyptians. Condi is going up to New York, he concluded. In fact, not only Condi but also the French and British foreign ministers, Bernard Kouchner and David Miliband, headed for New York. The three began to meet at the UN, for hours each day, disconnected it seemed from their own capitals. Within hours of the Bush-Merkel conversation, we learned from the Israelis that Rice had just called Olmert and asked him to declare an immediate ceasefire. That was not at all what the president was saying. At one point, Hadley instructed me to call the Israelis and make clear what the president's views were, in effect telling me to contradict the secretary of state. I did so, shaking my head at where we had ended up in this last month in office.

Sarkozy and his national security advisor, Jean-David Levitte, were telling us they were now inches from a deal. On January 5, Sarkozy had visited Egypt and then Israel, and then returned to Egypt once again. Here was the plan, Levitte informed us: On January 6, Sarkozy and President Mubarak would hold a news conference at which Mubarak would deliver some carefully negotiated language about stopping arms smuggling. We knew Levitte well because he had been the French ambassador to the United Nations in 2001 and 2002, and then France's ambassador in Washington until 2007, and we trusted him. The idea was simple: A mechanism would be established on the Egyptian side of the border to stop the smuggling; European help and even forces on the ground would be available to make it work. The Netherlands and Denmark actually did offer to provide troops for such a border force. Once the mechanism was agreed, Israel would declare a ceasefire.[13]

The press conference did indeed take place, but Mubarak did not say what was expected; instead, he called only for an immediate ceasefire. The fine words about stopping smuggling were spoken – but only by Sarkozy. Instead of establishing a mechanism first, the ceasefire – and opening of the border crossings – would come first. This was not at all what Sarkozy had discussed when in Israel, nor was it what Levitte had discussed with me. It was perhaps the reaction to carnage that day when Israeli shells had killed dozens of Palestinians near a UN school.

But negotiations were continuing and Olmert spoke to Sarkozy again on Wednesday, January 7. Sarkozy again promised to block any action in the UN Security Council. Olmert dispatched a senior military figure, Gen. Amos Gilad, to Egypt to try to elicit a serious commitment against smuggling on which Israel could rely – and then it could declare a halt to the war. Hadley told me he had spoken to Condi, who would stay up in New York. Olmert needs to just declare victory, Hadley said, and call the president and say he's stopping – right now. I knew that was Rice's position, and it seemed Hadley was now adopting it rather than trying to force Rice back into line with the president's views. Condi says the situation will come unstuck, Hadley told me, at Friday prayers when so many crowds will gather all across the Middle East. Of course,

Friday prayers in the Middle East occurred before the business day began in New York, and that meant the ceasefire would have to come not on Friday but on Thursday – the following day, Thursday, January 8. I thought this was another classic NEA line now being swallowed whole; I had heard the "Friday prayers" threat so many times I could not count them.

The Revolt of the Foreign Ministers

On Thursday, Condi told us she wanted a Security Council resolution, so her position had officially changed from trying to resist one to trying to pass one. But the Israelis were still resisting and told us the French were too. According to the Israelis, Paris was saying a resolution could be resisted if only the United States would join them and remain firm. France and the United States were now in the same boat in at least one sense: There appeared to be one policy in their capitals, coming from their presidents, and another coming from their foreign ministers camped at the UN in New York. Rice and Olmert spoke that day, and the Israelis described the conversation as stormy. Tourgeman told us the French cannot understand why United States is pushing for a resolution; why isn't the United States supporting a delay? Rice called Olmert a second time and once again asked for a halt to all military action. She told Olmert there was no draft resolution circulating, which was inaccurate – the staff of our mission to the UN had just given one to the staff of the Israeli mission. Now the Israelis felt they were being deliberately misled. What was in the draft? Did it meet the president's requirement that it not suggest a moral equivalency between Israel and Hamas? I did not know because I hadn't seen it yet; we in the NSC had not been given a draft. Hadley told me he had spoken with Condi and she said the draft language was fine but, all things considered, that was not very reassuring.

It was important, Hadley and I agreed, that we make sure we know exactly what the French are doing, so we called Levitte. We needed to get the French view from the French, not via Israel. We put together a conference call with both Levitte and Tourgeman. Hadley told them we all agreed on delay in New York – but we all knew that at that moment Condi was not backing delay. She was pressing for a resolution to be adopted fast, as was Kouchner. There is a revolt of the foreign ministers, Levitte joked – but it was a perfectly accurate description. Hadley had told Rice of the call and halfway through she joined it. There is an agreed text now, she said, and we can't delay any more. An agreed text? Agreed by whom? Hadley asked. Have the Israelis seen it? No, Condi admitted. My own sources at the UN had told me the Arab states had gotten the text and indeed had made some edits in it, but like the Israelis, we in the White House had not seen it yet.

What was going on in New York? Eliot Cohen, counselor to the State Department, described the scene this way: "We were all exhausted. We had not planned on being there for several days. Those things count. We kept on staying. . . . The Arabs were putting a lot of pressure on us. In retrospect it might have made more sense to back off and let our UN mission handle it."[14]

Meanwhile, Kouchner and Miliband put on additional pressure, and at least in the case of Kouchner he did so without coordinating his actions with his own capital. Tourgeman now called back to say Olmert had just spoken with British Prime Minister Gordon Brown and had called the text shameful, insulting, and a victory for terrorism. Why? It did not call for the release of Gilad Shalit or for an end to terrorism against Israel and Israelis. It did not even mention Hamas, much less condemn it, condemn its weapons smuggling, or condemn the thousands of rockets and mortars fired into Israel. It called Gaza occupied territory and made no reference to the Israeli pullout of all bases and settlements in 2005. It called for opening all the passages into Gaza, a key Hamas goal. Finally, by encouraging "intra-Palestinian reconciliation," it called for reconciliation between the PA and a terrorist group, Hamas.

Here is the text of Resolution 1860, as adopted on January 8, 2009:

The Security Council,

Recalling all of its relevant resolutions, including resolutions 242 (1967), 338 (1973), 1397 (2002), 1515 (2003) and 1850 (2008),

Stressing that the Gaza Strip constitutes an integral part of the territory occupied in 1967 and will be a part of the Palestinian state,

Emphasizing the importance of the safety and well-being of all civilians,

Expressing grave concern at the escalation of violence and the deterioration of the situation, in particular the resulting heavy civilian casualties since the refusal to extend the period of calm; and *emphasizing* that the Palestinian and Israeli civilian populations must be protected,

Expressing grave concern also at the deepening humanitarian crisis in Gaza,

Emphasizing the need to ensure sustained and regular flow of goods and people through the Gaza crossings,

Recognizing the vital role played by UNRWA in providing humanitarian and economic assistance within Gaza,

Recalling that a lasting solution to the Israeli-Palestinian conflict can only be achieved by peaceful means,

Reaffirming the right of all States in the region to live in peace within secure and internationally recognized borders,

1. *Stresses* the urgency of and *calls for* an immediate, durable and fully respected ceasefire, leading to the full withdrawal of Israeli forces from Gaza;

2. *Calls for* the unimpeded provision and distribution throughout Gaza of humanitarian assistance, including of food, fuel and medical treatment;

3. *Welcomes* the initiatives aimed at creating and opening humanitarian corridors and other mechanisms for the sustained delivery of humanitarian aid;

4. *Calls on* Member States to support international efforts to alleviate the humanitarian and economic situation in Gaza, including through urgently needed additional contributions to UNRWA and through the Ad Hoc Liaison Committee;

5. *Condemns* all violence and hostilities directed against civilians and all acts of terrorism;
6. *Calls upon* Member States to intensify efforts to provide arrangements and guarantees in Gaza in order to sustain a durable ceasefire and calm, including to prevent illicit trafficking in arms and ammunition and to ensure the sustained reopening of the crossing points on the basis of the 2005 Agreement on Movement and Access between the Palestinian Authority and Israel; and in this regard, *welcomes* the Egyptian initiative, and other regional and international efforts that are under way;
7. *Encourages* tangible steps towards intra-Palestinian reconciliation including in support of mediation efforts of Egypt and the League of Arab States as expressed in the 26 November 2008 resolution, and consistent with Security Council resolution 1850 (2008) and other relevant resolutions;
8. *Calls for* renewed and urgent efforts by the parties and the international community to achieve a comprehensive peace based on the vision of a region where two democratic States, Israel and Palestine, live side by side in peace with secure and recognized borders, as envisaged in Security Council resolution 1850 (2008), and recalls also the importance of the Arab Peace Initiative;
9. *Welcomes* the Quartet's consideration, in consultation with the parties, of an international meeting in Moscow in 2009;
10. *Decides* to remain seized of the matter.

I agreed with Olmert; I thought the terms shameful and believed the president should not allow the United States to support them. But there was obviously a huge problem here: Rice had herself negotiated the terms with the British, the French, and the Arabs. Had the text been negotiated the usual way, by diplomats up in New York while Rice was in Washington, she would not have had so much invested in it. During the course of Thursday, January 8, our own internal battle raged. Because the Security Council was not meeting until 9:15 pm, phone calls and meetings continued throughout the day. Olmert called the president around dinner time (coincidentally, a dinner the president was hosting for some Americans Jews who had been among his most loyal supporters). Hadley and I had several discussions during the day, and Hadley concluded, in the end, that we could not vote for this language. I believe he might have urged a veto were it not for Condi's role. She and I had an unhappy conversation as I drove home from work around 8 pm. What's wrong with this language, she asked; she did not see what Olmert was screaming about, and all UN language is always a compromise.

The Last Vote

The president, I believe, would have happily vetoed this resolution and left office with that veto as his last act in the United Nations. But that would have meant that his last act was a repudiation of Condi, and he did not wish to do that. He cut the baby in half and abstained, an extremely rare action for the United States in the Security Council. If we were going to abstain, it would be better not to be alone, and Tourgeman told me the French would abstain with us. He had just spoken to Levitte, he said, and Kouchner had been instructed to abstain if we did. This was too important to leave to hearsay, so I phoned Levitte – at 1:00 am Paris time. Yes, he assured me, the instruction had gone out from the Foreign Ministry, the Quai D'Orsay. But to be sure, he had personally spoken with Kouchner to tell him of President Sarkozy's decision. We will be with you if you abstain, he said.

But France voted for the resolution; the final vote was 14 in favor, none against, and the United States as the sole abstention. I could not resist calling Levitte the next morning to ask what had happened. He told me he had twice phoned Kouchner to instruct him to join us in abstaining, and Kouchner simply disobeyed his instruction. Perhaps. Perhaps not. Rice's own reaction to her instruction to abstain was not, of course, to disobey – but her explanation of her vote was clearly the speech in support of the resolution she and her staff had prepared before the president had made up his mind. She explained that we were abstaining only because we thought the resolution was premature: We should all have waited to see the outcome of the Egyptian mediation effort. She uttered not a word of criticism of the resolution and in fact said, "We decided that this resolution – the text of which we support, the goals of which we support and the objectives of which we fully support – should indeed be allowed to go forward." This was as close as she could come to saying the president had called it wrong and she disagreed with the vote she had just cast.

That was the last act for the Bush administration's involvement in the Israeli-Palestinian conflict. It was a sad ending, offering confusion when the president himself had so staunchly, for eight years, resisted international pressure in the UN and outside it. He had vetoed 10 resolutions in the Security Council, 9 of them dealing with the Arab-Israel conflict; one more would have changed little in the region but would have been a fitting way to end, a reminder of his dedication to the war on terror and to the defense of Israel's security. For the Israelis, it was a sad symbol of the divisions they had since the Second Lebanon War experienced between State and the White House, and of the contrast between the constant tension with Rice and the constant support from Bush. For me, it was an ironic reminder of the remark Hadley had made when I had agreed to stay at the NSC: The White House is ultimately where Middle East policy is made. The comment was true but not the whole truth, not in an administration where the secretary of state had become so dominant in foreign policy. There were still red lines set by the president's deepest beliefs, and not even Condi's own role in the drafting of Resolution 1860 could bring the president to allow a vote for it. But I thought back to his conversation with Blair and his agreement that a Palestinian state had to be built from the bottom up – that reality had to shape the diplomacy and not vice versa. There too he had expressed a view that might have led to a different policy, one focused on building a state in the West Bank rather than on the slim chance of getting a signed agreement in the year left to us after Annapolis. But it was nearly January 20 now, and Middle East policy was no longer my job. It was time to pack.

Notes

1. Rodman, *Presidential Command*, 233, 249.
2. Turbowitz, interview, pp. 8–9.
3. Matti Friedman, "Former Israeli Premier Details Failed Peace Offer," *Associated Press*, September 19, 2010, http://www.washingtonpost.com/wp-dyn/content/article/2010/09/19/AR2010091901014.html.
4. Rice, *No Higher Honor*, 650–52.
5. Olmert, interview, pp. 2–4.
6. Saeb Erekat, television debate excerpts, Al-Jazeera TV, transcribed by MEMRI, March 27, 2009, http://www.memri.org/report/en/0/0/0/0/0/0/3241.htm.
7. Mahmoud Abbas, "I Reached Understandings with Olmert on Borders, Security," *Middle East Media Research Institute*, November 16, 2010, http://www.memri.org/report/en/0/0/0/0/0/0/4770.htm.
8. Shalom Tourgeman, email exchanges with the author, November 16, 2010.
9. Dennis Ross, Margaret Warner, and Jim Hoagland, "From Oslo to Camp David to Taba: Setting the Record Straight," *Washington Institute for Near East Policy*, August 8, 2001, http://www.washingtoninstitute.org/templateC07.php?CID=172.
10. Rice, *No Higher Honor*, 724.
11. Ibid.
12. Bush, *Decision Points*, 409–10.
13. Barak Ravid, Avi Issacharoff, and Assaf Uni, "Israel and Egypt to Begin Negotiations on Gaza Truce," *Jewish Daily Forward*, January 7, 2009, http://www.forward.com/articles/14874/.
14. Cohen, interview, p. 9.

Lessons Learned

On January 19, I went to the Oval Office to say goodbye to President Bush and then handed in my White House pass, my diplomatic passport, and my White House Blackberry and secure phones. I signed a statement promising to keep classified information secret and agreed to run any manuscript (including this one) by the NSC for approval so that it did not inadvertently reveal classified information. On Inauguration Day, January 20, 2009, my wife and I flew off to California for a much-needed vacation. Now the Middle East would be someone else's job, and the question was what to make of the Bush years – what lessons to learn from our successes and failures.

A key conclusion, one that I have tried to illustrate in the preceding chapters, is that every president should organize the White House staff to keep the key decisions in his own hands. The National Security Council staff should be instructed not to homogenize policy disputes and seek a consensus. The president should keep in mind Margaret Thatcher's famous 1981 comment: "To me consensus seems to be the process of abandoning all beliefs, principles, values and policies in search of something in which no one believes, but to which no one objects."[1] Too often I had heard officials who were confronting a dispute among cabinet principals say, "We can't go to the president like this; we have to work this out." On the contrary, just as the Supreme Court does not review all court of appeals decisions but does take those where the various circuit courts have come out with conflicting decisions, so the president should insist on knowing of and on deciding the issues where his principal advisers are in conflict.

The president should also assume that bureaucracies have strong views and very capable and knowledgeable top officials. It is not a criticism of those career officials to say that by the time they reach the top, their life experiences will have molded them; a top general and a top diplomat will not, after 30 years in the field, see the world the same way. Nor will they necessarily see it the president's way, and that is the point. That is why the president should demand that his national security agencies, primarily State, Defense, and the NSC staff, be peopled with political appointees who know and support his views. As I have noted, this was George Shultz's approach, and one must assume it was deliberate; Condi Rice took a different view and explains in her memoir that her approach was deliberate as well. I recall how Shultz would react, back in the days of the Reagan administration, when a top career diplomat complained that he thought a particular policy of Reagan's was wrong. He would as always listen carefully, but at the end he would say, "You know, you may be right and maybe we should do it your way. But first you are going to have to get yourself elected president. For now, Ronald Reagan is president, so we are going to do it his way." I heard Shultz argue with the president many a time and he was not reluctant to state his views, but he made sure the bureaucracy understood that policy was made in the White House.

My own staff at the NSC – indeed, all the staff of the NSC – consisted mostly of career people from State (career Foreign Service officers), Defense (career military officers), and the CIA. One reason every White House favors getting such officers seconded to the NSC is budgetary: They are "freebies" to the White House, with their salaries paid by their home agencies, whereas the NSC often carried the full freight for political appointees. Whenever I interviewed career officers for an NSC position, I would tell them that they had no doubt heard this was for them the chance of a lifetime to work at the White House. It isn't, I would say; you're here because your peers think so well of you, and if this doesn't work out, you'll probably get another invitation in a few years. So, do not come to work for a president whom you really do not like or with whose views you are uncomfortable. There will be another president in 4 years, or 8, or 12, with whom you may be more comfortable, and you'll have a better time. Don't tell me your politics; I hope you say yes to this offer, but just think about this before you do so.

The goal should always be to make decisions as the president would want them made and to prevent people from substituting their judgment for his. When there are significant decisions to be made, and especially when his top appointees have differing views, the answer is to present them all to him. The thousands of smaller decisions that must be made – what precisely to say on the occasion of some country's National Day celebration, what to say to a visiting delegation and in what tone, how to word a cable of instructions to an ambassador, what signal the White House press secretary should send about the tone of a presidential phone call – cannot be presented to the president, so the goal is to ensure that the officials making those decisions are aware of and loyal to his views. The assumption that career officials will always subordinate their own views to his is mistaken. In the Bush NSC in 2004, one ranking officer quit one day and signed on to the Kerry campaign the next; another top official left and soon began denouncing his former colleagues. They were free to do this and right to leave when they disagreed with policy, but how faithfully were they following the president's policy views in the days, weeks, and months before they left? They were presumably doing what they thought best for the country, but the system works only when presidential appointees do what the elected president thinks best for the country.

No system, no set-up, no procedures will substitute for this. As Peter Rodman wrote, "we need to allow for the possibility that to search for a *procedure* that assures the right decision is to pursue a mirage."[2] We saw this in another sense (and probably closer to what Rodman meant) in the handling of the Syrian nuclear reactor. There, the procedures in place were ideal, but from my point of view, the decision taken was mistaken. Yet at least it was the president's decision, and the procedures guaranteed that he had heard all the arguments and that the policy reflected his considered view.

These comments relate to organizing the government, but what of policy? What, again, is to be learned from our successes and failures in the Middle East during the Bush years? The first lesson is to avoid subordinating all regional issues to the Israeli-Palestinian conflict. Doing so contradicts reality as Arabs and Israelis see it, and it leads the United States to give more weight to Arab officials' statements on that conflict than to the realities of their rule and of their countries' situations.

Without suggesting that the Israel-Palestine issue is unimportant to Arab populations or to Arab governments, it is one among many issues. For many Arab leaders, the central issue of these years has been the rise of Iran – an issue on which most see eye to eye with Israel. For Sunni Arab regimes, especially those in the Gulf, Israel is not an enemy, not a source of potential antiregime protests or violence, not a potential or current claimant of disputed lands, islands, or oil and gas reserves. It is not an ideological or religious rival. But Iran is all these things, so the apparent American obsession with the Israeli-Palestinian conflict is a mistaken priority. Moreover, Iran's influence and actions make an Israeli-Palestinian peace much harder: Israel is unlikely to take additional risks with its own security when a defiant Iran is building up the strength of Hamas and Hizballah every day and – as I write – moving ever closer to a nuclear weapon.

Moreover, the advent of the Arab Spring revolts in 2011 should have put paid to the view that all Arab politics revolves around Israel. For what happened in Tunisia was about Tunisia, and the same was true in Egypt, Libya, Syria, and Bahrain. Our ability to cope with, indeed, even to see clearly, the realities of life in Israel and the West Bank and the challenge of Iran to the region can be compromised by the prism through which we analyze events. That prism is not a new invention: The view that in the Middle East the one central issue is the Israeli-Palestinian conflict has for decades been an article of faith in the State Department's Near East bureau and to many academic analysts.

In the Bush years, Egypt's succession crisis, its decrepit authoritarian regime, its vast millions of desperately poor *fellahin*, and its declining influence in the region were increasingly ignored after 2006 as we turned to Annapolis and "the Annapolis process." Only Egypt's attitude toward Israel-Palestinian peace talks counted. Similarly in the Obama administration, the president honored Mubarak by making Egypt the location of his first Middle East trip and his speech to the entire Muslim world, while remaining silent about the miserable situation inside the country. Then George Mitchell, the Middle East peace negotiator, paid court to the vicious Assad regime in Syria, visiting repeatedly in 2009 and 2010 in an effort to improve the regime's attitude toward Israeli-Palestinian talks and get it back into direct peace talks with Israel. Syria's internal repression, its role in Iraq (where it supported jihadi groups trying to kill Americans and Iraqis), its support for Hamas and Palestinian Islamic Jihad (both headquartered there) and Hizballah, and its alliance with Iran were all viewed as secondary.

Too often, bilateral relations with everyone take a back seat once the goal of comprehensive peace is put on the table. The only important thing about a nation's policies becomes whether it appears to play ball with the big peace effort. As we saw in the latter part of the Clinton and Bush administrations, once you commit to a major effort at an international peace conference or attempt to broker a comprehensive Middle East peace, then those goals overwhelm all others. The net result of such an approach is to obscure reality, to ignore the immense complexities Arab countries face, and to concentrate instead on what their foreign ministries say about Israel and the Palestinians.

This approach also led the United States to pay more attention to what Arab officials said abroad, especially to us, about Israel and to ignore what they said to their own people. The Egyptian case is once again illustrative: Mubarak was seen as a peacemaker in Washington while for 30 years his regime fed the Egyptian people a steady diet of anti-Israel and anti-Semitic hatred. Israel's peace treaty was with Sadat and Mubarak, while it had no such understanding with the people of the country. With the demise of the Mubarak regime, the views of the Egyptian people will count for much more – and their views have been formed largely by government media spewing hate.

So the first lesson is that Arab political life does not revolve around Palestine. It is one issue among many and never the determining factor in any Arab nation's actions and even in its relations with the United States. The best example: the United States under Clinton and Bush had far closer relations with Israel than the Obama administration maintained, yet simultaneously had closer relations with Saudi Arabia as well.

The second lesson is that Israel will be more flexible when it is certain of American support for its security than when that assurance is in doubt. Martin Indyk, Clinton's ambassador to Israel and then assistant secretary of state for NEA, summed this up succinctly: "The record . . . suggests that American presidents can be more successful when they put their arms around Israeli prime ministers and encourage them to move forward, rather than attempt to browbeat them into submission."[3]

Some analysts would deny this assertion. Did not President Carter make great progress despite his unhappy relationship with Prime Minister Begin and the Israeli government, and didn't President George H. W. Bush arrange the Madrid Conference despite a good deal of friction with Israel? Although a fair account of those events would take too many pages, and has in both cases given rise to many articles and books, neither case suggests that the United States will get what it wants through, as Indyk put it, trying to browbeat the Israelis into submission. President Sadat and Prime Minister Begin began negotiating not because President Carter pressed them hard to do so but rather despite his efforts to stop them. He preferred a very large Geneva Conference and had convened one jointly with the Soviet Union. Sadat and Begin opposed bringing the Soviets into Middle East peacemaking, and neither man thought any progress would be made if the goal were a comprehensive Israeli-Arab peace settlement rather than an Egyptian-Israeli deal. Those two statesmen were acting in opposition to U.S. pressure, not in submission to it. In the Madrid case, the United States did get the international conference it sought, but obviously it did not lead to peace; by the end of the Bush administration in January 1993, any apparent momentum for peace had disappeared. The most direct U.S.-Israel confrontation in the George H. W. Bush years came over the denial of American loan guarantees for Israeli borrowing to build housing for the massive inflow of Soviet Jews. The guarantees were denied as pressure to force a change in Israeli settlement policy, but the net result did not change Israeli Prime Minister Shamir's conduct on settlements. Rather, the confrontations with Bush and Secretary of State Baker, and what in his view seemed to be a tilt toward the Arabs, embittered Shamir and led him to distrust the United States. This conditioned his behavior before, during, and after the Madrid Conference; led him to oppose a central American role in any ensuing negotiations; and surely was one key reason the fanfare at Madrid resulted in no real progress. So in neither case did a distancing from Israel produce what the United States wanted.

It is difficult to see Ariel Sharon making the decision to leave Gaza, form a new political party, or (if his colleagues are right) formulate plans or at least intentions to begin a withdrawal from large parts of the West Bank, if he did not believe America had his back. We saw this again when Ehud Olmert argued to his cabinet that there was a need to act fast – while George Bush was still president. This does not mean that Israeli decisions are to be supported regardless of their effect, and President Bush drew red lines (such as preventing the assassination of Yasser Arafat) and criticized Israel in public as well as in private ("when I say now I mean now" or "these remarks are unacceptable"). But he conveyed a deep commitment to Israel's security and stayed with it ("Israel has the right to defend itself"), even when almost the entire world was criticizing Israeli counterterrorism tactics.

Bush understood that his goal of "no daylight" between the United States and Israel would maximize his leverage there. He also understood the impact of any perceived gap between the United States and Israel on Israeli security. Given the amount of anti-Semitism and hostility to Israel, any suggestion that the United States is distancing itself and less inclined to defend Israel has an immediate impact: There are more expressions of anti-Jewish sentiment and of hostility to Israel. The net effect, of course, is to make Israelis feel less secure and less likely to respond to American pleas that Israel "take risks for peace."

There is another way of stating this principle. As we saw regarding the Israeli withdrawal from Gaza, the "compensation" Israel received for that move did not come from the Palestinians. Because its withdrawal was unilateral, what Sharon needed was "political" or "ideological" compensation from the United States to swing the Israeli political system toward supporting disengagement. This example is not unique. Because Israel is a strong state locked into struggle with a weak nonstate entity, many of the moves we want it to make will be unrequited or at least not evenly matched by Palestinian moves. Warm, even fulsome, American support can even the score and make such moves possible, whereas a cold or bitter relationship makes them less likely. Thus, the distancing between our two governments can hinder our ability to convince Israel to take steps we may think wise.

Neither President Bush nor President Clinton was uncritical of Israel, but both understood the need for Israeli trust in them – and used that trust to advance their policies. Because countries only have one set of leaders at a time, the corollary third lesson is to maintain the best possible personal relations with Israeli officials. This is never easy in international politics, and President Bush had troubled relations with President Chirac of France and Chancellor Schroeder of Germany. But he tried to manage his relations with Israeli leaders so as to maximize his leverage on them, as the incident in which he called Sharon "a man of peace" revealed.

President Bush was always cognizant of the fact that foreign leaders are not primarily diplomats, even or perhaps especially when they are visiting him or meeting with him; like him, they are politicians. Most foreign ministers are elected politicians themselves (many of whom later seek the prime minister position) though our secretaries of state rarely are, so that very often discussions between American and foreign officials are between career diplomats on our side and politicians on theirs. When I listened to or participated in meetings with Middle Eastern or European leaders, I was always struck by the way President Bush wove in American politics and asked them about their own. He was seeking to explain the context in which he worked and to understand theirs better, as well as to express his understanding that they all faced constraints and could perhaps help one another deal with them. This always elicited better understanding and almost always efforts to forge better cooperation. Putting a foreign leader on the defensive, hurting him or her in domestic politics, is by contrast a sure-fire way to weaken our ability to attain American policy goals.

The fourth lesson is that it is always an error to concentrate on negotiations rather than real progress on the ground. The Bush administration had committed this error when all its influence was directed toward the "Annapolis process" rather than to helping Salam Fayyad make progress in the West Bank. As Tony Blair had told President Bush in late 2008, "Building Palestinian capabilities is key. We should push ahead and not put all our eggs into the basket of diplomacy. Look, reality on the ground will shape an agreement, not vice versa."

In fact, the lack of real-world progress actually threatens any talks that may be underway because Palestinians will give them no credence if the context is a worsening of the conditions under which they live. Talks may then appear to be an Israeli trick, a means of prolonging the occupation. Moreover, whatever may be achieved at the negotiating table will be meaningless unless the Palestinian Authority is strong enough to enforce any agreement that is reached. One effect of a lack of American attention to real life under the PA is the PA's financial condition: The PA has repeatedly faced cash crises over the years because of the lack of Arab state financial support. One example occurred in 2010. American and EU financial support is reasonably steady and predictable; Arab support comes in fits and starts and depends to some degree on American pressure and pleading. By September 2010, Saudi contributions for the year totaled only $30.6 million, compared to $241.1 million in 2009. The United Arab Emirates, which contributed $173.9 million in 2009, paid nothing in 2010 until September, when it forwarded $42 million. It is impossible to believe this would have been the situation if the United States had been paying adequate attention and exercising adequate pressure. But it is what happens if an administration concentrates on ceremonies and not on how the PA will meet its payroll.

This is not an argument against diplomacy nor against the view that, even at their worst, Israeli-Palestinian negotiations can provide a useful cover for other activities such as the building of Palestinian institutions. The very existence of a negotiating track can allow Arab and European governments to reduce the shrillness of their attacks on Israel and to prod the Palestinian side toward moderation. But unless the negotiations are really moving toward success – and in my view, that condition never existed during the Bush years because of the PLO's unwillingness or inability after Arafat as under Arafat to sign a compromise agreement – they cannot be the main American goal. Instead, we should be trying to create the conditions that may someday make peace possible. President Bush did this when he broke with Arafat and demanded a decent, competent Palestinian government opposed to terror in all its forms. It was only when this happened that Ariel Sharon, leader of the Israeli right, committed himself to supporting Palestinian statehood. Similarly, building Palestinian institutions such as security forces and a functioning judicial system is a real step toward statehood.

The trade-offs can be very direct. As I have related, sometimes we asked the Israelis for symbolic concessions to the Palestinian Authority to make some meeting go more smoothly or at least appear to do so, instead of asking for moves that would actually provide concrete progress for Palestinian citizens. Because there is only so much traffic to be borne by any Israeli government (which will always face criticism for any concessions that are unrequited by Palestinian moves), to ask for one move is often to abandon or delay another – another that may have greater long-term impact on the ground.

As I have noted, everyone in Washington thought the state-building efforts Salam Fayyad was making were terrific, but they never became the focus of our policy. They were marginal, supplemental, and never central; in contrast, negotiations were central, and the success being recorded in them was very often exaggerated. The "peace process" can in this sense become the enemy of progress or even of peace. I tried to eliminate the term from every White House document, though this effort met with mixed success, and I never used it myself. To me it meant the endless series of sessions that overlooked or even obscured realities on the ground: the inability of the PA to defeat terror, its financial crises, the growing popularity of Hamas, the endemic corruption of Fatah, and the party's inability to win public support. We needed a process that overcame those obstacles to statehood, and the "peace process" often led us to discuss instead where the next conference would be held.

What is the proper American part to play? The fifth lesson is to avoid an overly intrusive American role. My own experience with trilateral meetings had made it clear that no negotiating takes place in the presence of the Americans. Both sides posture, seeking our approval and support. The serious negotiations are bilateral, and indeed in the case of Oslo were purely bilateral and kept secret from the United States. During the Bush years, efforts to insert the United States actually made bilateral Israeli-Palestinian negotiations harder. It is one thing to press the Israelis and Palestinians to negotiate but quite another to think that things will go more smoothly if we are physically present.

The sixth lesson is to avoid an obsession with a settlement "freeze," which the United States far more than the Palestinians or Arab states has made the sine qua non for progress toward peace – or even to sitting down to negotiate. A freeze had never been a Palestinian precondition for negotiations, and they had negotiated for years, under Arafat, while there was not only construction in settlements but also new settlements being built.

This is not to say that the settlement issue is an unimportant one but rather that a demand for a complete construction freeze in settlements *and* in Jerusalem (which became the U.S. position in 2009) is not realistic, nor is it a prerequisite for peace. It is unrealistic because no Israeli government will ever freeze all construction in large portions of the nation's capital or bar natural growth of populations in the settlements. In the Bush administration, we saw this and negotiated an arrangement with Israel that would allow some construction but not the expansion of Israel's footprint in the West Bank. As described in detail in Chapter 3, the agreement reached with Prime Minister Sharon was that all inducements to move to settlements (such as cheap mortgages) would end, there would be no new settlements at all, and new construction would be only in already built-up areas. That way, no additional land would be taken and Palestinian interests would not be prejudiced: Construction would only be *inside* existing settlements. This was a sensible approach to coping with the settlement issue.

The seventh lesson is that the remarkable assumption that the issues in the Israeli-Palestinian conflict are actually pretty simple to resolve is simply a fallacy. This is the belief that one need only get the parties to the table and once there, they would make quick progress and continue the talks until a final status agreement was reached. The only question would be where to place that table: Camp David, Taba, Annapolis, or Oslo. This was not an analysis but a nearly religious belief; it was faith-based diplomacy. The usual way this belief was put was that the parties were inches apart, all the major issues had been nearly agreed, and everyone understood what an agreement would look like, so there was not much more work to be done. This was a refrain heard often in the years after Oslo, including throughout the Bush years.

This was a remarkable and wrong-headed view. Listening to George Mitchell refer time after time after time to his experience as a negotiator on Northern Ireland, it seemed to me that he was drawing an exactly wrong analogy. In Northern Ireland, the interests of the two parties (Protestant and Catholic) had by the end become reconcilable, but the negotiators and leaders did not know each other and could not find a way to get together and hash out a deal reflecting those now mutual interests. Getting them in a room, breaking the ice, cajoling and leading, and not least providing a smoothing American presence were all important. In the Middle East, the negotiators had known each other for 20 years and got along fine; when they met, there was back-slapping and hugging, joking and storytelling. It often surprised Americans new to the region how well they all related – and how little they needed us. Getting them to the table and getting a negotiation going was, in the Clinton and Bush years, the easy part.

If indeed all the issues were so clear and all the solutions so obvious, it seemed to me that we have to learn something from the decades of failure by the parties to embrace those "obvious" solutions. Namely, we must learn that the "obvious" solution was unacceptable to both sides. That obvious solution could, of course, change over time, but Arafat's refusal at Camp David and Abbas's reaction to Olmert's offer suggested that even an offer that seemed most generous in Israeli terms might be completely insufficient for the Palestinian leadership. Similarly, could an Israeli prime minister agree to some of the "obvious" final status conditions the Palestinians wanted, such as the movement of many thousands of Palestinian "refugees" to Israel and the division of the Old City in Jerusalem?

Moreover, was it true that all the conditions of a final status agreement were so clear? I had never understood the basis for that claim. Certainly, it was not true with respect to Jerusalem. It was also not true when it came to security, so vital for Israel; it would be an endlessly complex matter to negotiate. The eight points that Defense Minister Barak had handed to President Bush and called absolutely essential for Israel were all likely to be rejected by the Palestinians. Determining final borders, at least in the Jerusalem suburbs, would also be immensely difficult. The parties were not "an inch away," and it was never accurate that "everyone understands what the final deal will look like." That was not an argument against negotiations nor a counsel of doom but rather a suggestion that a final status was not around the corner – and that therefore the actual life being lived by Palestinians was not a temporary condition soon to be transformed. Now, 45 years after the 1967 War, this should hardly be a great revelation, but too often its implications are ignored. The difficulty of negotiating a final status agreement should suggest that far more emphasis be placed instead on changing the conditions under which Palestinians live today and on building the institutions under which they are governed. That is a far surer road to reconciliation and to peace. To focus on what progress is possible today and what dangers lurk tomorrow is not an abandonment of American responsibility but an assertion of reality. And peace will be built on reality, not on hope.

Notes

1. Notable & Quotable, "Margaret Thatcher on What 'Consensus' Really Means," *Wall Street Journal*, October 6, 2009, http://online.wsj.com/article/ SB10001424052748704471504574445072280951620.html.
2. Rodman, *Presidential Command*, 24 (emphasis in original).
3. Indyk, *Innocent Abroad*, 408.

13

Conclusion

Will there ever be peace between Israelis and Palestinians, or is there still (as the story I told in the introduction suggests) hope but no chance?

More than a century of violence between Israelis and Arabs in the area once called Mandatory Palestine has finally produced a broad consensus that two entities should exist there – Israel and Palestine. At least since the Arab or Saudi Plan of 2002, Arab states appear to have given up hope of destroying Israel. The PLO leadership has long since sought a deal with Israel that would lead to its withdrawal from the West Bank and to the creation of a Palestinian state. And since the days of Ariel Sharon's leadership, most of the Israeli right has joined the center and left in believing that Israel should separate from the Palestinians and allow them to rule themselves in their own entity.

Yet progress since the Oslo Agreement of 1991 has been very slow. This is generally viewed as a great problem, but I am inclined to see it as both inevitable and salutary. In the Oslo Agreement, Israel took a defeated and exiled Yasser Arafat and placed him back in the West Bank at the top of Palestinian politics. This was quite similar to the disastrous British decision to appoint Haj Amin al Husseini as Mufti of Jerusalem in 1921, which also elevated a terrorist and poisoned Palestinian political life for a generation. Both decisions were avoidable errors, and both led to years of violence and many Jewish and Arab deaths. For like Husseini, Arafat saw the murder of Jews as a reasonable tactic to achieve his goals. And as in the case of Husseini, the "Palestinian self-rule" that was one of Arafat's key goals meant not that the people would rule themselves but that he himself would rule them.

So Arafat crushed the Palestinian civic life that had grown up after 1967 under Israeli rule. By 1995, it was estimated that there were seven hundred NGOs in the West Bank and Gaza – before they were systematically eliminated. Arafat's "security" organizations, which Sharon rightly called "security-terror organizations," reported only to him and engaged in violence and corruption. The reigning theory was that handing him Palestine to govern was smart because he would use that muscle to protect Israel from terrorist groups (that were also his enemies) without the human rights limitations that bound Israeli forces. It was with this in mind that Yitzhak Rabin appeared ready to give Arafat a state, perhaps concluding as well that in view of President Clinton's passionate commitment, it would be unwise for Israel to cross its greatest ally. This calamity was avoided only because Arafat himself was not ready for any compromise, preferring to end his life believing in his own myth rather than helping his fellow Palestinians.

It was only after the collapse of Camp David and Arafat's return to terror that the United States abandoned the idea that an Arafat state could somehow lead to peace. As has been explained here, President Bush's conclusion that Arafat must go was viewed by most of the world as an outrageous step away from peace. But Bush understood that it was in neither Israel's interests nor our own to permit a terrorist state in Palestine, and he understood as well that Israel would, after the first and second intifadas, never permit such a state. So in 2002, he began to articulate a new policy, demanding reform as the price of Palestinian statehood.

He thought in 2002 that such a state could be built during his presidency. This was overly optimistic because it was not possible to push Arafat aside, and real progress began only after his death. In Bush's second term, progress was slower than might have been possible because of the determined focus on diplomacy, as if diplomacy would create the sinews of Palestine self-government. It did not and could not because as Tony Blair articulated, reality on the ground would dictate the diplomatic progress and not vice versa. State-building is an arduous task and four years were not sufficient to accomplish it.

Progress has also been endangered by the strength of Palestinian terrorist groups, above all Hamas, whose coup in Gaza has now split the Palestinians in two. That strength is hard to measure because Hamas depends so greatly on outside support, largely from Iran. More broadly, the PA leadership under Prime Minister Fayyad is trying to create a moderate, responsible Palestinian politics – for the first time in history – at a moment when Islamist extremism has been spreading in the entire Muslim world. In that sense, he is rowing against strong currents. The changes that are visible in the PA are nevertheless striking, not least the creation (with help from American trainers) of security forces that maintain law and order and fight terror. The PA leadership is moving, as Blair has put it, from a resistance mentality to a government mentality. This is critical if diplomacy is ever to have a chance, and in an interview Blair explained why:

The only way [the Palestinians] will ever feel strong enough to make the compromises is if what is happening on the ground leads people to believe that actually if we keep going, we're *really* going to get a state.... The Palestinians have to create the circumstances in which these compromises are possible. The only way of doing that is if the people actually within the Palestinian Territories are feeling sufficiently positive about life and what is happening that they say, "Well, OK then. Let's go for it." You see, the people who are actually within the West Bank – and I suspect even within Gaza too – they don't have many illusions about what they can get or what they can't get. The illusions are all outside. But for the Palestinians, what they've got to do is, they've got to give up that kind of dream. Now, it may be an illusory dream, but it's a dream. If you ask them to give it up in exchange for a theoretical agreement, then they say, "Well, why?" If what you're doing is you're actually creating the circumstances in which not the dream, but nonetheless a very substantial and clear gain is in prospect, then I think they will go for it. That's why the political consequence of this building from the bottom up is so important.[1]

Thus, nothing would contribute more to progress than a reorientation of American priorities – and those of Israel, the Arab states, and the EU – away from the obsessions with diplomacy and with settlement construction and toward actually building the bases for Palestinian self-government. And progress there would have another byproduct of great value: allowing a return to Palestinian politics. It is impossible to build a democratic Palestinian state without democratic political parties and free elections that create legitimate governments. It is impossible to create legitimate governmental institutions if the Palestinian parliament does not meet and pass laws. Through the Bush years and into the Obama administration, the Fatah Party emerged as an obstacle to democracy, its own incompetence and intractable resistance to reform leading it to prefer rule by decree to electoral tests. Moreover, it viewed Fayyad and his work as a threat, choosing to struggle against the PA rather than seeking to enhance and take credit for its achievements. But it is reasonable to believe that continuing advancement in the credibility of PA institutions and improvement in the standard of living in the West Bank will allow, sooner rather than later, a return to free elections. This can create a virtuous cycle between the political system and the PA institutions, each enhancing the other; conversely, if this cannot be achieved, if Fatah not only attacks but also weakens or even destroys the work of the PA, independence will be much further off.

Salam Fayyad has described his own views of the process of state-building:

The idea was to impart a sense of possibility about what might happen, what we would want to see happen: an end to the Israeli occupation and an opportunity for Palestinians to be able to live as free people in a country of our own.... It's the power of ideas translated into facts on the ground – taking Palestinian statehood from abstract concept to reality.... [I]f we manage to create that kind of critical mass of positive change on the ground, I imagine it would be very difficult for anyone looking at us fairly to then still argue that Palestinians aren't capable of managing something that looks like a state.... I'd argue that the strength of our program derives, at least in part, from its transformative potential, in the sense that it really begins to allow people to see a state in the making – in a way that grows on them, not happens to them, or for them. Often, people come to the conclusion that it's hopeless. I understand that. But they're thinking about things in a static way. The state-building program goes well beyond the world as it is now. You begin to move; you begin to act; you begin to create new realities; and that in itself provides a much better dynamic. All this, I believe, feeds into a sense of inevitability that undercuts the pervasive feeling of despair.[2]

I am not an optimist about negotiating a final status agreement because the compromises are terribly difficult for both Palestinians and Israelis. It is often said that the outlines of a compromise deal are very clear and have been clear for 20 years, so that finishing the negotiation must be simple. The opposite is true: Both sides do see what a compromise must look like and neither side appears to want it. Both, or at least the political leadership on both sides, prefer the status quo. This is another reason why progress on the ground is so important: A final agreement is not in sight. How people actually live in the years before one is possible should depend not on the bad feelings produced by endless failed efforts at diplomacy but on genuine change in their lives: On the Palestinian side, that means more prosperity, more mobility, and less Israeli intrusiveness, and on the Israeli side it means more security. All that can be achieved.

If it is achieved, it will undercut Hamas's rule in Gaza. No one has a "solution" for the situation there, unless it is the eventual collapse of the Iranian regime, the end of its support for Hamas and other terrorist groups, and the defeat for Islamic radicalism that the Iranian regime's demise would mean. But steady improvements in political and economic life in the West Bank combined with Hamas repression of dissent and imposition of sharia in Gaza will surely lead a good majority of Gazans to hate Hamas rule and wish to end it. They cannot achieve that now, but we should do all we can to erode support for Hamas by showing another, competing model for Palestinian life.

What kind of entity will Palestine be? Once upon a time, optimists believed that Gaza, freed from Israeli rule, could be the model. It is, in its way: That is one kind of Palestine. That kind will be prevented in the West Bank by Israel – and by Jordan, whose security is also at stake. The greatest single issue for Palestine being security – internal security (given the threat from Hamas and other terrorist groups) for the new state and the security of Israel and Jordan – it is hard to avoid wondering about Jordan's future role. This is a taboo subject and has been since King Hussein "abandoned" Jordan's claims and role in the West Bank in 1988. "We respect the wish of the P.L.O., the sole legitimate representative of the Palestinian people, to secede from us in an independent Palestinian state," the king said then. But what if the new, independent Palestinian state has another wish – to have a more organic relationship with Jordan? Surely, the two states would have an economic union; surely, Jordan would serve as Palestine's bridge to the world, via Amman rather than Tel Aviv, or via Aqaba rather (or at least far more) than Eilat or even Ashkelon. Surely, the two states would cooperate fully on security matters, having a long and easily crossed border. One can easily envision that the "international forces" that would assist the young Palestinian entity in maintaining security might be substantially Jordanian.

The question is whether intimate economic and security ties would lead further, to some form of political connection. This too is a taboo topic, but the subject ought to be broached. The Jordanian government fights hard to defeat the view that "Jordan is Palestine," but the goal would not be eliminating the Hashemite Kingdom and subsuming it to the Palestinian state. Rather, it would be some form of link, perhaps a Habsburg-like dual monarchy where one king reigned but two prime ministers governed two independent states, each having its own parliament, cabinet and executive bodies, and judicial system. If Palestinians on both sides of the Jordan River became convinced that this formula would best provide security as well as decent, legitimate, efficient government, the taboo would slowly disappear.

Whatever its relationship with Jordan, would the Palestinian state be a decent democratic society? This is perhaps a tougher challenge even than building reliable institutions. As one scholar wrote, "Having rejected a separate state in 1947, Palestinians fell under Jordanian and Egyptian occupation. In the ensuing years, they built a national identity founded on anger, 'steadfastness,' self-pity, resentment, and entitlement."[3] The key Israeli goal in any final status agreement is the "end of conflict" with Palestinians and all Arab states, and this will require not only the right phrases in a signed agreement but also a transformation of Palestinian attitudes and sense of identity. In Israel, there has been a decade-long untrammeled debate over the conditions of a final status agreement, but nothing of this sort has occurred on the Palestinian side. The PA and PLO have not prepared the Palestinian people for the national concessions that any final status agreement with Israel will require. If such concessions are understood as unjust and evil steps that are acceptable only in the context of "ending the occupation," and if establishment of an independent state is understood only as a stage in the elimination of Israel and recovery of "all Palestinian lands," Palestinian statehood is a guarantee of more conflict rather than its end. It is in this context that both Israeli complaints about "incitement" (usually meaning gross anti-Semitism and celebration of violence and those who commit it) in the Palestinian media and Israeli demands about recognition of Israel as a Jewish State should be understood. The underlying question is whether Palestinians are agreeing to a permanent peace and wish to move from a military and political struggle with Israel to a lasting compromise. Given the strength of the Palestinian groups expressly supporting irredentist views (not least Hamas), Israelis are wise to demand proofs and protections from the entities, presumably the PLO and PA, with which they are dealing and which will be running a Palestinian state. For, after all, the goal of all these decades of negotiations is not a paper peace treaty – it is peace.

The lesson of the Bush years is that the road to peace may not be the path that has been taken most often, is accepted most widely, and is safest politically. When President Bush defied conventional wisdom, he was at his most effective, and the United States truly brought peace closer. The conferences and ceremonies that got the most applause did not do so. Peace will not be the product of fanfare and speeches; it will be won through tough decisions and tougher actions.

Notes

1. Blair, interview, pp. 5–6.
2. Salam Fayyad, "Why I'm Building Palestine," *Foreign Policy*, November 29, 2010, http://www.foreignpolicy.com/articles/2010/11/29/why_im_building_palestine.
3. Alex Joffe, "The Discreet Coyness of Salam Fayyad," *Jewish Ideas Daily*, December 3, 2010, http://www.jewishideasdaily.com/content/module/2010/12/3/main-feature/1/the-discreet-coyness-of-salam-fayyad.

Index

Abbas, Mahmoud (Abu Mazen)
  generally, 140, 155–156, 244
  Abrams and, 131–132, 135, 170, 208–209,
    292
  Annapolis Conference and, 249, 250,
    253–255, 256
  appointment of, 62, 63
  Arafat and, 65, 68, 79, 83, 99, 101
  Bush and
    generally, 121
    Annapolis Conference, 253–255, 256
    Arafat compared, 63–64
    doubts regarding Abbas, 124
    final status negotiations, 271
    Hamas participation in Palestinian
      elections, 146
    initial conversations with, 70
    national unity government, 206
    negotiations, 232–233
    on Olmert, 285–286
    terrorism, 69, 75–76
    visits to Washington, 79–81, 132–133
  disengagement and, 135
  Document of National Accord and, 176
  election of, 119–120, 122
  emergency government appointed by,
    232–233
  Fatah and, 121, 122, 270
  final status negotiations and, 68, 121,
    216–217, 234, 250, 267, 270,
    271–272, 277–278, 279–280
  Gaza Strip and, 266, 270–271, 272
  Hadley and, 271–272
  Hamas and, 124, 125–126, 210
  Hamas takeover of Gaza Strip and, 228

  hesitancy of, 124
  international conference approach and,
    208–209
  Jerusalem, and status of, 275
  leadership of, 120
  Mecca Agreement and, 222
  national unity government and, 206, 209,
    218, 220, 228, 229
  negotiations with, 121
  Netanyahu and, 311–312
  Olmert and
    Annapolis Conference, 249
    final status negotiations, 270
    Gaza Strip, 266, 270–271, 272
    negotiations, 210, 258, 260, 286–287
    political weakness of Olmert, 232–233,
      234
    West Bank, 270–271
  Palestinian elections and
    generally, 132–134, 136, 151, 165–166,
      209–210
    Hamas participation in, 145–146
  Qurie and, 248–249
  at Red Sea Summits, 69, 71, 72, 75–76
  refugees and, 291
  resignation of, 83–84, 163
  Rice and
    disengagement, 135
    final status negotiations, 267, 271–272,
      277–278, 279–280
    Mecca Agreement, 222
    national unity government, 209, 220
    on Olmert, 286
    terrorism, 77
  Roadmap and, 213–216

Abbas, Mahmoud (Abu Mazen) (*cont.*)
  settlements and, 311
  Sharon and, 78, 79, 82, 83, 123
  suspension of peace talks by, 267
  terrorism and, 69, 75–76, 77
  Tourgeman and, 290
  trilateral meeting with Olmert and Rice,
    220–221
  Turbowitz and, 290
  visits to Washington, 79–81, 132–133
  weakness of, 121, 160
  Welch and, 144, 170, 208–209
  West Bank and
    generally, 270–271, 274–275
    rejection of Olmert offer, 289–293,
      312
Abdallah (Saudi King)
  generally, 132
  Bush and, 35–36, 63, 65, 287
  Gaza Strip and, 217, 242
  Israeli withdrawal from occupied territories
    and, 29
  normalization with Israel and, 29
  Palestinian refugees and, 29
  Powell and, 14–15
  at Red Sea Summits, 69, 71
  Second Intifada, Saudi plan to end, 28–29
  secret letter to US, 15
Abdullah (Jordanian King)
  generally, 132
  "April 14th letter" and, 111
  Bush and, 62, 63, 73, 169, 275
  Obama and, 305
  at Red Sea Summits, 69, 71, 73
  Rice and, 110–111
  Roadmap and, 49–50
  summits hosted by, 123
Abramowitz, Aaron, 252
Abrams, Elliott
  generally, 119, 126, 129, 159, 226, 233,
    252, 258
  Abbas and, 131–132, 135, 170, 208–209,
    292
  al-Kibar nuclear reactor and, 237
  Annapolis Conference and, 196, 248–251
  "April 14th letter" and, 103
  Arafat and, 60–61
  Bandar and, 198
  Bush and, 59, 61, 202–203
  Cheney and, 59
  departure from government, 304
  final status negotiations and, 117, 213–214,
    216, 317

Hadley and, 61, 116–117, 124, 223, 239,
    275, 298
  Hamas and, 167
  hitkansut (convergence) policy and,
    171–172, 173
  international conference approach and, 196,
    197, 210, 232, 242, 246
  Lebanon War and, 195
  Mecca Agreement and, 219
  in NSC, 59–61
  Olmert and, 160–161, 173–174, 207–208,
    288–289
  Palestinian elections and, 152
  Qurie and, 115
  Rice and
    generally, 124
    appointment of Abrams, 59
    decision not to follow Rice to State
      Department, 116–117
    Lebanon War, 195
    loyalty to Rice, 59, 61
    "off the record" remarks by Abrams,
      224–225, 226
    settlements, 115–116
  Roadmap and, 213–214
  in second Bush Administration, 116–117
  settlements and, 67–68
  Sharon and, 65–66, 88, 90, 101–102,
    103–104, 132, 136–138, 154
  Tourgeman and, 202, 214, 216, 276, 296
  Turbowitz and, 188, 202, 214, 216
  visits to Israel, 269–270
  Weissglas and, 88, 90, 101, 102, 137, 149
  Welch and, 170, 176, 223–224
Abu Ala'a. *See* Qurie, Ahmed (Abu Ala'a)
Abu Mazen. *See* Abbas, Mahmoud (Abu
    Mazen)
Agency for International Development, 169
Agreement on Movement and Access, 148–151
Ahmadinejad, Mahmoud, 257
Al Aqsa Martyrs Brigade, 101
Al Jazeera, 289–290, 292
al-Kibar nuclear reactor
  generally, 200, 249
  Abrams and, 237
  Bush and, 238–239, 246–247
  Cheney and, 227, 236, 237
  debate regarding, 235–236
  diplomatic option, 236–239
  disclosure of information regarding, 271
  Hadley and, 227, 236
  intelligence regarding, 227–228
  Israeli bombing of, 246–248

military option, 236, 237
North Korea and, 227–228, 236, 271
Olmert and, 227, 246–247
Rice and, 236, 237–238
Security Council and, 236, 238, 246
al Qaeda, 163
Alexandria Statement, 114
American Israel Public Affairs Committee, 10
American Jewish Historical Society, 202–203
Annan, Kofi
generally, 135, 192, 207, 226, 241–242
Geneva Initiative and, 85
on killing of Yassin, 102
Palestinian elections, and Hamas
participation in, 143, 144, 166, 167
Roadmap and, 58
Annapolis Conference
Abbas and, 249, 250, 253–255, 256
Abrams and, 196, 248–251
Bush and, 249, 253–255, 256
Fayyad and, 249
final status negotiations and, 251, 255–256,
259–260
Hadley and, 248–251
Livni and, 250, 251
Olmert and, 249, 250–251, 253, 255
origins of, 196
overemphasis on, 309
Rice and, 251
Tourgeman and, 253
Turbowitz and, 253
United Nations and, 253
Annapolis Declaration, 255–256
"April 14th letter"
Abdullah and, 111
Abrams and, 103
Arab League and, 110
Arab reactions to, 109–113
Blair and, 110
borders of Israel and, 108–109
Burns and, 103
Bush's commitments in, 107–109
disengagement and, 106
final status negotiations and, 107–109
Hadley and, 103
Jordan and, 110–112
Muasher and, 110–112
Mubarak and, 111
need for new Palestinian leadership and,
106
Obama and, 308
Qurie and, 109–110, 112
refugees and, 108

Rice and, 112
Roadmap and, 107–108
security of Israel and, 108
settlements and, 107, 108–109
Sharon's commitments in, 106–107
terrorism and, 108
Tourgeman and, 103
Weissglas and, 103, 109
West Bank fence and, 107, 109
Aqaba Summit, 71–76. *See also* Red Sea
Summits
The Arab Center (Muasher), 110–112
Arab Human Development Report, 114
Arab League
Annapolis Conference and, 253
"April 14th letter" and, 110
"Arab Plan" and, 29
PLO and, 129
"Arab Plan," 28–31
"Arab Spring," 306–307
"Arabists" in State Department, 19, 43, 176
Arafat, Moussa, 140, 160
Arafat, Yasser
generally, 113–114, 155–156, 165
Abbas and, 65, 68, 79, 83, 99, 101
Abrams and, 60–61
Blair and, 43
Burns and, 30
Bush and
abandonment of Arafat, 43, 58, 315
attacks on Arafat in speeches by, 34
death of Arafat, 119
distrust of Arafat, 26–27
Camp David negotiations and, 6, 120, 312
Cheney and, 27, 30–31
Clinton and, 4–5, 34, 45, 76
comeback of, 84
corruption of, 314–315
death of, 119, 315
Hadley and, 43
Hannah and, 30
Hizballah and, 25
Iran and, 25
Israeli attacks on facilities of, 24, 37
Karine A affair and, 25–27
Libby and, 30
marginalization of, 52
medical condition of, 116
mini-rebellion against, 56–57
Oslo Accords and, 314
Palestinian elections and, 56–57
Powell and, 6–7, 9, 24, 33
Qurie and, 90, 101

Arafat, Yasser (*cont.*)
  reputation as statesman, 24–25
  Riedel and, 8
  Roadmap and, 56–57
  Second Intifada, calling for, 5
  settlements and, 311
  Sharon and, 24, 54–56, 119
  siege of headquarters, 31, 82
  terrorism, commitment to, 101
  unwillingness to agree to peace, 291, 292,
      310, 312
  as "victim," 28
  Zinni and, 30–31
Ariel (settlement), 85, 276–277, 278, 280
Armitage, Richard, 83
Assad, Bashar, 227, 247, 248, 306–307
Assad, Hafez, 21
Ayalon, Ami, 84
Ayalon, Danny
  generally, 215
  Bush-Sharon relationship and, 11, 12
  Karine A affair and, 25
  Lebanon War and, 190
  Operation Defensive Shield and, 31
  Rice and, 22, 77, 200
  Roadmap and, 50
  Sharon's expectations of Bush and, 9, 10

Baker, James, 61, 197, 308
Ban Ki-moon, 241–242
Bandar (Saudi Prince), 15, 17, 69, 181, 198
Barak, Ehud
  generally, 194, 254, 291
  Bush and, 263, 312
  Camp David negotiations and, 250
  Clinton and, 4
  defeat of, 60
  Gaza Strip and, 266–267
  Hadley and, 266–267
  Palestinian Authority and, 266, 270
  Rice and, 244–245, 267
Barghouti, Mustafa, 128, 163
Bassem, Haji, 25
Beckett, Margaret, 184
Begin, Menachem, 101–102, 307, 308
Beilin, Yossi, 85, 86, 142
Ben Gurion, David, 137
Bin Laden, Osama, 20
Blair, Tony
  generally, 104, 119, 132–133, 266, 315
  "April 14th letter" and, 110
  Arafat and, 43
  Bush and, 241, 274, 282–283, 302, 309

  on democratization of Middle East, 87
  Iraq War's relationship to Middle East
      situation and, 38, 39
  on killing of Yassin, 102
  Lebanon War and, 183, 184
  London Conference and, 125
  Palestinian Authority and, 315–316
  peace process and, 57
"Blue curtain," 127–128
Bolten, Josh, 192, 199, 234, 241
Bombings in Israel
  generally, 53–54, 69–70, 77, 83
  decline in, 122
  by Fatah, 101, 102
  by Hamas, 76–77, 102, 116, 146, 172
  by Islamic Jihad, 146, 150–151
  "Park Hotel Massacre," 30
  during Second Intifada, 13, 21, 22, 24,
      27–28, 30, 37, 41
Bottom-up negotiations, 259
British Broadcasting Corporation, 43
Brown, Gordon, 300
Brzezinski, Zbigniew, 113, 114
Burns, William J.
  generally, 126
  "April 14th letter" and, 103
  Arafat and, 30
  Israeli view of, 51
  at Red Sea Summits, 69
  Roadmap and, 50, 51
  Saudi Arabia and, 15
  visits to Israel, 83
Bush, George H.W., 16, 35, 43, 61, 307, 308
Bush, George W.
  Abbas and
    generally, 121
    Annapolis Conference, 253–255, 256
    Arafat compared, 63–64
    doubts regarding Abbas, 124
    final status negotiations, 271
    Hamas participation in Palestinian
        elections, 146
    initial conversations with, 70
    national unity government, 206
    negotiations, 232–233
    on Olmert, 285–286
    terrorism, 69, 75–76
    visits to Washington, 79–81, 132–133
  Abdallah and, 35–36, 62, 63, 65, 73, 169,
      275, 287
  Abrams and, 59, 61, 202–203
  al-Kibar nuclear reactor and, 238–239,
      246–247

Annapolis Conference and, 249, 253–255, 256
"April 14th letter" (*See* "April 14th letter")
Arab world expectations of, 8–9
Arafat and
  abandonment of Arafat, 43, 58, 315
  attacks on Arafat in speeches by, 34
  death of Arafat, 119
  distrust of Arafat, 26–27
Barak and, 263, 312
Blair and, 241, 274, 282–283, 302, 309
campaign of, 4
Clinton and, 5
constancy of, 64
conventional wisdom and, 318
Dahlan and, 75
democratization of Middle East and, 86–87, 122–123
disengagement and, 99–100, 130–131
Egypt and, 306
Europe and, 20
evolution of new Middle East policy, 44–45
Fayyad and, 275
final status negotiations and, 223, 271
Geneva Initiative and, 86
Hadley and, 275
Hizballah and, 180
Hussein and, 57
international conference approach and, 232, 239–242
Israeli helicopter attacks and, 77
Jones Report and, 293–295
killing of Yassin and, 103
as lame duck, 260, 279
leadership of, 64
Livni and, 169, 262–263, 274
Mecca Agreement and, 219
Merkel and, 297–298
moral claims of Palestinian people and, 43
Mubarak and, 104–105
national unity government and, 206
need for new Palestinian leadership and, 40, 41–42, 62
"no daylight" strategy, 308
Olmert and
  al-Kibar nuclear reactor, 246–247
  Annapolis Conference, 249, 255
  initial conversations, 158–159
  Jones Report, 293–295
  Mecca Agreement, 219
  military aid to Israel, 234
  Palestinian statehood, 233–234
  peace talks, 269

  personal relationship, 225, 264–265
  on Rice, 280
  support for, 264
  Syria, 269, 276
  terrorism, 268–269
  West Bank offer, 292–293
Operation Defensive Shield and, 31
Palestinian elections, and Hamas participation in, 146
Palestinian statehood and, 16–17, 42, 232, 233–234, 315
Peres and, 262
personal relationships with leaders, 309
"Quartet" and, 58
Qurie and, 121
at Red Sea Summits, 71, 74, 76
reelection of, 116
relations with Israel, 309
Rice and, 35, 198–200, 225, 226
right of return and, 74–75
Roadmap and, 55, 58, 81–83, 87, 204–205
Saudi Arabia, relationship with, 14–15
Security Council and, 297
settlements and, 58, 311
Shalom and, 63
Sharon and
  on Abbas, 70
  "April 14th letter," 105
  characterization of Sharon as "man of peace," 35
  disengagement, 99–100, 130–131
  expectations of, 9–13
  meetings with, 36–37
  need for new Palestinian leadership, 62
  personal relationship, 11–12, 154
  reaction to break with Arafat, 44
  at Red Sea Summits, 74, 76
  Roadmap, 55, 58, 81–83
  strokes suffered by Sharon, 153
  at United Nations, 142
speeches regarding Middle East situation, 41–42
speeches to Knesset, 273–274
terrorism and, 69, 75–76, 268–269
Tourgeman, and Sharon's perception of, 9–10
at United Nations, 142
United Nations speeches, 22, 196–197, 201–202, 203
visits to Israel, 262–265
vocabulary of, 64

Camp David Accords (1978), 16, 158

Camp David negotiations (2000)
  generally, 43
  Arafat and, 6, 120, 312
  Barak and, 250
  borders and, 108–109
  Clinton and, 4–5, 150
  collapse of, 44–45, 315
  Palestinian statehood and, 16
  State Department and, 195
Cantor, Eric, 224–225
Carter, Jimmy, 16, 85, 307, 308
Cheney, Dick
  Abrams and, 59
  al-Kibar nuclear reactor and, 227, 236, 237
  Arab world expectations of, 9
  Arafat and, 27, 30–31
  Clinton and, 5
  foreign policy and, 198–199, 200
  Karine A affair and, 26
  need for new Palestinian leadership and, 41
  Olmert and, 235
  Palestinian statehood and, 16–17
  peace talks and, 38
  Powell and, 34
  Rice and, 283
  Sharon and, 131
Chirac, Jacques, 110, 206, 309
Christian Science Monitor, 56
Clinton, Bill
  generally, 104, 155, 201, 213, 238, 291
  approaches to peace-making, 43
  Arafat and, 4–5, 34, 45, 76
  Barak and, 4
  Bush and, 5
  Camp David negotiations and, 4–5, 150
  Cheney and, 5
  diplomatic activity of, 241
  errors made by, 255
  failure of Middle East talks under, 4–5
  military aid to Israel, 234
  Palestinian statehood and, 16, 315
  Powell and, 5
  relations with Israel, 307, 309
Clinton, Hillary, 306
Cohen, Eliot, 190–191, 192, 195, 299
Conference of Presidents of Major American
  Jewish Organizations, 232, 308
Connor, Bull, 245
Consensus, 304
Convergence (*hitkansut*) policy, 171–174
Cunningham, Jim, 287

Dagan, Meir, 227, 236, 246–247

Dahlan, Mohammed
  generally, 140, 244
  Bush and, 75
  Fatah and, 115
  Hamas and, 115
  Hamas takeover of Gaza Strip and, 228,
    229
  Palestinian Authority and, 77, 115,
    135–136, 137
  Palestinian elections and, 132–136, 151,
    152, 159
  terrorism and, 78, 83
  weakness of, 160
  Wolf and, 77, 83
D'Alema, Massimo, 184
Danin, Rob, 117, 151–152
Dayton, Keith, 214, 228–229, 231, 241, 249,
    259–260, 266
de Gucht, Karel, 308
de Soto, Alvaro, 134–135, 144, 167, 226
Defense Department
  political appointees *versus* career personnel
    in, 304–306
  Presidential control of decision making,
    importance of, 304–306
DeLay, Tom, 133
Demographics, 92
Disengagement
  Abbas and, 135
  "April 14th letter" and, 106
  Bush and, 99–100, 130–131
  doomed to failure, 159–161
  evolution of, 87–93
  Giladi and, 91, 120, 154
  Hamas takeover of Gaza Strip and,
    231–232
  IDF and, 93, 135, 139, 230, 231–232
  implementation of, 139
  Israeli approval of, 112–113, 125
  Kaplinsky and, 89, 154
  Meridor and, 100–101, 121
  "Quartet" and, 134–135, 142–143
  Rice and, 100, 135, 136–137, 154
  Sharon and, 89, 93, 94, 98–100, 130–131,
    136–137
  State Department and, 99
  strengthening of Hamas during, 159–161
  Tourgeman and, 89–90
  Weissglas and, 89, 90, 92–93, 136,
    154–155, 160
  West Bank, coupling with, 100
Diskin, Yuval, 269–270
Document of National Accord, 176

Dulles, John Foster, 237

Edelman, Eric, 30, 49
Egypt
  Bush and, 306
  Gaza Strip and, 103, 297
  Obama and, 306–307
el-Baradei, Mohammed, 237
Elections. *See also specific election or person*
  Palestinian elections (*See* Palestinian
    elections)
Erekat, Saeb
  generally, 110, 287, 292
  Jerusalem, and status of, 272
  Livni and, 258, 276, 291
  Olmert and, 286, 289–290
  Powell and, 56
  Rice and, 267
  West Bank and, 288, 290–291
European Union in "Quartet." *See* "Quartet"
Evolution of new Middle East policy, 44–45
*Extraordinary, Ordinary People: A Memoir of
  Family* (Rice), 245

Faris, Qaddurah, 85
Fatah
  Abbas and, 121, 122, 270
  bombings in Israel by, 101, 102
  corruption in, 164–165
  Dahlan and, 115
  democracy and, 316
  difficulty in reforming, 128
  Document of National Accord and, 176
  Fayyad and, 316
  Karine A affair and, 25
  military strength of, 77
  national unity government with Hamas,
    206
  overview, 129
  Palestinian Authority and, 270
  Palestinian elections and
    defeat in, 163, 164–166
    participation in, 126, 127, 131
    reasons for defeat in, 164–166
  polls regarding, 152
  Qurie and, 270
  rationale for saving, 128–129
  secular nature of, 165
  tension with Hamas, 128
  truce with Hamas, 125–126
  war with Hamas, 140, 176–177, 206–207,
    209–210, 212, 226–227
Fayyad, Salam

  generally, 209, 244
  Annapolis Conference and, 249
  appointment of, 38
  Bush and, 275
  commitment to reform, 124, 129
  economic situation of Palestinian Authority
    and, 170, 272–273, 278–279
  Fatah and, 316
  financial support to, 133
  Hamas takeover of Gaza Strip and, 228
  moderation of, 315
  Palestinian elections and, 163
  state-building and, 316
  US support for, 80, 128, 239, 259, 276,
    282, 309, 310
  West Bank and, 265, 266, 267
Feith, Douglas, 19–20, 38–39, 40–41, 49
Feltman, Jeffrey, 84
Final status negotiations
  Abbas and, 68, 121, 216–217, 234, 250,
    267, 270, 271–272, 277–278, 279–280
  Abrams and, 117, 213–214, 216, 317
  Annapolis Conference and, 251, 255–256,
    259–260
  "April 14th letter" and, 107–109
  Bush and, 223, 271
  Giladi and, 91
  Hadley and, 67
  Jerusalem, status of and, 312–313
  Jordan, role of, 317–318
  Olmert and, 222–223, 233, 234, 270
  Palestinian Authority and, 317–318
  PLO and, 317–318
  Rice and, 209, 212–213, 215, 216–217,
    267, 271–272, 277–278, 279–280
  Tourgeman and, 216
  Turbowitz and, 216
  Welch and, 216, 223–224
Fischer, Joschka, 21, 33, 113
The Forward (Jewish newspaper), 224
Fractured Palestinian leadership, 129
France at Security Council, 299, 302
Fraser, William M., 259–260
Friedman, Thomas, 28–29, 30

Gates, Robert, 236, 237, 238
Gaza Strip
  Abbas and, 266, 270–271, 272
  Abdallah and, 217, 242
  Agreement on Movement and Access,
    148–151
  attacks on Israel from, 265, 266, 267, 269,
    287, 295

Gaza Strip (*cont.*)
  Barak and, 266–267
  chaos in, 139–140
  crossing to and from, 148–151
  disengagement (*See* Disengagement)
  Egypt and, 103, 297
  greenhouses in, 134, 135, 140
  Hamas rule in, 315, 317
  Hamas takeover of, 228–232
  IDF in, 77, 92, 100, 106
  Iran and, 228
  Israeli attacks in, 226–227, 266, 267, 269,
    295
  Israeli withdrawals from, 79
  military difficulties in occupying, 92, 93
  Olmert and, 266, 270–271, 272
  Operation Autumn Clouds, 207
  Operation Cast Lead, 295
  Palestinian Authority and, 159–161
  Rice and, 272
  security forces in, 77
  Tourgeman and, 287
  truce in, 78, 278
  US position on Israeli withdrawal from, 44
G8 (Sea Island) summit, 113–114
Geneva Initiative, 85–86, 272
Genger, Arie, 10, 22, 77
Germany and peace talks, 33
Gerson, Michael, 11, 38
Gilad, Amos, 135, 298
Giladi, Eival, 91, 120, 154, 172–173, 190
Givat Ze'ev (settlement), 276–277, 278
Goldstone Report, 311
Gulf Cooperation Council, 215

Haaretz (Israeli newspaper), 98, 99, 311–312
Haass, Richard, 6, 19
Hadley, Steve
  generally, 127, 132, 197, 200, 216, 233,
    252, 258
  Abbas and, 271–272
  Abrams and, 61, 116–117, 124, 223, 239,
    275, 298
  al-Kibar nuclear reactor and, 227, 236
  Annapolis Conference and, 248–251
  "April 14th letter" and, 103
  Arafat and, 43
  Bandar and, 198
  Barak and, 266–267
  Bush and, 275
  final status negotiations and, 67
  Hizballah and, 180
  Karine A affair and, 25
  Mecca Agreement and, 219

  Meridor and, 219, 223
  military aid to Israel, 234
  need for new Palestinian leadership and, 39,
    40
  at NSC, 59
  Olmert and, 174, 286
  policy and, 133, 302
  Qurie and, 103, 115
  Rice and, 199, 224–225, 226, 283–284,
    294, 298–299
  Roadmap and, 49, 50, 53, 216–217
  Security Council and, 297, 299
  settlements and, 67–68, 139
  Sharon and, 65–66, 67, 101–102, 103–104,
    129, 154
  Tourgeman and, 208, 296–297
  Turbowitz and, 189, 201–202, 208
  visits to Israel, 119, 269–270
  Weissglas and, 101, 102
Haig, Alexander, 285
Hamad (Bahraini King), 71
Hamas
  Abbas and, 124, 125–126, 210
  American policy to weaken, 170–171
  anti-Semitism in, 140–142
  armed struggle, dedication to, 165
  bombings in Israel by, 76–77, 102, 116,
    146, 172
  Dahlan and, 115
  disengagement, strengthening of during,
    159–161
  Document of National Accord and, 176
  financial restrictions on, 163–164
  Iran and, 229
  Islamist nature of, 165
  Israeli attacks on, 83
  legal restrictions on, 163–164
  Livni and, 126
  majority in Palestinian Legislative Council,
    169–170
  Mecca Agreement and, 217–218
  military strength of, 77, 135–136
  national unity government with Fatah, 206
  Olmert and, 296–297
  Palestinian elections and
    participation in, 126, 131, 140–142,
      143–144, 159
    victory in, 163–164, 169–170
  PLO and, 75
  polls regarding, 152
  "Quartet" and, 230
  rule in Gaza Strip, 315, 317
  Syria and, 306–307
  takeover of Gaza Strip, 228–232

tension with Fatah, 128
terrorism and, 84
as terrorist group, 163–164
truce with Fatah, 125–126
truce with Palestinian Authority, 78, 82
war with Fatah, 140, 176–177, 206–207, 209–210, 212, 226–227
war with Israel, 177
war with Palestinian Authority, 115, 140
Haniyeh, Ismail, 167, 170, 176, 200, 208–209, 218, 228
Hannah, John, 27, 30, 192–193
Hariri, Rafik, 121, 124–125, 180, 182
Hariri, Saad, 180
Hayden, Michael, 236
Hitkansut (convergence) policy, 171–174
Hizballah
  generally, 25
  Arafat and, 25
  Bandar and, 181
  Bush and, 180
  Hadley and, 180
  Iran and, 180, 189
  Lebanon War (*See* Lebanon War)
  military strength in Lebanon, 180
  overview, 179
  Rice and, 180
  Sheba'a Farms and, 184–186
  Syria and, 189, 306–307
Hoenlein, Malcolm, 308
Howard, John, 104
Hussein, Saddam, 57, 63
Hussein (Jordanian King), 317
al Husseini, Haj Amin, 314

IDF. *See* Israeli Defense Forces
Independent Palestine Party (Palestinians), 163
Indyk, Martin, 307–308
International Atomic Energy Agency, 236–237, 238, 246, 248
International Monetary Fund, 253
International Red Cross, 228
Intifada. *See* Second Intifada
Introduction, 1–3
Iran
  Arafat and, 25
  Gaza Strip and, 228
  Hamas and, 229
  Hizballah and, 180, 189
  Lebanon War and, 184, 188
  nuclear program of, 238, 239
  Rice and, 189, 200–201
  strategic challenge from, 306
  strategic imperative regarding, 200–201

Iraq War
  attention devoted to, 192
  relationship to Middle East situation, 38–39
  Rice and, 63, 192
  Roadmap and, 57–58
Islamic extremism, 20
Islamic Jihad
  bombings in Israel by, 146, 150–151
  Document of National Accord and, 176
  Hamas-Fatah war and, 207
  Syria and, 306–307
  truce with Palestinian Authority, 78, 82
Israeli Defense Forces
  generally, 205, 231, 234, 241
  disengagement and, 93, 135, 139, 230, 231–232
  in Gaza Strip, 77, 92, 100, 106
  "Jenin Massacre" and, 31
  Lebanon War and, 181
  Qana attack and, 186–187
  Rice and, 190
  Second Intifada and, 13
  siege of Arafat by, 28
  in West Bank, 79
  West Bank fence and, 101
Ivanov, Igor, 33

Jackson, Henry M., 59–60
Javits, Jacob, 60
"Jenin Massacre," 31
Jerusalem, status of
  Abbas and, 275
  Erekat and, 272
  final status negotiations and, 312–313
  Powell and, 23
  Qurie and, 272
  Rice and, 272, 280
Jerusalem Post, 24, 162
Jewish Agency, 216
Jones, James L., 259–260, 282, 294
Jones Report, 294, 295
Jordan
  "April 14th letter" and, 110–112
  final status negotiations, role in, 317–318
  Palestinian statehood and, 317–318
  Roadmap and, 49–51

Kadima Party (Israel)
  election of, 170, 174
  formation of, 88–89, 150
  Livni and, 279, 284
  Olmert and, 158, 159, 223–224, 264, 278
Kaplinsky, Moshe, 10, 21, 89, 153–154
Karine A affair, 25–27

Karzai, Hamid, 121
Katsav, Moshe, 8
Kemp, Jack, 44
Kerry, John, 305
Kimche, David, 85
Kirkpatrick, Jeane, 285
Kissinger, Henry, 60
Koizumi, Junichiro, 104
Kouchner, Bernard, 298, 300, 302
Kurtzer, Daniel, 132, 137, 138, 139

Labor Party (Israel), 86, 114–115, 138, 147,
    150, 174
Lavrov, Sergei, 135, 221–222, 266
Lebanon War
    Abrams and, 195
    Arab reaction to, 181
    Ayalon and, 190
    Blair and, 183, 184
    Giladi and, 190
    Hizballah in aftermath of, 189
    humanitarian issues, 185
    IDF and, 181
    Iran and, 184, 188
    Livni and, 184, 185
    Olmert and, 177, 181, 183–185, 189–191
    overview, 179
    Qana attack, 186–189
    Rice and, 177, 179, 181, 182–186,
        189–191, 195
    Rome Conference, 181, 184
    Siniora and, 182–183, 184
    UNIFIL, 179, 182, 186, 189
    Winograd Commission, 223–224, 233
Lessons learned
    intrusive US role, avoiding, 311
    Israeli flexibility dependent on firm US
        support, 307–309
    personal relationships with Israeli leaders,
        importance of, 309
    Presidential control of decision making,
        importance of, 304–306
    primacy of Israeli-Palestinian situation,
        avoiding overemphasis on, 307
    reality on ground as more important than
        negotiations, 309–311
    settlement "freeze," avoiding overemphasis
        on, 311–313
Levitte, Jean-David, 298, 299, 302
Libby, I. Lewis ("Scooter"), 16–17, 26, 30,
    283
Likud Party (Israel), 88–89, 98, 102, 103, 115,
    137, 139

Livni, Tzipi
    generally, 194, 222, 272
    Annapolis Conference and, 250, 251
    Bush and, 169, 262–263, 274
    election campaign of, 274, 282, 286
    Erekat and, 258, 276, 291
    Hamas and, 126
    Kadima Party and, 279, 284
    Lebanon War and, 184, 185
    Olmert and, 223–224
    Qurie and, 258, 276, 277–278
    refugees and, 262–263, 293
    Rice and, 185, 205, 206, 220, 268,
        276–277, 279, 295–296
    Roadmap and, 205
    settlements and, 252
    Siniora and, 181
    West Bank and, 276–277, 291
London Conference, 125

Ma'ale Adumim (settlement), 67, 139, 275,
    276–277, 278, 280
Maariv (Israeli newspaper), 23–24
Madrid Conference, 195, 197, 307, 308
McConnell, Michael, 236
Mecca Agreement, 217–219
Meretz Party (Israel), 86, 142
Meridor, Sallai, 100–101, 121, 215–216, 219,
    223, 252
Merkel, Angela, 132–133, 167, 283, 297–298
Meshal, Khaled, 168, 220–221
Middle East Partnership Initiative, 114
Miliband, David, 298, 300
Military aid to Israel, 234–235
Mitchell, George, 7, 24, 306–307, 311–312
Mitchell Report, 7, 12, 13, 23, 45, 67
Moeller, Per Stig, 49
Mofaz, Shaul, 25, 279
Mofaz, Shlomo, 25
Moral equivalence, 28
"More for more," 102
Muasher, Marwan, 15, 49–50, 51, 87,
    110–112
Mubarak, Hosni
    generally, 132, 266
    "April 14th letter" and, 111
    Bush and, 104–105
    demise of, 307
    Obama and, 305, 306–307
    Powell and, 104
    at Red Sea Summits, 69, 71
    Rice and, 104
    Roadmap and, 63, 65

Sarkozy and, 298
summits hosted by, 123
Mughniyah, Imad, 25, 265
Mughrabi, Adel, 25
Muslim Brotherhood, 229

Nasser, Gamal Abdel, 165
National Democratic Institute for
  International Affairs, 126
National Endowment for Democracy, 86,
  114
National Religious Party (Israel), 98, 112–113
National Security Council (NSC)
  political appointees *versus* career personnel
    in, 304–306
  Presidential control of decision making,
    importance of, 304–306
National Union Party (Israel), 98–99
National unity government, 206, 209, 218,
  220, 228, 229
Negroponte, John, 195
Nehustan, Ido, 252
Netanyahu, Benjamin
  Abbas and, 311–312
  election campaign of, 279
  first term as Prime Minister, 271
  Obama and, 305–308, 309
  positive actions toward Palestinians, 252
  settlements and, 312
  Sharon and, 137, 139
  in Sharon government, 62, 158
Neubach, Karen, 44
9/11 attacks
  effect on US Israeli policy, 20–21
  Haass and, 19
  Powell's reaction to, 19, 20
  Riedel and, 19
  Tourgeman and, 24
Nixon, Richard M., 60
"No daylight" strategy, 308
North Korea, al-Kibar nuclear reactor and,
  227–228, 236, 271
Northern Ireland, Middle East compared, 312
Nusseibeh, Sari, 84

Obama, Barack
  Abdullah and, 305
  "April 14th letter" and, 308
  Cairo speech, 306
  Egypt and, 306–307
  election of, 287
  intrusiveness of US role under, 311
  Israel, relationship with, 307, 308–309, 311

Israeli suspicions of, 306
Jones and, 294
moral equivalency and, 306
Mubarak and, 305, 306–307
Muslim world and, 306
Netanyahu and, 305–308, 309
peace talks and, 306–307
settlements and, 74, 311–312
Olmert, Ehud
  generally, 194
  Abbas and
    Annapolis Conference, 249
    final status negotiations, 270
    Gaza Strip, 266, 270–271, 272
    negotiations, 210, 258, 260, 286–287
    political weakness of Olmert, 232–233,
      234
    West Bank, 270–271
  Abrams and, 160–161, 173–174, 207–208,
    288–289
  al-Kibar nuclear reactor and, 227, 246–247
  Annapolis Conference and, 249, 250–251,
    253, 255
  background, 158
  Bush and
    al-Kibar nuclear reactor, 246–247
    Annapolis Conference, 249, 255
    initial conversations, 158–159
    Jones Report, 293–295
    Mecca Agreement, 219
    military aid to Israel, 234
    Palestinian statehood, 233–234
    peace talks, 269
    personal relationship, 225, 264–265
    on Rice, 280
    support for, 264
    Syria, 269, 276
    terrorism, 268–269
    West Bank offer, 292–293
  campaign of, 159
  Cheney and, 235
  corruption charges against, 260, 264, 273,
    278
  election of, 170
  Erekat and, 286, 289–290
  final status negotiations and, 222–223, 233,
    234, 270
  Gaza Strip and, 266, 270–271, 272
  Hadley and, 174, 286
  Hamas and, 296–297
  hitkansut (convergence) policy and,
    171–174
  importance of US support for, 308

Olmert, Ehud (*cont.*)
  international conference approach and, 175,
    207–208, 233, 246
  Jones Report and, 293–295
  Kadima Party and, 158, 159, 223–224, 264,
    278
  Lebanon War and, 177, 181, 183–185,
    189–191
  Livni and, 223–224
  Mecca Agreement and, 218, 219
  optimism of, 282–283
  Palestinian statehood and, 233–234
  Qana attack and, 187–189
  refugees and, 270, 288
  resignation of, 278, 284
  Rice and
    generally, 174
    attempts to circumvent, 257–258
    cease fire, 298
    friction between, 187–189, 219, 220,
      222–223, 254, 256–257
    Gaza Strip, 272
    international conference approach, 175,
      233, 246
    Jones Report, 293–295
    Lebanon War, 177, 183–184, 189–191
    military aid to Israel, 234–235
    misunderstanding between, 245
    personal relationship, 193
    Roadmap, 214–215
    Security Council, 299
    at Security Council, 296
  Roadmap and, 205–206, 212–213,
    214–215
  Sarkozy and, 298
  Security Council and, 296–297, 300
  settlements and, 260
  in Sharon government, 62
  Siniora and, 181, 186
  succeeding Sharon, 158
  terrorism and, 268–269
  trilateral meeting with Abbas and Rice,
    220–221
  Turbowitz and, 284–285
  visits to Washington, 174–175, 287–289,
    293–295
  Welch and, 160–161, 174, 207–208
  West Bank and
    generally, 161–162, 191, 203–204, 210,
      270–271
    offer regarding, 287–289
Omar (Mullah), 20
al-Omari, Ghaith, 84, 155

Operation Autumn Clouds, 207
Operation Cast Lead, 295
Operation Defensive Shield, 31
Operation Summer Rains, 177
Oren, Michael, 64
Organization for Security and Cooperation in
    Europe, 65
Oslo Accords, 26, 129, 142, 314
Oslo Interim Agreement, 126–127
Otte, Marc, 151

PA. *See* Palestinian Authority
Pace, Peter, 236
Palestine Liberation Organization
  final status negotiations and, 317–318
  Hamas and, 75
  "Jenin Massacre" and, 31
  Karine A affair and, 25–27
  Mecca Agreement and, 217–218
  negotiations with, 129
  negotiations with Israel, 217–218, 242, 258
  Palestinian statehood and, 314
Palestinian Authority
  Barak and, 266, 270
  Blair and, 315–316
  Dahlan and, 77, 115, 135–136, 137
  economic situation of, 266, 272–273,
    278–279, 310
  elections and, 119–120
  emergency government, 232–233
  Fatah and, 270
  final status negotiations and, 317–318
  foreign aid to, 123, 133, 170
  Gaza Strip and, 159–161
  military strength of, 135–136, 137
  national unity government, 218, 228, 229
  security forces, 77
  training of security forces, 214, 228–229,
    265, 266
  truce with Hamas, 78, 82
  truce with Islamic Jihad, 78, 82
  war with Hamas, 115, 140
  West Bank and, 125–126, 129
Palestinian elections
  Abbas and
    generally, 132–134, 136, 151, 165–166,
      209–210
    Hamas participation in, 145–146
  Abrams and, 152
  Annan and Hamas participation in, 143,
    144, 166, 167
  Arafat and, 56–57
  Bush and Hamas participation in, 146

complaints regarding, 120
Dahlan and, 132–136, 151, 152, 159
Fatah and
  defeat of, 163, 164–166
  participation by, 126, 127, 131
  reasons for defeat, 164–166
Fayyad and, 163
Hamas and
  participation by, 126, 131, 140–142,
    143–144, 159
  victory of, 163–164, 169–170
Palestinian Authority and, 119–120
"Quartet" and, 143–144, 152, 166,
    167–168
Qurie and, 132–136
results of, 163
Rice and
  generally, 152
  Hamas participation in, 144–145,
    147–148, 152, 166–168, 169
Sharon and, 147–148
Tourgeman and
  generally, 152–153
  Hamas participation in, 144–145
Weissglas and, 131, 151
  generally, 126–127
  Hamas participation in, 144–145
Palestinian Legislative Council
  Abbas and, 63
  elections (*See* Palestinian elections)
  Hamas victory in, 163–164, 169–170
  militias and, 145
  national unity government, 218
  Roadmap and, 56–57
Palestinian statehood
  Bush and, 16–17, 42, 232, 233–234,
    315
  Camp David negotiations and, 16
  Carter and, 16
  Cheney and, 16–17
  Clinton and, 16, 315
  as conditional on new Palestinian
    leadership, 42
  G.H.W. Bush and, 16
  Jordan and, 317–318
  Libby and, 16–17
  Olmert and, 233–234
  PLO and, 314
  possible shape of, 317–318
  Powell and, 23
  Reagan and, 16
  Rice and, 32, 133
  Riedel and, 16, 17

Security Council Resolutions regarding, 32
Sharon and, 16, 310
"Park Hotel Massacre," 30
Pensioners Party (Israel), 174
"People's Choice" plan, 84–85
"People's Voice" plan, 84–85
Peres, Shimon, 24, 91–92, 114–115, 147, 150,
    262
Peretz, Amir, 147
PLC. *See* Palestinian Legislative Council
PLO. *See* Palestine Liberation Organization
"Political horizon" theory, 203–204
Popular Front for the Liberation of Palestine,
    163, 176, 207
Portman, Rob, 234
Powell, Colin
  generally, 59, 83
  Abdallah and, 14–15
  Arab reaction to speeches of, 23–24
  Arafat and, 6–7, 9, 24, 33
  Bush's pro-Israeli position and, 35
  Cheney and, 34
  Clinton and, 5
  divergence from Bush Administration, 6–7,
    20, 34–35, 48
  Erekat and, 56
  Geneva Initiative and, 85, 86
  Genger and, 10
  Israeli view of, 51
  Jerusalem, and status of, 23
  Karine A affair and, 25, 26
  marginalization of, 198–199
  Mubarak and, 104
  need for coherent policy and, 22–23
  need for new Palestinian leadership and, 40,
    41
  9/11 attacks, reaction to, 19, 20
  outreach to Arab world, 8
  Palestinian statehood and, 23
  "Quartet" and, 48–49
  at Red Sea Summits, 69, 76
  Rice and, 7, 283
  Roadmap and, 49–50, 56, 57–58, 87
  Second Intifada and, 6–7, 23
  settlements and, 23, 58, 67
  Sharon and, 9, 10, 24, 33
  terrorism and, 23, 77–78
  visits to Israel, 83
  visits to Middle East, 32–33, 45
Power, Faith, and Fantasy (Oren), 64
Presidential Command (Rodman), 284
Preventive Security Organization, 228
Principals Committee, 34

Prisoners, 252
Putin, Vladimir, 132–133, 135

Qaddoumi, Farouk, 121
Qana attack, 186–189
Qawasmeh, Abdullah, 77–78
"Quartet"
    Bush and, 58
    disengagement and, 134–135, 142–143
    formation of, 32–33
    Hamas and, 230
    Mecca Agreement and, 217–219
    Palestinian elections and
        generally, 152
        Hamas participation in, 143–144, 166,
            167–168
    Powell and, 48–49
    Roadmap and, 49, 50, 58
    Sharon and, 58
    Welch and, 143
Qurie, Ahmed (Abu Ala'a)
    generally, 120, 272
    Abbas and, 248–249
    Abrams and, 115
    appointment of, 83–84
    "April 14th letter" and, 109–110, 112
    Arafat and, 90, 101
    Bush and, 121
    Fatah and, 270
    Feltman and, 84
    Hadley and, 103, 115
    Jerusalem, and status of, 272
    Livni and, 258, 276, 277–278
    offer of resignation, 115
    Palestinian elections and, 132–136
    resignation of, 163
    Rice and, 111–112, 267–268, 271–272,
        279, 280
    weakness of, 160

Rabbo, Yasser Abd, 85, 272
Rabin, Yitzhak, 137, 201, 238, 315
Rantisi, Abdel Aziz, 76–77, 111
Reagan, Ronald, 16, 59, 86, 285, 305
Red Sea Summits
    Abbas at, 69, 71, 72, 75–76
    Abdallah at, 69, 71
    Abdullah at, 69, 71
    Aqaba Summit, 71–76
    Burns at, 69
    Bush at, 71, 74, 76
    Mubarak at, 69, 71
    Powell at, 69, 76

Rice at, 69–70, 76
    Sharm el-Sheik Summit, 69–71
    Sharon at, 69, 71, 72–73, 74, 76
    Weissglas at, 73–74
Refugees
    Abbas and, 291
    Abdallah and, 29
    "April 14th letter" and, 108
    Livni and, 262–263, 293
    Olmert and, 270, 288
Ribicoff, Abraham, 60
Rice, Condoleezza
    generally, 59, 66, 83, 84, 129, 135, 233,
        266
    Abbas and
        disengagement, 135
        final status negotiations, 267, 271–272,
            277–278, 279–280
        Mecca Agreement, 222
        national unity government, 209, 220
        on Olmert, 286
        terrorism, 77
    Abdullah and, 110–111
    Abrams and
        generally, 124
        appointment of Abrams, 59
        decision not to follow Rice to State
            Department, 116–117
        Lebanon War, 195
        loyalty to Rice, 59, 61
        "off the record" remarks by Abrams,
            224–225, 226
        settlements, 115–116
    al-Kibar nuclear reactor and, 236, 237–238
    Annapolis Conference and, 251
    "April 14th letter" and, 112
    Arabs, influence of, 194
    attitude toward Israel, 274
    Ayalon and, 22, 77, 200
    Bandar and, 181, 198
    Barak and, 244–245, 267
    Bush and, 35, 198–200, 225, 226
    Cheney and, 283
    civil rights analogy and Palestinians, 245
    on democratization of Middle East, 87,
        146–147
    disengagement and, 100, 135, 136–137,
        154
    Erekat and, 267
    final status negotiations and, 209, 212–213,
        215, 216–217, 267, 271–272,
        277–278, 279–280
    foreign officials, influence of, 192–193

Gaza Strip and, 272
Genger and, 10, 22, 77
Hadley and, 199, 224–225, 226, 283–284, 294, 298–299
Hannah and, 192–193
hitkansut (convergence) policy and, 174
Hizballah and, 180
IDF and, 190
international conference approach and, 175, 191, 195–198, 207, 210, 232, 233, 241, 246
Iran and, 200–201
Iraq War and, 63, 192
Jerusalem, and status of, 272, 280
Jones Report and, 293–295
Karine A affair and, 26
on killing of Yassin, 102–103
Lavrov and, 221–222
Lebanon War and, 177, 179, 181, 182–186, 189–191, 195
legacy of, 191–192
Livni and, 185, 205, 206, 220, 268, 276–277, 279, 295–296
London Conference and, 125
Mecca Agreement and, 218–219, 222
media, influence of, 192
Meridor and, 215–216
Mubarak and, 104
national unity government and, 209, 220
need for new Palestinian leadership and, 33–34, 37, 40, 62
Olmert and
    generally, 174
    attempts to circumvent, 257–258
    cease fire, 298
    friction between, 187–189, 219, 220, 222–223, 254, 256–257
    Gaza Strip, 272
    international conference approach, 175, 233, 246
    Jones Report, 293–295
    Lebanon War, 177, 183–184, 189–191
    military aid to Israel, 234–235
    misunderstanding between, 245
    personal relationship, 193
    Roadmap, 214–215
    Security Council, 296, 299
Operation Defensive Shield and, 31
optimism of, 282–283
Palestinian elections and
    generally, 152
    Hamas participation in, 144–145, 147–148, 152, 166–168, 169

Palestinian statehood and, 32, 133
peace talks and, 38
"political horizon" theory and, 203–204
post-Iraq War peace process and, 64–65
Powell and, 7, 283
prisoners and, 252
Qana attack and, 186–189
Qurie and, 111–112, 267–268, 271–272, 279, 280
at Red Sea Summits, 69–70, 76
return of dead bodies and, 252
Roadmap and, 49–50, 87, 213–215, 216–217
Rumsfeld and, 283
Saudi Arabia and, 15
Second Intifada and, 5
Security Council and, 297, 299, 302
settlements and, 67–68, 74, 251–252, 260
Sharon and
    crossing to and from Gaza, 148–151
    disengagement, 136–137
    distrust of Rice, 10
    English comprehension by Sharon, 12
    friction between, 130
    Hamas participation in Palestinian elections, 147–148
    personal relationship, 154
    visits to Israel, 78–79, 123–124, 135
Siniora and, 182–183, 186–187
in State Department, 116
State Department personnel, influence of, 193–194
statesmanship of, 226
terrorism and, 77
Tourgeman and, 194–195, 200, 201, 220, 223, 252
trilateral meeting with Abbas and Olmert, 220–221
Turbowitz and, 200, 201–202
Weissglas and, 77, 79, 83, 87–88, 90, 102–103, 139, 257, 263
Welch and, 193–194
West Bank and, 288, 292
West Bank fence and, 78
Wolfensohn and, 150
Riedel, Bruce
    Arab world expectations of Bush and, 8–9
    Arafat and, 8
    9/11 attacks and, 19
    Palestinian statehood and, 16, 17
    Saudi Arabia and, 14–15
    Second Intifada and, 6
Right of return, 74–75

Roadmap
   Abbas and, 213–216
   Abdullah and, 49–50
   Abrams and, 213–214
   Annan and, 58
   "April 14th letter" and, 107–108
   Arafat and, 56–57
   Ayalon and, 50
   Burns and, 50, 51
   Bush and, 55, 58, 81–83, 87, 204–205
   delay in release of, 62–63
   Edelman and, 49
   Feith and, 49
   goals of, 51–52
   Hadley and, 49, 50, 53, 216–217
   Iraq War and, 57–58
   Israeli approval of, 70–71
   Israeli objections to, 68–69
   Jordan and, 49–51
   Livni and, 205
   marginalization of Arafat, 52
   Muasher and, 49–50, 51, 87
   Mubarak and, 63, 65
   Olmert and, 205–206, 212–213, 214–215
   overview, 48–49
   Palestinian Legislative Council and, 56–57
   phases of, 52
   Powell and, 49–50, 56, 57–58, 87
   "Quartet" and, 49, 50, 58
   Rice and, 49–50, 87, 213–215, 216–217
   sequence of, 203
   settlements and, 67–68
   Sharon and, 50, 53–55, 56, 58, 70–71,
      81–83
   Tourgeman and, 50, 203, 212–214
   Turbowitz and, 203, 212–213
   Weissglas and, 50, 68–69
Rodman, Peter, 198–199, 284, 306
Rome Conference, 181, 184
Ross, Dennis, 16, 291, 292
Rove, Karl, 192
Rudman, Warren, 7
Rumsfeld, Donald, 33–34, 38, 41, 198–199,
   283
Russia
   Mecca Agreement and, 218, 221–222
   in "Quartet" (*See* "Quartet")
   Syria and, 237

Sadat, Anwar, 307, 308
Sana'a Declaration, 114
Sarkozy, Nicolas, 297, 298, 302
Saud (Saudi Prince), 253

Saudi Arabia
   Burns and, 15
   relationship with Bush, 14–15
   Rice and, 15
   Riedel and, 14–15
   Second Intifada, Saudi plan to end, 28–31
Schroeder, Gerhard, 309
Scowcroft, Brent, 197
SCUD missiles, 63
Sea Island (G8) summit, 113–114
Second Intifada
   Abdallah and Saudi plan to end, 28–29
   "Arab Plan" to end, 28–31
   Arafat calling for, 5
   bombings in Israel, 13, 21, 22, 24, 27–28,
      30, 37, 41
   efforts to stop, 5–7
   Haass and, 6
   IDF and, 13
   Powell and, 6–7, 23
   Rice and, 5
   Riedel and, 6
   Saudi plan to end, 28–31
   Sharon and, 13
Security Council
   al-Kibar nuclear reactor and, 236, 238, 246
   Bush and, 297
   Hadley and, 297, 299
   moral equivalence in, 28
   Olmert and, 296–297, 300
   Palestinian statehood, Resolutions
      regarding, 32
   Resolution 242, 173
   Resolution 1515, 87
   Resolution 1701, 179, 189
   Resolution 1860, 300–301
   Rice and, 297, 299, 302
   Tourgeman and, 299, 300, 302
   US abstentions in, 301–303
   US vetoes in, 12
Settlements. *See also specific settlement*
   Abbas and, 311
   Abrams and, 67–68
   "April 14th letter" and, 107, 108–109
   Arafat and, 311
   Bush and, 58, 311
   "freeze," avoiding overemphasis on,
      311–313
   Hadley and, 67–68, 139
   hitkansut (convergence) policy, 171–174
   Livni and, 252
   Netanyahu and, 312
   Obama and, 74, 311–312

Olmert and, 260
Powell and, 23, 58, 67
Rice and, 67–68, 74, 251–252, 260
Roadmap and, 67–68
Sharon and, 74, 95, 138, 311
Weissglas and, 74, 139
Settlers' Council, 98
Shahak, Amnon Lipkin, 85
Shalit, Gilad, 177, 220–221, 230, 300
Shalom, Silvan, 63, 213, 214
Shamir, Yitzhak, 308
Sharansky, Natan, 125
Sharm el-Sheik Summit, 69–71. *See also* Red
    Sea Summits
Sharon, Ariel
    generally, 155–156, 238, 314
    Abbas and, 78, 79, 82, 83, 123
    Abrams and, 65–66, 88, 90, 101–102,
        103–104, 132, 136–138, 154
    "April 14th letter" (*See* "April 14th letter")
    "Arab Plan," reaction to, 29–30
    Arafat and, 24, 54–56, 119
    Bush and
        on Abbas, 70
        "April 14th letter," 105
        characterization of Sharon as "man of
            peace," 35
        disengagement, 99–100, 130–131
        expectations of, 9–13
        meetings with, 36–37
        need for new Palestinian leadership,
            62
        personal relationship, 11–12, 154
        reaction to break with Arafat, 44
        at Red Sea Summits, 74, 76
        Roadmap, 55, 58, 81–83
        strokes suffered by Sharon, 153
        at United Nations, 142
    centrality of, 95–96
    Cheney and, 131
    in coalition government, 114–115
    demographics and, 92
    disengagement and, 89, 93, 94, 98–100,
        130–131, 136–137
    election of, 9
    elections called by, 54
    English comprehension by, 12
    first election of, 60
    flexibility of, 95–96
    Geneva Initiative and, 86
    Gerson and, 11
    Hadley and, 65–66, 67, 101–102, 103–104,
        129, 154

importance of US support for, 308,
    309–312
Kaplinsky and, 153–154
Karine A affair and, 25
London Conference and, 125
medical condition of, 153–154
Munich, comparisons to, 21
need for new Palestinian leadership and, 62,
    88
negotiations with Palestinians, 27–28
Netanyahu and, 137, 139
Operation Defensive Shield and, 31
Palestinian statehood and, 16, 310
police investigations of, 105
political troubles of, 115–116
Powell and, 9, 10, 24, 33
"Quartet" and, 58
at Red Sea Summits, 69, 71, 72–73, 74,
    76
reelection of, 61–62
Rice and
    crossing to and from Gaza, 148–151
    disengagement, 136–137
    distrust of Rice, 10
    English comprehension by Sharon, 12
    friction between, 130
    Hamas participation in Palestinian
        elections, 147–148
    personal relationship, 154
    visits to Israel, 78–79, 123–124, 135
    right of return and, 74–75
    Roadmap and, 50, 53–55, 56, 58, 70–71,
        81–83
    Second Intifada and, 13
    settlements and, 74, 95, 138, 311
    strokes suffered by, 153, 154
    Syria and, 88
    terrorism and, 13, 21
    Tourgeman and, 154
    at United Nations, 142
    visits to Crawford, 129–132
    visits to Washington, 9–10, 81–83, 131
    on vulnerability of Israel, 66–67
    Weissglas and, 10, 12, 153
    West Bank fence and, 78–79
Sharon, Gilad, 158
Sharon, Omri, 24
SHAS Party (Israel), 174
Sheba'a Farms, 182–186, 269
Shikaki, Khalil, 152
Shin Bet, 84, 205, 231, 234, 241, 269–270
Shubaki, Fouad, 25
Shultz, George, 59, 266, 305

Siniora, Fouad
  lack of Israeli support for, 180–181
  Lebanon War and, 182–183, 184
  Livni and, 181
  Olmert and, 181, 186
  Qana attack and, 186–187
  Rice and, 182–183, 186–187
  US support for, 180
Solana, Javier, 148, 149–150, 167, 207
Soliman, Omar, 83, 103, 228
State Department
  anti-Israel attitudes in, 176
  "Arabists" in, 19, 43, 176
  Camp David negotiations and, 195
  disengagement and, 99
  Feith and, 19–20
  Karine A affair and, 26
  political appointees *versus* career personnel
    in, 304–306
  Presidential control of decision making,
    importance of, 304–306
  Rice in, 116
  shift in Administration policy toward,
    198–200
Syria
  al-Kibar nuclear reactor (*See* Al-Kibar
    nuclear reactor)
  Hamas and, 306–307
  Hizballah and, 189, 306–307
  Islamic Jihad and, 306–307
  Russia and, 237
  secret peace talks with Israel, 271, 276
  Sharon and, 88
Syria Times, 23

Talansky, Morris, 278
Tenet, George, 12, 13, 23, 24, 45
Terrorism. *See also specific terrorist group*
  Abbas and, 69, 75–76, 77
  "April 14th letter" and, 108
  Arafat, commitment of, 101
  bombings in Israel (*See* Bombings in Israel)
  Bush and, 69, 75–76, 268–269
  Dahlan and, 78, 83
  9/11 attacks (*See* 9/11 attacks)
  Olmert and, 268–269
  Powell and, 23, 77–78
  Rice and, 77
  seminary attack, 268–269
  Sharon and, 13, 21
Thatcher, Margaret, 304
Third Way Party (Palestinians), 163
Times of London, 140, 309

Top-down negotiations, 259
Tourgeman, Shalom
  generally, 194, 258, 287, 296, 299
  Abbas and, 290
  Abrams and, 202, 214, 216, 276, 296
  Annapolis Conference and, 253
  "April 14th letter" and, 103
  "Arab Plan," reaction to, 29–30
  Bush, and Sharon's perception of, 9–10
  disengagement and, 89–90
  final status negotiations and, 216
  Gaza Strip and, 287
  Hadley and, 208, 296–297
  hitkansut (convergence) policy and,
    171–172
  9/11 attacks and, 24
  in Olmert government, 170
  Palestinian elections and
    generally, 152–153
    Hamas participation in, 144–145
  Rice and, 194–195, 200, 201, 220, 223, 252
  Roadmap and, 50, 203, 212–214
  Security Council and, 299, 300, 302
  Sharon and, 154
  Welch and, 214, 216
  West Bank and, 290–291
Turbowitz, Yoram
  generally, 194, 258
  Abbas and, 290
  Abrams and, 188, 202, 214, 216
  Annapolis Conference and, 253
  final status negotiations and, 216
  Hadley and, 189, 201–202, 208
  hitkansut (convergence) policy and, 173
  Olmert and, 284–285
  prisoners and, 252
  Rice and, 200, 201–202
  Roadmap and, 203, 212–213
  Welch and, 214, 216
Turki (Saudi Prince), 8–9, 15

United Arab Emirates, financial support to
  Palestinian Authority, 310
United Nations
  Annapolis Conference and, 253
  Bush at, 142
  Bush speeches at, 22, 196–197, 201–202,
    203
  Development Program, 114
  General Assembly, 285
  Human Rights Council, 311
  in "Quartet" (*See* "Quartet")
  Security Council (*See* Security Council)

Sharon at, 142
UNIFIL, 179, 182, 186, 189

Waldheim, Kurt, 285
Walker, Edward S., Jr., 8
Walles, Jake, 128, 145, 164, 229–230,
    248–249
Ward, William E. "Kip," 124, 137, 214,
    228–229
Washington Post, 43, 56, 99–100
Weissglas, Dov ("Dubi")
    generally, 66
    Abrams and, 88, 90, 101, 102, 137, 149
    "April 14th letter" and, 103, 109
    disengagement and, 89, 90, 92–93, 136,
        154–155, 160
    Hadley and, 101, 102
    hitkansut (convergence) policy and,
        171–172, 173
    Iraq War and, 63
    in Olmert government, 170
    Palestinian elections and
        generally, 126–127, 131, 151
        Hamas participation in, 144–145
    reaction to Bush's break with Arafat,
    at Red Sea Summits, 73–74
    Rice and, 77, 79, 83, 87–88, 90, 102–103,
        139, 257, 263
    right of return and, 74–75
    Roadmap and, 50, 68–69
    settlements and, 74, 139
    Sharon and, 10, 12, 153
    visits to Washington, 62
    West Bank fence and, 79
Welch, David
    generally, 144–145, 159, 226, 233, 235,
        249, 252
    Abbas and, 144, 170, 208–209
    Abrams and, 170, 176, 223–224
    final status negotiations and, 216, 223–224
    Hamas and, 167
    hitkansut (convergence) policy and,
        171–172
    international conference approach and, 232
    Olmert and, 160–161, 174, 207–208
    prisoners and, 252
    "Quartet" and, 143

Rice and, 193–194
Tourgeman and, 214, 216
Turbowitz and, 214, 216
visits to Middle East, 126, 131–132
West Bank
    Abbas and
        generally, 270–271, 274–275
        rejection of Olmert offer, 289–293, 312
    disengagement, coupling with, 100
    Erekat and, 288, 290–291
    Fayyad and, 265, 266, 267
    fence (*See* West Bank fence)
    hitkansut (convergence) policy, 171–174
    IDF in, 79
    Israeli military advances into, 28, 37
    Israeli withdrawals from, 79, 82
    Livni and, 276–277, 291
    Olmert and
        generally, 161–162, 191, 203–204, 210,
            270–271
        offer regarding, 287–289
    Operation Defensive Shield, 31
    Palestinian Authority and, 125–126, 129
    Rice and, 288, 292
    Tourgeman and, 290–291
    US position on Israeli withdrawal from,
        44
West Bank fence
    "April 14th letter" and, 107, 109
    IDF and, 101
    Israeli plans to build, 37, 68, 78–79
    Rice and, 78
    Sharon and, 78–79
    Weissglas and, 79
Winograd Commission, 223–224, 233, 264
Wolf, John, 76, 77, 79, 83
Wolfensohn, James D., 134–135, 148, 150
Wollack, Ken, 126
World Bank, 134–135, 253
World Zionist Organization, 216

Yahya, Abdel Razak, 38
Yassin, Sheikh, 102–103, 111

Zelikow, Philip, 197–198, 200, 201
Zinni, Anthony, 23, 24, 25, 30–31
Zoellick, Robert, 195